Disciplinary Applications of Information Literacy Threshold Concepts

edited by
Samantha Godbey, Susan Beth Wainscott, and Xan Goodman

Association of College and Research Libraries
A division of the American Library Association
Chicago, Illinois 2017

The paper used in this publication meets the minimum requirements of American National Standard for Information Sciences–Permanence of Paper for Printed Library Materials, ANSI Z39.48-1992. ∞

Cataloging-in-Publication data is on file with the Library of Congress.

Copyright ©2017 by the Association of College and Research Libraries.
All rights reserved except those which may be granted by Sections 107 and 108 of the Copyright Revision Act of 1976.

Printed in the United States of America.

21 20 19 18 17   5 4 3 2 1

Table of Contents

vii .... Foreword
Ray Land

1 .... Introduction
Samantha Godbey, Susan Beth Wainscott, Xan Goodman

11 ..... Section One. Authority is Constructed and Contextual

13 .... Chapter 1. Teaching Inclusive Authorities: Indigenous Ways of Knowing and the Framework for Information Literacy in Native Art
Alexander Watkins

25 .... Chapter 2. "But How Do I Know It's a Good Source?" Authority is Constructed in Social Work Practice
Callie Wiygul Branstiter and Rebecca Halpern

37 .... Chapter 3. Exploring Authority in Linguistics Research: Who to Trust When Everyone's a Language Expert
Catherine Baird and Jonathan Howell

51 .... Chapter 4. Evidence and Authority in Health and Exercise Science Research
Michelle Twait

63 ..... Section Two. Information Creation as a Process

65 .... Chapter 5. Common Ground: Communicating Information
Beate Gersch

79 .... Chapter 6. Using the Frame Information Creation as a Process to Teach Career Competencies to Advertising Students
Megan Blauvelt Heuer

93 .... Chapter 7. Moving Public Health Learners to the Skeptical Edge with Information Creation as a Process
Xan Goodman

109 ..... Chapter 8. Teaching Source Selection in Public Affairs Using Information Creation as a Process
Christina Sheley

121 ... Section Three. Information Has Value

123 ..... **Chapter 9.** Information Privilege in the Context of Community Engagement in Sociology
Heidi R. Johnson and Anna C. Smedley-López

135 ..... **Chapter 10.** Images Have Value: Changing Student Perceptions of Using Images in Art History
Courtney Baron, Christopher Bishop, Ellen Neufeld, and Jessica Robinson

149 ..... **Chapter 11.** Mining for the Best Information Value with Geoscience Students
Susan Beth Wainscott and Joshua Bonde

163 ..... **Chapter 12.** Teaching the Teachers: The Value of Information for Educators
Jess Haigh

175 ... Section Four. Research as Inquiry

177 ..... **Chapter 13.** Empowering, Enlightening, and Energizing: Research as Inquiry in Women's and Gender Studies
Juliann Couture and Sharon Ladenson

191 ..... **Chapter 14.** Framing the Visual Arts: The Challenges of Applying the Research as Inquiry Concept to Studio Art Information and Visual Literacy
Marty Miller

205 ..... **Chapter 15.** Integrating the ACRL Threshold Concept Research as Inquiry into Baccalaureate Nursing Education
Kimberly J. Whalen and Suzanne E. Zentz

223 ..... **Chapter 16.** Action Research as Inquiry for Education Students
Samantha Godbey

237 ... Section Five. Scholarship as Conversation

239 ..... **Chapter 17.** Performance as Conversation: Dialogic Aspects of Music Performance and Study
Rachel Elizabeth Scott

251 ..... **Chapter 18.** Framing the Talk: Scholarship as Conversation in the Health Sciences
Candace Vance

263 ..... **Chapter 19.** Widening the Threshold: Using Scholarship as Conversation to Welcome Students to Science
Rebecca Kuglitsch

275 ..... **Chapter 20.** Theater as a Conversation: Threshold Concepts in the Performing Arts
Christina E. Dent

287 ... Section Six. Searching as Strategic Exploration

289 ..... **Chapter 21.** From Novice to Nurse: Searching For Patient Care Information as Strategic Exploration
Elizabeth Moreton and Jamie Conklin

303 ..... **Chapter 22.** Leveraging the Language of the Past: Searching as Strategic Exploration in the Discipline of History
Jamie L. Emery

317 ..... **Chapter 23.** Mapping the Chaos: Building a Research Practice with Threshold Concepts in Studio Art Disciplines
Ashley Peterson

331 ..... **Chapter 24.** Teaching Future Educators Exploration through Strategic Searching
Michelle Keba

343 ..... **Chapter 25.** Threshold Concepts, Information Literacy, and Social Epistemology: A Critical Perspective on the ACRL Framework with Reference to Psychology
Tony Anderson and Bill Johnston

359 ... Bibliography
361 ... About the Authors

Foreword

Ray Land

This volume marks a significant new departure in the development of the threshold concepts analytic framework. We find a nationwide community of practitioners not only negotiating consensus on a set of practice-specific threshold concepts, or "frames," but, further, purposefully employing these overarching concepts to inform curriculum design and enhance learning within other disciplinary communities. The twenty-five chapters of this volume are eloquent testimony to this endeavour, ranging across disciplines and specialisms that include Arts and Humanities, Social Science, Empirical Science, Business, and Health.

Research into the nature of threshold concepts is a project, now, of some fifteen years duration. The characteristics of thresholds have been debated and discussed in considerable depth in earlier volumes.[1] Proposed as an analytic framework to explore ways of thinking and practicing within the disciplines, this research maintains that there are particular concepts in *any* given discipline (a large claim, of course) that cannot easily be assimilated or accommodated within one's existing meaning frame. They present a form of troublesome knowledge which requires not only a difficult reconceptualization, but a letting go of one's existing meaning frame and the prevailing conceptions of which it is constituted. Ironically, as Kuhn has pointed out, "our meaning frame is often the mechanism which brings the anomalous nature of a given phenomenon to light, but then proves inadequate to resolve the problems raised by its existence ... and must be reformulated."[2]

The reformulation of such a powerful frame also effects a shift in the learner's subjectivity.[3] It often provokes a state of *liminality*, a transitional period of uncertainty in which the learner may oscillate between existing and emergent understandings. Learning thresholds are often the points at which students experience difficulty and anxiety. There is, of course, a safety in staying in the known.

The early work on thresholds identified their principal characteristics as being transformative, integrative, irreversible, re-constitutive (of one's subjectivity), discursive (in terms of requiring the use of new discourse), and often troublesome. Must all these characteristics *always* pertain? The superordinate and non-negotiable characteristic of a threshold concept would seem to be its *transformative* capacity. Without transformation, in this framework, there will be no threshold crossing. However, the transformation would seem to be effected by the integrating function of threshold concepts, in the sense of their bringing what formerly appeared to be disparate conceptual elements into a coherent relationship, much as the addition of a particular jigsaw piece may bring other pieces together to provide a new and meaningful perspective:

> Adding a new concept to a learner's collection can affect the understanding of other concepts in that collection, so that over time the whole collection develops and changes. The threshold concept can be a conceptual straw that breaks the camel's back—or a piece in a jigsaw of concepts that causes them to coalesce and produce a step change in perception.[4]

The characteristics of thresholds have never been posited as an essentialist or definitive exercise. As Felten points out, the intention has been "to provoke and suggest, not to prove and conclude."[5] That said, without the transformative and integrative elements, it would seem difficult to envisage learning thresholds. In some instances, ontological shifts precede epistemological shifts. Though we would not see the identification of other threshold characteristics as a scoring exercise, nonetheless the personally reconstitutive effects of such radical shifts in perspective and ontology appear ratchet-like and unlikely to be easily reversed. They are also most likely to require the use of new language to name what we have come to know, or even to produce such knowing.[6] Whether these transitions are troublesome will obviously depend to a great degree on the individual learner's prior knowledge and experience. The transition could, of course, be exhilarating and absorbing. The massive archive of published material on thresholds across some 250 subject areas in over forty-five countries, maintained at University College London,[7] compellingly suggests, however, that such encounters with challenging new understandings and modes of practice tend to be difficult. And the threshold concepts framework has always emphasised the role of conceptual difficulty in significant learning. As Cousin points out:

> In resisting the market call for "satisfaction surveys," threshold concept researchers do not ask students "Did you like my teaching?" Rather their question is more likely to be "What did you find difficult?" They seek a conversation with stu-

dents about mastery, which does not yield to a Likert scale survey but promises instead to build a mutually productive relationship.[8]

Indeed, we would argue that a key strength of the threshold concept framework is that it draws in the interest and participation of subject experts, educationalists, and students in what Cousin terms a "transactional" relationship.[9] The ACRL threshold of *Scholarship as Conversation,* and such applications in this volume as Rachel Scott's *Dialogic Aspects of Music Performance* and Candace Vance's exhortation *Let's Talk,* provide nice examples of this quality.

What we observe also in the diverse contributions within this volume are how the six "frames" identified within the ACRL *Framework for Information Literacy for Higher Education* serve (as does the threshold concepts framework more broadly) as an example of what Perkins has termed *Action Poetry.*[10] This is the notion that for an idea to have traction and portability it should a) have relatively straightforward main premise and b) be capable of application to a wide range of educational contexts quickly and without too much difficulty. In this way, it has both explanatory and actionable potential.

The six ACRL framings, moreover, would seem to be pertinent examples of what Hokstad and Gundrosen have termed "complex threshold concepts,"[11] having an overarching or permeating quality which informs or underpins other (disciplinary) concepts or areas of knowledge. Such concepts require particular dispositions, such as the confidence to challenge, living with uncertainty, and dealing with complexity. Such dispositions are intertwined and nested.

There have, naturally, been cogent criticisms of the recent ACRL initiative and the threshold concept framework. But such challenges are intrinsic to academic endeavour and, in our view, strengthen the standing of these initiatives. A framework that did not attract such criticism, it might be argued, could hardly be having a serious effect at classroom level.

The Framework was initially concerned with teacher perspectives on threshold concepts as a tool of curriculum analysis and design to better understand ways of thinking and practising within the disciplines. It has since widened to encompass student experiences of conceptual difficulty, explorations of the nature of liminality, aspects of academic and professional identity, the role of language in assisting new understanding, the affective and dispositional dimensions of transformation, and the analysis of complex threshold concepts. A further future priority is also the assessment of threshold concepts, rendered problematic by the fact that they are both transformative across time, as well as embodied. In many respects, our conventional modes of assessment appear like "mismatched frames" that don't quite fit the picture. A "big rethink" would appear to be on the cards to accommodate the kinds of shifts and transformations in disciplinary thinking that are discussed in the chapters that follow in this welcome addition to the burgeoning literature on threshold concepts.

> Ray Land is Professor of Higher Education and Director of the Centre for Academic Practice at Durham University in Durham, England

Notes

1. Jan H. F. Meyer and Ray Land, eds. *Overcoming Barriers to Student Understanding: Threshold Concepts and Troublesome Knowledge* (London: Routledge Falmer, 2006), 3–18; Ray Land, Jan H. F Meyer, and Jan Smith, eds. *Threshold Concepts Within the Disciplines* (Rotterdam: Sense Publishers, 2008); Jan H. F. Meyer, Ray Land, and Caroline Baillie, eds. *Threshold Concepts and Transformational Learning* (Rotterdam, Boston & Taipei: Sense Publishers, 2010); Ray Land, Jan H. F. Meyer, and Michael T. Flanagan, eds. *Threshold Concepts in Practice* (Rotterdam, Boston & Taipei: Sense Publishers, 2016).
2. Thomas S. Kuhn, *The Structure of Scientific Revolutions*, 3rd ed. (Chicago, IL: University of Chicago Press, 1996), 122.
3. Jan H. F. Meyer and Ray Land, "Threshold Concepts and Troublesome Knowledge (2): Epistemological Considerations and a Conceptual Framework for Teaching and Learning," *Higher Education* 49, no. 3 (2005): 374.
4. Peter Vivian, "A New Symbol-Based Writing System for Use in Illustrating Basic Dynamics" (unpublished doctoral thesis, Coventry University, 2012), 55.
5. Peter Felten, "On the Threshold with Students," in *Threshold Concepts in Practice*, eds. Ray Land, Jan H. F. Meyer, and Michael T. Flanagan (Rotterdam, Boston & Taipei: Sense Publishers, 2016), 4.
6. Linda Adler-Kassner and Elizabeth Wardle, eds. *Naming What We Know: Threshold Concepts of Writing Studies* (Logan: Utah State University Press, 2015).
7. Michael T. Flanagan, "Threshold Concepts: Undergraduate Teaching, Postgraduate Training, Professional Development and School Education: A Short Introduction and a Bibliography," accessed December 22, 2016, http://www.ee.ucl.ac.uk/~mflanaga/thresholds.html.
8. Glynis Cousin, "Foreword," in *Threshold Concepts in Practice*, eds. Ray Land, Jan H. F. Meyer, and Michael T. Flanagan (Rotterdam, Boston & Taipei: Sense Publishers, 2016), ix.
9. Ibid.
10. David Perkins, "Minding the Gap" (presentation, ESRC Enhancing Teaching-Learning Environments (ETL) Project, Edinburgh University, Edinburgh, 2000).
11. Leif Martin Hokstad and Stine Gundrosen, "'Cause soon, it will be real': Medical Simulation as Change Space in Interprofessional Training" (presentation, 6th Biennial Threshold Concepts Conference: Thresholds on the Edge, Dalhousie University, Halifax, Nova Scotia, June 17, 2016).

Introduction

Samantha Godbey, Susan Beth Wainscott, Xan Goodman

As its title suggests, this book explores information literacy threshold concepts in the context of subject disciplines. For most academic librarians, the term "threshold concept" is a recent addition to their professional vocabulary. Described as a portal, transition, or threshold to additional learning and deeper understanding for a learner, threshold concepts were first defined by Meyer and Land in 2003[1] and have been explored in libraries starting around 2010. In February 2015, the Association of College and Research Libraries (ACRL) officially filed the Framework for Information Literacy for Higher Education (Framework),[2] offering a new approach to information literacy based on threshold concepts. This document draws on the threshold concept analytic framework, proposing six threshold concepts for information literacy. Since the initial drafts of the Framework were shared in 2014, many librarians have struggled to make sense of the document and to identify ways in which they can apply these concepts in their own professional settings. With the rescinding of the Information Literacy Competency Standards for Higher Education by the ACRL Board of Directors in June 2016, librarians are engaging even more with the Framework and its threshold concepts.

The editors' interest in threshold concepts predates the first drafts of the Framework, inspired by a session at the 2013 ACRL Conference about the work of Korey Brunetti, Amy R. Hofer, Silvia Lin Hanick, and Lori Townsend, who were, and are, conducting a Delphi study in order to identify threshold concepts in information literacy.[3] At that point, we began to integrate threshold concepts into our library instruction practice and research agendas. We began to discuss threshold concepts with librarian and disciplinary faculty colleagues. We have since led multiple workshops on the Framework, helping librarians to understand the threshold concepts it contains and attempt to integrate one or more of these concepts into a traditional one-shot library session. Through these workshops, we have directly observed librarians' efforts to understand the Framework and their desire to learn from one another's experiences with threshold concepts. As subject librarians in a range of disciplines, namely education, engineering, and health sciences, we are personally familiar with the rewarding and challenging aspects of applying these concepts in disciplinary settings.

In this book, we wanted to provide a space for librarians to explore threshold concepts as an idea and the specifics of what the threshold concepts contained in the Framework might look like in disciplinary contexts. We have worked with our authors to provide a balance of the theoretical and practical in order to help readers both conceptually and pragmatically with their work in supporting student learning. In this introduction, we provide background on threshold concepts, the Framework, and this book.

Defining threshold concepts

The definition of threshold concepts has been expanded over the years based upon the work of many educational scholars and practitioners,[4] and includes both characteristics of the concepts and the process a novice may undergo while learning. Threshold concepts are currently defined by the following characteristics:

- Transformative: Threshold concepts will alter the learner's view of the world and how they seek to understand and make sense of new information within their discipline, or even how they feel about or perform within the practices of their discipline.[5] This is the characteristic that is consistently described by Meyer, Land, and their coauthors as a defining characteristic and of primary importance to the discovery of threshold concepts.[6] Threshold concepts are not simply important facts, theories, or laws; they change the learner and how the learner will approach inquiry and the acceptance of new information. The threshold concept may even alter the learner's sense of professional identity.[7]
- Integrative: Many threshold concepts are also integrative in that they reveal patterns or connections between information that were not previously apparent,[8] like a connect-the-dots puzzle that previously had several dots lacking numbers. Once a learner accepts the threshold concept, the picture in the puzzle is made clear. Thus, threshold concepts tend to demarcate a plateau in student learning where students might not progress beyond defining and memorizing until the integrating concept is grasped.
- Irreversible: Threshold concepts may also irreversibly change the learner and be difficult to unlearn.[9] Once the learner has been transformed, they, now more comfortable with a particular threshold

concept, may find it difficult to relate to the perspective of those who are not similarly transformed.
- Bounded: Each threshold concept generally has more or less definable conceptual boundaries to its usefulness.[10] Sometimes one or more of the boundaries of a threshold concept will coincide with or be indicative of the boundaries between one discipline and others.[11] Additionally, learners who have crossed a threshold may also use jargon or discourse that is less accessible to those who have not crossed that threshold.[12]
- Troublesome: For many learners, the transformation required to understand a threshold concept will cause them to struggle. The process of accepting a threshold concept will be troublesome because it may require a learner to abandon a prior view of the world.[13] Additionally, there may be jargon to learn,[14] and the new relationships revealed by an integrative threshold concept may upset other aspects of the learner's worldview.

Meyer cautions those looking for potential threshold concepts within their knowledge domain that this list of common characteristics is not useful when simply used as a diagnostic or a rubric to identify threshold concepts.[15] He emphasizes that the characteristics are best used to provide guidelines for considering what each individual learner may be experiencing when faced with concepts that challenge their worldview, and how to best support each of their learning processes when some but not all may be struggling with this fundamental disruption.[16]

This process of transformation will be unique to, and troublesome to different extents for, each learner. The transformation process is most fully described in Meyer, Land, and Baillie's 2010 book, *Threshold Concepts and Transformational Learning*.[17] Here, three states are described: the preliminal, liminal, and postliminal, with acknowledgement that some learners experience these states in a cyclical manner, recursively, or oscillating between worldviews.[18]

The preliminal state is the original status of the novice learner, unperturbed by what they are unaware that they do not know, or "the unknowable unknown."[19] Before an encounter with the threshold concept, the novice is in the blissful state of ignorance of any other potential, and potentially disruptive, view of the world. The learner's shift out of the preliminal state is provoked upon being made aware of the threshold concept.[20] The threshold concept disturbs their understanding of the world, and if they do not immediately reject it out of hand, they have entered the liminal state, and their potential for transformation has begun.

Within the liminal state, the learner considers that this threshold concept and foreign way of sense-making may be true, and their world is shaken by what this possibility holds. They may feel instability due to an awareness that their prior knowledge was incomplete or simply wrong. They may be prompted to reject prior understandings outright or to significantly adjust the context. They may attempt to deconstruct their prior worldview and find a way to incorporate the new threshold concept information or viewpoint.[21] This adjustment to a different way of thinking can be disruptive to a learner's affective state.[22] Some learners may even experience a stall or plateau in their learning as they become stuck[23] within a liminal state while they struggle to accept or resist[24] the threshold concept.

The postliminal state is the world that lies beyond the conceptual threshold or boundary.[25] Previously known and accepted facts may remain, but the connections to other facts or the context that forms knowledge are forever altered for the learner. As a learner more deeply accepts the concept and becomes more familiar with the language used in the field to discuss and use the concept, it may change the way they make sense of the world.[26] They may simultaneously be accepting the threshold concept and this expert perspective as part of their professional identity.[27] Thus, while the process of shifting through these states is internal, if a learner crosses over to the postliminal state, one observable signal or symptom of the transformation is a change in their discourse.[28]

The Framework

The Framework for Information Literacy for Higher Education consists of an introduction, six frames structured around six threshold concepts, and several appendices.

The six threshold concepts within the Framework are, in alphabetical order:

- Authority Is Constructed and Contextual
- Information Creation as a Process
- Information Has Value
- Research as Inquiry
- Scholarship as Conversation
- Searching as Strategic Exploration

The introduction and appendices explain some of the theory undergirding the document, including metaliteracy[29] and the work of Wiggins and McTighe[30] on essential questions and backward design. Each frame is comprised of a threshold concept followed by knowledge practices and dispositions for that threshold concept. The *knowledge practices* are defined as "demonstrations of ways in which learners can increase their understanding of these information literacy concepts," while the *dispositions* "describe ways in which to address the affective, attitudinal, or valuing dimension of learning."[31] It is important to note that the Framework authors stress that these knowledge practices and dispositions are not meant to be prescriptive in terms of local application of the Framework. They note that "each library and its partners on campus will need to deploy these frames to best fit their own situation, including designing learning outcomes."[32]

In the introduction to the Framework, the authors note that the term "framework" was chosen deliberately to emphasize that "it is based on a cluster of interconnected core concepts, with flexible options for implementation, rather than on a set of standards or learning outcomes, or any prescriptive enumeration of skills."[33] The Framework authors therefore caution readers against using this document as a prescriptive document, instead encouraging individuals to take the Framework and work with it in order to make it fit their own situations. In the following chapters, you will find examples of librarians who are doing just this.

The editors appreciate that the adoption of the Framework and the rescission of the Standards is a controversial topic for many. The Framework has prompted robust debate among academic librarians as well as other library and information science professionals. We editors have taken a pragmatic approach to the Framework and look at it as a document that has inspired dialogue about our teaching and helped us in conversations with one another and with disciplinary faculty. We do not believe that the Framework is a perfect document, but we and others have found inspiration here. We also recognize that the idea of threshold concepts has its critics. We appreciate threshold concepts not as an edict, but as one way of thinking about learning. This, to us, is one way of approaching information literacy among others. These threshold concepts have given us language to start with as we explore the questions of what challenges our students are likely to face in their learning. We also appreciate the inclusion of the dispositions, which address the affective dimension of learning, and which we have found to be tremendously important in our interactions with students around troublesome points in learning.

The adoption of the Framework has been disruptive within our professional community. Some of our colleagues have rejected the Framework and underlying philosophy; some may agree in principle but are unable to put it into practice due to inertia or organizational culture at their institutions. Some are still testing out threshold concepts and considering whether they can be added to their practice, and others have fully embraced the Framework and discarded prior practices. This is all reminiscent of a learner's process when encountering a troublesome or threshold concept. Land, Meyer, and Baillie emphasize the importance of a supportive environment during the liminal phase.[34] We editors have adopted a supportive stance in recognition of the critical importance of each individual's distinct process with engaging with the Framework. As a result, we do not take a position on whether the Framework should replace or supplement existing practices, guidelines, or standards. We present here examples of colleagues' work in order to explore the proposed information literacy threshold concepts as depicted in the Framework. We believe it is for the reader and their home institution to determine if the ideas presented in this book would be useful to try within their own professional contexts.

This book

We organized the chapters in six sections aligned with the Framework because we want this to be a useful and approachable text. Readers might focus on chapters that align with their job duties and subject assignments, or readers might choose to read all the chapters on a specific threshold concept that draws their interest. Nonetheless, readers will notice the title of this book very deliberately refers to threshold concepts and not to the ACRL Framework. We wanted to emphasize the threshold concepts themselves over the precise language in the current version of this document. Many, but not all, authors explored specific language from the Framework and its knowledge practices and dispositions, but we wanted to provide flexibility to our authors in the extent to which they would focus on the Framework language as it currently exists. We also worked with authors to think and write about these ideas as threshold concepts, not simply as statements that had been put out by ACRL. We editors have been inspired especially by certain aspects of threshold concepts—the acknowledgement of the messy liminal space, the recognition of the different paths learners can take in the learning process, and the recognition of the affective dimension of learning, and we wanted to emphasize these ideas as threshold concepts and not exclusively as frames. Finally, it is our hope that the Framework will continue to evolve as librarians grapple with these and other information literacy threshold concepts.

The chapters cover a range of disciplines, including the humanities, social sciences, life sciences, and physical sciences, and a range of students, from first-year undergraduates to doctoral students. Readers will encounter chapters in which librarians have designed learning outcomes aligned with the frames as presented in the latest version of the Framework. Some authors have used knowledge practices or dispositions as outcomes, and others have generated outcomes independent of these specifics in the Framework. With these examples, we share different approaches to working with information literacy threshold concepts and how librarians are making them work not only within their institutional contexts, but within those disciplinary contexts that vary within institutions. In addition, there are chapters in which authors draw on or propose discipline-specific threshold concepts, using the common characteristics of threshold concepts to identify troublesome areas within subject disciplines.

In the following chapters, authors describe their experiences with negotiating an information literacy threshold concept within a discipline and provide suggestions for addressing that threshold concept in that disciplinary context. Many chapters are by a single academic librarian, others by two or more librarians at one or more institution, and several are co-authored by a librarian and a disciplinary faculty member. Chapter authors include those who have enthusiastically embraced the Framework and others who approach the document and threshold concepts with skepticism. All, however, have found ways of using the Framework's threshold concepts to think about information literacy in a different way. We asked authors to authentically explore their experience with threshold concepts within the specific disciplinary context in which they interact with learners. In these chapters, authors span the theoretical and practical, which, in our opinion, is key to fully taking advantage of the potential of threshold concepts to improve student learning experiences in impactful ways.

We hope this book will be helpful to academic librarians involved in instruction and reference, especially those who work with particular disciplines as subject liaisons. We hope it will help our readers to develop or enrich expertise regarding threshold concepts and approach interactions with students and faculty in new ways. We hope these chapters will provide inspiration and provoke discussion that moves librarians' work forward and enhances student learning. We look forward to continuing to engage with you about these and other troublesome concepts.

Notes

1. Jan H. F. Meyer and Ray Land, "Threshold Concepts and Troublesome Knowledge 1 – Linkages to Ways of Thinking and Practising," in *Improving Student Learning 10: Improving Student Learning Theory and Practice - 10 Years On*, ed. Chris Rust (Oxford, England: The Oxford Centre for Staff & Learning Development, Oxford Brookes University, 2003), 412–424.
2. Association of College and Research Libraries (ACRL), *Framework for Information Literacy for Higher Education*, February 2, 2015, http://www.ala.org/acrl/standards/ilframework.
3. See Lori Townsend, Amy R. Hofer, Silvia Lin Hanick, and Korey Brunetti, "Identifying Threshold Concepts for Information Literacy: A Delphi Study," *Communications in Information Literacy* 10, no. 1 (2016): 23–49.
4. Ray Land, Jan H. F. Meyer, and Michael T. Flanagan, eds. *Threshold Concepts in Practice* (Rotterdam, Boston & Taipei: Sense Publishers, 2016), xi. See also the online bibliography: Michael T. Flanagan, "Threshold Concepts: Undergraduate

Teaching, Postgraduate Training, Professional Development and School Education: A Short Introduction and a Bibliography," accessed December 22, 2016, http://www.ee.ucl.ac.uk/~mflanaga/thresholds.html.
5. Meyer and Land, "Threshold Concepts and Troublesome Knowledge 1," 412, 415.
6. The importance of this characteristic is described in strong terms: "Hence the superordinate and non-negotiable characteristic of a threshold concept is its *transformative* capacity." Land, Meyer, and Flanagan, *Threshold Concepts in Practice*, xii.
7. Jan H. F. Meyer and Ray Land, "Threshold Concepts and Troublesome Knowledge: Issues of Liminality," in *Overcoming Barriers to Student Understanding: Threshold Concepts and Troublesome Knowledge,* eds. Jan H. F. Meyer and Ray Land (London: Routledge, 2006), 21–22.
8. Meyer and Land, "Threshold Concepts and Troublesome Knowledge 1," 416.
9. Ibid.
10. Ibid.
11. Ibid.
12. Ibid., 420–421.
13. Ibid., 419
14. Ibid., 420–421.
15. Jan H. F. Meyer, "Helping Our Students: Learning, Metalearning, and Threshold Concepts," in *Taking Stock: Research on Teaching and Learning in Higher Education*, eds. Julia Christensen Hughes and Joy Mighty (Montreal: McGill-Queen's University Press, 2010), 205.
16. Ibid, 210.
17. Ray Land, Jan H. F. Meyer, and Caroline Baillie, "Editors' Preface," in *Threshold Concepts and Transformational Learning*, eds. Jan H. F. Meyer, Ray Land, and Caroline Baillie (Rotterdam: Sense Publishers, 2010), xi–xiii.
18. Ibid., xi; Meyer and Land, "Threshold Concepts and Troublesome Knowledge: Issues of Liminality," 24.
19. Leslie Schwartzman, "Transcending Disciplinary Boundaries: A Proposed Theoretical Foundation for Threshold Concepts," in *Threshold Concepts and Transformational Learning*, eds. Jan H. F. Meyer, Ray Land, and Caroline Baillie (Rotterdam: Sense Publishers, 2010), 22.
20. Land, Meyer, and Baillie, "Editors' Preface," xi.
21. Ibid.
22. Ray Land, "Toil and Trouble: Threshold Concepts as a Pedagogy of Uncertainty," in *Threshold Concepts in Practice,* eds. Ray Land, Jan H. F. Meyer, and Michael T. Flanagan, (Rotterdam: Sense Publishers, 2016), 14–16.
23. Ibid.; Schwartzman, "Transcending Disciplinary Boundaries," 33.
24. Schwartzman, "Transcending Disciplinary Boundaries," 33.
25. Land, Meyer, and Baillie, "Editors' Preface," xi.
26. Ibid.
27. Meyer and Land, "Threshold Concepts and Troublesome Knowledge: Issues of Liminality," 21–22.
28. Land, Meyer, and Baillie, "Editors' Preface," xi.
29. Thomas P. Mackey and Trudi E. Jacobson, "Reframing Information Literacy as a Metaliteracy," *College and Research Libraries* 72, no. 1 (2011): 62–78, doi: 10.5860/crl-76r1.

30. Grant Wiggins and Jay McTighe, *Understanding by Design* (Alexandria, VA: Association for Supervision and Curriculum Development, 2004).
31. ACRL, *Framework*.
32. Ibid.
33. Ibid.
34. Land, Meyer, and Baillie, "Editors' Preface," xiv.

Authority is Constructed and Contextual

Section One

CHAPTER 1*

Teaching Inclusive Authorities:
Indigenous Ways of Knowing and the Framework for Information Literacy in Native Art

Alexander Watkins

Embedded in the frame Authority is Constructed and Contextual is an important social justice theme: that "authority is constructed in that various communities may recognize different types of authority," and that there are "biases that privilege some sources of authority over others."[1] These short sentences encapsulate an important idea that we as librarians need to expand on and teach more fully and inclusively. Often when we teach this frame, the communities that define authority are solely Western communities: academia, government, business, etc. While who and what counts as authority in these communities differ, they are all based on Western systems of knowledge and ways of knowing. It is imperative to look at authority cross-culturally, to examine and consider authorities based on other cultures' ways of knowing, because the systems of knowledge that construct authority are cultural artifacts rather than universal truths. When librarians teach only Western authority, we are complicit in perpetuating a hegemonic concept of authority that only recognizes one way of knowing, one system of knowledge. This dominant authority

---

* This work is licensed under a Creative Commons Attribution 4.0 License, CC BY (https://creativecommons.org/licenses/by/4.0/).

is marked by specific and exclusive indicators: peer review, scholarly journals, PhDs, etc. Alternative knowledge from other cultural contexts are not eligible for these markers of Western authority and are therefore all too often excluded from consideration, from credibility, and from scholarly discourse, impoverishing the conversation and perpetuating inequity. How can we teach learners to value many kinds of knowledge and evaluate multiple authorities in a richer system of knowing?

This question is inherently difficult to answer because in order to effectively teach the concept, we must ask students to understand several interlocking concepts. Students need to understand knowledge systems and their resultant conceptions of authority. The idea of multiple culturally constructed authorities fits many of the requirements of a threshold concept. Although just one part of this frame, it is more discrete and coherent than the frame as a whole. Once understood, it changes the way the learner views and understands authority. No longer is it a neutral arbiter of quality marked by a few key indicators, but a result of culturally specific knowledge systems. Realizing that the ultimate goal is moving students to an understanding of this threshold has fundamentally changed how I teach authority. Students cannot just follow a formula or go through a checklist to determine authority; instead, they require cultural knowledge and understanding. As an art librarian, I see the need to embrace teaching a more inclusive authority, especially in classes that deal with the art of other cultures.

In this chapter I will specifically explore teaching multiple authorities in indigenous art, where the culture that created the art varies drastically in knowledge practices from the culture now interpreting that art. When researching the art of non-Western and indigenous cultures, the concept of multiple culturally-constructed authorities becomes crucial to creating inclusive scholarship and interpretations. Researchers that only use Western markers of authority to evaluate information will find a one-sided perspective because academic sources are most often written about these communities rather than by them. Reliance on Western authority effectively silences the voices of indigenous people who made the artwork under study, who used it in their rituals or daily life, and whose traditions that art belongs to. Under this Western hegemony, interpretation of native cultures is denied to members of that culture and reserved for those with Western authority. As Linda Tuhiwai Smith so searingly recounts in the introduction to her book, the Western monopoly on interpretation is incredibly painful to indigenous cultures: "It galls us that Western researchers and intellectuals can assume to know all that is possible to know of us… It appalls us that the West can desire, extract, and claim ownership of our ways of knowing, our imagery, the things we create and produce, and then simultaneously reject the people who created and developed those ideas…."[2] This sentiment should spur us as librarians to fight against colonialist constructions of authority that deny voice and agency to indigenous peoples, and to teach the validity of indigenous perspectives.

The differences between Western and indigenous ways of knowing means different traits are seen as markers of authority. According to Barnhardt and Kawagley, native knowledge systems are often based on long histories of accumulated experiences with the world. The particulars and specifics of this knowledge are related to the whole as native knowledge is often holistic and interrelated. This knowledge is passed on through stories, demonstrations, and trial.[3] Mastery depends on practical application of knowledge and indeed is tested through everyday survival: "Knowledge is something you do; not a pre-existing tool independent of the person holding it, nor of the uses it might be put."[4] This can be contrasted with Western knowledge, which is typically compartmentalized, taught in detached and decontextualized settings, and indirectly measured with tests rather than judged based on one's ability to put that knowledge into practice.[5] Thus, in traditional native knowledge systems there is respect and trust for inherited wisdom, often communicated through an oral tradition, and for knowledge that has proved its utility in everyday practices. There is respect for stories that connect the particulars of knowledge to holistic worldviews, values, and life ways. Knowledge is collective, evolving in a community of users, knowers, and actors. Authority is not conferred via systematic processes of Western bureaucracy, but rather through community decision making and respect for the knowledge and authority of elders.[6] It's important to point out that both knowledge systems have advantages, that they reinforce and fill in gaps, rather than one being superior to the other. But because of these differing systems, indigenous knowledge is often kept out of traditional academic publications because it lacks the markers of authority librarians so often teach: credentials, peer-review, or citations to the written record; it instead relies on the wisdom of elders, community agreement, and oral tradition. However, there is still much common ground in how both traditional and Western knowledge are built: reliance on observations of the natural world, recognizing patterns, then verifying and predicting.[7] It should then be possible to teach students to value and evaluate information from indigenous authorities.

Certainly, indigenous cultures are not the only groups who are excluded from Western authority, especially in art history. Patriarchal histories and systems often keep women out of the conversation. The emphasis on scholarly and analytical approaches in the Western tradition frequently devalues the embodied, tacit knowledge of artisans because it is often based on tradition and physical skill. Looking at the art of indigenous cultures, we should not be surprised that there are intersectional biases. Indigenous artisans are often women of color, whose voices are frequently silenced and ignored. The knowledge of craftspeople has special resonance in indigenous knowledge systems.

Native artisans' skills are passed down, applied in everyday situations, and what they make is tied to ways of living but also intimately related to spiritual systems. Knowledge is made, embedded in, and carried on through the baskets, songs, rituals, and other art forms of the native culture.[8] The importance of this knowledge and the array of factors lining up against its inclusion in scholarship only makes it more vital to proactively ensure the voices of native artisans are heard and given the credence and authority that they deserve.

The frame of Authority is Constructed and Contextual is an important but imperfect tool for incorporating indigenous authorities into library instruction. The first important point made by the Framework is that "Experts understand that authority is a type of influence recognized or exerted within a community."[9] From this quote, the conclusion can be drawn that authority is a relative, culturally constructed concept. But the frame does not seem to fully embrace the implication of this assertion: that no one type of cultural authority is natural or superior. While there may be a hierarchy of authority among communities within the same culture, once there is a cross-cultural comparison, hierarchies become colonializing and culturally supremacist. Western systems of knowledge devalue information from culturally diverse authorities. Despite the frame's insistence that experts understand multiple types of authority, it does not recognize that they also have incentives to protect and police the boundaries of their authority. This makes it difficult to move information from an indigenous source to an academic arena, where that information is not considered authoritative.

The frame also implicitly recognizes a certain kind of authority as important and marginalizes other kinds: "Experts know how to seek authoritative voices but also recognize that unlikely voices can be authoritative, depending on need."[10] Here, certain voices are always authoritative, while marginalized voices can (in unlikely situations) be authoritative if there is a specific need for it. This begrudging recognition should be rejected, especially in native arts, where indigenous views should be considered as, if not more, authoritative as academic ones. Indeed, in many cases, indigenous knowledge is more authoritative, especially when it comes to the making and uses of art objects. One disposition of learners outlined in this frame is that they "question traditional notions of granting authority and recognize the value of diverse ideas and worldviews."[11] Although this disposition has good intentions, it is unclear what it means by "traditional," but by pairing it with "diverse ideas" it implies that this traditional authority is somehow non-diverse and "others" any additional and diverse worldviews. The conclusion we must draw is that the Western conception of knowledge is the traditional default, despite the existence of indigenous knowledge traditions, whose origins predate the academic tradition by many hundreds of years. It sets up a dichotomy: there is the default Western academic knowledge (which needs to be questioned) and other diverse knowledge (whose value is generally unrecognized). Despite the Eurocentric phrasing in this disposition, the frame importantly shifts evaluation from being carried out entirely in a Western framework to the possibility for considering different conceptions of authority. It is also a reminder to be wary of positioning one kind of authority as the default. It points to two core ideas: that there are multiple authorities that are each cultural constructs (and therefore none are natural) and there are benefits to seeking out multiple authorities.

Teaching authority with this degree of nuance is challenging in a typical one-shot library instruction session. We want students to broaden the perspectives they consider, develop a more inclusive concept of authority, and be able to evaluate diverse sources of information. Teaching this threshold concept will often require working closely with the course instructor in order to hook into class themes and assignments. Clearly, there is little point of discussing alternative authorities if the instructor will accept only academic sources and has little interest in broadening the perspectives they would like students to consider, so it is key to identify instructors whose values, interests, and course objectives align with exploring this concept. Hopefully, in classes on indigenous arts this will be rare. Rather, instructors are likely to be teaching students about indigenous world views already. Indeed, it may be that understanding native world views and the profound impacts they have on understanding and interaction with the world is a threshold concept for indigenous studies. Talking to instructors about threshold concepts and how the library can be a partner in teaching indigenous ways of knowing can be a good way to propose a collaboration. The library session can then both reinforce and expand this concept, and students will already be primed and ready to apply the idea of native world views to evaluating indigenous authority. Thus, together the instructor and the librarian can help students step through this threshold of understanding world views, while also making progress on understanding the constructed nature of authority. Teaching inclusive authority may also be bolstered by many art history students' awareness of debates over the Western canon, the Eurocentric narrative of the development of art, as well as moves to add "non-Western" art into art history. Knowledge of this historical pattern of exclusion and the default positioning of the Western is transferable to concepts of authority.

Ideally, a library session will allow students to think through ideas about authority themselves via guided exploration and discussion. Given some prompting through worksheets or questions, students are certainly capable of reaching many of the important conclusions on their own. They may readily recognize the importance of indigenous points of view, the different kinds of information they get from these voices, and realize they need to evaluate these sources using different criteria. Students may be able to come up with some of the ways of researching indigenous knowledge, including finding articles written by indigenous people or in indigenous magazines, finding interviews, seeking out oral histories, or, depending on the nature of the project, conducting their own field research. This last option, however, can be problematic due to the colonial history of research on indigenous peoples.

While we want to encourage students to seek out indigenous voices, there are problematic dynamics that come into play when researchers go to indigenous people for answers. Linda Tuhiwai Smith lays out the connection of research to colonialism and imperialism, and the pain and hurt research has caused and continues to cause indigenous peoples.[12] To ameliorate this painful dynamic, it is vital to ensure that research empowers native voices rather than exploits them. Native ideas should not be treated as raw materials needing packaging and analysis by Western scholars before they constitute authoritative knowledge, but as inherently authoritative. It is also important to recognize that indigenous voices can come from many places, especially the all-too-common exclusion of Western-educated natives because they are not considered to be writing from an "authentic" indigenous perspective.[13] One important notion for researchers seeking indigenous voices is the idea of "reporting back," that there should be information reciprocity, cooperation, and mutual benefit.[14] In most cases, students at the undergraduate level should be relying on already available indigenous perspectives, rather than conducting original research. Indeed, the library session can help students avoid making these mistakes by teaching students how to find indigenous voices in various formats, from articles to oral histories. It will still be important to discuss and be aware of the issues inherent in research on indigenous communities, so that students accord indigenous voices appropriate respect, dignity, and authority.

Teaching that Authority is Constructed and Contextual has to be more than teaching learners how to evaluate and identify scholarly articles. Such learning objectives only skim the surface of the frame and indeed do not reflect the core idea of varying cultural authorities. Classes should get students to grapple with multiple ways that different cultures and communities construct authority, as well as the ways the West systematically marginalizes and trivializes alternate forms of authority. Teaching academic authority on an equal footing with indigenous knowledge can help demonstrate the concepts embedded in this frame. There are quite a few potential learning objectives for teaching inclusive authorities.

Here are some possible learning objectives for teaching indigenous authority in art history:

- Students understand that authority is constructed based on cultural systems of knowledge and ways of knowing.
- Students understand that indigenous authority is different from but not less than Western conceptions of authority.

- Students question the Western system of authority as default or natural.
- Students can identify and explain the different markers of authority in Western and indigenous cultures.
- Students seek out native voices and can articulate how and why native understandings of art are different from Western interpretations.
- Students are aware of the colonial nature of research on indigenous cultures.

It will be difficult to teach all of these learning objectives in a typical one-shot session, where it may be competing for time with other learning objectives. However, if an entire class session can be devoted to this frame only, its goals might be for students to begin to understand indigenous perspectives, for students to explore the differences between academic and indigenous knowledge, and to understand the importance of these alternate viewpoints. For the University of Colorado Boulder's World Art Studies II class, the second semester survey, I worked with the professor and teaching assistants to integrate these concepts into a unit on Maya art. Each of the five teaching assistants (TAs) dedicated one of their recitation sessions to discussing indigenous knowledge and the Authority is Contextual frame. They based the session on a lesson plan and worksheet I designed, and this structure built on the "train the trainer model for information literacy" instruction we have in the art survey classes.[15] First, the students were assigned to read a scholarly article about Mayan art. In the discussion session, students watched a video interview with a native artisan. TAs set up these as two concrete examples of different kinds of knowledge and used a worksheet to guide students in thinking about these issues. First, teams of students filled out a matrix (Chart 1) to compare indigenous knowledge to scholarly knowledge. A completed matrix was given to TAs in order to facilitate assessment, but not to students. Interestingly, students struggle with answering the questions in regard to scholarly knowledge just as much as for indigenous knowledge. While it can be helpful for students to already be familiar with Western sources, this is not necessary, and, in fact, a lack of entrenchment may make this a particularly good moment to address the question of authority. The exercise helps students understand scholarly discourse, but does not present it as the only place authority is vested.

Students then work through three further questions:
- What are three clues or ways that you can tell that a source is scholarly?
    This question is not necessarily tied to understanding indigenous knowledge, but to reinforce the ability to identify scholarly sources.

- How might you gather indigenous or practitioner knowledge? How might these methods avoid problematic researcher/indigenous subject dynamics?

    This question asks students to think about how they could get indigenous perspectives, while asking them to recognize issues in doing indigenous research.
- Do you think that scholarly and indigenous knowledge are compatible? Why or why not? What might be some of the barriers to indigenous knowledge being valued in a scholarly context?

    This question is particularly important. It asks students to think about how indigenous knowledge is excluded from scholarly discourse. Working through this question with students can be used as formative assessment by gauging how well students can articulate the differences and barriers. Then the instructor can add or modify important points that were missed by the students.

Finally, student groups were asked to explain or describe a work of art from an imagined scholarly or indigenous perspective. Groups were assigned alternating perspectives, and then one group from each side was asked to present their description. This task allows students to be creative, practice presentation skills, and use role-playing to imagine themselves in the shoes of an academic writer or indigenous artisan. This activity can be used to assess whether students demonstrate an understanding of the divergent ways these two groups interact with art. I would expect to see students who grasp the divergent interactions with art presenting a construction of an academic perspective using visual analysis, jargon, and references to academic theories, while those presenting the indigenous perspective should reference use, tradition, and religious or cultural significance.

In many cases, a full session focusing on indigenous authority may not be an option. However, it is still certainly possible to introduce students to indigenous voices in a one-shot session. This might mean folding indigenous voices into a larger context of various competing voices on native art. For example, for a native North American art class, the professor was concerned with student reliance on Internet sources, especially Wikipedia and gallery websites. Because of this concern, it made sense to incorporate various voices and their modes of communication, one of which would be native peoples. So in this class, students worked in groups to fill in a matrix where each row contained a different community that communicates about native art, and students answered a series of questions about information from that community (Chart 2). Each group was assigned one row and had to report out their answers. These reports are an opportunity for assessment, where the instructor can stress important points and correct mistakes. This approach has both advantages and drawbacks. We were able to cover many of the communities that communicate about native art, discuss different information creation processes, and have students recognize different types of authority, while addressing the professor's initial concerns about students' overreliance on the web. This approach of connecting a broader understanding of the threshold concept to a professor's specific concern can be an effective vehicle for beginning a conversation with faculty and students. However, one drawback to this approach is that most of the communities covered were Western and draw on the same knowledge system, reducing the time to focus on the threshold concept and differences in authorities created by multi-cultural ways of knowing. This can be partially remedied by explicating and drawing contrasts between the various Western authorities and indigenous authority, as well as spending additional time on native authority.

When students understand that authority is constructed and contextual, they realize that there are cultural systems that create authority, that important information can come from multiple different authorities, and that understanding is enriched by listening to voices from various cultures. Despite its problematic construction, the frame can help librarians teach a concept that is so important for rectifying the exclusion and marginalization of non-Western voices in academia. Indeed, it is increasingly untenable to do otherwise. Teaching only the Western construction of authority suggests that these sources are the only authoritative sources for information and Western criteria are the only criteria with which to judge authority. Librarians should not be complicit in the hegemony of Western knowledge practices, and instead should contribute to a diverse and inclusive conception of authority. We can be allies to native voices, helping them to be recognized as the experts they are. We should want learners to hear and value native stories and explanations, not to assume that all that can be known about these objects can be found in Western texts. Instead, they need to understand that "each object contains memories of the person who made it, the knowledge of how to gather and prepare materials, the prayers and songs, the philosophies and metaphors for making sense of the world."[16]

CHART 1.1
Matrix comparing indigenous and scholarly authority

	Scholarly Knowledge	Indigenous Knowledge
How or in what form is this knowledge disseminated/communicated?	Books and scholarly articles	Oral tradition, interviews, apprenticeships. Passed down through tradition, training, and stories.
What kind of people are considered to be authorities in these spheres of knowledge? What qualifies them to be authorities?	Scholars, professors, others with PhDs. Qualified by study/education/research	Elders, religious leaders, master artisans. They are qualified by their years of experience, expertise, role in the community, and respect of community.
Who's the audience of this knowledge?	Other scholars	Community members, tribe members, trainees
What is the purpose of this type of knowledge?	Explain and interpret art from a scholarly perspective. Apply academic theories to art. Analyze cultures and their history through their art.	Pass on traditions and explain art in a way meaningful to the community. Knowledge of how to use art in traditions, rituals, ceremonies. Knowledge of how to create art via traditional techniques, motifs, etc.
How is each type of knowledge useful in interpreting and understanding art?	Get theory and analysis, get archival research, get art historical perspective	How the community views and uses the art. How the art was created. The art's meaning to the community.

CHART 1.2
Matrix for comparing the output and authority of various communities who communicate about indigenous art.

Communities	Who is considered an authority in this community and why?	Through what means do each of these groups communicate?	For what purpose or needs would you use information from this community?	Pros of using information from this community:	Cons of using information from this community:
Wikipedia					
Gallery					
Museum					
Indigenous					
Academic					

Notes

1. Association of College and Research Libraries (ACRL), *Framework for Information Literacy for Higher Education*, February 2, 2015, http://www.ala.org/acrl/standards/ilframework.
2. Linda Tuhiwai Smith, *Decolonizing Methodologies: Research and Indigenous Peoples* (London: Zed Books, 1999), 1.
3. Ray Barnhardt and Angayuqaq Oscar Kawagley, "Indigenous Knowledge Systems and Alaska Native Ways of Knowing," *Anthropology & Education Quarterly* 36, no. 1 (2005): 8–23.
4. Christopher Jocks as quoted in Deborah Doxtator, "Basket, Bead and Quill, and the Making of 'Traditional' Art," in *Basket, Bead and Quill*, ed. Janet E. Clark (Thunder Bay, Ontario: Thunder Bay Art Gallery, 1996), 12.
5. Angayuqaq Oscar Kawagley and Ray Barnhardt, "Education Indigenous to Place: Western Science Meets Native Reality," 1998, http://eric.ed.gov/?id=ED426823.
6. Ibid.
7. Barnhardt and Kawagley, "Indigenous Knowledge Systems and Alaska Native Ways of Knowing."
8. Doxtator, "Basket, Bead and Quill, and the Making of 'Traditional' Art."
9. ACRL, *Framework for Information Literacy for Higher Education*.
10. Ibid.
11. Ibid.
12. Smith, *Decolonizing Methodologies*.
13. Ibid., 13–14.
14. Ibid., 15.
15. Alexander Watkins and Katherine Morrison, "Can Only Librarians Do Library Instruction? Collaborating with Graduate Students to Teach Discipline-Specific Information Literacy," *The Journal of Creative Library Practice*, February 2015, http://creativelibrarypractice.org/2015/02/27/can-only-librarians-do-library-instruction/.
16. Doxtator, "Basket, Bead and Quill, and the Making of 'Traditional' Art," 14.

CHAPTER 2*

"But How Do I Know It's a Good Source?"
Authority is Constructed in Social Work Practice

Callie Wiygul Branstiter and Rebecca Halpern

Social workers, like librarians, tend to be a skeptical bunch. Social workers serve in a variety of professional roles ranging from therapists to program directors to human resources managers. Regardless of the setting in which a social worker is employed, they are often required to make important clinical or policy decisions. On a micro, or clinical level, social workers often have to determine the best treatment model for their clients. Some decisions clinical social workers need to make are: Given what the client is suffering from and the client's own dispositions and beliefs, what are the best approaches for treatment? Which types of clinical settings, such as in-patient programs, group therapy, or school-based programs, are going to have the greatest impact? On a macro, or community-level, social workers may help to make policy decisions about wellness and mental health initiatives, such as low-cost health care clinics, low-income housing, or recreation activities. Some decisions social workers in the policy sector may need to make are: Which resources are their communities lacking? Who are the important constituents or stakeholders? What laws exist to help or hinder the initiative?

---

* This work is licensed under a Creative Commons Attribution-NonCommercial-NoDerivatives 4.0 License, CC BY-NC-ND (https://creativecommons.org/licenses/by-nc-nd/4.0/).

When making these decisions, social workers employ an evidence-based practice (EBP) approach. The social work EBP approach has its roots in other clinical and practitioner-based professions like medicine and nursing. This approach advocates decision-making as a conversation among the practitioner's expertise, the dispositions of the client or community of focus, and, of course, research evidence. For social workers, these decisions have potential real and lasting impact on what are often underrepresented or marginalized communities. EBP educators encourage burgeoning social workers to ask: "Whose evidence and for what purpose?"[1] Social workers understand that even a highly evaluated or widely recognized treatment model won't be appropriate for all clients, and that any evidence-based decision must be contextualized within the client's sociopolitical realities. For librarians teaching in the social work discipline, engaging students in that "whose evidence skepticism" is the forefront of much research instruction. In particular, the Authority is Constructed and Contextual information literacy frame bridges library research strategies and social work ethos.

The University of Southern California's (USC) School of Social Work is a heavily evidence-based program, designed to prepare students to be able to judiciously locate, assess, and employ evidence on macro-, messo-, and micro-levels of decision making. Indeed, the Council on Social Work Education "recognizes that teaching social work students how to access, analyze, interpret, and appropriately employ evidence is critical to effective social work practice."[2] Interestingly—for both social workers and librarians—what the profession considers "best evidence" is highly dependent on a number of factors, including, unsurprisingly, the methodology used to generate that evidence. As indicated by models like the hierarchy of evidence,[3] EBP practitioners recognize that not all research evidence constitutes "best evidence." The hierarchy of evidence is a pyramid to visually represent methodologies that provide the strongest evidentiary case for clinical decision-making. This model visualizes that for most social science research, so-called filtered research methodologies—like meta analyses and systematic reviews—provide "stronger" evidence than, say, qualitative studies.[4] So while students are prompted to consider the source of the evidence, who published it, where it was published, the purpose or use of the evidence, and how the evidence was generated, they are also being told that their professional expertise and clients' dispositions matter, too. This paradox forms the basis for the paradox of social work education. It should be noted that EBP generally, and the hierarchy of evidence specifically, is contested in the field of social work. One argument against a heavy focus on systematic reviews and meta-analyses is that it privileges one kind of knowledge over another—namely, academic, quantitatively gathered evidence. The argument goes that EBP privileges research above clients, and that perhaps a better term for EBP is instead "research supported."[5] Nevertheless, the School of Social Work, where the authors of this chapter work, is an EBP program training EBP practitioners, with issues of community representation in research literature woven throughout the curriculum.

In traditional models of primary and secondary education, students are taught to yield to professional literature and/or "expert" opinions, as well as synthesize these arguments into their own argument. However, in the context of social work practice, students will use their own professional expertise and opinions to diagnose and develop a treatment plan for patients, instead of simply consulting traditional evidence and research published in peer-reviewed journals. Unlike their colleagues in medicine, social workers predicate treatment plans on a combination of traditional research interventions, client preferences, and cultural ethics.[6] In particular, social work education unravels and exposes the political underpinnings of "systems that grant authority, including their faults, along with considerations of when, where, and why these systems are used."[7] Social work education provides a rich backdrop for understanding how authority of evidence is a situational, contextual, and, indeed, political negotiation.[8]

When information literacy educators are grappling with the Authority is Constructed and Contextual frame, we are mostly speaking to an information source's cognitive authority (as opposed to political or administrative). Cognitive authority refers to the believability of a source based on who the source is. Simply put, some information is more credible than others simply because the person who told you "knows what they're talking about."[9] Unlike, say, political authority, cognitive authority is concerned with a source's "trust and credibility,"[10] as well as reputation of the source. As Wilkinson points out, authority in this context is not synonymous with expertise, though "authorities [sometimes] obtain their credibility by being experts or reliable sources for knowledge."[11] The distinction between cognitive authority and other authorities is crucial. Social work educators, and the librarians who work with them, want students to recognize that "unlikely voices can be authoritative," and that students "are developing their own authoritative voices in a particular area."[12] Social workers trained in EBP thinking come to understand that source authority is a mediation between evidentiary (how the source was produced and by who) and experiential (what the practitioner knows about their client) spheres of knowledge.

When we first familiarized ourselves with the Framework, the Authority is Constructed and Contextual frame immediately seemed like there would be a clear connection between the dispositions therein and the type of research social work students do. Evidence-based practice work requires students to "evaluate [information sources] based on the information need and the context in which the information will be used."[13] What we took for granted, though, is just how troubling the terms "authority" and "contextual" truly are. Indeed, it has been quite a struggle to reorient our teaching practices away from strictly scholarly, peer-reviewed sources and not just for us, but for teaching faculty, too. If authority is constructed and contextual, does that mean anything goes? The transformative and troublesome nature of the threshold concept within the Authority is Constructed and Contextual frame seemingly operates in opposition to the constructed and contextual nature of evidence-based practice.

The librarians in this program grapple with teaching "that some kinds of expertise are more worthy than others without privileging certain sources of knowledge."[14] In fact, the term "evidence" itself presents its own problematic connotations. If experts are expected to "remain skeptical of the systems that have elevated that authority and the information created by it," how do we reconcile the hierarchy of evidence, which asserts some ways of producing knowledge are better than others, with the understanding that many of the populations served by social workers do not, and may never have, peer-reviewed, meta-analytical research about them? In fact, this incongruity illuminates the troublesome nature of the threshold concept, as well as general lamentations that have surrounded this frame from its conception: "Novices may understand evidence and authority as unchangeable and can struggle to relate their own use of evidence in daily life to scholarly or professional approaches to evidence."[15] Clearly defining what constitutes evidence in social work practice to new MSW students sets their standards for defining their research methods throughout their program.

It is important to distinguish between authority and expertise when considering evidence-based practice in social work research. One of the central critiques of this frame, at least initially, was the conflation of authority with expertise.[16] For example, community stakeholders, such as civic leaders, may have the highest credibility and historical understanding of a community. This credibility naturally lends itself to authority. Often, students look toward such authoritative members of a community during their community tours in order to gain historical insight to synthesize with demographic information in their papers. But authority is not the same as expertise and, as the frame explains, "Experts understand that authority is a type of influence recognized or exerted within a community. Experts view authority with an attitude of informed skepticism and an openness to new perspectives, additional voices, and changes in schools of thought."[17] Experts have specific, concrete knowledge bases; authoritative beings have credibility within a sphere of influence.[18] In this example with community stakeholders, these leaders are authoritative sources of information because they have influence recognized within a community, but these stakeholders are not necessarily experts. Distinguishing these characteristics in knowledge practices is challenging, but nevertheless a good exercise is understanding authority in scholarship and communities.

In addition, the concept of authority is laced with many political and social problems. For example, the widely used Beck Depression Inventory is considered one of the premier authoritative tools for measuring depression, but has real limitations. The original sample upon which BDI-II was developed was largely Caucasian and greatly misrepresentative of the United States population, as well as many other countries. Additionally, the inventory fails to recognize factors that determine how other cultural groups might experience depression. It is therefore up to the social worker to determine if this inventory is an appropriate measure for their client.[19]

About the USC School of Social Work

The USC School of Social Work is deeply committed to introducing students to a contextual, evidence-based way of thinking about information, as evidenced in a curriculum update. The School recently implemented new foundation curriculum based on updated Council of Social Work Education (CSWE) standards. The new curriculum "places a stronger emphasis on the science of social work and leadership" and "reflects feedback from employers and alumni, who cite a need for additional training in analyzing results, thinking critically about complex problems, embracing and managing increasing demands for accountability and data-informed decision-making, budgeting, effectively collaborating with colleagues across settings and institutions and with professionals trained in other disciplines...."[20] The heart of the Framework for Information Literacy for Higher Education is in accepting that "students have a greater role and responsibility in creating new knowledge, in understanding the contours and the changing dynamics of the world of information, and in using information, data, and scholarship ethically."[21] Thus, critical thinking, data-based decision-making, and steering through the structures and understanding the purposes of information, as implicated by the new CSWE standards, align with many of the tenets of information literacy. From the beginning of this program, students engage with a myriad of both scholarly and popular resources to refine their knowledge of social work principles and trends. Students are also tasked with identifying authoritative sources upon their entry into the program during the School's welcome week. This skill is reinforced during their foundation year courses (i.e., first-year courses), during which students must compare and assimilate an author's arguments into the findings of other sources, articulate their own argument, and evaluate sources.

In one such foundation-year course, SOWK 536: Policy and Advocacy in Professional Social Work (SOWK 536), students engage with contextual authority in their first assignment, a community immersion research paper. This paper builds on students' experiences touring an assigned community in Los Angeles before the first week of class. They are expected to merge these experiences with the scholarly, popular, and anecdotal sources that describe the socio-economic and political underpinnings of each community. Rather than merely documenting their experiences in each community, students are expected to synthesize their original conclusions with the documented findings of traditional sources of information, such as government resources, newspapers, and scholarly journal articles. In addition, the assignment instructions urge students to come to a conclusion of how well (or not) their communities function, supported by evidence they have uncovered during their research. The assignment prompt encourages students to compare and contrast how their perceptions of the community differ from published research on the areas. Students are also encouraged to share only the data they believe to be most important or representative of their communities.

In this particular assignment, because students are expected to develop an analysis of a community based on many different types of information from a variety of sources, they demonstrate their ability to "define different types of authority," "use… indicators of authority to determine the credibility of sources," recognize the sometimes informal nature of authoritative content, acknowledge their own expertise in an area of the social work discipline, and "understand the increasingly social nature of the information ecosystem."[22] They also begin to determine the utility of and/or bias within each source. Because this is the first assignment in a foundation-year course students complete within their first semester of the program, students must rely on their own conceptions of authority and expertise, as well as the librarians' presentations of authority and expertise, including an explanation of the discrepancies between the two. The Authority is Constructed and Contextual frame helps to explain the convoluted nature of this process, which "includes points of disagreement where debate and dialogue work to deepen the conversations around knowledge"[23] and, thus, aligns with the learning objectives and outcomes of this course.

The student learning outcomes for this course complement many frames well, but they complement the Authority is Constructed and Contextual frame particularly effectively. One core competency for this course is critical thinking, wherein students are expected to apply critical thinking to inform and communicate professional judgments and the related student learning outcome indicates students will "distinguish, integrate, and appraise multiple sources of knowledge."[24] The onus is on the librarians to help students understand that all reputable sources, regardless of type, use evidence, but each uses such evidence in different ways. Though the assignment description does not explicitly make connections to evidence-based practice, the fact that this is an inaugural assignment in a heavily EBP-focused program is apparent. Throughout the assignment, students are encouraged to use research evidence to make connections between issues facing their communities of focus to epidemiological data, or potential interventions. The expectation to weave research evidence into a community analysis introduces students to the complexity of evidence-based practice in that students need to "appraise multiple sources of knowledge" within the context of a specific community. The following section outlines how the social work librarians address this task in our instruction sessions.

What we do

The School has two librarians embedded into its program—one on-campus and one distance librarian. The librarians supplement these library sessions with course-integrated tutorials and videos. One-shot sessions are offered on a voluntary basis to the approximately sixty-seven course sections; most, but not all, sections receive in-class library instruction. In addition to the tutorials and videos, the librarians recorded a lecture for students whose instructors do not opt into library instruction.

Each library instruction session focuses on how to use evidence in the community immersion paper. For example, the librarians explain that finding a peer-reviewed article about their specific community is unlikely and that, in fact, finding location-specific scholarly information isn't necessary for the assignment. Instead, it is more likely that students will find articles pertaining to topics that can be applied to their communities, such as the connections between violent crime and availability of social service centers or food deserts and the number of children who receive free/reduced lunches. In social work parlance, the librarians emphasize that peer-reviewed information is helpful for macro-level analysis, whereas location-specific information is often used for micro-level analysis. The librarians also focus on introducing students to evidence-based practice, which is a tenet of social work research. Although the program also includes a course solely focused on evidence-based practice, and many students opt to enroll in that class concurrently with SOWK 536, students must demonstrate an aptitude for illuminating consistencies or discrepancies between published research and their opinions of the communities they study.

The librarians also highlight the fact that a source's reputability depends on how it will be used. For example, a community organizer may be the most authoritative voice in a community and may provide incisive historical commentary that will not be found in a journal article or other scholarly sources. Or, if such commentary is found in a scholarly source, students must analyze the power structures inherent in traditional media sources during certain times throughout history. Thus, informal, first-person commentary from a community organizer who has lived in a community for decades may lend credence to a particular argument or, at the very least, provide important context to accounts in traditional media sources. This opens the floor for conversations about the way privilege influences the perception of a source's perceived authority.[25]

Methods of teaching the frame

The librarians discovered that one major source of anxiety for students is distinguishing between reputable and non-reputable sources. Unsurprisingly, many students simply want to know the best sources to use and frequently ask the librarians, "But how do I know if my source is good?" To be able to help students through the Authority is Constructed frame, the librarians have to begin by framing popular and scholarly sources as equal (one is not necessarily better than the other) and explaining that they both serve different purposes. For example, while students might not find demographic research about their communities in library databases, they may find it in popular sources. In fact, specific information about their community, such as demographics and statistics, will likely be found in a popular source of information, such as a blog, city council website, or even a government resource, such as the United States Census Bureau's website. The librarians go on to explain the differences in purpose, authorship, audience, and availability between scholarly and popular sources. One analogy the librarians use is that so-called "popular sources" are used to answer the who, what, where, and when questions about a community (questions that are typically answered by demographic data and newspaper stories); whereas so-called "scholarly sources" are used to answer "so what?" or to make connections between those who-what-where-when questions. This distinction helps students recognize that peer-reviewed or scholarly works are not necessarily the most authoritative or appropriate source for every kind of question they'll ask.

Understanding authority as a construct largely depends on understanding its function. The audience of a blog is likely different than the audience of a scholarly journal article. Again, the librarians reiterate that a journal article is not necessarily "better" than a blog—it only serves a different purpose. From here, the librarians have the opportunity to introduce the conversation surrounding power structures inherent in typical scholarly publishing processes, which further contextualize the construct of authority. In particular, the librarians reiterate that many of the underrepresented, under-resourced communities they will often work with are not well included in traditional scholarly publications. In those cases, looking at information produced by local or indigenous sources can be better than peer-reviewed scholarship.

The next step of the process involves the flow of information. The librarians explain that it is important for students to do some legwork when deciding which sources to include in their paper—that simply telling them which sources are best isn't straightforward. Sources should be written by a knowledgeable author, meaning one who is considered an authoritative source within the field of social work or who can otherwise authoritatively speak to a topic without bias. Also important is that the information found within should be corroborated with other sources. By demonstrating or discussing methods to corroborate information with other sources, the librarians offer a method for evaluating sources.

The next step involves identifying where information "lives." This is considered part of the nuts and bolts of the assignment, where students explain that popular sources of information are likely freely available, while many scholarly sources are paywalled behind library database subscriptions. This provides another opportunity to "identify authoritative information sources based on need."[26] To that end, the librarians developed a library guide for this assignment to provide students with a jumping-off point. In that guide are interactive tutorials we designed called "Knowing Where to Look" and "Evaluating Sources." These tutorials provide practice exercises where students begin to identity where to look for different types of information and how to evaluate the usefulness of information based on the information need and assignment requirements. Students are encouraged to complete these tutorials prior to the live sessions. Throughout the live sessions, we design activities to let students practice identifying where different types of information live in the information landscape. For online sessions, the librarian uses the Poll Pod in Adobe Connect to ask students to identify the most appropriate place to look for local crime statistics, population demographics, or research on the impact of gentrification. By highlighting that there is no "one right source" or place to look, students begin to realize the complexity and nuance of information-seeking for social work research. This understanding is highlighted in the learning activities; when we see that students disagree about where to look for, say, information about the effects of food insecurity, we encourage a discussion among those students until they reach a level of mutual understanding. Moreover, these exercises underscore that authority depends on much more than simply who wrote an article, but also on the function and use of that article. For example, when looking for information related to the number of veterans under the age of forty employed in a specific county, we advise students that the United States Department of Veteran Affairs or the United States Bureau of Labor Statistics websites are authoritative sources for this information, but they may also find pertinent information through local nonprofit veterans advocacy websites.

Conclusion

Shifting from a lesson plan primarily concerned with showing students library resources for their research to one where we encourage them to engage with the concepts in the Authority is Constructed and Contextual frame is not without its obstacles. While restructuring our in-class sessions and digital learning objects to support the frame has brought increased engagement in our instruction among students, there were some challenges in working with social work faculty. Like most instruction librarians, we faced some resistance from social work faculty who simply wanted us to teach students where to go to get the resources they need. For some, talking about authority and the politics of publishing is outside the scope of what they're used to getting from librarians. The most effective approach for implementing this frame is through collaboration with, and education for, disciplinary faculty. Having frank conversations about their and our expectations for the session, as well as articulating how the Authority is Constructed and Contextual frame (without necessarily calling it that by name) supports the learning objectives for the course, program, and discipline as a whole, especially as it relates to the training of evidence-based practitioners, can be beneficial. Often these conversations would start by asking faculty what they felt their students had a hard time grasping and going from there. The librarians would talk about the Authority is Constructed and Contextual frame and the dispositions therein, and connect the language of the frame to the language instructors used to describe the sources their students used. Also, of course, for many instructors the proof of the pudding is in the eating. Shifting our focus away from simply instructing students where to go toward addressing how authority is constructed and contextual leads to better-researched, more nuanced papers, as indicated through our various channels of instructor feedback. Some of those channels include sitting in on the faculty meetings for instructors of the course, receiving midterm grade reports from student advisors, and simply asking instructors, once that first assignment has been graded, to reflect on the types of sources their students used.

When introducing any information literacy concept into a disciplinary arena, it is essential to connect the dispositions of that concept to the ethos of the discipline. For social workers, the need to be able to locate the best possible information for their clients is well aligned with the skills and dispositions brought on by thinking about authority in a contextual way. For a profession centered on EBP, the need to be able to critically investigate how authority, expertise, and evidence manifests in information sources is a crucial skill. Again, evidence-based social work practice demands that practitioners ask, "Whose evidence and for what purpose?" Our jobs as information literacy professionals is to equip students with the ability to ask—and answer—that question. While evidence-based practice is not without its criticisms and limitations,[27] an EBP ethos of skepticism, interrogation, and sociopolitical contexts makes way for a bridge connecting a disciplinary practice to information literacy.

Notes

1. Stanley L. Witkin and W. David Harrison, "Editorial: Whose Evidence and For What Purpose?" *Social Work* 46, no. 4 (2001): 293.
2. "Teaching Evidence-Based Practice," Council of Social Work Education, accessed May 16, 2016, http://www.cswe.org/CentersInitiatives/CurriculumResources/TeachingEvidence-BasedPractice.aspx.
3. Patricia B. Burns., Rod J. Rohrich, and Kevin C. Chung, "The Levels of Evidence and Their Role in Evidence-based Medicine," *Plastic and Reconstructive Surgery* 128, no. 1 (2011): 305; B. A. Petrisor and M. Bhandari, "The Hierarchy of Evidence: Levels and Grades of Recommendation," *Indian Journal of Orthopaedics* 41, no. 1 (2007): 11.
4. Mark Petticrew and Helen Roberts, "Evidence, Hierarchies, and Typologies: Horses For Courses," *Journal of Epidemiology and Community Health* 57, no. 7 (2003): 527.
5. Anna Charlotta Petersén and Jan Ingvar Olsson, "Calling Evidence-Based Practice into Question: Acknowledging Phronetic Knowledge in Social Work," *British Journal of Social Work* 45, no. 5 (2014): 1581.
6. "Evidence-Based Practice," Social Work Policy Institute, accessed May 20, 2016, http://www.socialworkpolicy.org/research/evidence-based-practice-2.html.
7. Lori Townsend, Amy R. Hofer, Sylvia Lin Hanick, and Korey Brunetti, "Identifying Threshold Concepts for Information Literacy: A Delphi Study," *Communications in Information Literacy* 10, no. 1 (2016): 33.
8. Ibid.
9. Patrick Wilson, *Second-Hand Knowledge: An Inquiry into Cognitive Authority* (Westport, Conn.: Greenwood, 1983).
10. Lane Wilkinson, "Is Authority Constructed and Contextual?" *Sense and Reference*, July 22, 2014, https://senseandreference.wordpress.com/2014/07/22/is-authority-constructed-and-contextual.
11. Ibid.
12. Association of College and Research Libraries (ACRL), *Framework for Information Literacy for Higher Education*, February 2, 2015, http://www.ala.org/acrl/standards/ilframework.
13. Ibid.
14. Lori Townsend, Korey Brunetti, and Amy R. Hofer, "Threshold Concepts and Information Literacy," *portal: Libraries and the Academy* 11 (2011): 862.
15. Townsend, et al., "Identifying Threshold Concepts for Information Literacy: A Delphi Study," 34.
16. Wilkinson, "Is Authority Constructed and Contextual?"
17. ACRL, *Framework for Information Literacy for Higher Education*.
18. Wilkinson, "Is Authority Constructed and Contextual?"
19. David J. A. Dozois and Roger Covin, "The Beck Depression Inventory-II (BDI-

II), Beck Hopelessness Scale (BHS), and Beck Scale for Suicide Ideation (BSS)," in *Comprehensive Handbook of Psychological Assessment: Volume 2 Personality Assessment and Psychopathology*, series ed. M. Hersen, volume eds. D. L. Segal and M. Hilsenroth (New York, NJ: Wiley), 50–69; Paul Richter, Joachim Werner, Andres Heerlein, Alfred Kraus, and Henrich Sauer, "On the Validity of the Beck Depression Inventory: A Review," *Psychopathology* 31, no. 3 (1998): 160–168; David J. A. Dozois and Roger Covin, "The Beck Depression Inventory-II (BDI-II), Beck Hopelessness Scale (BHS), and Beck Scale for Suicide Ideation (BSS)," 60; Brad Hagen, "Measuring Melancholy: A Critique of the Beck Depression Inventory and Its Use in Mental Health Nursing," *International Journal of Mental Health Nursing* 16, no. 2 (2007): 108–115, doi:10.1111/j.1447-0349.2007.00453.x.
20. University of Southern California School of Social Work, Master of Social Work Curriculum, accessed June 2, 2016, https://sowkweb.usc.edu/master-social-work/msw-degree/curriculum.
21. ACRL, *Framework for Information Literacy for Higher Education*.
22. Ibid.
23. Ibid.
24. Ibid.
25. University of Southern California, "Information Literacy Outcomes for Undergraduates," accessed June 1, 2016, https://libraries.usc.edu/research/instructional-services/learning-outcomes.
26. Ibid.
27. Anna Charlotta Petersén and Jan Ingvar Olsson, "Calling Evidence-Based Practice into Question," 1581.

CHAPTER 3*

Exploring Authority in Linguistics Research:
Who to Trust When Everyone's a Language Expert

Catherine Baird and Jonathan Howell

Many instruction librarians use the CRAAP test or a similar pneumonic tool as a regular activity in information literacy instruction classes. This involves having the students in the class select one or more sources and instructing them to answer a series of questions about these sources, as prompted by a simple checklist. Is the selected source Current, Relevant, Authoritative, Accurate and What is its Purpose? The goal is to help the students ascertain whether or not they should select this source and use it for an assignment. On occasion, a student will raise a hand and ask a simple question: "What do you mean by authoritative?" This is the central question we will deal with in this chapter.

Our disciplinary context is the field of linguistics. As in other disciplines, the local information landscape exhibits particular nuances and idiosyncrasies which allow exploration of information literacy more globally. The cost of entry into the local information landscape, for students and librarians alike, is particularly high in linguistics because, as we will elaborate, the discipline is not widely known and, for various reasons, scholars of linguistics have a fragmented distribution.

---

* This work is licensed under a Creative Commons Attribution-NonCommercial-ShareAlike 4.0 License, CC BY-NC-SA (https://creativecommons.org/licenses/by-nc-sa/4.0/).

For a librarian and a linguist, threshold concepts provided us the common language to engage in productive, sustained discussion, between each other and in the classroom. We therefore adopt the language of threshold concepts in this chapter, recognizing, however, that the validity of threshold concepts is a matter of continued debate in librarianship.[1]

In addition to exploring the local information landscape, we also examine parallels between a discipline-specific threshold concept, Linguistic Authority is Constructed and Contextual, and the information literacy threshold concept Authority is Constructed and Contextual.

In the following section, we introduce our understanding of the information literacy threshold concept Authority is Constructed and Contextual. Next, we compare features of the discipline-specific threshold concept Linguistic Authority is Constructed and Contextual with the information literacy threshold concept Authority is Constructed and Contextual. In the remaining sections, we provide a case study from an introductory course on phonetics and phonology, with exercises that were intended, first, to confront students with troublesome knowledge, second, to lead them through the liminal space and, third, to help them understand their own role as emerging experts. We conclude with a reflection about the nature of collaboration between librarian and faculty member and the promise that teaching for transfer holds for advancing information literacy.

What is authority?

Before librarians began working with threshold concepts, largely through the introduction of the Framework for Information Literacy for Higher Education[2] (Framework), a typical discussion of authority would have included the following topics, some or all of which would likely be touched upon during a typical library instruction session:

- Reviewing the concept of peer-review
- Comparing popular and scholarly literature
- Considering the match between an information need and respective level of authority sought
- Recognizing information may contain bias/prejudice and may be affected by cultural, political, or other contexts

Students would likely leave such a session understanding that they should prefer information created in the academic culture (e.g., published in a peer-reviewed journal) and develop a critical stance to information created in other spheres (e.g., popular media.) Given the time pressures of the one-shot model, a librarian would spend more time on the first two points as listed above and less time on the latter two. However, a deeper, more nuanced discussion of authority would not have taken place, as the need to demonstrate library databases, the library catalog, and citation styles and mechanics would fill the remainder of the instruction time.

The scenario described above, particularly under the time pressures noted, promotes dualistic thinking.[3] There simply is no threshold for students to cross. They do not encounter any troublesome knowledge, but likely accept as fact that some information sources are inherently better than others. Learning which ones to trust is accomplished by relying on a checklist of indicators of authority, such as whether a source is published in a peer-reviewed journal or written by a university professor. As long as students cite peer-reviewed sources in their assignment or paper, some degree of success in learning about authority is deemed to have taken place.

In contrast, we approached the concept of authority, not as a set of skills to be learned during a visit to the library, but as a semester-long discussion. This began by introducing troublesome knowledge early on in the semester through activities discussed below. After the introduction of troublesome knowledge (i.e., that there was no easy way to determine authority of an information source through simple indicators of quality), the authors had to be comfortable allowing the students to be uncomfortable as they grappled with the new knowledge. For the librarian, who is used to wrapping up a one-shot instruction session with a tidy assessment and some indication of successful learning, this was particularly challenging.

Moreover, through the semester-long discussion, we needed to guide students to an understanding of how and why authority is complex—namely, that Authority is Constructed and Contextual in at least the following ways:
- Authority is partially constructed through reputation, such as author affiliation and publication record, publication venue/distribution channel (e.g., well-known journal, academic blog, television news report), and demonstrated impact (e.g., citation counts).
- Authority is partially constructed through credentials.
- Authority is relative to a community in that different communities recognize different authorities.
- No authority is without some degree of bias.
- Authority can be demonstrated through subject expertise and the ability to communicate that expertise in a persuasive manner.
- Authority, particularly within an academic discipline, is likely to change over time as new knowledge is created and community values change.

The indicators of authority referenced in the CRAAP test reflect various considerations an expert may take into account. Unlike the novice learner, however, the expert does not treat all indicators equally and does not give them equal weight in all contexts. The introduction of the Framework and of threshold concepts into the information literacy classroom has changed the authority conversation. Instead of asking students to answer simple questions about authority (who is the author?, what are an author's credentials?), we are prompting them to ask deep questions about the nature and provenance of authority, how it might be tempered, and why it should be questioned.

Undoubtedly, there are several possible instructional models that might replace the skills-based one-shot with something that promotes discussion over an extended period. The instruction we describe in this chapter follows a model of collaboration between an information literacy expert and an expert in another discipline, i.e., a librarian and a linguist. Given this model, we were particularly concerned with identifying overlapping or complementary pedagogical goals. Specifically, we wondered whether the information literacy threshold concept Authority is Constructed and Contextual was entirely distinct from concepts of authority in linguistics. Noting many similarities between the two, we hypothesized that guiding a student through one liminal space would help them pass through the other.

In the next section, we introduce authority in the context of linguistics, guided by Meyer and Land's discussion of kinds of troublesome knowledge[4] (alien, ritualized, inert, tacit) and identify parallels between the threshold concept Linguistic Authority is Constructed and Contextual[5] (henceforth linguistic authority) with the information literacy threshold concept Authority is Constructed and Contextual.

Parallels between linguistics and information literacy: Two authority threshold concepts

For most students entering the linguistics classroom, it is simply common sense that there is a *right way* to speak and write a language. The dictionary tells us whether something is a word, what it means, and how it should be pronounced, and English teachers and stylebooks tell us which words can and can't be strung together into sentences. Rarely do people ask who it is that decides what language is good and what is bad.

As it turns out, it's not linguists. In contrast to *prescriptivists*, who explain how language ought to be used, linguists are said to be *descriptivists*. Investigating language from a scientific perspective, linguists aim not to lay judgment on language use, but to describe and ultimately explain language. Contrary to the assumption of most laypeople, there is no absolute authority on language. As in other scientific fields, linguists make a hypothesis, they follow a set of procedures to test the hypothesis, and they and their peers then evaluate the strength of the evidence in support of the hypothesis. Linguistics is therefore a scientific authority concerned with evaluating theories of language. Prescriptive authority, the kind most people take for granted, is entirely socially constructed.

This conception of linguistic authority is foundational in linguistics. For the learner, it can be quite troublesome because it is alien to them. For better or worse, the educational system recognizes only one particular variety of language as standard. What the system fails to recognize (although many individual educators may) is that language changes and has many varieties. There is a wealth of evidence, since at least Roman times,[6] of older generations complaining about younger generations and their destruction of language. (It hasn't happened yet.) Even in the USA, with its predominance of monolingual English speakers, one finds regional variation. Although there is nothing inherently wrong with recognizing a standard variety of a language, the choice typically privileges one group, i.e., educated, white middle/upper class men, while stigmatizing others.

The information literacy threshold concept Authority is Constructed and Contextual is similarly alien. In a preliminal state, students are dualistic thinkers in both domains. Information is classified into good and bad just as language is classified into good and bad. In both domains, this apparently straightforward binary contrast is revealed instead to be something complex. In both domains, the contrast is revealed as socially constructed rather than inherent.

Linguistic authority is also troublesome because it can become ritualized and remain inert. After several semesters studying linguistics, students may easily repeat certain talking points—e.g., all language varieties are equally complex, there is no primitive language—while failing to understand the motivation behind them. In an attempt to reconcile the troublesome knowledge with their preliminal state, students may at times adopt nihilistic and subjectivist positions. For example, rather than seeing linguists as investigating a complex human phenomenon scientifically, they may explain the linguist's task as finding ways to validate bad language. They may conclude that language is completely unconstrained and therefore not something that can be studied systematically. They may also fail to transfer the knowledge to their daily lives. Students continue to encounter and participate in social judgments, including linguistic discrimination, without recognizing them as socially constructed.

Similarly, with respect to information literacy, a student may be able to name indicators of authority but may fail to attach the indicators to any kind of meaning. For example, *peer-reviewed* is literally a box that must be checked, but there is no sense of what it means or how it might be related to authority in the student's own life. Students may be able to recite that there is no such thing as unbiased information but continue to utilize information as if it is unbiased. Again, and in order to reconcile the troublesome knowledge about constructed and contextual authority, they become mistrustful of all information, even while continuing to select and use information tacitly.

Linguistic authority can be troublesome because it requires students to access tacit knowledge. We all use more than one variety of language and, for the most part, we know which contexts require which variety. Bilinguals, for example, know when to use which language when speaking with other bilinguals, sometimes switching within the same sentence. We know how to talk to people inside and outside of our geographical community, our community of practice, our age group, or our gender. The authorities in each context—the people who judge the social appropriateness of our language—are different. We know how and when to change our language, but this knowledge is largely tacit.

Similarly, students are not blank slates with respect to information. No one treats all information equally. In their daily lives, students frequently make determinations about the authority of information, e.g., whether to take an umbrella based on the information presented in the weather app on a smart phone. Clearly, they use criteria (indicators) to arrive at these determinations, but these criteria are tacit: they do not access them consciously and may struggle to identify them explicitly when prompted.

Once students see linguistic authority as constructed and contextual, rather than absolute and invariant, their perception of language is radically transformed. Language is no longer a discrete set of skills to be mastered from experts; rather, language is exposed as a complex natural and social phenomenon investigated scientifically by a community of scholars. Having crossed this threshold, an individual is unlikely to return to a view of language as inherently right and wrong.

In addition to being troublesome, then, the concept that linguistic authority is constructed and contextual is transformative, integrative, and irreversible—four of the five likely characteristics of a threshold concept identified by Meyer and Land. Whether it has the property of boundedness is less clear. Indeed, we have emphasized this threshold concept in linguistics precisely because it shares so many similarities and parallels with the related information literacy threshold concept Authority is Constructed and Contextual and lends itself to transferability for the learner. We also note that Meyer and Land did not intend their set of characteristics as an exhaustive checklist.

Entering two liminal spaces

Given the parallels we had identified between the two threshold concepts of authority, we designed an exercise, the purpose of which was twofold: to confront our students with the complexity of authority as it relates to linguistic authority; and to confront them with the complexity of authority as it relates to information.

We begin, briefly, with some background about a linguistic phenomenon called *vocal fry*. The sounds of language vary according to different settings of our vocal tract. One of these settings is the configuration of our vocal folds, which we use to distinguish between words like *fat* and *vat*. At this point, we invite you to hold your hand to your throat and make a *ffffffffffff* sound, followed by a *vvvvvvvvvvvv* sound. The [f] sound is produced with the vocal folds held apart. The [v] sound is produced with vibration. These are the most common ways of manipulating the vocal folds, but the focus of this assignment was a configuration of the vocal folds called vocal fry. People liken vocal fry (a.k.a. creaky voice) to the sound of a creaky door or bacon frying in a hot pan.

The motivation for using vocal fry in English is not well understood, but linguists note that laypeople have a strong reaction to it, and the phenomenon has received a lot of attention, not just from academics but also the media (e.g., *The New York Times*, *The Today Show*, NPR, *Science*, *Time*.)[7] For this reason, it provided a nice opportunity to engage students in a discussion of authority. Having already discussed the mechanics of vocal fry, we introduced students to a set of carefully chosen sources, in a deliberate order, beginning with two television news clips.

In the first clip,[8] an anchor explains that experts believe reality television (especially the Kardashians) could be to blame for a new fad called vocal fry. The piece features two scientific authorities: an Ear, Nose, and Throat physician and a speech language therapist. One asserts that vocal fry "probably started back with Meredith Grey and Grey's Anatomy where she had this very tired sounding voice." The other describes a so-called treatment. The reporter narrates the piece with judgmental language: vocal fry is "creeping in" to the conversations of young women and you need to "catch yourself doing it" to reverse it.

In the second clip,[9] the host questions a guest panel about challenges faced by millennials, including vocal fry and its potential impact on employment. The panelists, all over forty, include a clinical psychologist/television personality, a senior executive from Monster Worldwide, and a journalist. Again, reality television is blamed as well as the poor social skills and immaturity of millennials.

During the subsequent in-class discussion, it was clear that the students were used to approaching news media with skepticism, but did so, initially, in a perfunctory manner, where they recited the "right" answer, e.g., there was bias in media reports because of the need to sell advertising/attract viewers. With some prompting, students noted that some of the experts had subject expertise, but the students nonetheless disagreed with the experts' claims, some visibly offended at the targeting of young women. One student pointed out how the media reports took advantage of the (constructed) authority that our society lends to doctors and scientists. It became clear that indicators of authority—in particular, credentials, reputation, subject expertise—were imperfect and context-sensitive.

Subsequent classes required students to read two research papers[10] which spurred the media interest around vocal fry (both peer-reviewed articles from outside the discipline of linguistics), an episode of the podcast *This American Life*,[11] and two blog posts by academic linguists.[12] Reading the articles, students discovered that neither claimed that vocal fry was more common now than in the past and neither claimed that vocal fry was more prevalent among youth or women. The podcast explicitly discusses some of the misreporting, and the blog posts detail many shortcomings of the original research articles themselves.

In many respects, this exercise resembles the kind of information literacy activity that librarians have been leading for many years, well before any discussion of threshold concepts. We do believe, however, the exercise is innovative in two ways. First, approaching our teaching via threshold concepts allowed us to move away from a one-shot model for information literacy instruction and instead to anticipate that students would take different paths through the liminal space. We designed the exercise not expecting students to acquire a skill by the end; rather, we designed the exercise to introduce troublesome knowledge and to promote a discussion around it, which could continue throughout the course of a semester rather than a single meeting.

Second, we anticipated and encouraged transfer. With respect to linguistic authority, the vocal fry exercise challenged students to move through a liminal space from a binary understanding of language as inherently good and bad toward an understanding that judgments about language are complex and socially constructed. At the same time, students were moving through a liminal space from a binary understanding of information as inherently good and bad to an understanding of information as complex and socially constructed. Passing through one space, we hoped, would help the student to pass through the other.

On this subject, we are influenced by the work of Kuglitsch, for whom teaching for transfer is a primary goal of the information literacy instructor: "If our aim is to teach students the generalized skills of information literacy, educational research suggests that the best way to do so is to explicitly situate those generalized skills of the Framework in a domain familiar to students. Students can then use their local knowledge of the domain to support and abstract the general principles of information literacy."[13]

In addition to situating the information literacy threshold concept Authority is Constructed and Contextual locally within the domain of linguistics, we are going one step further and relating it to a distinct threshold concept in the discipline of linguistics.

CRAAP: From checklist to discussion prompt

In the next exercise, approximately a week later, we aimed to move the discussion from simply recognizing information literacy authority as complex (i.e., non-binary) to exploring the specific ways in which it is complex (i.e., constructed and contextual) in the context of the discipline of linguistics.

The context for this exercise is a presentation in which students must choose an unfamiliar language and prepare an authoritative, engaging, and focused fifteen-minute presentation that provided the class with general background information about the language (such as language family, sound inventory) and a discussion on the week's topic.

In preparation for their presentation, we asked students to search for resources on the phonetics and phonology of their language, first in the Linguistics and Language Behavior Abstracts (LLBA) database, and then the following week on the web. Students also annotated their selections with a CRAAP score and a brief note about how the resource might inform their presentation.

Importantly, our purpose in introducing the CRAAP test was not to give students an easy tool or shortcut for identifying authoritative sources; rather, we intended the CRAAP test as a conversation starter. The student submissions were graded only for completion, and we did not provide students with a correct answer. We then chose a handful of these resources and required all students to review that same set of resources, to post their score, and publish their rationale on the course website. The postings formed the basis of an in-class discussion.[14]

The decision not to provide a correct or model answer proved troublesome for many students. Some students were also distressed by the considerable variation and inconsistency in scores between and among individual students. The scores of authority were, like authority itself, constructed and contextual.

The discussion of students' rationale was particularly fruitful. Collectively, students identified a wealth of positive and negative indicators of authority. For students still uncomfortable with the understanding of authority as complex, i.e., those who desired sources to be either good or bad, finding indicators provided a point of entry into the conversation. On the other hand, they and their peers quickly discovered that different students valued the indicators differently.

As one example, we discussed Ethnologue,[15] a web resource cataloguing statistics on 7,457 languages. Most students noted that it was currently in its nineteenth edition, had been in publication since 1951, and was updated within the previous year. Students recognized these as indicators of reputation and recency and thus as positive indicators of authority. In many cases, however, the individual facts presented on a language entry were not credited to specific individuals. A subset of students viewed this as a negative indicator of authority. This flowed into a discussion about the authority of organizations. Ethnologue is published by SIL International, a non-profit Christian missionary organization with close ties to the Wycliffe Global Alliance of Bible translation organizations. Some students worried that the missionary goals of the organization negatively influenced Ethnologue's authority, while other students maintained that the influence, if any, was marginal. Nearly all students agreed that, for the particular context of the presentation, Ethnologue was sufficiently authoritative to be used as a resource. Without taking a position ourselves, we happily pointed out that the class mirrored the field of linguistics itself, which uses Ethnologue widely for many pragmatic purposes but is divided in the amount of authority it accords to Ethnologue, for many of the same reasons identified by the students.

Unlike the vocal fry exercise, the CRAAP exercise was more actively metacognitive. In the vocal fry exercise, bloggers and podcasters did a lot of the work identifying specific critiques of authority. In this exercise, students had to generate their own set of indicators and determine the appropriate weight of each indicator.

We intended the vocal fry exercise described in the previous section to move students away from binarity into the liminal space. We intended the CRAAP exercise, and others omitted here for space, to guide students through the liminal space by refining their understanding of information literacy authority as constructed and contextual. We were challenged, however, when it came to determining how to recognize when students had left the liminal space and crossed the threshold. To what extent were students thinking like an expert, either like an information studies scholar or a linguist? True expertise is arrived at by, among other things, an extended period of time studying a specific subject, and so it was unreasonable to expect that students would exhibit true expert behavior.

In the following final instructional example of this chapter, we exposed students to the academic culture of the discipline of linguistics. We designed an exercise, first, to emphasize how authority may change over time, as new knowledge is created and community values change, second, to situate information literacy authority in the context of the discipline of linguistics, and third, to help students see themselves as co-constructors of authority, as emerging members of the disciplinary community.

Joining the community of experts

In academia, as in the world at large, the discipline of linguistics is often little known. Although many universities have a separate department of linguistics, people researching language in higher education may also be found in departments of anthropology, classics, computer science, education, English, law, philosophy, psychology, speech language pathology, sociology, and of specific languages, to name a few.

There are at least three reasons for this fragmented distribution. First, the breadth and depth of subfields reflect the considerable complexity of human language. Many aspects of language are regular and rule-governed, like the laws of physics or the functions of biological systems. This is true for at least the subfields of phonetics, phonology, syntax, and semantics. Other aspects of language are, by contrast, influenced by human culture. This is true especially for at least the subfields of discourse analysis, anthropological linguistics, and sociolinguistics.[16] For this reason, linguistics departments may be variously housed in colleges of humanities, social sciences, cognitive sciences, behavioral sciences, or physical sciences.

Second, modern linguistics, conceived of as the scientific study of language, consolidated as a discrete discipline relatively late, in the last half of the twentieth century.[17] The founding of modern linguistics as a separate and unified discipline is usually credited to MIT linguist and philosopher Noam Chomsky and his work in the 1950s that challenged B.F. Skinner's behaviorism.

Third, Chomsky has in some ways been equally as divisive as he has been unifying. Chomsky and his followers championed the informal collection of introspective judgments as a primary source of data in linguistic theory. Introspective judgments provide negative evidence, such as the ungrammaticality of sentences like *I'd like to can swim* or words like *bnick* and *psab* (compare: *blick* and *prab*). Chomsky pronounced that experimental laboratory methodologies of the type used in psychology were "a waste of time and energy,"[18] and Chomsky was equally critical of corpora (i.e., collections of naturally occurring text or speech), dismissing them as useless and "wildly skewed."[19] Chomsky's strong positions alienated language scholars using other methodologies, and an environment of hostility both from and against so-called armchair linguists like Chomsky dominated until the 1990s with the emergence of interdisciplinary research cultures.

The novice, of course, knows little if any of this, including the librarian. Faced with a list of search results from Google Scholar or LLBA, how can the novice determine which works will be considered more or less authoritative? Yet this is exactly the context that an expert brings to bear in evaluating authority.

Focusing particularly on the division created by Chomsky around research methodology, we selected a set of abbreviated quotations from Chomsky and other historically prominent linguists and presented them in class as Twitter posts. As an in-class activity, students also read and discussed work by academic linguists who use recently developed methodologies, such as experiments that use crowdsourcing like Amazon Turk, to question the validity of more traditional introspective methods used by Chomsky and his followers. Finally, in a homework assignment, students were asked to search the LLBA and propose several different methodologies that might be appropriate for their own final research project and to anticipate how each methodology would be received by different communities of linguists.

Because students had been exposed to the disciplinary culture and history, students were more successful in selecting an appropriate methodology from recently published linguistics articles. Rather than viewing the choice as unquestionably authoritative because it appeared in a peer-reviewed journal or arbitrary because all choices were equally scientific, they were able to recognize that their choice aligned them with a particular community of scholars. By choosing a methodology, the student was effectively granting more weight to the authority of one community over another.

Conclusion

We want students to be able to both understand and transfer generalized information literacy knowledge such as Authority is Constructed and Contextual to different contexts. By situating information literacy learning within a discipline and even seeking parallels to disciplinary threshold concepts, we set up the students to transfer their understanding.

Threshold concepts provide us with a common language to talk about our pedagogical goals, moving the librarian-faculty collaboration from superficial to substantive. Lacking the disciplinary context, the librarian's role in the authority conversation would have been marginalized, with authority being presented in an oversimplified and generic fashion, and less interesting and engaging for the students. Lacking the information literacy context, the linguist would likely have failed to recognize Authority is Constructed and Contextual as a concept needing to be taught, and the opportunity to connect to the linguistic threshold concept, Linguistic Authority is Constructed and Contextual would be lost.

We realize that this is not the only path to teaching for transfer. However, we found that the language of threshold concepts significantly changed the tenor and substance of our collaboration, which was immediately reflected in the way we approached our teaching and had a direct impact on student learning. It also helped to mitigate some of the typical barriers to librarian-faculty collaboration. Faculty spend less time reflecting about their teaching, given the value institutions place on scholarship. Faculty may sometimes be aware of disciplinary blind spots, but they are less likely to recognize the extent and nature of their own expert information literacy. Finally, there are stereotypes about library instruction and faculty expectations of this instruction as skills-based, orientation sessions that must be overcome.

Our approach, in many respects, was totally unremarkable. The students searched databases and they evaluated sources. Students used the CRAAP test, keyword searching, and a specific citation style. These and other touchstones remained but were in service of something bigger, as we were liberated to focus on the learner's journey and enjoy the rewards and challenges of teaching big ideas.

Notes

1. See, for example, Ian Beilin, "Beyond the Threshold: Conformity, Resistance, and the ACRL Information Literacy Framework for Higher Education," *In the Library with the Leadpipe,* February 25, 2015, http://www.inthelibrarywiththeleadpipe.org/2015/beyond-the-threshold-conformity-resistance-and-the-aclr-information-literacy-framework-for-higher-education.
2. Association of College and Research Libraries (ACRL), *Framework for Information Literacy for Higher Education*, February 2, 2015, http://www.ala.org/acrl/standards/ilframework.
3. For discussion, see, Maura Seale, "Information Literacy Standards and the Politics of Knowledge Production: Using User-Generated Content to Incorporate Critical Pedagogy," in *Critical Library Instruction: Theories & Methods,* eds. Maria T. Accardi, Emily Drabinski and Alana Kumbier (Duluth, MN: Library Juice Press, 2010), 221–235.
4. Jan Meyer and Ray Land, *Threshold Concepts and Troublesome Knowledge: Linkages to Ways of Thinking and Practising in the Disciplines* (Edinburgh: Enhancing Teaching-Learning Environments in Undergraduate Courses, May 2003), http://www.etl.tla.ed.ac.uk/docs/ETLreport4.pdf.
5. Threshold concepts are not widely recognized in linguistics. We identified this threshold concept in the course of our own discussions.
6. The earliest example is usually credited to Horace, Book III of *Odes.*
7. Douglas Quenqua, "They're Like, Way Ahead of the Linguistics Curve," *New York Times,* February 27, 2012, http://www.nytimes.com/2012/02/28/science/young-women-often-trendsetters-in-vocal-patterns.html; "New Speech Pattern of Young Women: Vocal Fry," *Today Show* video, 3:39, December 15, 2011, http://www.today.com/video/today/45681263; Laura Starecheski, host, "Can Changing How You Sound Help You Find Your Voice?" *All Things Considered* radio broadcast, 7:46, October 14, 2014, http://www.npr.org/blogs/health/2014/10/14/354858420/can-changing-how-you-sound-help-you-find-your-voice; Marissa Fessenden, "Vocal Fry Creeping into U.S. Speech," *Science,* December 9, 2011, http://news.sciencemag.org/social-sciences/2011/12/vocal-fry-creeping-u.s.-speech?ref=hp; Katy Steinmetz, "Get Your Creak

8. On: Is 'Vocal Fry' a Female Fad?" *Time*, December 15, 2011, http://healthland.time.com/2011/12/15/get-your-creak-on-is-vocal-fry-a-female-fad/.
9. Melissa Reid, "Vocal Fry on the Rise: Way of Talking Blamed on Pop Culture," *Fox 8 News Cleveland* video, November 21, 2013, http://fox8.com/2013/11/21/vocal-fry-on-the-rise-way-of-talking-blamed-on-pop-culture/.
9. "Like, Millennial Probs: Vocal Fry Hurting Job Prospects," *Fox Business News* video, June 3, 2014, http://video.foxbusiness.com/v/3603797521001/like-millennial-probs-vocal-fry-hurting-job-prospects/?#sp=show-clips.
10. Lesley Wolk, Nassima B. Abdelli-Beruh, and Dianne Slavin, "Habitual Use of Vocal Fry in Young Adult Female Speakers," *Journal of Voice* 26, no. 3 (2012): e111–e116; Anderson, Rindy C., Casey A. Klofstad, William J. Mayew, and Mohan Venkatachalam, "Vocal Fry May Undermine the Success of Young Women in the Labor Market," *PLoS ONE* 9, no. 5 (2014): e97506.
11. Ira Glass, host, "If You Don't Have Anything Nice to Say, SAY IT IN ALL CAPS," *This American Life* podcast, 58:52, January 23, 2015, http://www.thisamericanlife.org/radio-archives/episode/545/if-you-dont-have-anything-nice-to-say-say-it-in-all-caps.
12. Mark Liberman, "Real Fry," *Language Log* (blog), June 19, 2014, http://languagelog.ldc.upenn.edu/nll/?p=13047; Christian DiCanio, "Vocal Fry Probably Doesn't Harm Your Career Prospects," *Language Log* (blog), June 7, 2014, http://languagelog.ldc.upenn.edu/nll/?p=12774.
13. Rebecca Z. Kuglitsch, "Teaching for Transfer: Reconciling the Framework with Disciplinary Information Literacy," *portal: Libraries and the Academy* 15, no. 3 (2015): 457–470.
14. See Candice Benjes-Small, Alyssa Archer, Katelyn Tucker, Lisa Vassady, and Jennifer Resor Whicker, "Teaching Web Evaluation: A Cognitive Development Approach," *Communications in Information Literacy* 7 no. 1 (2013): 39–49 for a similar activity.
15. M. Paul Lewis, Gary, F. Simons, and Charles D. Fennig, eds., *Ethnologue: Languages of the World, 19th Edition* (Dallas: SIL International, 2016).
16. William O'Grady, Michael Dobrovolsky, and Mark Aronoff, *Contemporary Linguistics: An Introduction* (New York: St. Martin's, 1989).
17. Mark Liberman, "The Future of Linguistics" (invited plenary address, Annual Meeting of the Linguistic Society of America, Anaheim, CA, January 4–7, 2007).
18. Noam Chomsky, *Language and Mind* (New York: Harcourt Brace Jovanovich, 1972).
19. Noam Chomsky, *Syntactic Structures* (The Hague: Mouton, 1957).

CHAPTER 4

Evidence and Authority in Health and Exercise Science Research

Michelle Twait

Introduction

In our everyday lives, healthcare providers are often viewed as authority figures based on their education and training. Their professional journey begins at the undergraduate level, where they first begin to wrestle with questions of authority and evidence. How do their research experiences help them understand the constructed and contextual nature of authority?

The author, liaison to the Health & Exercise Science (HES) department at a small private liberal arts college, will explore this question through various examples from HES courses and their relevance to librarians. For instance, how might librarians help students understand external authority without diminishing students' own sense of authority as developing researchers and thinkers? And how do we help students think about authority in the context of one discipline while acknowledging those "rules" might be different in other subjects? Finally, how do HES faculty perceive students' grasp of threshold concepts?

The author provides instruction to undergraduate students pursuing the following majors or minors: health and physical education, health fitness, athletic training, coaching (minor), and public health (minor). The HES department strives to "facilitate student-faculty research" and encourages students to "conduct and present the results of research at scholarly conferences."[1] Each major takes a different approach to achieving this goal. In part, this can be attributed to the requirements of the different accrediting bodies or professional associations for each major and minor. For example, one of the national competencies for athletic training education is to "describe and differentiate the types of quantitative and qualitative research, research components, and levels of research evidence."[2] These information literacy standards or competencies are typically built into methods courses in the major, and this is often where students will receive library instruction.

Library instruction for HES courses

The author has worked with each of the majors within the HES department. Instruction has primarily been offered through one-shot sessions and supplemented with handouts or online pathfinders. In particular, instruction efforts have been focused on two courses: HES 220: Research and Statistics in Health and Exercise Science and HES 203: Introduction to Athletic Training.

Library instruction efforts with HES 220 (Research and Statistics in Health and Exercise Science) are consistent and ongoing. This class introduces students to research and statistical methods in the discipline and asks them to identify a topic, explore potential research methods, and design a hypothetical study. Students are encouraged to grapple with the notion of authority in the context of their research proposals. In this context, they learn that their authority as researchers is connected to the authority of the sources they cite. Students learn that the literature review situates their study within the larger context of HES research and that this involves acknowledging other authorities or experts. During the session, we discuss how to distinguish among scholarly and non-scholarly sources, since the assignment requires students to use peer-reviewed journals. Although I provide a brief explanation of the peer review process, I lack the time to engage students in a conversation about the constructed nature of peer review and those who criticize the system. The session has focused on understanding what peer review is and how to recognize it when searching; a threshold concepts approach may provide opportunities for more in-depth instruction.

More recently, the author has developed a relationship with HES 203 (Introduction to Athletic Training), as the standards and requirements for the program have evolved. In this course, students are introduced to research in the field and, in particular, the notion of a "hierarchy of evidence." In the context of athletic training, the top of the hierarchy is regarded as the most authoritative. Students' understanding of the contextual nature of authority is also framed by the available evidence. As we discuss the hierarchy of evidence, students consider when and why each type of evidence might be appropriate. For instance, students are asked to think about why a randomized, controlled clinical trial might not exist for a particular topic and in what circumstances might an observational study be the best available evidence. During the session, we also compare and contrast trade publications and scholarly journals, which requires students to assess the role of expert opinion. Students learn that expert opinion may be the best evidence in certain contexts. Finally, the LibGuide for the course includes the Board of Certification exam references. Although students will not sit for the exam until their senior year, including this information acknowledges this board's authority in their undergraduate studies and as future professionals.

After the session, students are asked to evaluate the evidence they found (including anecdotes or opinions from Preceptors) and to determine, if possible, an answer to their research question. This step shifts students from a basic understanding of the hierarchy of evidence to analysis and application, which addresses the contextual nature of authority. Furthermore, by asking students to both seek support for and question their conclusions, this part of the assignment helps students develop a sense of their own authority as researchers.

Like the HES 220 session, one hour is not enough time to discuss the constructed nature of the hierarchy of evidence and its assumptions about authority. Nor am I able to discuss the Board of Certification, its members, and how one comes to serve on the board. In both courses, students understand authority as defined by their discipline but may not fully appreciate the constructed or contextual nature of authority.

Faculty perspectives on threshold concepts

While individual sessions for specific courses are a key component of our instruction program, the author and her colleagues wanted to think more broadly about student learning. While most of the conversations about threshold concepts and information literacy have centered on the librarian's role, we must acknowledge that disciplinary faculty are our partners in this work. In 2014, our library received a grant giving faculty members from various disciplines the opportunity to explore threshold concepts related to using information to conduct inquiry. Through a series of conversations and a summer workshop, we asked participants to collectively identify critical points where students wrestle with problems related to their use of information.[3] By involving faculty from many disciplines in the process of identifying 1) which threshold concepts are common to all disciplines and 2) the best ways to nudge students across those thresholds, the librarians hoped to fill a significant gap in this emerging theoretical framework. By discussing points where students get stuck, the librarians could look for threshold concepts that are generalizable while also identifying how these concepts are manifested in different disciplines.[4]

During the first faculty conversation, participants suggested that format and authority are closely linked. One faculty member from the English department pointed out that there is a hierarchy of authority based on format, noting that her discipline uses the term "genre" instead of format. Likewise, an art professor commented that similar examples could be found in her field; for instance, with the Mona Lisa, there is the original work, online images, or reproductions on post cards. A faculty member from the math department mentioned that authority in her field is "Where did it come from?" and "Who produced it?" Similarly, a geology professor explained that disciplinary associations produced the first databases in her field and that affiliation lends credibility and authority to those databases.

Faculty members also proposed two threshold concepts related to authority. First, they argued that the willingness and ability to question authority is a threshold concept. In other words, helping students understand that people, review boards, and editorial boards are fallible; they are sometimes wrong, bad research gets published, and good research goes unpublished. Secondly, faculty members believe that students cross a threshold when they embrace their own sense of authority. As one of the faculty participants told us, it's important for students to believe, "I have a voice. I have something to say."

During the second faculty conversation, faculty asserted that every exchange of information requires an act of judgment, arguing that one makes decisions about who to pay attention to and what value one believes their ideas have. Participants also pointed out that valuable ideas are sometimes overlooked because those proposing new ideas lack power. This tension between upholding tradition and originality reflects a tension related to authority.

Faculty interviews

Inspired by these conversations, the author interviewed four faculty members in the Health and Exercise Science department during the spring semester of the 2015–16 academic year. The main purpose of the interviews was to explore faculty perspectives on HES students' understanding of authority as a threshold concept. The interviews included questions about research opportunities within the major, places where students get "stuck," pedagogical approaches, and faculty perspectives on assessment.

Most interview subjects mentioned encouraging both attendance and presentation at professional conferences. In the case of health fitness, a research project and presentation are a requirement. Similarly, the capstone course for the Athletic Training major involves an extensive literature review and presentation. Faculty view presentations as a way for students to develop their own sense of authority while also exposing students to the contexts of authority construction in a particular field. One professor mentioned "the transformation" he sees when students present at conferences. By interacting with experts and listening to other presentations, students are being socialized into a profession, i.e., this is what authority looks like in our discipline.

When asked about places where students get stuck in terms of thinking about authority or evidence, one faculty member commented, "I think it's mostly that they make claims and don't even think to find it.... You can't just say 'there's a need,' you have to establish that or cite that." Two of the professors said that students struggle with assessing the authority of a source or mistakenly assume that information found on Wikipedia is reliable. This illustrates the troublesome nature of authority: what is acceptable evidence in one situation may not be in another context. Interestingly, one faculty member noted that students are intimidated or overwhelmed by the sophisticated vocabulary or technical language in research studies and have sometimes "shied away from authority in literature, in their searches, because it's hard to read."

Faculty often mentioned pedagogical approaches to helping students understand authority and evidence. For example, one professor explained that she initiates a conversation with students about their research needs and helps them break down the components of a scholarly article. Another faculty member stressed the importance of "revisiting" or providing ongoing exposure to these ideas in order to move students across the threshold. Unfortunately, as this professor acknowledged, the structure of many majors does not allow for a great deal of overlap among courses. One faculty member hopes to create an assignment that asks students to explore the question, "What is 'research' in xyz discipline?" For example, HES students would compare their assumptions about authority and evidence to those in art or history. Similarly, one of the faculty members interviewed commented that her own views on authority have been challenged through her work with a student majoring in political science. A few faculty members talked about bringing people's experiences into their teaching as a means of highlighting the contextual and constructed nature of authority. For example, one professor encourages students to interview practitioners, hoping to teach students that "life experiences... have value and meaning and we should honor that." This illustrates, as the Framework notes, how "various communities may recognize different types of authority."[5]

When asked about assessing students' grasp of authority as a threshold concept, one faculty member acknowledged that traditional assessment measures (e.g., test questions) were insufficient. Instead, he argued, that "seeing them apply it, seeing it in action" was the best way to determine if students had crossed that particular threshold. Another professor said, "I always like when someone starts to realize who an important authority is on a topic." In other words, the student has internalized some of the disciplinary views on authority. That faculty member also acknowledged the difficulty inherent in assessing threshold concepts: "I think … you almost end up having to project onto the students that this is supposed to be a transformational moment …. I don't know if the student would necessarily define them as transformational." This suggests that teaching metacognitive skills would complement any instruction related to threshold concepts.

Three of the faculty members interviewed mentioned the tension between practitioners and scholars. It is interesting to note that, in these pre-professional programs, authority is not only constructed and contextual, but also contested. As one faculty member noted, "I think the practitioners don't necessarily take the [theoretical into consideration] … they become the authority." This appears to be an issue within the discipline of athletic training as well. For example, Mark Merrick asserts that athletic trainers "tend to think of people who do research as being a different group than clinical practitioners."[6] In these pre-professional programs, students are typically required to do internships or practicums. As these students have one foot in the classroom and the other in the field, these opportunities may provide a rich environment for students to grapple with the contextual nature of authority. Related to the authority of practitioners, one professor believes this is why she does not see as much growth in students' research skills over the four years. She believes students hold up former teachers and coaches as role models and resist learning new methods or strategies.

Interview subjects were asked how they explain external authority while, at the same time, trying to encourage students to develop their own sense of authority as budding scholars. One faculty member mentioned that athletic training students have a unique opportunity to develop their own sense of authority, pointing out that evidence-based practice is relatively new to the field, and students are often teaching their "preceptors and supervisors about these concepts." This same professor mentioned that, since the hierarchy of evidence includes opinion, students are encouraged to find their own voice as an authority. Another professor said that he tries to help students work through that struggle to find their voice, especially during one-on-one sessions:

> "They always worry about … 'Is it good enough?' I say, 'Well, what is your rationale?' and then I try to get them to think about… 'Is it something new? Are you adding to the body of knowledge? Are you developing a question about something that you want to know that hasn't been answered?'

Once students work through that crisis of faith, he notices that "it gets to where solving one question … builds to more questions, then I know they've got it." This might be likened to the irreversibility of threshold concepts in that, once grasped, students embrace their role as an authority.

One professor noted that students may develop a bias toward their own discipline's views on authority, saying that he has overheard students harshly criticize research conducted in the humanities and social sciences. Another faculty member also mentioned this issue, saying, "I think we've probably trained them that a peer-reviewed, randomized, controlled trial would trump whatever comes below [on the hierarchy of evidence] for whatever topic under the sun. It's probably to our detriment." These comments further illustrate the importance of helping students understand the constructed and contextual nature of their views in order to avoid the development of prejudices related to evidence and authority.

Interestingly, one professor mentioned that students' own sense of authority is eroded by stereotypes and misperceptions of the discipline. In particular, physical education and health education students "feel like they're always put down." A different professor brought up the same issue, saying, "I think it really wears on the confidence of [students], especially in the education realm … and maybe they feel more defensive." As noted in the Framework, grasping "authority" as a concept involves developing certain dispositions, including maintaining "an open mind when encountering … conflicting perspectives" and recognizing "the value of diverse ideas and worldviews."[7] In moving across this threshold, learners may need to explore the origins of these stereotypes in order to better understand their own authority.

Implementation and assessment

The ideas and themes raised by faculty provide fruitful starting points for thinking about integrating and assessing threshold concepts. On the author's campus, recent conversations related to curricular reform present an opportunity to discuss the Framework. Similarly, the move toward a focus on evidence-based practice in the field of athletic training has created opportunities for the author to work more closely with that program. This change has led some athletic training faculty to argue that information literacy is "a fundamental component" and should be embedded throughout the curriculum.[8]

Implementation. In my liaison work, I often approach my work in terms of the department or program, rather than a collection of related, but unique majors. As I discuss threshold concepts with faculty, I recognize the need to invest more time in understanding the needs and goals of specific majors. I realize that I have a limited amount of information about how authority and evidence are discussed within the context of courses. I might see an assignment or the syllabus, but I am not privy to the day-to-day lectures or one-on-one conversations with students. Shulman used the term "signature pedagogies" to describe how this tacit knowledge is conveyed to students and noted that signature pedagogies "define the functions of expertise in a field, the locus of authority, and the privileges of rank and standing."[9] Understanding these signature pedagogies in the majors and minors represented in the HES department will help me introduce threshold concepts.

Just as I may not be informed about all the details for a particular course, instructors may not be aware of my knowledge and experience as a librarian. For example, in one of my interviews, a faculty member mentioned that he allows students to cite non-refereed sources in their methodology section because the articles might provide models for their experimental design. However, he noted that all other sources must be peer-reviewed. This distinction makes sense to an experienced researcher and, in fact, illustrates the contextual nature of authority. However, a novice researcher might be confused and wonder, "Why is non-refereed okay sometimes and not at other times?" Although HES students learn about peer-reviewed journals or the hierarchy of evidence, their understanding of authority may be limited. As a liaison librarian, I can share what I know about scholarly publishing, disciplinary differences, and students' research habits.

My conversations with faculty also highlighted the need to talk to students about their research experiences and how their understanding of authority is shaped by those experiences. Lynn Clouder also suggests that faculty members be "ready to listen to students who wish to share their experiences and legitimizing uncertainties can only be helpful in moving students forward towards or through the threshold."[10] As the HES liaison, I am well-positioned to listen to students in the classroom or at the reference desk as they process their experiences.

As I look for ways to introduce HES students to the concept of "authority is constructed and contextual," I would like to incorporate the following ideas:
- Help students understand the contextualized nature of authority by asking them to think about audience, purpose, and context as it relates to their sources.
- Continue to advocate for alternatives to the one-shot session. Faculty from the grant-funded conversations expressed interest in looking at how "baby steps" to threshold concepts could be introduced in various courses. Perhaps I can work with HES faculty to incorporate multiple sequenced sessions, serve as an embedded librarian for a course, or utilize a flipped classroom model. In addition, I would like to redesign my online guides in a way that provides scaffolding for student learning related to authority and evidence.

- Expose HES students to disciplinary differences in authority. Students are being socialized into the research practices of a discipline as they progress through their major. At the same time, students are simultaneously taking courses in a variety of subjects in order to meet general education requirements or as they pursue secondary majors or minors. As the liaison librarian, I can help them understand and appreciate the differences they see.
- Ask HES students to analyze an article in terms of the "the now common practice of funding disclosures and conflicts of interest statements in publications and presentations."[11]
- Provide a forum for discussing why scholars cite sources (not just the mechanics of citation styles) and how citation practices represent structures of authority.
- Model "questioning authority" for students by offering examples of controversies involving retracted papers in medical journals.
- Acknowledge the structures and information ecosystems that created commonly used tools within the discipline (e.g. the Cochrane Library for systematic reviews).

Like many other instruction programs, the author's library devotes a significant amount of time and energy on first-year students, primarily through first-term seminar program. As I look ahead, I predict a shift in emphasis to the later years, when students have developed a greater capacity for ambiguity and the HES students are also more likely to be engaged in experiential learning activities. As Barbara Fister points out, "… in that first year, students aren't ready to think deeply about the big picture. They don't have the knowledge base or the experience to think about the systems that influence how knowledge is produced and shared, or about how they can become authorities themselves."[12] This issue was hinted at in my interviews with HES faculty. As one professor said, "The biggest part we really try to get out of that beginning class is how do you even know what question to ask, then how do you use your question to do your search, and then it goes into we start to talk more about the quality of evidence in the junior classes, and then the senior classes are really about pulling it all together." This same professor also noted that patient care experiences, which happen in later years, give students a more nuanced understanding of evidence. This shift will require close collaboration with faculty and a deeper understanding of the curricula of specific programs and majors.

Assessment. Much like the implementation of disciplinary applications of threshold concepts, assessment is also an activity best done in consultation with faculty. In the case of HES or other related programs, one might find commonalities with the Framework and shared goals. For example, as Deborah Begoray, Gillian Rowlands, and Doris Gillis point out, "the field of health literacy... will need measures that capture the wider range of skills inherent in more complex concepts, are sensitive to change, and enable us to make comparisons across contexts."[13] Whereas previous information literacy assessment tools have been task-based or skill-based, assessing threshold concepts is a far more complex and nuanced initiative. As Eamon Tewell points out, "the Framework appears to reject North American higher education's climate of continual standardized assessment measures by moving away from easily quantifiable outcomes."[14] Interviews, observational studies, focus groups, and portfolios may play a larger role in the assessment of threshold concepts.

According to one study, "students learn in the classroom by learning to reflect in the classroom, which they in turn learn from reflecting on what they do beyond the classroom."[15] If metacognitive skills and reflection are an important factor in students' understanding of threshold concepts, we should consider incorporating journals or learning logs into student assessment. For example, one might prompt students to explain why they choose the source they did and reflect on what that choice says about their views on authority.

Students' reflections can be a valuable source of information for instructors and librarians. After all, these are troublesome concepts, and undergraduate students, who are presumably in the midst of crossing these thresholds, can offer very different perspectives than people who cannot recall a time when they did not understand the constructed and contextual nature of authority. Similarly, it might be valuable to target alumni in assessment efforts, who may be able to recognize (in hindsight) and reflect on their threshold moments.

Conclusion

As illustrated by the previous sections, student research is contextualized by concentric circles of authority: the students' own sense of authority, their professor's authority, course requirements, departmental requirements, accreditation or association authorities, and the broader disciplinary views on authority. If students are to gain a rich and nuanced understanding of authority, the importance of faculty-librarian collaboration cannot be underestimated. Ideally, graduating seniors would be able to critically appraise the authorities within their own discipline while also understanding and appreciating other approaches. For librarians, this may mean greater involvement in upper-level courses, along with a deepening and strengthening of our liaison relationships.

What will not change is the need to meet the learners where they are; students' backgrounds, experiences, and prior knowledge will play a role in their readiness to engage with threshold concepts. Therefore, we must listen to and learn from our students. By working together with our colleagues, faculty, and students, we can foster an environment in which students can engage with troublesome concepts, integrate their knowledge, and explore boundaries.

Notes

1. Gustavus Adolphus College, "Department Mission," https://gustavus.edu/hes/gen-info.php.
2. National Athletic Trainers' Association, *Athletic Training Education Competencies*, 2011, https://www.nata.org/sites/default/files/competencies_5th_edition.pdf.
3. For more on "bottlenecks" in student learning, see, for example, Jill R. Sturts and Rasul A. Mowatt, "Understanding and Overcoming 'Bottlenecks' in Student Learning," *Schole: A Journal of Leisure Studies and Recreation Education* 27, no. 1 (2012): 39–45.
4. See Amy R. Hofer, Lori Townsend, and Korey Brunetti, "Troublesome Concepts and Information Literacy: Investigating Threshold Concepts for IL Instruction," *Portal: Libraries and the Academy* 12, no. 4 (2012): 387–405; see also Jan Meyer and Ray Land, *Overcoming Barriers to Student Understanding: Threshold Concepts and Troublesome Knowledge* (New York: Routledge, 2006).
5. Association of College & Research Libraries (ACRL), *Framework for Information Literacy for Higher Education*, February 2, 2015, http://www.ala.org/acrl/standards/ilframework.
6. Mark Merrick, "I Can't Believe We Don't Know That!" *Journal of Athletic Training* 41, no. 3 (2006): 231.
7. Association of College & Research Libraries (ACRL), *Framework for Information Literacy for Higher Education*, February 2, 2015, http://www.ala.org/acrl/standards/ilframework.
8. Mary Romanello and Malissa Martin, "Information Literacy in Athletic Training: A Problem-Based Approach," *AT Education* 11, no. 3 (May 2006): 40.
9. Lee Shulman, "Signature Pedagogies in the Professions," *Daedalus* 134, no. 3 (Summer 2005): 54.
10. Lynn Clouder, "'Caring as a 'Threshold Concept:' Transforming Students in Higher Education into Health(care) Professionals," *Teaching in Higher Education* 10, no. 4 (2005): 514.
11. Maureen Knapp and Stewart Brower, "The ACRL Framework for Information Literacy in Higher Education: Implications for Health Sciences Librarianship," *Medical Reference Services Quarterly* 33, no. 4 (2014): 464.
12. Barbara Fister, "Looking Deeper and Reaching Further with Threshold Concepts," (presentation, Kentucky Joint Spring Conference, April 2016), http://barbarafister.com/KY.pdf.
13. Deborah L. Begoray, Gillian Rowlands, and Doris E. Gillis, "Concluding Thoughts and the Future of Health Literacy," in *Health Literacy in Context: International Perspectives*, eds. Deborah L. Begoray, Doris E. Gillis, and Gillian Rowlands (New York: Nova, 2012), 158.

14. Eamon Tewell, "A Decade of Critical Information Literacy," *Communications in Information Literacy* 9, no. 1 (January 2015): 37.
15. Brian Hendrickson, "A Second Wave: Metawriting in the Composition Classroom," *PraxisWiki* (2014), http://kairos.technorhetoric.net/praxis/tiki-index.php?page=C-CCC2014_M25.

Information Creation as a Process

Section Two

CHAPTER 5*

Common Ground:
Communicating Information

Beate Gersch

This chapter discusses two subject areas that intersect naturally with information literacy: journalism and media studies. Both involve the communication, interpretation, and evaluation of information. While some academic institutions have separate departments for journalism and media studies, frequently these courses are offered under the umbrella of communication, which also includes classes in rhetoric, interpersonal, and organizational communication. Communication is the glue that binds them all, whether students learn to create a news report, a PR campaign, give a speech, study the dynamics of communication within business organizations, or learn about communication differences across cultures. However, identifying the proper academic home for journalism, media studies, and other communication courses has often involved fierce debate between their respective faculty and administrators. Journalism, traditionally, has been regarded as a skills-based vocational trade. With the transition into the twenty-first century, academic institutions have argued for the integration of journalism courses into larger communication or media studies departments, often for budgetary reasons, but also because of the necessity to redefine professional journalism in the face of digital platforms, social media, and citizen journalism. Not all journalism practitioners and journalism faculty embrace this blend of journalism and media studies. Although a deeper discussion of the arguments falls outside the scope of this chapter, some conceptual differences between a professional trade like jour-

---

* This work is licensed under a Creative Commons Attribution-NonCommercial-NoDerivatives 4.0 License, CC BY-NC-ND (https://creativecommons.org/licenses/by-nc-nd/4.0/).

nalism and an interdisciplinary field like media studies play a role in the way they connect to information literacy, which informs library instruction for these courses. Despite their differences, it is clear that both journalism and media studies are in the business of teaching students to communicate information and thus are inextricably linked to concepts of information literacy.

The idea of "information creation as a process" is nothing new to those teaching and learning in journalism and media studies. Traditionally, budding journalists are instructed in the craft of collecting and producing information, condensing it, editing it, and distributing it. Similarly, students of media have focused not only on the analysis of content creation but also its reception among varied audiences in different contexts. In that sense, for learners in journalism and media studies "information creation as a process" is an essential element, i.e., a threshold concept in becoming an expert in their field. Meyer and Land's threshold concepts theory[1] posits that learners become experts in a discipline by gradually passing certain thresholds in that discipline through internalizing, if you will, threshold concepts that open up a new way of thinking for learners within the discipline. The defining characteristics of these threshold concepts are that they are transformative, troublesome, bounded, integrative, and irreversible. For journalism students, "information creation as a process" becomes a defining part of their professional identity, and they embrace the challenges of creating information in different formats and for different audiences. As in other disciplines, students are often challenged by the conventions of journalistic inquiry and writing, since they are quite different from the essay writing they may have learned in high school or early college composition classes. Particularly with the rise of digital platforms and social media, the lines between professional journalism, citizen journalism, and other expressions in the public sphere have been blurred, as have the boundaries between industry, education, and entertainment. The distinction between consumers and producers of information is now a fluid one, and journalism students consciously need to redraw some of those lines in order to develop their craft. For media studies students, the experience of passing this particular threshold of "information creation as a process" is perhaps a bit different, as they do not necessarily aspire to become creators of media but critics, users, and sometimes just informed consumers. One of the most challenging things in media analysis is to get students to "see" what is not there—whose voice is not heard, whose identity is not represented, which ideology is absent in media content? The answers to these questions undoubtedly reveal important elements in the process of information creation. It is not uncommon to hear students say that a class in media studies has "ruined" their ability to enjoy media anymore because they cannot help but see the underlying processes of media production when consuming media content, no matter what the context.

Interdisciplinary fields: Friends or foes?

In their first publication on threshold concept theory, Meyer and Land posit that threshold concepts are "possibly often (though not necessarily always) *bounded* in that any conceptual space will have terminal frontiers, bordering with thresholds into new conceptual areas."[2] Since information literacy is typically taught within the context of other disciplines, the boundedness of information literacy threshold concepts is relative. While threshold concepts in natural sciences may be very clearly bounded, the demarcation is less clear in social sciences, let alone interdisciplinary fields, like gender studies, cultural studies, or media studies. Information literacy is interdisciplinary in nature, in that it draws on theories and methods from other fields, such as education, psychology, and information science. While the interdisciplinary character of information literacy deprives us of clear boundaries with regard to vocabulary, methods, and theories, it provides us with opportunities to enrich our field through conceptual overlaps with other subject areas. Journalism and media studies are two such subject areas, as they involve the creation, interpretation, and evaluation of information.

Information Creation as a Process

Although today's digital containers of information, in particular, mask the creation process, as librarians our task is to unveil these processes in order for learners to recognize how they affect the information product and its reception among various types of users. The ACRL Framework identifies Information Creation as a Process as a threshold concept for information literacy[3] and thereby formally acknowledges the significance of the relationship between information and ways of communicating it. The frame asks students to "develop, in their own creation processes, an understanding that their choices impact the purposes for which the information product will be used and the message it conveys."[4]

As a past instructor in media studies, I required even students in non-production classes to produce some media content themselves in the form of short videos, mockups of magazines, or storyboards, depending on the course topic. This process of information creation asked students to think about the audience and purpose of information, as well as the production parameters and restraints. The experience of producing information themselves fosters students' critical thinking and deeper analysis of information.

Although students in journalism and media studies early on learn to examine underlying creation processes, most of them do not readily apply their journalistic skills and/or knowledge of media to other areas of information seeking or evaluation, for example, when asked to explore library resources for their assignments, whether in journalism and media courses or other classes. They typically compartmentalize journalistic or media studies skills and information literacy skills as serving different purposes in their academic career—the former as the end goal of their journalism or media studies education, the latter at best as a means to that end, and at worst as a required "nuisance" they must endure in the form of a library instruction session, while their instructor is out of town to attend a conference.

Another challenge comes from journalism and media studies faculty who often believe that information literacy instruction is simply a waste of time because "we are already teaching that." It is not an easy task, but as librarians we need to communicate to faculty how we can offer distinctly different gateways into the concept of information creation, which will not only help students succeed in their class but be able to integrate their newfound knowledge and skills into their overall academic and professional lives. As part of the Framework,[5] the threshold concept of Information Creation as a Process offers new opportunities for librarians to collaborate with journalism and media studies faculty to reveal ways in which this threshold concept crosses the boundaries between academic tool and professional identity. Meaningful assignments and exercises help students tackle this "troublesome" threshold concept.

The next section addresses conceptual intersections between information literacy and the areas of journalism and media studies, specifically through the lens of information creation. This includes specific examples of assignments that focus on information creation as a process. The chapter concludes with a call to deepen our collaboration with course instructors in these subject areas through strengthening our common ground.

Journalism

The first principle of the Society of Professional Journalists Code of Ethics is to "seek truth and report it."[6] Ideally, journalists are expected to serve as the watchdogs of democracy, ensure that all voices are heard, and that news reporting does not become a pawn to economic or other specific interests and promotions. Journalism students are not only being trained to recognize "information creation as a process" but, more important, to partake in this process. Journalism *is* information creation. A recent long-term study of journalism students at a Canadian university showed that, over time, these students "develop an understanding of their roles both as producers and consumers within multiple information ecosystems."[7] While most academic classes help students to develop the art of academic writing for the purpose of becoming participants in disciplinary (scholarly) discourse, journalism students learn, among other skills, to communicate disciplinary (scholarly) information to a general audience. MacMillan observes that, "These students are keenly aware of their role as creators; to them content creation for external audiences is the end to which IL [information literacy] is the means."[8]

One of the knowledge practices of the Information Creation as a Process frame is to "recognize that information may be perceived differently based on the format in which it is packaged."[9] Journalism students are trained to produce information in different formats, e.g., a daily news beat, an in-depth report, breaking news, etc. Most of these information products exist in a digital format and are readily available online. However, they all come with different timelines and different rules on how to create them. A breaking news item requires immediate information output, while a dossier in a monthly or quarterly magazine allows for more in-depth research and crafting of the information with regard to organization and choice of content, as well as wording. This understanding of the publication cycle is essential to journalism students as they prepare to enter the profession. In honing their craft, they inadvertently practice some information literacy skills, such as accessing, evaluating, selecting, and incorporating information. However, it typically takes the collaboration between the course instructor and the instructional librarian for students to see the interrelatedness of journalistic and information literacy skills. As practitioners of information creation, ideally, they eventually develop the ability to recognize the underlying creation processes of information in other contexts, much like a professional photographer sees the world through photographic frames, even without a camera at his or her disposal. This becomes a professional habit, which is often the result of having struggled with a troublesome threshold concept earlier in their career or studies. The key for information literacy educators is to help students apply these skills of information creation to recognizing these processes in any information products they consume, not only in their professional training but in other contexts and for other purposes as well, whether in their academic or personal lives.

The Accrediting Council on Education in Journalism and Mass Communications states that graduates of accredited programs should "conduct research and evaluate information by methods appropriate to the communications professions in which they work."[10] Working for a popular magazine requires different professional skills from working for a trade magazine. Specifically, journalism students learn how to "write correctly and clearly in forms and styles appropriate for the communications professions, audience and purposes they serve."[11] Many academic subject areas follow specific formulas in their written assignments (for example, writing in science versus humanities), the product of which ideally contributes to existing disciplinary knowledge. Journalism students, on the other hand, adopt specific professional standards that fall outside of conventional academic writing. For example, the traditional model for a news story is the inverted pyramid in which the most important information about an event should be given right away, followed by pertinent details and, finally, other relevant information. In practicing this model, journalism students develop one of the Information Creation as a Process frame's knowledge practices, to "develop, in their own creation processes, an understanding that their choices impact the purposes for which the information product will be used and the message it conveys."[12] This is at the core of journalism education, and therefore positions journalism students perfectly to reflect on this process in their own consumption of information, even outside a professional context.

Journalism classes offer an ideal opportunity for librarians to infuse information literacy into the Communication curriculum. One example is to turn the library instruction session into a press conference, where students can reflect on aspects of information literacy through practicing their journalistic research and writing skills.

The press conference. This assignment, which works best in a face-to-face library instruction session, is ideal for newsgathering or newswriting courses, where the focus is on gathering information, doing research, and creating a "story" according to specific parameters provided by the course instructor. Students are asked to attend a "press conference"/instruction session in the library hosted by the "press speaker"/instruction librarian and write a news report that focuses on a "news item" presented during the "press conference." This can be an information resource, such as a database, a service like the writing center, or an event like Banned Books Week. Students are asked to prepare for the session by doing some initial research and formulating questions they plan to ask about the news item.

At the "press conference," the librarian provides a ten- to fifteen-minute presentation about the news item. This should include a few facts, a brief demonstration or presentation of images, and a news point, i.e., an important aspect of the presentation that can serve as a hook for the audience of the news report. The course instructor and the librarian collaborate to determine the news point and the extent of the information provided about the news item. Depending on the type of news assignment, students are informed about the news item two days or more before the "press conference," at which point they can begin with their background research. This can include any information resource available to them as budding journalists.

After the presentation by the instruction librarian, the "press corps" of students is required to ask questions related to the news item in general or the presentation in particular. This can lead to further demonstration of whatever information resource may have been the subject of the "press conference." Following the "press conference," students are asked to write a report on the news item presented to them based on their research and the "press conference." These reports are based on particular parameters of journalistic writing, such as the inverted pyramid style, an online blog, or other types of journalistic writing. While the course instructor will grade the students' reports based on his or her own grading rubric, ungraded copies are provided to the librarian for assessment of what students perceive to be the most important information about the news item, what other information they included, and the language they choose to describe it. The student reports reveal the "muddiest point" in the instruction and help the librarian make adjustments to the presentation in the future, which might include the clarification of library terms or the selection of resources to be presented.

Ideally, the collaboration between the course instructor and the librarian goes beyond the one-shot "press conference" and leads to a reflection exercise that can occur either in the classroom, in an online discussion forum, or in the form of a written homework assignment. Students share their rationale for the identification, placement, and omission of any information the librarian shared during the "press conference." Similarly, the librarian provides a rationale for her or his choices of content and language in the presentation. Through discussing their perspectives and potential differences, students, librarian, and course instructor together can identify some of the knowledge practices articulated for the Information Creation as a Process frame. Within this context, students are asked to reflect on whether and how a different medium, context, or audience would have changed the information product they created. This discussion can serve as a stepping stone to the last part of this assignment, where students research information resources and reflect upon the information creation processes from which they emerged. This works best as a guided exercise where students are given a specific topic and specific resources (or, if they are more advanced, categories of information resources, such as books, websites, etc.). Setting limitations like this makes it easier for students to compare their differences and similarities; it also allows the librarian to model the process for the students with familiar resources.

This course-integrated assignment promotes the knowledge practices and supports the learners' dispositions for the Information Creation as a Process frame. It merges journalism and information literacy skills to foster the multiple roles of the metaliterate learner, such as researcher, participant, translator, producers, author, etc.[13] Having students reflect on their own process of creating information develops their ability to recognize specific characteristics of information products that reveal their creation process.

Media studies

Unlike journalism, which can be regarded as a professional trade with specific guidelines, rules, and ethics, media studies is an interdisciplinary field. It draws on models and concepts from various subject areas, including political and economic theory, psychoanalytic theory, rhetoric, visual arts, film theory, journalism, as well as literary and cultural studies. While there is no specific set of parameters for studying media, an array of approaches exists which connect students to those other disciplinary knowledge areas. Aside from applied courses in media studies, such as video production, the goal of media studies is to teach students aspects of media literacy, which, according to Hobbs, is "a constellation of life skills that are necessary for full participation in our media-saturated, information-rich society."[14]

Information literacy and media literacy have existed in parallel conceptual universes for quite some time. In 1992, the Aspen Institute Report of the National Leadership Conference on Media Literacy defined media literacy as "the ability to access, analyze, evaluate, and create media in a variety of forms."[15] These skills are akin to those in the ACRL Information Literacy Competency Standards adopted in 2000,[16] which were based on the idea that an information literate individual should "recognize when information is needed, and have the ability to locate, evaluate, and use effectively the needed information."[17] Media literacy has traditionally involved a critical analysis of media industries, media content, and media audiences. Inevitably, this included, among other things, a look at media ownership, censorship, stereotypes, and media effects (particularly the concern about depictions of violence in the media). Initially, these concerns were based on a broadcast model of traditional media (e.g., television, radio, and print) in which the lines between producers and consumers of media were clear. However, the emergence of new technologies and ways in which people engage with information has led to a reconceptualization of both media literacy and information literacy. The model of a hierarchical linear flow of information to a unified audience has long given way to the idea of information reception as a complex process informed by social systems and (power) relationships. Students in media studies are encouraged to take a contextual approach to media messages beyond privileging content. A critical analysis requires media users to take into account the political-economic system in which the content was produced, the rules that govern the medium through which the content is disseminated, and the various ideological positions of a diverse audience decoding the content. "At the heart of digital and media literacy, education is not the mere transmission of facts and information about media industries, audiences and effects, but the goal of promoting a deep understanding of the concept of constructedness."[18] The same is true for information literacy, and the Information Creation as a Process frame speaks exactly to this notion of constructedness.

While an extensive discussion of theories of media effects goes beyond the scope of this chapter, suffice it to say that effects research has evolved from the assumption of direct effects (information sent = information received) to a more complex notion of audience reception that focuses on the ideological position of the audience and the context in which the interaction between audience and media (or information resource) occurs. Similarly, creators of media, or information in general, also operate in specific contexts and occupy ideological positions, all of which may affect the information product. As stated earlier, information does not have utility and value in itself. These are determined by and remain fluid through the context in which information is produced and consumed. Media studies is a broad field and offers many opportunities to connect with information literacy. One of the gateways for students to hone their media and information literacy skills is through the textual analysis of media content. The assignment described below utilizes the representation of information as a starting point to address how media industry, media producers, and media users all shape the process of information creation.

Looking for clues. This assignment works best in a face-to-face setting, but can also be conducted online with some adjustments. It is suitable for any class in which media analysis is part of the curriculum. No specific preparation is needed on the part of the students. The instruction session will involve analysis, discussion, exploration, and creation of information.

In preparation for the instruction session, the librarian creates three different versions of a news report or story on the same topic. This can be a fictional or actual news item, a fictional segment of a movie, or a scene from a fictional television drama. It is advisable to do this exercise early on in the course while students are still novices at media analysis. The topic should be something that is not currently a news item in order to avoid students already having preconceived notions about it. More important, the story should include a specific location, a dispute (or competing interests) of some kind, and a proposed solution, some or all of which should be altered in each of the different versions.

At the beginning of the instruction session, students are divided up into at least three groups. Each group is given a different version of the same topic. Students are instructed to read the text and, as a group, identify 1) the main characters, 2) the location, 3) the dispute, 4) who is to blame for it, and 5) the potential solution to the dispute. The librarian creates five columns with these story elements on a whiteboard and has each group write their answer(s) in the appropriate column. It should soon be evident that, based on the version they read, students provide different answers to these five aspects of the story. The librarian then engages the class in a discussion about what specific information in the story is different (word choices, order of events, omissions, or additional information). The librarian leads the discussion further to have students think about what factors could have played a role in the creation of the different versions of the story, such as the gender, race, or sexual orientation of the writer or editor, the company or person funding the story, or the location of the anticipated audience. Students are also invited to create other potential versions of the story. The librarian then helps students think about how they would find clues about those elements that are part of the creation process. For example, depending on the type of media, IMDb as a resource for movies, the "About" page of a website, etc., would be appropriate. It may be useful to keep a list of clues for such information on the whiteboard, so students are able to refer to it for the last part of the exercise. Finally, the key is to have students apply their insights gained from the exercise to information resources about a new topic, which should be based on their class assignment and chosen in collaboration with the course instructor. The librarian assists students in identifying clues about the creation process of the information resources they explore. At the end of the session, or as a homework assignment, students can write a brief reflection on three of their resources and any information they were able to find about the creation process of these resources. For example, if their chosen topic for the assignment is the representation of racial stereotypes in recent Disney animated movies, they might choose to look at the Disney web site, a scholarly article in a media studies journal, and a review in a newspaper. While their instructor will require them to focus on the content of these information resources, for the information literacy component students will be asked to explore some of these questions:

- What type of information resource is this: a blog, an article, a press release?
- What other information does this resource contain that may or may not be relevant to the task at hand?
- What sources did the authors consult, if any, and how are they documented?
- What is the tone of the resource: casual, scholarly, factual, entertaining?
- Who might be the audience?
- What amount of time and effort appear to have been put into the information?
- What is the purpose of the information?

Beginning students may offer some basic surface clues that are easily identifiable, for example, the level of sophistication in the language of the content and the credentials of the author. Advanced students might point out how the composition of an editorial board and the scope of a particular journal affect the content.

Cross-pollination and turf wars

This chapter offered two specific examples of incorporating the Information Creation as a Process frame into journalism and media studies courses. Certainly, different types of classes, even within the same subject area, require different types of approaches to introducing information literacy threshold concepts to the students and faculty. Information Creation as a Process is not the only frame relevant to these subject areas. While engaged in information creation as a process, journalists are also doing "research as inquiry" and "searching as strategic exploration." When analyzing hegemonic processes in the media, a discussion of "authority" and how it is "constructed and contextual" is an important aspect of the curriculum, alongside the notion that "information has value." It is clear that, while our instruction sessions may privilege one specific frame, it is likely that we will also touch on one of the others. When looking at the curriculum in their subject area, librarians should map out when and where to introduce students to each of the frames in the Framework. Presenting students (and faculty) with the entire Framework at once is daunting and not conducive to student learning. Focusing on one frame at a time does not mean other threshold concepts cannot be thrown into the conversation. However, knowledge practices and dispositions take time to develop; students should be given an opportunity to explore one frame at a time. This can occur with different assignments over the course of a semester if the librarian is continuously embedded in the class or in one-shot sessions in different courses throughout the students' course of study. Ideally, by the time they graduate, students will have been introduced to all six frames (and perhaps others that librarians felt important to add), be able to recognize their interrelatedness, and integrate their newly honed knowledge practices into their academic work, even beyond their specific subject area.

There is much common ground between Communication (as a field of study), communication (as a practice), and information literacy. This chapter only discussed two communication areas: journalism and media studies. However, other courses in communication focusing on rhetoric, public speaking, organizational communication, etc., offer similar opportunities for librarians to incorporate the Information Creation as a Process frame into their instruction. As stated in the introduction of this chapter, without information there is nothing to communicate, and information only becomes meaningful through communication. Collaborating with communication instructors is a logical extension of our information literacy efforts, as the areas of study within that field are also in the information business, so to speak. Such collaboration does not always come easy because some communication instructors feel that librarians are encroaching on their territory and that they are perfectly capable of teaching information literacy themselves. After all, they teach students to access, analyze, evaluate, and even create information. What can we as librarians possibly add? The Information Creation as a Process frame offers an ideal gateway for collaboration with faculty in the field of Communication, because Information Creation as a Process is a shared threshold concept in subject areas like journalism and media studies, as well as information literacy. Although not all subject faculty might identify Information Creation as a Process as a threshold concept, it still provides a shared concern about student learning. It is always easy to start a conversation with a phrase such as, "I've noticed that students seem to struggle with…" or "I am interested to get your opinion on…."

The ACRL Framework also offers the frames as a way to start a conversation with faculty about a holistic approach to student learning that goes beyond disciplinary knowledge. The conceptual overlap between knowledge areas in the field of communication and information literacy make it particularly easy for librarians to literally engage in "scholarship as a conversation." Subject librarians need to approach teaching faculty as instructors and scholars who share their commitment to student learning. The Framework in its current form does not "sell well" as a document. Therefore, it is up to us as librarians to communicate its concepts and philosophical underpinnings to subject faculty and find our common ground to help students succeed. Faculty might already engage in the knowledge practices of some of the frames, but sometimes it is much harder to change their dispositions than those of the students, especially if they've been teaching a particular course for decades and see no critical deficiencies in their students' learning.

Our appeal should not be about information literacy as merely a tool for students currently enrolled in one particular course. Rather, the key is to demonstrate our role as partners in supporting metaliterate learners for whom information literacy is on par with media, visual, digital, and other literacies, as they navigate through various communication territories—as researchers, collaborators, and producers—in their academic, professional, and personal lives.

Notes

1. Jan H. F. Meyer, Ray Land, and Caroline Baillie, eds., *Threshold Concepts and Transformational Learning* (Rotterdam, Netherlands: Sense Publishers, 2010), ix–xv.
2. Jan Meyer and Ray Land, "Threshold Concepts and Troublesome Knowledge: Linkages to Ways of Thinking and Practising Within the Disciplines," Enhancing Teaching-Learning Environments in Undergraduate Courses Project, (Edinburg, Occasional Report 4, 2003): 5.
3. Association of College and Research Libraries (ACRL), *Framework for Information Literacy for Higher Education*, February 2, 2015, http://www.ala.org/acrl/standards/ilframework.

4. Ibid.
5. Ibid.
6. Society of Professional Journalists, *Code of Ethics*, September 6, 2014, http://www.spj.org/ethicscode.asp.
7. Margy E. MacMillan, "Fostering the Integration of Information Literacy and Journalism Practice: A Long-Term Study of Journalism Students," *Journal of Information Literacy,* 8 no. 2 (2014): 15.
8. Ibid., 16.
9. ACRL, *Framework*.
10. Accrediting Council on Education in Journalism and Mass Communications, *Professional Values and Competencies*, 2013, http://www2.ku.edu/~acejmc/PROGRAM/STANDARDS.SHTML#std2.
11. Ibid.
12. ACRL, *Framework*.
13. Tom Mackey and Trudi Jacobson, *Metaliteracy: Reinventing Information Literacy to Empower Learners* (Chicago: Neal-Shuman, 2014), 92.
14. Renee Hobbs, *Digital and Media Literacy: A Plan of* Action (Washington, DC: Aspen Institute, 2010), vii.
15. Patricia Aufderheide, *Aspen Institute Report of the National Leadership Conference on Media Literacy* (Washington, DC: Aspen Institute, 1992).
16. ACRL, *Information Literacy Competency Standards for Higher Education*, 2000, http://www.ala.org/acrl/standards/informationliteracycompetency.
17. American Library Association Presidential Committee on Information Literacy, *Final Report* (Chicago, IL: American Library Association, 1989).
18. Renee Hobbs, "The State of Media Literacy: A Response to Potter," *Journal of Broadcasting & Electronic Media* 55, no. 3 (2011): 427.

CHAPTER 6*

Using the Frame Information Creation as a Process to Teach Career Competencies to Advertising Students

Megan Blauvelt Heuer

Because information source types in advertising are dynamic and numerous, teaching Information Creation as a Process represents a critical part of information literacy education for students in advertising and marketing programs. Since these programs place great emphasis on career skills, addressing this frame should be situated within an awareness of professional practice. The transfer of information skills from college to career is not necessarily a simple corollary. There is evidence that information skills are situational, and that the transfer of skills from education to work only occurs at basic levels.[1] Annemaree Lloyd, a prolific researcher in the area of workplace information literacy, argues that information literacy is not a set of discrete skills but rather a socially constructed set of concepts, practices, and values, and that educators should be aware of other information contexts outside of the bounded world of college in order to teach the transfer of those competencies.[2] Fortunately, the *Framework for Information Literacy for Higher Education* (Framework) allows us to address this transfer through the focused instruction of underly-

---

* This work is licensed under a Creative Commons Attribution-ShareAlike 4.0 License, CC BY-SA (https://creativecommons.org/licenses/by-sa/4.0/).

ing concepts of information and how those concepts might apply in varying contexts. This chapter will look at how students struggle with the concept of Information Creation as a Process, give an overview of the advertising information landscape, and present progressive learning activities with suggestions for possible assessments.

Moving students through the threshold concept

Information Creation as a Process is a foundational concept that, when learned, leads to better execution of research activities by addressing deeper research problems. Unlike other frames, it cannot be directly tied to a specific research activity, such as looking for information, using search tools, or choosing good sources, though it is related to all of those. Understanding this concept enables students to search for information more strategically (Searching as Strategic Exploration) and to recognize how a source's method of publication may impact an evaluation of authority and usefulness (Authority is Constructed and Contextual). At the heart of Information Creation as a Process is the idea that information is delivered to a particular audience by means of a publication method that is selected with intention. How we find, evaluate, and use information is impacted by the way the information was created and for whom it was created. The foundation of this frame is the understanding of information as rhetorically situated. By this I mean recognizing the intended audience, the typical conventions of the genre, and the motivations behind producing that type of information as more important than the superficial characteristics, such as how one accesses that information.

Experts recognize and classify information, albeit perhaps unconsciously, by how it is created, whereas students tend to see information as a blur. While this might have always been true for college students, the digitization and "Googlization" of the information world has only compounded the problem.[3] Different types of information are much easier to distinguish when physically manifested and placed in different locations within a library. However, databases and web-scale discovery aggregate various types of information into one interface, blurring the boundaries further, making source differentiation even more difficult for students. In my experience, students, even well-informed ones, place more emphasis on the database in which the information was found or that it was found on the open web than on the method in which it was created—not surprising given that the boundaries of means of access seem better defined.

It is easy to get caught up in the importance of teaching students to recognize format, but it is essential that they understand why they are doing so beyond the requirements of an assignment sheet or a checklist. Search engines have fundamentally changed students' native information-seeking behavior, and they are quite comfortable relegating information search—and evaluation for that matter—to an algorithm. Librarians' awareness of the effect of Google on student research is well documented in Hofer, Townsend, and Brunetti's study on applying threshold concepts.[4] Therefore, in grasping this particular threshold concept, a student must first grasp the need to approach research strategically as a motivation to learn to recognize how and why information is created. This means addressing why this should matter to them; otherwise, teaching format turns into a meaningless requirement. This could be accomplished by demonstrating research strategies connecting need to source type so that they see how strategy can be more effective.

Once students understand why they should care to distinguish between sources, the problem of source differentiation can be addressed through discussing how and why different information types are produced, identifying ways students might determine how a piece of information is produced, and comparing source types that on the surface seem very different but share similar creation processes. For example, having students find the same information type, like newspaper or trade magazine articles, using different tools can help them move past the tendency to classify information by means of access. Including recognition of source type any time sources are discussed, such as in annotated bibliographies or research journals, can also help reinforce recognition of information creation processes. Given that the information landscape will probably look very different in their professional lives, doing this kind of work with college students is essential in the transfer of concepts and practices to multiple settings.

Once students are able to distinguish between different types of information, they need to recognize when certain information products may be preferred. As Seeber suggests, it is important that we do not present any one type of information as better than another.[5] For example, presenting peer-reviewed articles as the most authoritative source without connecting to the context of use can elicit black and white thinking about authority on the part of the student. When working with students in evaluating information, students can compare pieces of information that may seem similar on the surface but represent different levels of usefulness. Also, having students compare the types of information sources preferred in different contexts and build awareness of the information products preferred within their chosen discipline helps them to refine their understanding.

The language of the frame may seem to suggest that we teach the entire information creation process for different information types, like newspaper articles, trade articles, journal articles, collected essays, etc. This may feel prohibitive within the scope of undergraduate instruction and is indeed impractical if there is a need to teach many source types beyond the scholarly research article, as is the case in advertising. Grounding instruction in an awareness of information as message and discussing the process of creation for specific types commonly used in the discipline should be sufficient. It is also important to note that not every information creation process is as extended as the scholarly publication cycle, so the emphasis on process can seem contrived for certain types of information. At a graduate level, it is potentially more critical for students to have a more refined understanding of information creation processes, particularly as they embark on becoming authors themselves.

The advertising information landscape

For advertising students new to the discipline, the types of information that might be used for research can be mystifying. Information sources are wide-ranging and represent both formal and informal publishing processes: market research, proprietary and free data sources, scholarly research, trade/industry publications, general media publications, association or special interest group publications, and varying primary information sources. These sources are created for widely varying purposes and audiences and are distributed in a myriad of ways, and this directly affects how we search for and use this information. Furthermore, the advertising industry is fast-paced, requiring professionals to keep up with emerging information products.

Business sources are usually utterly unfamiliar to incoming students and, in fact, they usually lack general knowledge of business practices that inform the information creation process. Students have admitted to me that the freshmen-level information literacy instruction they received felt very remote from the experience of researching within their major, a good argument for the disciplinary application of information literacy instruction the Framework promotes. The fact is that instruction on the scholarly publication process has only some bearing on secondary research in advertising. While there is a representative body of scholarly inquiry in marketing and advertising, there is a divide between academic research and the information products preferred by practitioners. Some faculty members emphasize the importance of theoretical literature or scholarly research on practical application, and some do not. Either way, much research in advertising exists outside traditional academic publishing. Information sources created by marketing firms and industry associations tend to have the same glossy look as popular sources on the web. This puts further importance on students understanding the information creation process, given that acceptable and unacceptable sources more closely resemble each other on a superficial level.

High value is placed on specific advertising industry publications, recent consumer data, and good market analysis; students should learn to recognize preferred source types. In advertising, the more specific and comprehensive the information is to the target market, the better. Expensive proprietary resources, like market research reports or national consumer data, include extensive primary research with much greater specificity than free information online. Sometimes, these sources will post limited teaser reports online for free, but this type of information potentially represents a lack of competitive edge for an advertiser. For finding data sources, students must strategize information search based on the specificity of their need as well as identify how the data was created in determining usefulness.

The difference in resources available to students and those available to professionals potentially makes the transfer of information literacy skills from the university to the workplace difficult. Some information products for advertising are intended for corporate purchase and may not provide a university license. On the other hand, the amount and quality of information to which a student has access often outstrips that available in the professional world, depending on the size and type of the employer. An agency may subscribe to specific consumer data sources but not the large business information databases available through a library. As a result, it is critical that students learn what information types are proprietary and how to supplement with free and public library sources.

Talking to faculty

The Framework shifts information literacy from a set of explicit tasks to essential concepts, but faculty may not understand teaching research as addressing concepts. Some of the work involved with reaching out to faculty is to reshape traditional conceptions of information literacy education, particularly if existing university learning outcomes are based on the Information Literacy Standards for Higher Education.[6] This particular frame is difficult to communicate to faculty because it is not directly tied to an explicit research function. I have found the best way to create a common language with the faculty is to start by discussing the problems that they see evidenced by their students' work and then supplying the threshold concepts that might lead to those problems. The top problems mentioned by my faculty relating to this frame are a lack of strategic thinking in research, an overreliance on Google, overreliance on one type of source, and a lack of awareness of the quality sources valued in the profession. As one professor put it, she constantly has to tell her students, "Stop surfing and start searching."

I help faculty understand that students do not strategize in their research partly because they cannot distinguish between different types of sources in a meaningful way. Expert problem solvers perceive underlying principles, whereas students do not, and experts employ strategy and planning, whereas students do not plan or adjust for failure.[7] This can partly be connected to a lack of domain knowledge—in this case, how disciplinary information is created. In educating students to become expert researchers, which is certainly a type of problem solving, we must teach how and why information is created.

Another selling point for this type of instruction to faculty is that it is critically important for students to recognize and classify information in a meaningful way because they will probably be accessing market information through different tools after graduation. Furthermore, even if they intend to enter a career path unrelated to research, students still need the ability to read and understand marketing information and recognize the creation process is part of that. Clearly, understanding this frame is essential in the transfer of research skills to the professional world.

Engaging the students

The following learning activities represent a sequence that builds understanding of this frame and other related frames progressively. They are designed to create an active learning environment and to address the transfer of concepts to professional practice. These learning activities generally follow a four-step process for teaching concepts: presenting a concept, modeling application of the concept, practicing application of the concept in a low-stakes setting, and finally engaging students in the transfer of the concept to other contexts.

Learning activity 1: Resource comparison chart

Student learning outcomes:
- Identify the uses, advantages, disadvantages, specificity, and means of access for various information sources used in advertising.
- Match research needs to potential information types and search tools.

This learning activity introduces students to the various types of advertising information, encourages recognition of the intended audience and purpose of each type, and emphasizes why these matter. Before this activity, students need at least minimal knowledge of accessing business resources, which may be accomplished through a pre-session online tutorial. The research guide also represents an important piece of scaffolding for the students.

Before students begin the source comparison chart, it is important that the purpose for the exercise is discussed. One essential element of transfer for students is to be actively engaged in determining how concepts might look in other contexts.[8] I connect the work we are doing in the class as important to their future professional life in that the tools they will have may not be exactly the same ones they have as a student. It is difficult for students to completely understand what their research needs will be in their future professions, but this introduces the idea that their information environment will change. We also do a short activity demonstrating the importance of searching strategically for the purpose of transfer and motivation. This could involve having the students start with a background source, like an industry overview, and discuss how it could aid their research. Another option would be to compare information found by searching for a professional association versus information found by blind Googling. Once the students understand the importance of recognizing different source types, they are ready for the comparison chart.

Because there are so many possible source types, it is important to focus on the most essential ones for the chart, keeping in mind what might be needed for the course's research project. The questions on the chart include:
- Who is the intended audience?
- What are the essential characteristics of this information type, including how and why it was created?
- Describe at least two ways you can access this type of information.
- How might you use this type of source in your research?
- What are the advantages/disadvantages of using this type of source in your research?

It is important to model the kind of thinking that the students need to do in completing the chart by walking through the thought process needed to answer the questions for one source type. The students are then split into groups, assigned a specific information type, and tasked with answering all the questions on the chart for their assigned type. Using group work in this way is a method of scaffolding for the students, allowing them to think through the concept with others and with the librarian.

This activity is intended as introductory, and therefore it is not expected that students will be able to learn everything about the information creation process of every source type and how they might be used. Rather, the activity is intended to start students on the path of distinguishing among these source types. The groups each report out to the class, allowing the others to finish filling out their chart. As a closing activity, there needs to be a metacognitive exercise so that students can articulate what they have learned about the concept and how that might transfer to future research projects. This could be a one-minute written response or a quick discussion of how they might use what they learned in a given specific research scenario.

Learning activity 2: Problem-based case studies

Student learning outcomes:
- Identify the limitations of information on companies, industries, markets, and consumers.
- Match research needs to appropriate types of information.
- Solve an information problem through strategic search and critical thinking.

In this session, students learn more about the advertising information landscape with a particular emphasis on how that might limit what they can find and how to overcome those limitations. Before delivering this session, an online tutorial on different information types and how to find them may help students be successful in the class, particularly if it has been a while since their last interaction with advertising research or if students are unfamiliar with all the information types you present in the class.

The session begins with a quick discussion reinforcing the idea that information is created and published for specific reasons, and that knowing why it is created and who creates it is key to performing deep research. Then, a set of cards with information regarding the creation process for advertising resources are distributed to student groups, with each group receiving the same set of cards. These cards should match the content delivered through the pre-session tutorial, so they should have some familiarity with the content on the cards and how to find examples of those types of information. The topics for the cards include North American Industry Classification System (NAICS) codes, syndicated market research, government data, company hierarchy, business directories, professional association reports, national consumer surveys, business journals, etc. *Business Information Needs and Strategies* by Abels and Klein can be very helpful in putting these cards together.[9] Taking an example card, I think aloud as to how the fact on the card might impact research. The groups then split up the cards among themselves and each student does the same with their cards, reporting these ideas out to the group.

At this point, each group is given its own research case study to work with for the remainder of the class. I inform the students that these case studies are based on actual research projects from the professional world. The case studies identify a client, the client project, and what they need to know from secondary research. These studies are problematic in that the topics chosen do not have clear answers, given the way business information is produced. For example, one case study is secondary research for an ad campaign for the local transit system. The difficulties lie in the fact that transit is not a traditional consumer product, competitors are not clearly definable, and local information must be found. Problems to address might include a need for a different level of geographic specificity than might be available, finding non-traditional consumer products, a NAICS code that is too broad for the company, or a brand that is part of a larger corporation.

Before the students begin their research, they are provided guided questions to encourage strategic search. It has been shown that problem solvers who have deliberately created solution strategies tend to attribute challenges faced to a weakness in the strategy rather than to factors beyond their control.[10] Actively encouraging students to strategize is essential, given that many students tend to give up when research seems to hit a dead end. This could be accomplished by having them work through a set of guided questions:

- What specific questions need answering?
- What source types should we consider?
- What tools might be best?
- What problems do we foresee?
- What terms might we use for the search?

Once students have created a strategy, have them divide the tasks for search and begin their research. The information process cards, the list of requirements for secondary research in the case study, and a detailed research guide provide scaffolding. This activity gives the librarian the opportunity to work with individual groups in order to suggest other avenues of reframing research questions. As they work, students are asked to answer these questions to report out to the class:

- What types of information did you use for your research? Are there any new information type cards you would create?
- What problems did you encounter in performing your research? How did these problems relate to how or why information is created?
- How would you solve these problems?
- What ambiguities might remain that should be clarified through primary research?
- What advice would you give another student about performing secondary research in advertising?

These questions move students through recognizing information types, recognizing how the information creation process does impact how they should search, considering changes in strategy in order to perform deeper research, and reflecting and summarizing on what was learned. In reporting out to the whole class, the students benefit from seeing how different research problems might be resolved. This type of research takes much longer than a class length will permit, and it is critical to emphasize that point so students understand that research is a lengthy and iterative process. The significant point is that they explore the case study enough to articulate the challenges presented and discuss strategies for overcoming those challenges. In other words, students are focused on thinking through research rather than simply producing answers. This activity could be assessed by having students create applications cards on which they write how the concept might apply in their everyday experience, which can help a student to feel more personally engaged. Since it is difficult for students to picture the context of a professional scenario, it is enough that they recognize the concept and that they have the confidence to transfer it to another context, even if it is not a professional one.

This learning activity could be reframed to focus on Information has Value by giving the same case study to all groups, but giving them varying levels of access. For example, one group could represent a large firm with access to several expensive databases while another group could represent a small firm with only free Internet sources or public library sources. Students could also simply discuss how their research might change if they did not have access to the high-price resources.

Learning activity 3: Research deconstruction

Student learning outcomes:
- Can recognize perceived industry value of specific information sources
- Can match research needs to appropriate types of information
- Can break down complex information problems to solvable questions

This learning activity has students take a research artifact specific to the discipline and reverse engineer the research process by analyzing how sources inform the work, what information types are preferred, and what questions might have been asked. This activity works well for starting students on a major research project and connects to other frames, particularly Research as Inquiry. I have used this activity in disciplines other than advertising with simply a shift in the research artifact used for the class.

This is intended as an upper-level activity, so students should have a firm grasp of different business information sources and how to find them. Research artifacts in advertising include market research reports, scholarly literature reviews, trade articles, marketing plans, and campaign plans books. I have the students deconstruct a campaign plans book because it is something they are expected to create themselves, both in school and in the professional world. A plans book presents the campaign strategy, example advertisements, analysis, and media plan with supporting evidence from primary and secondary research. It is difficult to get a professional research artifact in advertising because this type of work is proprietary. In working with my faculty, I discovered that the plans books created by the winning teams in the National Student Advertising Contest work well for this activity, given that they are accessible, of high quality, and unlike professional plans books, include reference lists.

I like to start this activity with a few questions to prime students for what they are about to learn:
- How does secondary research inform an ad campaign?
- What types of sources are preferred for a campaign plans book?

They may not know the answers, but the research deconstruction will help them to answer these more fully. We also discuss the ways sources are used, based on Bizup's BEAM method.[11] This method was intended originally for academic writing, but used more broadly, the concept can be applied in this very different context. To illustrate how sources are used for the students, I give an example campaign and go through specific sources for that campaign that fall into the categories of background sources for establishing the context, exhibit sources, like data on which they perform their own analysis, and analysis sources that represent another's interpretation of exhibits. Using this method helps alleviate the confusion of primary and secondary sources with primary and secondary research and encourages students to think about how the different information types are functioning in their work.

After these initial discussions, students are broken into small groups with a copy of an advertising plans book for each group. They are to highlight places in the plans book where secondary research is evident. Because these plans books do not include formal citations, students must identify what types of sources might have been used, though the reference list can provide some help. Once the students finish their research deconstruction, they report out to the class. The group presentations can be guided by these questions:
- What research questions do you think were asked by this ad team?
- What types of sources, background, evidence, or analysis did they use to answer those questions?
- Do any source types seem to be preferred? Why do you think they are preferred?
- What source types are not being used? Why do you think they are not preferred?

After the students have engaged with an example of good secondary research, they move to creating a concept map for their own project, organized in any way that makes sense to them. An example concept map for the plans book the students deconstructed is helpful for those who may not have made a concept map before. On their map, the students must include major areas of research, specific questions for those areas, and possible sources that might answer those questions. The students' concept maps can be used to assess this activity by looking to see how well students matched their research questions to appropriate source types and how well they broke down all aspects of the problem. Using an online concept-mapping tool like Mindmapfree.com or

MindMeister allows students to send you a digital copy of their maps while keeping a copy as reference for their project. A one-minute response or quick discussion might also be included on how they made decisions about which sources to include on their concept maps and what sources were excluded, based on the processes used to create them.

Conclusion

Teaching recognition of the information creation process is certainly not a completely new idea to the Framework, but this document does encourage us to consider teaching this concept as a direct goal of information literacy instruction. In working toward becoming expert researchers, it is essential that advertising students learn concepts about the nature of information itself so that they may transfer their understanding to new contexts outside of college. This can be done through the active engagement of students in that transfer process. Though teaching threshold concepts may seem daunting, particularly for lower-level students, it is possible to break down the concepts into progressive learning goals. At lower levels, students need to acknowledge the importance of recognizing the information creation process and begin to discern differences among source types. As students move into the upper levels, the work that remains is to reinforce their understanding of the different types of information and how they can leverage that understanding for more sophisticated research. Keeping the theory of threshold concepts in mind, as instructors we can acknowledge that our students will not necessarily learn the concept within the space of a one-shot session, but we can inspire them to start thinking about information and research in a new way. Cementing that understanding and realizing its greater implications comes as students continue to practice research outside of the classroom.

Notes

1. N. Ferran-Ferrer, Juli Minguilln and Mario Prez-Montoro, "Key Factors in the Transfer of Information-Related Competencies between Academic, Workplace, and Daily Life Contexts," *Journal of the American Society for Information Science & Technology* 64, no. 6 (2013): 1112–1121.
2. Annemaree Lloyd, *Information Literacy Landscapes*, 1st ed. (Oxford: Chandos, 2010), 138.
3. W. Badke, "Remedial Information Literacy?" *Online* 35, no. 2 (2011): 52.
4. Amy R. Hofer, Lori Townsend, and Korey Brunetti, "Troublesome Concepts and Information Literacy: Investigating Threshold Concepts for IL Instruction," *portal: Libraries and the Academy* 12, no. 4 (2012): 395.
5. Kevin Patrick Seeber, "Teaching 'Format as a Process' in an Era of Web-Scale

Discovery," *Reference Services Review* 43, no. 1 (2015): 24, doi:10.1108/RSR-07-2014-0023.
6. Association of College and Research Libraries (ACRL), *Information Literacy Competency Standards for Higher Education*, 2000, http://www.ala.org/acrl/standards/informationliteracycompetency.
7. Barry J. Zimmerman and Magda Campillo, "Motivating Self-Regulated Problem Solvers," in *The Psychology of Problem Solving*, eds. Janet E. Davidson and Robert J. Sternberg (Cambridge: Cambridge University Press, 2003), 236.
8. Rebecca Z. Kuglitsch, "Teaching for Transfer: Reconciling the Framework with Disciplinary Information Literacy," *portal: Libraries and the Academy* 15, no. 3 (2015): 470.
9. Deborah Klein and Eileen Abels, *Business Information Needs and Strategies* (Bingley, UK: Emerald Group Publishing Limited, 2008).
10. Zimmerman and Campillo, "Motivating Self-Regulated Problem Solvers," 245.
11. Joeseph Bizup, "BEAM: A Rhetorical Vocabulary for Teaching Research-Based Writing," *Rhetoric Review* 27, no. 1 (2008): 72–86, doi:10.1080/07350190701738858.

CHAPTER 7

Moving Public Health Learners to the Skeptical Edge with Information Creation as a Process

Xan Goodman

Introduction

During the twentieth century, the discipline of public health benefitted from many notable achievements, including the discovery and application of antibiotics to treat infection, the development of a vaccine that allowed for the eradication of smallpox, and a vaccine for polio.[1] In this chapter, I will focus on two other notable public health cases of the twentieth century, as related to public health information creation. These cases hinge on a proposed threshold concept: social determinants of health (SDOH). Social determinants of health describe factors that influence population health behaviors and health outcomes. Poverty, socioeconomic status, stress, one's built environment—that is, whether a person's neighborhood has sidewalks or bike lanes—and one's race or ethnicity are all SDOHs. Even access to healthy food is a social determinant that affects the health status and health outcomes of populations. The Healthy People 2020 Initiative and World Health Organization have outlined more social factors that influence health.[2] This chapter explores SDOH as a threshold concept through the lens of the cases of Henrietta Lacks and the Tuskegee Experiment, as well as the information literacy threshold concept Information Creation as a Process.[3]

An understanding of social determinants of health is essential to students of public health, as these students will enter careers in epidemiology, environmental health, health promotion, and health care, where they will grapple with questions of how SDOH impact populations. Students will work as epidemiologists, community health workers, infectious disease experts, food inspectors, environmental health specialists, public health officers, professors, and sexual health educators, among many other careers. Students will encounter essential questions, such as: Is health care a human right? Additionally, public health dilemmas abound and are evident in multiple contexts, from viral disease outbreaks such as Zika to debates in the United States about universal healthcare coverage.[4] The aim of focusing on Henrietta Lacks and the Tuskegee Syphilis Study is to explore two well-known public health cases with library instruction that encourages students to adopt a new lens through which they view information and a skeptical approach to information creation in public health. At the same time, students will be encouraged to critically think about SDOH and information creation using instructor-selected reading materials and information sources, so they can apply what they learn. In this chapter, I propose lessons aimed at undergraduate students. Public health undergraduate students are poised to become contributors to policy, guidelines, and evidence-based research, and grasping these threshold concepts will be critical to their ability to positively affect the communities they will serve.

I am a liaison librarian at the University of Nevada, Las Vegas (UNLV) Libraries, where I support the Schools of Allied Health, Community Health Sciences, and Nursing. In my role, I work with professors and course coordinators to integrate library instruction into the curriculum. UNLV is located in Las Vegas, a city community with complex public health challenges. The city has a built environment, for example, that results in an excessively high number of pedestrian fatalities.[5] There is a paucity of fresh food grocers, and sixteen Las Vegas census tracts are designated as food deserts.[6] Systematic issues conspire to create an environment with low-quality public education, and low graduation rates that mostly affect lower socioeconomic populations.[7] These are just a few examples of the many public health challenges that our students will encounter as professionals.

The social determinants of health as a threshold concept

A threshold concept represents a foundational disciplinary concept a student will ideally grasp to achieve mastery in a discipline. As defined by Meyer and Land, threshold concepts have five primary characteristics, that they are: troublesome, bounded, transformative, integrative, and irreversible.[8] SDOH as a concept embodies these five characteristics. Students newly introduced to SDOH might experience feelings of discomfort, disbelief, and even anger about the SDOH. Students will necessarily struggle when introduced to this concept as their current ideas about health and health outcomes are upended. SDOH as a framework for understanding public health is troublesome, bounded, transformative, integrative, and irreversible. It is important to note that I found no existing research on what students tend to believe before being exposed to SDOH. Thus, I provide examples of direct classroom experience and assignment responses in this chapter.

SDOH are often troublesome when students first encounter the idea that factors such as low socioeconomic status or access to a built environment might affect health. Students will sometimes express doubt and exhibit an affective response of discomfort with this new knowledge. Besides discomfort, troublesome new knowledge might also represent a point in the learning process where a student gets stuck[9]—for example, when students are initially unable to grasp how the zip code of populations might determine incidence of disease or be strong predictors of mortality. The troublesome nature of SDOHs might present in the classroom from students who exhibit strong emotional responses. I experienced this directly in class discussions about health as a human right; students expressed that they did not "buy" the idea that health is a human right and were noticeably emotional in their discussion. Some did not want to pay for the health care of others and asked, *Why should I have to pay for someone else?* Others talked about personal responsibility and how people might be less responsible for their health if universal health care were available.[10] Some students were more nuanced and expressed that there is simply not enough money available to provide access to health care for all, so those who are unable to afford care might need to go without or find other options. As students grapple with understanding the significance of SDOH, they are discomforted by the potential ramifications of this idea.

A student who encounters troublesome knowledge is said to be in the space of liminality. The liminal space is one where a student thinks, where they mull over a new concept, sometimes tossing it aside, retreating, and returning to again pick it up. When first encountering SDOH, students might retreat from these concepts because they are troubling, slightly unbelievable, and difficult to grasp. To cross the liminal space and integrate new knowledge about SDOH, a student needs to experience a transformation in their thinking. Transformative thinking in a discipline represents a change in how a discipline is approached. To become a successful public health practitioner students need to integrate knowledge about the SDOH into their thinking. Integrative refers to a student adopting the ways of a discipline. They simply begin to think, for example, like an epidemiologist or a public health officer. Once new disciplinary knowledge is adopted, it is described as irreversible; once learned it cannot be unlearned.[11] Bounded refers to the knowledge boundaries of a discipline. The SDOH is a threshold concept that bounds the practice of public health; it is foundational to understanding how to do the discipline.

SDOH move a healthcare practitioner to examine the systems and structures that affect health outcomes. As an example, Dr. Adewale Troutman is an allopathic medical doctor who also has a graduate degree in public health. Dr. Troutman served as past president of the American Public Health Association and Director of Public Health in Louisville, Kentucky.[12] Dr. Troutman's work to map disease in Louisville, Kentucky, is grounded in the threshold concept of SDOH. Dr. Troutman examined why populations in particular zip code regions had higher incidences of mortality and rates of disease. His epidemiological exploration of population health and the role of health inequities led to a citywide initiative in Louisville to improve the health of communities.[13] A physician trained in public health will have an awareness of health disparities and health inequities and will approach the practice of medicine differently. Doctors often treat the individuals instead of focusing on disease prevention and populations.[14] Among physicians who have earned a degree in public health, their practice of health care often seems to have been affected by an understanding of the SDOH. Fineberg expressed this well: "A physician who appreciates the role and potential for public health interventions… has a deeper understanding of the conditions that preserve health, of the primacy of disease prevention, and of the interfaces between personal and medical care and community health protection," and Dr. Troutman's work provides one example.[15]

Information Creation as a Process

Policy, evidence-based papers, guidelines, and research are all forms of public health-related information created by different processes. Information Creation as a Process is one of six frames outlined in the Association of College and Research Libraries' (ACRL) *Framework for Information Literacy for Higher Education* (Framework). I will use this frame to explore how a librarian and a faculty member might partner to combine an information literacy threshold concept with a discipline-specific threshold concept to motivate students to question critically, take a skeptical approach to information, and apply what they learn to question the public health information they encounter. The Framework suggests that "experts look to the underlying processes of creation as well as the final product to critically evaluate the usefulness of the information."[16] Undergraduate students are novice learners who are encountering disciplinary content for the first time, and they will not move to expert level in one course. However, Information Creation as a Process can be introduced along with SDOH in a scaffolded manner to build this skill. In the Introduction to Public Health Course at UNLV, students read texts such as *Silent Spring* and *The Immortal Life of Henrietta Lacks*, in addition to other works. In librarian-designed lessons, students will be encouraged to delve deeper into the original medical data at the heart of the Henrietta Lacks case, so they will consider the processes that went into their creation. A potential collaboration between a faculty member and librarian can be established to allow students to explore the frame Information Creation as a Process through a skeptical approach to information, critically thinking about SDOH.

Public Health Education Standards

Undergraduate public health education is guided by standards established by the Council on Education for Public Health (CEPH). CEPH requires an institution offering a bachelor's degree in public health to offer a general education curriculum that addresses the following areas: scientific knowledge, including the biological and life sciences and concepts of health and disease; foundations of social and behavioral sciences; basic statistics; and the humanities and the arts. CEPH also describes foundational domains a student should acquire. Specific domains relevant to information literacy instruction include:

- The basic concepts, methods, and tools of public health data collection, use, and analysis, and why evidence-based approaches are an essential part of public health practice
- The socioeconomic, behavioral, biological, environmental, and other factors that impact human health and contribute to health disparities
- Basic concepts of legal, ethical, economic, and regulatory dimensions of health care and public health policy and the roles, influences, and responsibilities of the different agencies and branches of government[17]

CEPH has also issued two broad competency areas for undergraduate learners: "the ability to communicate public health information, in both oral and written forms, through a variety of media and to a diverse audiences" and "the ability to locate, use, evaluate, and synthesize public health information."[18] Students are also required to have an opportunity to engage in experiential activities and additional co-curricular experiences that expose students to life-long learning opportunities and other meaningful experiences, such as networking, professionalism, teamwork, and leadership.

University context

Within the health sciences programs at UNLV, the curriculum is intended to be scaffolded programmatically to provide an education, whereby concepts are introduced, enhanced, and reinforced. Thus, a first-year student who has indicated an interest in the health sciences will be enrolled in the first-year health sciences seminar course, HSC100. In the second-year seminar, PBH 205 students are introduced to public health and learn about SDOH. These undergraduate students are novice learners who are encountering disciplinary content for the first time. In PBH 205, they are required to read the *Immortal Life of Henrietta Lacks*. In PBH 330, students examine SDOH and their importance regarding global health. In their capstone course, PBH 495, students are required to complete either an independent research project or a project with a community partner. As a result of this requirement, students often select Las Vegas agencies that serve clientele who are affected by SDOH, and SDOH might feature prominently in any final project.

The following table identifies the core sequence of first-year, second-year, milestone, and capstone classes for the Bachelor of Science in Public Health as mapped to the frame Information Creation as a Process, SDOH, and CEPH foundational domains. As a liaison librarian, I have worked with each of the following courses in varying capacities: HSC 100, PBH 205, and PBH 330. I have developed the curriculum map below to use as a tool to pitch library instruction sessions modeled on the frame Information Creation as a Process to public health instructors; the courses included in this map do not represent all of the opportunities to introduce Public Health Education Standards in the curriculum. Table 7.1 includes other suggestions for mapping the SDOH to the frame Information Creation as a Process. In this chapter, the suggested lessons are for the second-year seminar course, PBH 205.

Henrietta Lacks

The story of Henrietta Lacks raises questions about Information Creation as a Process. Hers is the remarkable account of an African-American woman with a sixth-grade education unknowingly providing cells to science, making Henrietta and her cells immortal.[19] Her cells were described as immortal because they could be grown in laboratories and used in medical research practically in perpetuity.[20] Henrietta was treated at the renowned John Hopkins Hospital in the 1950s, at the time one of the only hospitals in Baltimore that would treat black patients.[21] Henrietta's race and socioeconomic status constrained her options to access health care, one of the key SDOH. At Johns Hopkins, she received treatment, but doctors initially misdiagnosed Henri-

Moving Public Health Learners to the Skeptical Edge 99

Table 7.1. UNLV Bachelor of Science in Public Health Program

UNLV Course	ACRL Frame Information Creation as a Process	Knowledge Practice	Disposition	SDOH	CEPH Bachelor's Degree Foundational Domains
First-Year Seminar HSC 100 Inquiry and Issues in the Health Sciences	Introduced	Recognize that information may be perceived differently based on the format in which it is packaged.	Accept that the creation of information may begin initially through communicating in a range of formats or modes.	Not introduced	General education course for health sciences. No specific public health content is covered.
Second-Year Seminar PBH 205 Introduction to Public Health	Introduced and connected to SDOH	Articulate the capabilities and constraints of the information developed thorough various creation processes. (Introduced)	Are inclined to seek out characteristics of information products that indicate the underlying creation process.	Introduced	The socioeconomic, behavioral, biological, environmental and other factors that impact human health and contribute to health disparities (Introduced)
		Develop their own creation processes, along with an understanding that their choices impact the purposes for which the information product will be used and the message it conveys. (Introduced)			Basic concepts of legal, ethical, economic and regulatory dimensions of health care and public policy and the roles, influences, and responsibilities of the different agencies and branches of government (Introduced)

Table 7.1. UNLV Bachelor of Science in Public Health Program

UNLV Course	ACRL Frame Information Creation as a Process	Knowledge Practice	Disposition	SDOH	CEPH Bachelor's Degree Foundational Domains
Milestone Course PBH 330 Global Health	Reinforced	Monitor the value that is placed upon different types of information products in varying contexts. (Introduced) Articulate the capabilities and constraints of the information developed thorough various creation processes. (Reinforced)	Are inclined to seek out characteristics of information products that indicate the underlying creation process.	Reinforced	The socioeconomic, behavioral, biological, environmental and other factors that impact human health and contribute to health disparities (Reinforced) Basic concepts of legal, ethical, economic and regulatory dimensions of health care and public policy and the roles, influences, and responsibilities of the different agencies and branches of government (Reinforced)

Table 7.1. UNLV Bachelor of Science in Public Health Program

UNLV Course	ACRL Frame Information Creation as a Process	Knowledge Practice	Disposition	SDOH	CEPH Bachelor's Degree Foundational Domains
Capstone Course PBH 495 Public Health	Enhanced	Develop their own creation processes, along with an understanding that their choices impact the purposes for which the information product will be used and the message it conveys. (Reinforced) Articulate the capabilities and constraints of the information developed thorough various creation processes. (Enhanced)	At this stage, students are creating their own capstone information product in the form of a research paper or report about their community partnership. Here, students should have acquired culminating skills.	Enhanced	The socioeconomic, behavioral, biological, environmental and other factors that impact human health and contribute to health disparities (Enhanced) Basic concepts of legal, ethical, economic and regulatory dimensions of health care and public policy and the roles, influences, and responsibilities of the different agencies and branches of government (Enhanced)

etta's cancer, and she died within six months. In the process, physicians acquired a sample of her tissue during the diagnostic process and more tissue during a cancer surgery. The tissue taken during Mrs. Lacks's surgery was done so without her consent. After her death, it appears that physicians deceived her husband into allowing an autopsy to take even more tissue samples from her body. Doctors at Johns Hopkins were experimenting with growing cancer cells in a laboratory environment, and they needed cells. Henrietta's cells were taken, cultured, and shipped to researchers around the United States and the world. Within less than a year of her death, a tissue culture enterprise had been established to sell Henrietta's cells to researchers for a profit.[22] The cells are still sold today for hundreds of dollars per vial.[23]

Henrietta's case embodies a common outcome that can result from SDOH, such as socioeconomic status or access to care—that because certain populations lack control over their options for the care, they may be coerced or unknowingly used as human subjects. Subjects might have little understanding of scientific research and are thus vulnerable targets for plunder and exploitation. For example, Henrietta's family was contacted in the early 1970s for blood tests, and in the 1980s parts of Henrietta's medical records were published without knowledge or consent from her family.[24]

The frame Information Creation as a Process encourages students who study this case to question the circumstances that allowed doctors to take tissue samples from an unsuspecting patient and cultivate them, even if they were helpful to science. Students are encouraged to question the information creation process for the source of this medical data. As with many human subjects, Henrietta's identity was unknown to researchers using the cells; the cell line developed from her tissue was merely referred to as HeLa cells, based on the first two letters of her first and last name.[25]

Tuskegee experiment

Sexually transmitted infections (STIs) are a stubborn public health dilemma. Students with interest in sexual health promotion, epidemiology, or local public health departments will become familiar with reporting structures for STIs and the extensive efforts to treat these infectious diseases, which have a high cost socially and within the healthcare system. The problem of STIs and their high cost for communities has been longstanding, which leads to the case of the Tuskegee Experiment, also known as the Tuskegee Syphilis Study and the Tuskegee Study of Untreated Syphilis in the Negro Male. It is a foundational public health study supported by the United States National Public Health Services in the mid-twentieth century.[26] This experiment provides an entry point for public health undergraduates to scrutinize the multiple roles of public health officials and thereby develop skepticism and critical thinking about the sources of public health knowledge.

The Tuskegee Experiment began in Macon County, Alabama in 1932 and ended in 1972. The study involved approximately 600 male subjects, of whom two-thirds had syphilis while one-third were a control group who did not have syphilis.[27] None of the subjects enrolled in the experiment were informed that they were part of a study; instead, they received false prognoses and were denied therapeutic care for syphilis. The men did receive some routine medical care that included "free physical examinations, free rides to and from the clinics, hot meals on examination days, [and] free treatment for minor ailments..."[28] but were explicitly denied care for syphilis. All of the participants had social factors that influenced their health outcomes. Most participants in the Tuskegee Experiment were from farming communities in rural Alabama, many were uneducated, and all subjects were African-American. Their socioeconomic status varied, but most were poor. Over the course of forty years, the men had medical tests, and some were only told they had "bad blood."[29] In the initial stages of the study, there was no known treatment for syphilis; however, even after the discovery of penicillin as a treatment, it was withheld from the men for over twenty years of the study.[30] The experiment was to watch men die from the effects of syphilis.

The environment of rural Macon County, Alabama from the 1930s to 1970s might be difficult for one to grasp. Students and readers might wonder why the subjects did not seek treatment for their disease outside of the county. The truth is that some did try. However, subjects enrolled in the study were outed to healthcare practitioners in the region as being a part of the Tuskegee Experiment; even if treatment was sought, subjects were denied.[31] The complexity of the Tuskegee Experiment is a fertile ground in which to explore the frame Information Creation as a Process. A focus on this case in Introduction to Public Health is aimed at encouraging students to question the foundations of public health practice with STIs. Even though the Tuskegee Experiment ended in the 1970s, there are other examples of studies that followed the progression of disease in patients without treating them, such as the Guatemala Syphilis Study and the New Zealand study of women with cervical cancer.[32]

Library instruction

In PBH 205, the second-year seminar, students are required to write reflection papers related to weekly readings. They answer the following questions: *What was the main point of the reading? What information did you find surprising and why? After reading the chapters, do you see the world differently? How?*

Why? How do you personally feel about what you read? These questions give students a chance to reflect on SDOH and to explore personal growth.

Librarians can partner with faculty to reinforce this trajectory of learning and create integrated library instruction sessions focused on the Tuskegee Experiment and HeLa cells as types of information to encourage students to view SDOH and the information creation process critically. The learning outcomes include a change in student thinking about SDOH and information creation and the development of healthy skepticism toward public health information.

In a one-shot lesson, these outcomes might be difficult to assess, but the librarian could do so later in the semester, if given access to student reflection papers. Ideally, I will integrate multiple library instruction sessions rather than a one-shot lesson. Students are already reading and reflecting about Henrietta Lacks, so the suggestion to add additional lessons on the SDOH and Information Creation as a Process seems feasible, given my prior instruction in public health courses.

Lesson one. Students will create a visual map of the SDOH to show relationships between the healthcare environments at the time of each case and how the SDOH influenced the introduction of Henrietta Lacks and the Tuskegee men into a system where they were used to create information without their permission. Students will question how African-American bodies were used to benefit others, and explore SDOH including socioeconomic status, racial, and health equity. The HeLa and Tuskegee cases each provide a useful opportunity to raise questions about data collection, including from whom and for use by whom the data was collected. A visual map could show the lack of options to equitable and quality care. It could include a decision-making tree that visually represents how Henrietta Lacks's cells were cultured and later commoditized for use globally in laboratories. Harms experienced by the Tuskegee men as a result of non-therapeutic treatment or harms suffered by the Lacks family due to Henrietta's unknowing contribution to science could also be mapped. Regarding the information creation process, students could be guided to question the validity of the researcher's sampling methods in targeting people without full access to care.

Lesson two. Next, students can explore the ethics of each case and informed consent, as they struggle with how to articulate the unique constraints that led to the development and subsequent use of men in the Tuskegee Experiment and the collection of Henrietta's cells. The frame Information Creation as a Process and its knowledge practices could be used to encourage students to critically question study design, subject enrollment, and SDOH as factors that influenced the health outcomes of the Tuskegee Experiment subjects and the collection of Henrietta's cells.

Students could complete a pre-reading assignment about informed consent to learn about guidelines for the treatment of human subjects. One possible source would be the Belmont Report,[33] which establishes ethical treatment of human subjects as outlined in the National Research Service Award Act of 1974.[34] Students can explore ethics of current and emerging public health information creation processes and compare the cases of Henrietta Lacks or the Tuskegee Experiment with the aim of promoting students' development of a skeptical, critical approach to Information Creation as a Process.

Lesson three. Lastly, students can examine the role of health professionals more closely in the development of information. For the Tuskegee Experiment, students could watch the documentary *Deadly Deception* in order to practice developing informed skepticism and critical questioning about the frame Information Creation as a Process. Foundational questions might center on the role of the Public Health Service in designing the Tuskegee Experiment, the role of public health officials in Alabama in continuing the deception, and the role of government and institutions of higher education such as the Tuskegee Institute as creators of information. This line of questioning also aligns with the frame Authority is Constructed and Contextual, but in focusing on Information Creation as a Process, students can interrogate the very sources of public health information—in this case, black men and the data taken from them while tracking the progression of the disease. A similar lesson can be designed using the HeLa cells, highlighting the plunder of the body of a black woman as an information source that was used in scholarly outputs, cures, commerce, and other research.

Conclusion

Information Creation as a Process in the Henrietta Lacks case and the Tuskegee Experiment link to how SDOH affect health outcomes. In each of these cases, poverty, lack of other healthcare options, socioeconomic status, race, health inequity, and health disparity all flowed together to produce bias in how information was created. Because of the nature of health information, students often do not even think about the information creation process, how the information came to be, and the importance of data to a population. Students might identify with the poverty of the subjects in each case or the struggle to find quality health care as a consumer. As such, there is a potential to connect the SDOH with their experiences and the stories of Henrietta Lacks and the men of the Tuskegee Experiment to move students to question information creation critically.

In Las Vegas, students live in a healthcare environment that is replete with health inequities and inequality, so much so that in 2016, UNLV and the University of Nevada, Reno hosted a conference to address health inequality,[35] and the UNLV student body has some characteristics outlined in the

SDOH. As of this writing, UNLV is the second most diverse campus in the United States, and many are first-generation college students who come from resource-limited backgrounds.[36]

When exposed to SDOH and Information Creation as a Process, students can begin to experience those characteristics of threshold concepts and start the journey to think differently about how the SDOH affect populations. They can be transformed through their exploration of stories about information creation and the use of populations with characteristics described by SDOH. Additionally, these are also communities that future students will serve in their careers. The lessons I proposed in this chapter are designed to encourage students to question critically, to interrogate how information is created with a skeptical lens, and to examine the use of humans as sources in the information creation process. I anticipate that students will experience the SDOH as a threshold concept and have their worldview transformed with regards to public health.

Henrietta Lacks's case is not merely about cancer cells. Her case represents an example of the intersection between SDOH and information creation. The use of human subjects in the Tuskegee Experiment, too, is not just about syphilis; it is about the confluence of SDOH in the production of information. Learning the language of SDOH and connecting this to Information Creation as a Process will be transformational for students once grasped. Students can begin to understand a foundational concept in public health and have the language with which to grapple with the types of information used in their careers. Equipping students with knowledge about SDOH will help them question research data collection, ethics of research, and the problematic nature of using vulnerable populations to advance public health. These cases occurred in the mid-twentieth century, but in the twenty-first century, pressing realities of unequal access to care still affect the poor and communities of color in the United States. These issues remain far-reaching and relevant to students at UNLV and across the nation.

Notes

1. Centers for Disease Control, "Ten Great Public Health Achievements United States, 1900–1999," *MMWR Weekly* 48 no. 12 (1999): 241–243.
2. Office of Disease Prevention and Health Promotion, "Social Determinants of Health," *Healthypeople.gov*, accessed December 17, 2017, https://www.healthypeople.gov/2020/topics-objectives/topic/social-determinants-of-health; Richard Wilkinson and Michael Marmot, eds., *The Social Determinants of Health: The Solid Facts*, 2nd ed. (World Health Organization, 2003), 10–29, http://www.euro.who.int/__data/assets/pdf_file/0005/98438/e81384.pdf.
3. Association of College and Research Libraries (ACRL), *Framework for Information Literacy for Higher Education*, February 2, 2015, http://www.ala.org/acrl/standards/ilframework.

4. Anna R. Plourde and Evan M. Bloch, "A Literature Review of Zika Virus," *Emerging Infectious Diseases* 22, no. 7 (2016): 1185–1192, https://dx.doi.org/10.3201/eid2207.151990; Jennifer Zipprich, Kathleen Winter, Jill Hacker, Dongxiang Xia, James Watt, and Kathleen Harriman, "Measles Outbreak—California, December 2014–February 2015," Centers for Disease Control and Prevention *Morbidity and Mortality Weekly Report*, (2015) 64, no. 6: 153–154, https://www.cdc.gov/mmwr/preview/mmwrhtml/mm6406a5.htm.
5. Sandra Gonzalez, "19 Pedestrian Deaths This Year Already in Nevada; New Prevention Campaign to be Unveiled," *3 News, Las Vegas*, March 6, 2016, http://news3lv.com/news/local/19-pedestrian-deaths-this-year-already-in-nevada-new-prevention-campaign-to-be-unveiled; "Las Vegas Close to Hitting Record Number for Traffic Fatalities," *3 New, Las Vegas*, December 1, 2015, http://news3lv.com/news/local/las-vegas-close-to-hitting-record-number-for-traffic-fatalities; Cassandra Keenan, "New Bill Aims to Protect Pedestrians in School Zones," *Las Vegas Review Journal*, November 15, 2015, http://www.reviewjournal.com/view/new-bill-aims-protect-pedestrians-school-zones.
6. Courtney Coughneour, Jennifer R. Pharr, and Shawn Gerstenberger, "Community Health Indicators in Southern Nevada," *Nevada Journal of Public Health* (2014) 11, no. 1, http://digitalscholarship.unlv.edu/njph/vol11/iss1/8; Karen Spears, "What is a Food Desert?" *University of Nevada Cooperative Extension* (2014) https://www.unce.unr.edu/publications/files/hn/2014/fs1405.pdf.
7. Janie Boschma and Ronald Brownstein, "The Concentration of Poverty in American Schools," *The Atlantic*, February 29, 2016, https://www.theatlantic.com/education/archive/2016/02/concentration-poverty-american-schools/471414/; Christopher B. Swanson, "Cities in Crisis 2009: Closing the Graduation Gap Educational and Economic Conditions in American's Largest Cities," *Editorial Projects in Education Research Center*, http://www.americaspromise.org/sites/default/files/legacy/bodyfiles/Cities_In_Crisis_Report_2009.pdf.
8. Ray Land, Jan H. F. Meyer, and Caroline Baillie, "Editors' Preface," in *Threshold Concepts and Transformational Learning*, eds. Jan H. F. Meyer, Ray Land, and Caroline Baillie (Rotterdam: Sense Publishers, 2010), ix.
9. Peter Davies and Jean Mangan, "Embedding Threshold Concepts: From Theory to Pedagogical Principles to Learning Activities," in *Threshold Concepts within the Disciplines*, eds. Ray Land, Jan H.F. Meyer, and Jan Smith (Rotterdam: Sense, 2008).
10. The fact that students equate personal responsibility with public health demonstrates that they are novices in their knowledge about the SDOH and public health. Public health is about populations not exclusively about individuals in the population.
11. Ray Land, "Toil and Trouble: Threshold Concepts as a Pedagogy of Uncertainty," in *Threshold Concepts in Practice*, eds. Jan H.F. Meyer and Michael Flanagan (Rotterdam: Sense, 2016), 14–18.
12. "Public Health Hero: Adewale Troutman," *Research America!*, accessed March 11, 2017, http://www.researchamerica.org/advocacy-action/public-health-thank-you-day/public-health-heroes/public-health-hero-adewale-troutman.
13. Adewale Troutman, "Creating Health Equity; Social Justice, Human Rights, and the Social Determinants of Health" (presentation at the Oregon Community Issues Forum, Portland, Oregon, October 8, 2009), accessed March 11, 2017, https://www.slideshare.net/unitedwaypdx/social-determinants-health-by-dr-adewale-troutman.

14. Harvey V. Fineberg, "Public Health and Medicine Where the Twain Shall Meet," *American Journal of Preventative Medicine* 41, no. 4S3 (2011): S150.
15. Ibid, S149.
16. ACRL, *Framework*.
17. Council on Education for Public Health (CEPH), "Accreditation Criteria: Schools of Public Health & Public Health Programs," (Silver Spring, MD: Council on Education for Public Health, October 2016), 26, accessed December 19, 2016, http://ceph.org/assets/2016.Criteria.pdf.
18. Ibid, 27.
19. Howard W. Jones, "Record of the First Physician to See Henrietta Lacks at the Johns Hopkins Hospital: History of the Beginning of the HeLA Cell Line," *American Journal of Obstetrics and Gynecology* 176, no. 6 (1992): S227–S228.
20. Rebecca Skloot, *The Immortal Life of Henrietta Lacks* (New York: Random House, 2010), 175–176.
21. Ibid, 89–91.
22. Ibid, 93–97.
23. See product page at American Type Cell Culture Collection, accessed March 13, 2017, https://www.atcc.org/products/all/CCL-2.aspx.
24. Skloot, *Immortal Life*, 334–335.
25. Ibid, 103.
26. Michael V. Uschan, *Forty Years of Medical Racism: The Tuskegee Experiments* (Farmington Hills, MI: Thomson Gale, 2006). The initial study was funded by the Julius Rosenwald Foundation. There is a complicated backstory to the Tuskegee Experiment; see the account of Allan M. Brandt, among others.
27. Allan M. Brandt, "Racism and Research: The Case of the Tuskegee Syphilis Study," *Hastings Center Report* 8, no. 6 (1978): 21.
28. James H. Jones, *Bad Blood: The Tuskegee Syphilis Experiment* (New York: The Free Press, 1981), 4.
29. Ibid, 5.
30. Ibid, 7–9.
31. Brandt, "Racism and Research": 25.
32. Charlotte Paul and Barbara Brookes, "The Rationalization of Unethical Research: Revisionist Accounts of the Tuskegee Syphilis Study and the New Zealand Unfortunate Experiment," *American Journal of Public Health* 105, no. 10 (2015): E12–E19.
33. National Commission for the Protection of Human Subjects of Biomedical and Behavioral Research, "*The Belmont Report*," Department of Health, Education, and Welfare, April 18, 1979, http://www.hhs.gov/ohrp/regulations-and-policy/belmont-report/.
34. *National Research Service Award Act of 1974*, Public Law 93-348, *U. S. Code* 42 (1974), 342–353, https://history.nih.gov/research/downloads/PL93-348.pdf.
35. Nevada Public Health Association, "Health Equity Aiming for the Highest Level of Health for All Nevadans," Conference Program, Springs Preserve, Las Vegas, Nevada, September 22–23, 2016, https://npha.wildapricot.org/resources/Pictures/2016NPHA_AgendaProgramBookv12.pdf.
36. Keyonna Summers, "UNLV Ranked Second Most Diverse Campus in the Nation," September 9, 2015, https://www.unlv.edu/news/release/unlv-ranked-second-most-diverse-campus-nation.

CHAPTER 8*

Teaching Source Selection in Public Affairs Using Information Creation as a Process

Christina Sheley

Introduction

Public affairs as an academic discipline is interdisciplinary in nature—merging many fields within the social sciences, including political science, management, and administrative science—and broadly encompassing the investigation and implementation of public and government policy. Schools or programs of public affairs often have concentrations in public policy, public affairs, public administration, and public and non-profit management. Public affairs concentrations, in contrast to the larger "public affairs" umbrella of schools or programs, tend to focus on the engagement of stakeholders to communicate about public policy issues or policy creation. Within all of these, there is typically an emphasis on preparing students for public services work at the undergraduate and terminal master's degree levels. Examples of the types of public services positions that a public affairs graduate might hold are: non-profit community program director, policy research analyst, city planning associate, and for-profit management analyst.[1]

The Information Creation as a Process frame is represented in the Association of College and Research Libraries Framework for Information Lit-

---

* This work is licensed under a Creative Commons Attribution 4.0 License, CC BY (https://creativecommons.org/licenses/by/4.0/).

eracy for Higher Education (Framework) as: "Information in any format is produced to convey a message and is shared via a selected delivery method. The iterative processes of researching, creating, revising, and disseminating information vary, and the resulting product reflects these differences."[2] Other important elements are the ability to articulate different informational attributes based on creation processes, assessing the fit between information product and research need, and understanding that information is valued differently depending on context.[3]

This chapter describes how the author has applied the Information Creation as a Process frame when teaching source selection in a public affairs course. This specific application stems from the author's broader understanding of threshold concepts and the Information Creation as a Process frame, evidence found in the literature, and context obtained from a project with public affairs faculty to define information literacy outcomes for this discipline.

Information Creation as a Process and public affairs

A threshold concept is fundamental disciplinary knowledge that upon understanding can act as a portal to new and previously inaccessible ways of thinking.[4] Often, students' mastery of threshold concepts allows for other disciplinary content to make sense. According to Meyer and Land, threshold concepts have five key characteristics in that they transform a learner's perspective and perhaps change the way a discipline is viewed, are irreversible or unforgettable, enable learners to integrate what was previously unseen, are bounded by the discipline and may help define disciplinary edges, and are likely to not be intuitive and involve forms of troublesome knowledge.[5]

The Framework as a whole is informed by the general idea of threshold concepts and draws upon previous work that identified threshold concepts in information literacy to develop the concepts at the core of each frame.[6] The Information Creation as a Process frame includes the following elements: understanding of the different information creation processes and their resulting products, formats, and delivery mechanisms; assessment of an information product's creation process and information need to determine how to use a product; understanding of evolving information creation processes to determine information quality; and recognition that information products are valued differently depending on context.[7]

In their book, *Teaching Information Literacy Threshold Concepts: Lesson Plans for Librarians*, Patricia Bravender, Hazel Anne McClure, and Gayle

Schaub, provide a more accessible explanation of the Information Creation as a Process threshold concept:

> With the advent of digital publishing, there are still a multitude of processes that underlie the creation of information objects. What is different is that the digital manifestations sometimes do not cue the user to the fact that they are, indeed, different types of information. In order to appreciate the timeliness, accuracy, complexity, and other attributes of information, people need to understand the purpose and processes behind its creation.[8]

This book also includes a curated set of lesson plans for each threshold concept represented in the Framework. In the introduction to the "Using Sources to Support a Claim" lesson in the Information Creation as a Process chapter, Dani Brecher relays the impact of the Information Creation as Process threshold concept on students' research abilities and processes when she states, "Understanding how and why information is created and how it is disseminated enables students to identify the best places to locate information and evaluate its value for their research."[9]

Intersection with public affairs. A review of the literature yields no theoretical or practical examination of the intersection between public affairs and the Information Creation as Process frame as represented in the Framework. This is not surprising, given its newness. The author also did not find any relevant works that addressed threshold concepts in general for public affairs.

Since academic librarians' work with threshold concepts largely intersects with information literacy instruction, the author looked at articles on this topic for public affairs to see if elements of the Information Creation as a Process frame were being discussed prior to or outside its formalized reference in the Framework. One such example is Rita Ormsby and Daniel W. Williams' article that applies information literacy criteria to a graduate "Ethics and Public Decision Making" course to analyze whether it meets existing accreditation standards. In the course of this analysis, the authors describe teaching students how to find books, peer and non-peer-reviewed articles, reports, and a variety of other information sources needed to complete a semester-long, ethical dilemma research project, and the struggle students encountered "when researching an interdisciplinary topic for the first time with information from numerous stakeholders in varied formats" to evaluate and select sources.[10] The article authors propose time could be spent giving "guidance about the preferred standards of books or articles, timelines, and guidelines" to address this struggle with variety and selection.[11] This reference to teaching preferred standards is interpreted by this author to mean the teaching of some aspects of information creation—why sources are produced, intended audience, and length of the production process—to clarify differences and support decision-making.

Michelle Pautz and Heidi Gauder's article analyzes the success of teaching information literacy concepts, using a variety of instructional interventions, to address deficiencies in source use in an undergraduate environmental policy course.[12] A portion of one of their information literacy instruction sessions was dedicated to having students examine how different information sources could be used to address a specific audience and purpose when arguing a position.[13] Information Creation as a Process was not explicitly identified, but this author believes that some aspects of information creation, such as who produced the source, for what audience and purpose was it produced, and what types of information are contained within the source, would need to be conveyed during this session in order for students to express thoughts about the intersection of information source and information need.

These articles provide some evidence of the intersection between the Information Creation as a Process frame and public affairs and indicate the discipline-specific information landscape and information literacy troubles that teaching creation processes can address. Students in public affairs often need to use an array of information sources—scholarly and practitioner literature, government and organizational documents, legal cases and regulations, and community data, to name a few—in the course of researching vast, interdisciplinary topics like healthcare, poverty, trade, climate change, and inequality. This variety is troublesome as students have a hard time distinguishing between different types of sources and, more important, the different information and perspectives represented within each. Further complications arise since most sources are delivered electronically; this obscures the source attributes that students use to distinguish between sources and make judgments about the value the information brings to course assignments.

Context from public affairs faculty. In addition to literature, a recent project with public affairs faculty provided discipline-specific context for the Information Creation as a Process frame and elevated the author's understanding of how it intersects with public affairs.

The School of Public and Environmental Affairs (SPEA) at Indiana University-Bloomington is nationally ranked and brings together the study of public affairs, environmental science, and policy, with a focus on governing and management aspects.[14] Undergraduate students investigate complex issues and critical problems in the School's Bachelor of Science in Public Affairs' degree program through majors in environmental management, human resources management, law and public policy, management, policy analysis, public financial management, nonprofit management and leadership, and public management and leadership.

In spring 2015, a faculty team from SPEA and the author applied for and received an Indiana University-Bloomington Libraries' Information Fluency Curriculum Grant. This two-year award supports the incorporation of information literacy learning outcomes, sequenced activities, and assessments into the School's non-profit management and human resources management majors so students can develop the skills and abilities needed to use and create information within a disciplinary context.[15] The non-profit management and human resources management majors will be a pilot for integration into other areas of the School.

In the initial stage of this project, discipline-specific information literacy learning outcomes were generated; these will be used in the second phase of the project to guide the integration of information literacy concepts into various parts of the curriculum. The Association for College and Research Libraries Information Literacy Competency Standards for Higher Education (these were still in use during this phase of the project) as well as the Framework were presented as general guiding documents for the development of these outcomes. A conversation about these documents occurred since they were foreign to the faculty involved, and an attempt was made to discuss individual standards and frames. However, this discussion was quickly abandoned because the faculty found it difficult to communicate about each in the absence of some disciplinary context or language. Instead, the following question guided the dialogue surrounding the generation of the information literacy learning outcomes: "What skills and/or abilities does an information literate graduate of the non-profit management program or human resources management program need to possess?"

As public affairs faculty answered this question, they indicated that information-literate public affairs graduates would need to be adept at working with information sources in the following ways: identify different types of discipline-specific information sources and recognize the type of information therein; identify different types of information important to a public affairs or sub-discipline's profession; determine the types of information needed to solve a problem; and build an argument informed by an exploration of relevant sources. The author believes that each of these skills and abilities requires an understanding of the Information Creation as a Process frame or an understanding of how information is created and disseminated. For example, knowledge of why information is created and for what purpose could assist students in strategically determining what types of information are needed to address a problem, instead of randomly conducting searches and haphazardly choosing sources.

This recognition by the author elevated the Information Creation as a Process frame in the project conversations with faculty, resulting in the following information literacy learning outcome: *Understand how information in various formats is created and distributed in order to analyze its relevance, credibility, and potential use for a specific purpose.* This outcome encapsulates many elements of the Information Creation as a Process frame, including understanding evolving information creation processes to determine information quality and comparing an information product's creation process to an information need in order to help decide how to use a product. In addition, the final phrase of the generated information literacy outcome—"potential use for a specific purpose"—indicates public affairs students should consider both content and context when selecting information sources for use.

Faculty also designated this outcome to be "foundational knowledge." They felt it should be addressed before or with other outcomes related to question development, search strategy, source evaluation, source use, and attribution, since its mastery could contribute to learning in these areas. This line of thinking is consistent with threshold concepts in general; students who grasp how and why information is created and disseminated could elevate their thinking about other information literacy concepts. For example, recognition of how and why scholarly journal literature is created and disseminated could spur students to think about which retrieval tools would be most appropriate to access this source type.

Because of this project's information literacy outcome and its designation as foundational knowledge for SPEA's public affairs students, I have begun using the concept of information creation processes to frame information literacy instruction related to information sources, information retrieval tools, and source selection. Using Information Creation as a Process is particularly well-suited when teaching source selection in public affairs because, as previously indicated, students in this discipline need to find and use a variety of information sources for course assignments, and they struggle with distinguishing between different types of sources and the information and perspective that result from these differences. Prior to this change in focus, the author's information literacy instruction focused on discipline-specific information retrieval tools and source evaluation. An example of how the author teaches source selection in a human resources management survey course using Information Creation as a Process follows.

Teaching source selection in public affairs

SPEA's human resources management major is designed to provide students with the professional development necessary to begin a successful career as a human resources practitioner in the public or non-profit sector. The program focuses on the general body of knowledge related to human resources management and expands students' conceptual foundation by developing understanding of the strategic link between organizational success and human resources management practices.[16] Key components of this curriculum include compensation strategy, selection and recruitment practices, diversity, application of employment law, ethics, managing change, and fundamentals of financial management.

The Human Resources Management in the Public Sector (V373) course provides students with foundational knowledge of the critical issues, concepts, and functions of human resources, as well as methods and perspectives of managers and human resources practitioners.[17] Business practice and regulatory factors that influence and direct the personnel actions of employers are also highlighted. V373 is a required course for all SPEA human resources management majors; typical enrollment is 210 students—principally sophomore and junior status—per semester.

V373's research-based assignment is a small group position paper that requires students to explore the background and various viewpoints surrounding a select list of human resources management issues. These issues are then turned into research questions, such as:

- Is affirmative action necessary?
- Do living wage ordinances work?
- Is the Family Medical Leave Act crippling employers?
- Was the American with Disabilities Amendments Act necessary?

Because of the interdisciplinary nature of the issues, research questions, and viewpoints, and the need to provide detailed feedback, the assignment is segmented into three stages. Students first conduct background research in order to produce a one-page summary of the human resources issue itself. Cohorts then identify and examine the conflicting viewpoints associated with their research question, producing a one-page outline of each viewpoint that is well supported with credible evidence. Finally, students take a position that responds to the research question and write a three-page analysis, using findings from the first two stages and additional evidence if needed.

Library instruction to support this assignment is delivered via a LibGuide and an in-class instruction session. The LibGuide reinforces basics about the varying source types—scholarly journal articles, practitioner articles, news articles, government documents and websites, legal documents, and general and organizational websites—that contain information about human resources management issues, and the disciplinary perspectives—political, social, economic, and legal—that may potentially impact the representation of viewpoints and positions. In addition, there are database and resource recommendations for gaining access to each source type. Students consult the LibGuide prior to the in-class instruction session and use it to find and read one information source that addresses the background and/or history of their assigned human resources management issue and one information source that addresses a viewpoint related to the research question. These sources are brought with the student to the in-class instruction session and are used during the discussion and exercises.

The teaching of source selection can encompass many things. The learning objective for this in-class instruction session is to introduce information creation processes within the context of human resources information and the final assignment in order to enhance student's ability to select sources for use in all aspects of the position paper. This is accomplished by introducing students to source types—articles, websites, government documents, organizational documents, and policy papers—and source characteristics—who produced the source, for what audience and purpose was it produced, and what types of information are contained within the source. In addition, students complete an exercise in which they spend time considering what value the sources they found prior to the in-class session will have in different contexts.

The in-class instruction session begins with a short lecture to orient students to the importance of understanding information creation processes and its potential impact on the outcome of the students' position paper. Students then explore this concept in small groups by engaging with the information sources they found prior to class to answer the following questions:

- Who produced this source?
- How long might it have taken to research and write this source?
- For what purpose was the source written and published?
- Where was the source published?
- Who is the audience for the source and publication?

Once students have identified characteristics for each source, the author asks them to compare and contrast source attributes and creation processes across all of the sources being examined by the group.

At the conclusion of this exercise, the students come back together as a class to discuss observations. At this time, the author often uses a concept-mapping tool to notate sources and creation processes to help students visualize nuance and relationships. For example, one arm of the map might be for government information and include such items as reports, data, news, blogs, work of the government (i.e., bills, Congressional hearings, etc.), laws, and department/organization/agency websites. Another arm might represent legal information and include primary sources, statutes or ordinances, cases, administrative materials, and secondary sources (i.e., law review articles, news, blogs, and commentary). The author can then point out the relationship between a legal document and a news or blog article that references a particular law.

A short lecture about information retrieval tools and access follows. The author transitions into this by explaining that since information has different creation processes, it is packaged and disseminated differently, which has an impact on where it can be accessed. For example, a scholarly journal article's creation processes dictate access to its full-text will principally be through subscription, library databases. The author then spends time explaining the list of information retrieval tools listed on a LibGuide and delineating which information source types are available in each tool.

The instruction session concludes with students examining the previously found information sources to assess how their assigned human resources issue is represented in each, or its perspective, and the types of information included (e.g., data and analysis in a scholarly journal article, personal accounts, and expert testimony in a news article) to construct this message. This portion of the session is guided by a worksheet. The author recommends the students draw upon their new understanding of each source's creation process to guide this examination. She also asks students to consider whether they would select each source for use in a specific context. For example, would students select their source(s) to include in the position paper if

- it was being presented to professionals at a Society of Human Resources Management meeting?
- it was being read by a group of faculty and graduate students? or
- it was being presented to a colleague who needed to make recommendations to the city mayor?

No formalized assessment has been conducted on the in-class instruction, the LibGuide, or the resulting position papers because this human resources management course is part of the larger assessment still being developed for the aforementioned information literacy curricular integration project. An informal examination of a sample of the position paper bibliographies, conducted by the faculty member who teaches this human resources management course and the author, indicated a higher variety of source selection and usage. Anecdotally, the faculty member has relayed that he believes students overall are selecting and using a wider variety of sources for inclusion in the position paper.

Conclusion

This example of teaching source selection in public affairs through examination of information creation processes stems from the author's evolving understanding of the Information Creation as a Process frame and its intersection with the discipline. Students in public affairs often need to use an array of information sources in the course of researching vast, interdisciplinary topics; however, this variety is troublesome as students have a hard time distinguishing between different types of sources and the information and perspective that result from these differences. The author's work with public affairs faculty from the School of Public and Environmental Affairs at Indiana University-Bloomington—specifically the development of an information literacy learning outcome focused on information creation that was flagged as foundational to other outcomes—also contributed to the development of this application. However, the author believes there are many other potential uses for public affairs besides source selection since the Information Creation as a Process frame can address many of this discipline's specific information literacy troubles relating to evaluation and use and may even serve to address those related to information retrieval and citation. Therefore, more examination of how this frame can be applied to public affairs is warranted.

Notes

1. Indiana University-Bloomington School of Public and Environmental Affairs, "Explore Careers and Outcomes," *Indiana University-Bloomington*, accessed June 14, 2016, https://spea.indiana.edu/career-development/explore-careers/index.html.
2. Association of College and Research Libraries (ACRL), *Framework for Information Literacy for Higher Education*, February 2, 2015, http://www.ala.org/acrl/standards/ilframework.
3. Ibid.
4. Jan Meyer and Ray Land, *Threshold Concepts and Troublesome Knowledge: Linkages to Ways of Thinking and Practising with the Disciplines* (Edinburgh: ETL Project, Universities of Edinburgh, Coventry and Durham, 2003), 1, https://kennslumidstod.hi.is/wp-content/uploads/2016/04/meyerandland.pdf.
5. Ibid, 4–5.
6. ACRL, *Framework for Information Literacy for Higher Education*.
7. ACRL, *Framework for Information Literacy for Higher Education*.
8. Patricia Bravender, Hazel Anne McClure, and Gayle Schaub, *Teaching Information Literacy Threshold Concepts: Lesson Plans for Librarians* (Chicago: Association of College and Research Libraries, 2015), 87–88.
9. Dani Brecher, "Using Sources to Support a Claim," in *Teaching Information Literacy Threshold Concepts: Lesson Plans for Librarians*, eds. Patricia Bravender, Hazel Anne McClure, and Gayle Schaub (Chicago: Association of College and Research Libraries, 2015), 89.
10. Rita Ormsby and Daniel W. Williams, "Information Literacy in Public Affairs Curriculum," *Journal of Public Affairs Education* 16, no. 2 (2010): 294.
11. Ibid, 299.
12. Michelle Pautz and Heidi Gauder, "Undergraduate Research Needs: Faculty-Librarian Collaboration to Improve Information Literacy in Policy Papers," Conference Papers—Southern Political Science Association (2016): 1–27.
13. Ibid, 9–10.
14. Indiana University-Bloomington School of Public and Environmental Affairs, "About Us," *Indiana University-Bloomington*, accessed June 17, 2016, https://spea.indiana.edu/about/index.html.

15. Indiana University-Bloomington Libraries Teaching & Learning Department, "Curriculum Grants," *Indiana University-Bloomington Libraries*, accessed June 8, 2016, https://libraries.indiana.edu/curriculum-grants.
16. Daniel Grundmann and Christina Sheley, "SPEA Information Literacy Curriculum Grant Application" (unpublished grant application, Indiana University-Bloomington, April 2015), 1–2.
17. Indiana University-Bloomington School of Public and Environmental Affairs, "Major in Human Resources Management," *Indiana University-Bloomington*, accessed September 13, 2016, https://spea.indiana.edu/undergraduate/degrees-majors/human-resource.html.

Information Has Value

Section Three

CHAPTER 9

Information Privilege in the Context of Community Engagement in Sociology

Heidi R. Johnson and Anna C. Smedley-López

Privilege can be broadly defined as advantages based on group belonging not extended to individuals outside of the group.[1] One type of privilege is information privilege, or unequal access to information due to paywalls, and this is a prevalent and persistent issue and injustice in our society, with paywalls blocking the general public from accessing potentially life-changing information. Ironically, a large percentage of that information is funded with taxpayers' dollars and is intended to benefit the public.[2]

The divide exists not only along socioeconomic lines but also between the scholarly community and the general public, as restrictions on access to important, impactful scholarly research persist. This divide is also evident between scholars in Western countries at institutions that can afford the costs of multiple, expensive journals and scholars at institutions in developing countries that have significantly smaller collections budgets.

The open-access movement has challenged the traditional publishing model, yet the traditional publishing model has proved to be resilient. The pushback from traditional publishing companies trying to turn a profit, the continual pressure on libraries to pay staggering prices for top-ranked journal titles, and the pressure for researchers to publish their research in those top-ranked journals, lacking the incentives and funds to pay the fees to publish open-access, all impede the movement and contribute to this digital divide and to information under-privilege.

The frame Information Has Value provides an approach to exploring the important concept of information privilege. The best way to understand information privilege and the frame Information Has Value is through firsthand experience and reflection, and students in SOC 205 Ethnic Groups in Contemporary Society (Ethnic Groups), a Sociology course with a heavy critical service learning component, have had opportunities to do just that.

Over the course of a semester, the authors, a librarian and sociology professor, developed working language around information privilege that framed privilege as access to potentially life-changing information not available to the general public. In the context of this course, students were tasked with providing various community partners—third parties unaffiliated with the university—with scholarly resources. However, they were only able to provide community partners the full text of open-access resources, not subscription-based resources that are subject to license agreements with vendors. This was severely restricting in terms of the types of information that could be made available to community members, who depend upon such information to secure their safety and well-being. Students thus had the opportunity to reflect on this experience and realize that, as students affiliated with a university, they have a form of privilege that the majority of people in this world do not: access to information that is behind paywalls.

Community partners: Information under-privilege in context

For this course, students work with community partners and provide them with annotated bibliographies listing both open-access resources and subscription-based resources. In order to determine policies around sharing library resources, the social sciences librarian first looked into electronic resources usage policies for non-authorized users. She found that UNLV University Libraries currently does not have a policy in place for electronic resources usage.[3] The de facto practice at UNLV University Libraries is for use of subscription electronic resources by authorized users only. Authorized users are not allowed to access and collect electronic resources for the purpose of handing them over to individuals unaffiliated with the university. This practice ensures that license agreements are followed.[4] Many license agreements, but not all, explicitly prohibit sharing of electronic resources with third parties unaffiliated with the university. There might be some room for interpretation in some license agreements that allow sharing with third parties for educational purposes. However, these exceptions apply only to sharing for situations in which community members would provide feedback to instructors about the quality of student work. The community partners actually needed these resources for personal purposes, so sharing with them was not an option, even according to these exceptions.

UNLV University Libraries does have public-use computers that allow access to subscription-based electronic resources. However, for many of the community members, UNLV University Libraries can be difficult to access due to issues such as limited access to transportation, the need to find child care, and language barriers. On the other hand, while public libraries can be physically accessed more easily by the general population, many community members may not be aware of Interlibrary Loan services through which they would be able to obtain scholarly research materials. Furthermore, accessing scholarly materials may be difficult because of language barriers or lack of library research skills.

Information professionals have addressed this issue of information privilege. In her blog, *Info-mational: On Technology, Media Literacy, and Librarians Who T-C-B*, Char Booth reflects on information privilege and what she calls information *under*privilege. She advocates for countering or circumventing information *under*privilege, writing the following:

> ...librarians and other information professionals are best equipped to shift the dynamic towards a freer flow of knowledge unattached to markers of access privilege.... Our responses take institutional as well as individual forms—consider Radical Reference, Creative Commons, the Open Access movement, and countless acts of community support and defiance that attempt to liberate constraints to informed inquiry in spite of the potential consequences.[5]

So there are many ways of countering information under-privilege, including the open-access movement, and some of those ways involve the individual while others involve institutions.

While there are many strategies countering information under-privilege, including activist strategies, we chose to transparently follow standard practices while offering a written critique of their many limitations. We could have chosen the route of defiance instead of choosing to follow the standard practice at UNLV University Libraries. We even discussed this, including potential consequences of choosing the route of defiance. Ultimately, we decided the students would be required to follow the standard practice. It was more important to be honest and transparent with everything related to the students' projects in this case because the projects would be very public, with student presentations in a public forum required as a part of the coursework, and with immigrants representing themselves in asylum cases in a public setting, presenting the students' research to judges. We did not want to break the law or violate terms of license agreements, risking penalties or other repercussions. The potential consequences could impede the great work that students were doing, and the Ethnic Groups professor did not want to jeopardize the entire project. Considering the context in which we would be providing electronic resources to community members, there was certainly a high likelihood that such an act of defiance would be discovered. Thus, we felt it was important to abide by standard practices.

Another reason for abiding by standard practices was our desire to partner and cooperate with administration on advocating for change in institutional practices and policy. Our alternative act of defiance has been to write about this injustice, here and elsewhere, as well as to advocate for changes in policy through discussions with the administration at UNLV University Libraries, who can engage in further conversations in the library community. As the result of our efforts, UNLV University Libraries has begun work on a policy regarding the sharing of resources. While acts of defiance are important on the ground and do mitigate the injustice of information under-privilege, injustices will persist unless there are changes in policy and practice at the institutional level. While we didn't necessarily involve students in these conversations, our plan is to involve them in these conversations more going forward.

In this context in which information under-privilege exists, the frame Information Has Value is especially pertinent. There are many dimensions of value that are evident in this frame. Information is a means of education and influence, and a means of negotiating and understanding the world for both students and community members. Looking specifically at "legal and socioeconomic interests," it is apparent that publisher/vendor interests play a major role in preventing community members from being able to access needed information resources. Students are prompted to think about these legal and socioeconomic interests. Through this experience, students come to understand information as a commodity in our world and come to reflect on what this means in terms of practical and ethical implications.

The context: Ethnic Groups and service learning in Sociology

The course, Ethnic Groups in Contemporary Society, is a community-based exploration of the experiences and social context of varying racial and ethnic groups in contemporary US society. The sociological analysis of race and ethnicity is especially important because it recognizes the profound role that both history and larger social forces, such as social institutions and social policy, play in shaping the lived experiences of different racial and ethnic groups. A community-based approach privileges the voices of the community members and situates them as the knowers and tellers of their own experiences.

In this course, we focus on learning to think about race and ethnicity sociologically while engaging directly with the different populations that we learn about. We do this in three ways. First, we engage in key sociological texts that discuss race and ethnicity from the sociological perspective. Second, we explore both academic and popular content by scholars of color and immigrant scholars. Third, we engage in a community-based research project driven by different local organizations that focus on race/ethnicity-based issues. Over the course of the semester, we rely heavily on several key theoretical frameworks and methodologies. These theoretical and methodological tools include: critical theory, feminist standpoint theory,[6] intersectionality,[7] and Community-Based Participatory Research (CBPR).

The Ethnic Groups course is part of Service Learning Initiative for Community Engagement in Sociology (SLICES), a larger service learning program that focuses on connecting classroom learning to the social environment, increasing critical thinking and research skills, fostering a commitment to lifelong community engagement, and fostering a social change model of leadership. SLICES relies on three key assumptions: that education can and should be intimately tied to social justice and the work of social change, that *all* students can make important contributions to the learning space and to learning activities, and that the engaged student is a successful student. While there is no consensus on the precise definition of service learning, generally service learning refers to civic engagement that is directly aligned with course learning objectives and has a reflection component.[8] In SLICES courses, we use a model of critical service learning that focuses our service on social justice issues, with an "aim to dismantle structures of injustice."[9]

The service-learning students worked with four different community partners over the course of the semester to complete community-based participatory research (CBPR) projects. Community-based participatory research projects are research projects that explicitly incorporate the community in identifying, designing, implementing, and disseminating research.[10] Two of our four projects were particularly impacted by information privilege. The Immigrant Justice Initiative (IJI) is a Las Vegas-based non-profit that focuses on providing legal representation and education for immigrants as they navigate the local immigrant court system. To better meet the needs of immigrants from El Salvador, Honduras, and Guatemala, IJI developed a series of workshops designed to teach asylum seekers about the local immigration court system and empower them to self-represent. Effective self-representation may be an important tool to asylum seekers in Las Vegas because only 3 percent of asylum cases represented by an attorney are won locally in comparison the national average of 48 percent.[11] The Ethnic Groups student research groups spend the semester researching and collecting evidence on country conditions from both empirical sources and popular sources that IJI clients can use when self-representing.

Mah'ha ga doo, or Gold Butte, Nevada, currently Bureau of Land Management property, is a sacred site to the Paiute Indian Tribe and home to the endangered Desert Tortoise. #SaveProtectButte is a collective initiative among local indigenous tribes, environmentalists, politicians, and other stakeholders that aims to have Gold Butte designated as a national monument to ensure cultural and environmental protection. The Gold Butte student research group gathered evidence in support of this site, such as peer-reviewed research and models from similar initiatives that had been successful in designating sacred sites or lands as national monuments.

The challenges associated with teaching the frame Information Has Value

To teach information privilege, the social sciences librarian introduced the concept in a ten-minute introductory presentation about the role of the library in the course. The social sciences librarian explained that students would not simply be able to hand over subscription-based electronic resources to community members, and asked students to reflect on this. Students then had the opportunity to experience their information privilege firsthand, as they had to distinguish between open-access resources and subscription-based resources as a part of their assignments, with the understanding that only the open-access resources could be provided to the community partners.

In addition to the knowledge practice "Learners who are developing their information literate abilities… recognize issues of access or lack of access to information sources," other knowledge practices that apply directly to this situation are "Learners who are developing their information literate abilities… understand how and why some individuals or groups of individuals may be underrepresented or systematically marginalized within the systems that produce and disseminate information" and "Learners who are developing their information literate abilities… inclined to examine their own information privilege."[12] When the students were forced to select only open-access resources for their projects, they were able to recall this idea of information privilege and realize the injustice of it—because this lack of access for community members impacts the health and well-being of these community members and the potential protection or lack of protection of sacred cultural sites. What could be more unjust than to deprive human beings of information that could secure their freedom, health, and well-being? Students had the opportunity to contemplate these injustices and realize how the traditional publishing system marginalizes the underrepresented groups with which they were working.

The best way to teach students about information privilege is to facilitate experiences in which information under-privilege is manifest—experiences in which students are inclined to examine their own information privilege. Ethnic Groups provided exactly that kind of scenario for the students. While the project was not designed with the sole intent of teaching information privilege, that has been an outgrowth of the course.

The course assignments: Meeting both the students' and the community partners' needs

Library research literacy, critical reading skills training, and library resources were integral for the service learning assignment, the final presentation to our campus community, and the report to our community partners. The integration began with intensive library research literacy training with the social sciences librarian. The students participated in training, which included an introduction to key databases, such as Google Scholar and newspaper databases, and critical reading training, during which students did close reading of a dense theoretical text and discussed and reflected upon it. The peer facilitators, past students of Ethnic Groups who returned to be group leaders for their peers in the current iteration of the course, participated in an advanced training on more targeted searching to find relevant sources in specialized databases.

Students then completed a class assignment that was designed to help them build effective literature review skills. We employed both a scaffolding strategy and a rewrite and resubmit strategy to facilitate deep learning. Each student conducted a mini literature review and found at least four peer-reviewed articles directly related to their research topic. The students then wrote individual annotated bibliographies from their selection of articles that were submitted to Professor Smedley-López for review. Extensive feedback on relevance to the topic and writing was given along with a preliminary grade, and then students were given the opportunity to rewrite and resubmit. After all revisions were made, revised annotated bibliographies were submitted to their peer facilitator to be included in the final report. A master annotated bibliography was then created and submitted as part of the final report to the community partner.

The individual annotated bibliographies were assessed in a similar way. A rubric was used that measured how well the students could identify the author's main argument and how useful the article was to the group's larger project. The final report narrative was assessed for how well it established the relevance of the group's research using supporting previous research.

Next, building off the annotated bibliography, the groups created an opening narrative on each topic that served as the introduction to the topic and relevance of the project. The narrative was used as the opening piece in the final report. The groups then used their collective literature review and incorporated an introduction into their poster presentation at the end of the semester service learning forum. In addition to the literature review activities, students completed and were given extensive feedback on weekly course reading summaries to facilitate the development of critical reading skills.

The IJI research group and the Gold Butte research group relied heavily on library resources for the bulk of their evidence, using both the UNLV University Libraries and the Wiener-Rogers Law Library. Actual library instruction in a computer classroom included one session on the library website and basic research literacy skills needed to find sources for their projects and one session on critical reading. The students were assigned many dense theoretical texts throughout the course, mostly by authors from the ethnic groups about which they were writing. For the critical reading instruction session, students went through a guided exercise, reading the beginning portion of, and answering comprehension and reflection questions about the 1995 article "Is the United States Postcolonial?: Transnationalism, Immigration, and Race" by Jenny Sharpe.[13] The learning outcomes of this assignment were for students to learn to slow down their reading and hear the author in their own voice and to practice making connections to prior knowledge. Students were also asked to reflect on the relevance of the twenty-one-year-old article today and reflect on its relevance to their experience in studying a particular ethnic group. For the course assignments, students were required to write reading summaries of some of their assigned texts, so this deep reading exercise prepared students for those assignments.

Effective critical reading skills and use of library resources were assessed throughout the semester. Following the critical reading workshop, the students' weekly reading summaries were assessed using a rubric designed to measure how well individual students could identify the author's main argument/s, offer critiques or criticisms of the readings, and discuss how readings contributed to a larger conversation about a given topic.

The social sciences librarian also arranged with a law librarian to provide the Gold Butte and IJI groups with instruction on finding legal resources. Thus, the project involved collaborations among librarians with different areas of expertise. The law library instruction provided students with the skills to find case law and research articles from law journals. The Gold Butte group needed to provide both peer-reviewed and popular sources as evidence focused on three areas: the importance of preserving indigenous sacred sites, legal precedents for preserving sacred sites, and a model of success.

The IJI research group needed to provide peer-reviewed and popular sources that could be used as evidence of country conditions for the three Latin American countries they were researching. Specifically, they were looking for evidence of gang violence, violence against women, violence against religious groups, violence against particular political affiliations, violence against children, or any other violence that would put an immigrant seeking refuge in the United States at risk of harm or death if they were not granted asylum. Helping to provide documented evidence of violence in country of origin to IJI's clients and workshop participants was important because the majority of the IJI's clients do not have proficient library research skills and are English language learners and need support collecting evidence in their new language.

Having access to library resources was important to both the students and the community partners for these two projects. The students' ability to effectively access and use library resources was key to meeting several of the course learning objectives. Library resources served as a means of education for the students, as through their library research all of the groups learned more about the population they were serving and the topic they were studying. Library resources also contributed to objectives for their community partners, as the annotated bibliographies were shared with and used by the community partners at the end of the course; for example, library resources were used as content for the IJI workshops.

Practical suggestions and future directions for teaching Information Has Value

There is no better way for students to learn about privilege and the frame Information Has Value other than through firsthand experience and reflection. Ever since Peggy McIntosh introduced the concept of white privilege in "White Privilege: Unpacking the Invisible Knapsack," scholars and students focused on studying cultural competence and racial justice have come to understand their own privilege through identifying practical experiences in which privilege is a predominating factor or determinant of that experience.[14] In order to understand privilege, students absolutely must reflect on their own experiences and interactions they experience with other people in order to understand those important concepts. The alternative is to understand them only abstractly, and not connect them with one's own experience, and this negates the pedagogical purpose of the concept, which is to bring systems of power and oppression to light in order to further the goals of social justice through making changes in one's behavior that reflect cultural competence and awareness. This poses a challenge to librarians who want to teach this frame but lack a context in which students experience their own information privilege or can observe information under-privilege. Few librarians have the opportunity to propose or develop courses in which critical service learning is a component, especially for the sole purpose of teaching Information Has Value.

Yet there are other ways and other contexts in which students can reflect upon their own information privilege. The concept of information privilege can be taught through helping students who are graduating to realize that they will not have the same access to subscription-based electronic resources that they have had as students.[15] Another alternative is to teach about information privilege is to focus on open sources of information rather than the experience of access restrictions. By focusing on open-access resources, students can grasp the fact that such resources are available to everyone, but this is not the case for subscription-based electronic resources that are available to them as students at an academic institution. Char Booth, for example, teaches about information privilege through Wikipedia assignments, demonstrating to students how they can leverage their privilege and treat it as a responsibility to share resources and expertise through "channeling" their work through an open resource.[16] She has been quoted as saying, "Teaching with Wikipedia helps students and faculty see that their access to resources and expertise carries with it a responsibility to the broader information ecology."[17] Thus, students do not simply have information privilege; they also have a responsibility to counter the injustices that it causes.

In the context of this course, we also determined some future directions to provide students with more of a knowledge base about the traditional publishing system and the open-access movement. This knowledge base will give them more context for understanding their information privilege and the complexity of the system in which information is a commodity. Thus, the social sciences librarian revamped her introductory lecture and library resources workshop to incorporate instruction on information under-privilege and the open-access movement. The lesson involved case studies representing a variety of perspectives on open-access. The case studies also pointed students to practical things they can do to participate in the open-access movement, such as how they can have conversations about Open Access and promote it through activism.[18]

Information privilege is real. It is a straightforward concept in that it refers very specifically to the situation of unequal access to information. Yet it is also a very significant form of privilege, one that can result in great injustice to community members who rely on certain types of scholarly information to secure their health, their well-being, and even their freedom—freedom to live in a place that they choose, where they experience safety and security. Ultimately, students learn best about information privilege when they experience it firsthand. In the case of Ethnic Groups, the injustice of information under-privilege was clear and unsettling, disrupting students' sense of comfort and ease with the status quo and further spurring their activist spirits. The critical partnership between UNLV University Libraries and SLICES in shaping the Ethnic Groups course, with the roles that library resources and the frame Information Has Value played throughout this course, allowed for these transformative experiences to happen among students.

Notes

1. Allan G. Johnson, *Power, Privilege, and Difference* (Mountain View, CA: Mayfield Publishing Co., 2001), 23.
2. SPARC (the Scholarly Publishing and Academic Resources Coalition), "Open Access," accessed December 5, 2016, http://sparcopen.org/open-access/.
3. Many universities do have such policies, including many other member institutions of the consortium to which UNLV University Libraries belongs, the Greater Western Library Alliance (GWLA). Arizona State University, for example, has a policy explicitly restricting the use of databases to Authorized Users, listing the categories of authorized users on the webpage that provides this policy. ASU Libraries, "Accessing Licensed Electronic Resources at Arizona State University," https://lib.asu.edu/policies/remote-access.
4. While "authorized users" may be defined differently in different license agreements, this term generally refers to currently enrolled or employed students, faculty, and staff. For example, see UNLV Libraries, "Accessing Library Databases from Off-Campus," accessed November 28, 2016. https://www.library.unlv.edu/help/remote.html.
5. Char Booth, "On Information Privilege," *Info-mational: On Technology, Media Literacy, and Librarians Who T-C-B* (blog), December 1, 2014, https://infomational.wordpress.com/2014/12/01/on-information-privilege/.
6. Feminist Standpoint Theory, or standpoint theory, is a methodological approach that argues that when studying the experiences of marginalized groups, researchers must turn to members of the marginalized group as the "starting point of the inquiry." Dorothy Smith, "Women's Perspective as a Radical Critique of Sociology," in *The Feminist Standpoint Theory Reader,* ed. Sandra Harding (New York and London: Routledge, 2004), 21–34.
7. Intersectionality is a term coined by Kimberle Crenshaw and refers to the ways in which different social identities interact leading to unique forms of oppression. Kimberle Crenshaw, "Demarginalizing the Intersection of Race and Sex: A Black Feminist Critique of Antidiscrimination Doctrine, Feminist Theory and Antiracist Politics," *The University of Chicago Legal Forum* 140 (1989): 139–167.

8. Tania D. Mitchell, "Traditional vs. Critical Service Learning: Engaging the Literature to Differentiate Two Models," *Michigan Journal of Community Service Learning* 14, no. 2 (2008): 50.
9. Ibid.
10. Sarah Banks, Andrea Armstrong, Kathleen Carver, Hellen Graham, Peter Hayward, Alex Henry, Tessa Holland, Claire Holmes, Amelia Lee, Ann McNulty, Niahm Moore, Nigel Nayling, Ann Stokoe, and Aileen Stracham, "Everyday Ethics in Community Based Participatory Research," *Contemporary Social Science* 8, no. 3 (2013): 263–277.
11. Executive Office for Immigration Review, U.S. Department of Justice, *FY 2015 Statistics Yearbook*, accessed December 8, 2016, page K2, https://www.justice.gov/eoir/page/file/fysb15/download.
12. Association of College and Research Libraries (ACRL), *Framework for Information Literacy for Higher Education*, February 2, 2015, http://www.ala.org/acrl/standards/ilframework.
13. Jenny Sharpe, "Is the United States Postcolonial?: Transnationalism, Immigration, and Race," *Diaspora: A Journal of Transnational Studies* 4, no. 2 (1995): 181–199.
14. Peggy McIntosh, "White Privilege: Unpacking the Invisible Knapsack," *Independent School* 49, no. 2 (1990): 31–36. Note: The original version of this article was published in the July/August 1989 issue of *Peace and Freedom*.
15. For more information about this type of instruction, here we point the reader toward the chapter in this book titled "Mining for the Best Information Value with Geoscience."
16. Eryk Salvaggio, "Information Privilege and Wikipedia: A Conversation with Char Booth (Part 1)," *Wiki Ed* (blog), February 22, 2015, https://wikiedu.org/blog/2015/02/02/char-booth-wikipedia-1/.
17. Ibid.
18. There are many ways students could get involved; for instance, see Adi Kamdar, "Three Things Students Can Do Now to Promote Open Access," February 1, 2013, https://www.eff.org/deeplinks/2013/01/three-things-students-can-do-now-promote-open-access.

CHAPTER 10*

Images Have Value:
Changing Student Perceptions of Using Images in Art History

Courtney Baron, Christopher Bishop, Ellen Neufeld, and Jessica Robinson

Recognizing images have value is an essential threshold concept for mastering the discipline of art history. Images are an important form of evidence in the history of art, second to viewing original works of art in person, and have transformed the academic study of art history. As digital copies of artworks, images document objects and make their representations readily accessible to anyone, anywhere.[1] The increased accessibility of images in the digital age has made the ability to study art possible for low-income individuals and historically underrepresented populations. This has led to diverse perspectives and fresh interpretations of works of art. Images have become the first step in the research process for an art historian and are used for quick reference on an as-needed basis and for in-depth study. Though in-person evaluation is generally preferred for study at the graduate or professional level, images are accepted and indeed expected for art historical research at all stages. Images provide a service to preserve fragile works of art in an accessible format. However, there are risks involved with using images as the basis of interpretation, since images with inferior quality or dubious authenticity can introduce misconceptions when reading a work. Digital images can be manipulated to enhance size, color, or contrast, which can lead to distorted stylistic and comparative argu-

---

* This work is licensed under a Creative Commons Attribution-NonCommercial-ShareAlike 4.0 License, CC BY-NC-SA (https://creativecommons.org/licenses/by-nc-sa/4.0/).

ments.[2] Scholars and students alike risk damage to their reputation by using lower quality images or not seeking permission to use images in publications. Therefore, images should be critically sourced, evaluated, and cited to ensure appropriate understanding of a work.

The shift in the library profession and among our teaching librarians from the Information Literacy Competency Standards[3] to the Framework for Information Literacy in Higher Education,[4] in conjunction with the Association of College & Research Libraries (ACRL) Visual Literacy Competency Standards,[5] provides new opportunities for combining library and visual literacy instruction.[6] Today, we live in a screen-based world where we are surrounded by visual media. However, the frequent exposure to visual content does not necessarily result in competency with visual materials. It has become essential for students to develop the skills needed to find, interpret, evaluate, use, and produce visual materials. Despite the prevalence of images and their importance in studying the history of art, students are not accustomed to treating images as a source of information and may not proceed with the same care they give other resources. The familiarity that comes from students' exposure to images on a daily basis compounds the widening gap between what they know about the differences between casual use and the critical sourcing of images for scholarly purposes. Librarians can help bridge the gap by showing art history students best practices for finding, evaluating, and citing images to aid the process of interpreting works of art.

Our thoughts on threshold concept theory

The application of threshold concepts in library instruction caused a shift in thinking among our teaching librarian team as we began to revise and reconsider the approaches we used with students. The adoption of threshold concepts was met with varying levels of skepticism by our teaching librarians because of the challenges associated with applying the concepts to one-shot sessions. Prior to the threshold concepts, our go-to exercises for library instruction classes included modeling searches, assisting with citation tools, and locating items in a catalog. We implemented the information literacy threshold concepts in the Framework by adapting our instruction to disciplinary needs, with the understanding that delivering all aspects of the concepts is not possible in a single session. Instead, we view our teaching as a journey that may not lead to a specific destination in a single class period, but provides the tools needed to facilitate mastery of the threshold concepts over time. The Information Literacy Competency Standards hindered our ability to deliver information literacy instruction that transcends traditional understandings of the librarian's role in the classroom. This change in thinking has empowered us to see ourselves as integral to the student's overall ability to grasp the information literacy threshold concepts. The flexibility of the threshold concepts affords us the ability to intentionally plan our instruction and legitimize our roles as teachers.

This change in thinking was especially important as we approached the frame Information Has Value because of the rapid changes taking place in delivery, availability, and attribution of digital images. For example, sharing our expertise and understanding of the components of the Information Has Value concept has led to new opportunities for library instruction that fully involves the major aspects of this frame in our art history classes, made possible by garnering faculty support through discussion in formal and informal settings. Since we teach freshmen and sophomores, we accept that these students probably have never considered images as a commodity or informational product, and may not be aware of the consequences for plagiarizing, misusing, or misinterpreting images. Our challenge is to provide patrons with access to information while simultaneously protecting them as both information creators and consumers. We believe this threshold concept is particularly essential for mastering art history.

Ultimately, our use of threshold concepts in library instruction is very much dependent on our status as guest instructors. In many instances, we are given a single class period to cover a wide range of information that is often informed by the faculty member who has invited us to present. In this capacity, we can deliver information that assists students in grasping aspects of a concept, but it is unrealistic to fully transform a student's understanding of even one troublesome threshold concept in a one-shot session. Instead, we are focusing our efforts on working with faculty who see the value in information literacy threshold concepts as integral to student learning, while still serving faculty who prefer skills-based library instruction. We have created a bridge between Information Literacy Competency Standards-based library instruction and the Framework by using a "yes, and" approach to incorporate three key topics through active learning strategies into skills-focused instruction: critically sourcing images, evaluating and interpreting images, and ethical and legal use and citation of images. We continue to deliver skills-based instruction as our foundation but incorporate a scaffolding approach to facilitate understanding of the information literacy threshold concepts in our teaching.

Critically sourcing images

Art historians must critically source images as evidence for forming interpretations. Art history students must first master the skill of finding high-quality images to study a particular work of art. We have observed that students are often unaware of authoritative sources and instead use easily accessible repositories such as Google Images, a search engine specifically for locating images on the web. They often download the first image from the results, which typically are of poor quality and have minimal or absent metadata. In an age when it is possible to find thousands of images with one click, the difficulty lies not merely in locating images but finding high-quality and accurate representations of artworks.

The movement from procuring images through controlled avenues, such as print sources and cataloged image libraries to less mediated online sources, has eliminated many quality control avenues. This has created a need for librarians to discuss issues related to quality, depth of image description, and authority to students who may be less knowledgeable about the characteristics of an image when formulating and refining search terms. Issues related to image retrieval for lesser known art by well-known artists, contemporary works, less prominent artists, and items related to a work that may have significant meaning, such as documentation, ephemera, and historical items, require the use of varied discovery platforms and search methods, including print sources and physical image repositories. Just as students may need to consult multiple databases to find scholarly articles on a topic, there is no "one-stop shop" for locating images. Librarians may discuss using comparative analysis of image results from multiple image sources and show how the best result will vary depending on the contextual qualities of the work of art.

Finding images. Librarians can show a variety of resources for locating images: subscription databases, museum repositories, web search engines, and social media. Artstor Digital Library, a subscription database, offers more than two million high-quality images with extensive image information from authoritative sources. The database offers features such as 360-degree panorama views, performance art footage, zoomable images that showcase fine details, and the ability to compare works. All images have been cleared for educational reuse. Museum and library websites are great alternatives, since they are free and usually offer high-resolution photographs of works or digitized materials along with contextual and difficult to locate information, such as the provenance of the artwork and acquisition date.

Web search engines tend to be the first place students look for images.[7] Student preference for Internet search engines is understandable since it is easy to quickly find content. Rather than direct them away from a resource that has been successful for past searches, librarians should teach students when it is appropriate to use Google to find images and how to use it more effectively. Library subscription resources will not contain all the images a student needs, and librarians can discredit themselves by perpetuating the notion that libraries are gatekeepers of information. Social media sites, such as Flickr and Instagram, focus on visual media and will be familiar to most students. Librarians can compare the purpose of these sites, which emphasize connecting and engaging with others through visual content, with the use of images in an academic context to help students select the most appropriate resource for art history images. Students should learn the strengths and weaknesses of online image sources and understand methods that will yield high-quality image results.

Best practices. When a general search engine such as Google Images is used, the need to critically source images is imperative. The search may return thousands of images but it is difficult to filter results by image resources. Teaching students to utilize Google's powerful search engine to find authoritative websites will lead to higher quality images. Using the advanced search options in web search engines can eliminate less authoritative sources from discovery and can guide students to content on museum websites that includes controlled metadata and higher quality standards. Emphasis on the use of synonyms, related terms, truncation, and Boolean operators to locate needed images in general search engines is especially important. Google's reverse image search feature allows students to use a picture to search for related images around the web as opposed to searching through keywords. This helps students find other online sources featuring an image of the work they are studying so they can locate higher quality images from more authoritative sources. Alternatively, if students are unfamiliar with a work but have an image in hand, they can use this search function to learn more about the work.

An endorsement of established image databases as superior to general search engines may imply that students should encounter no difficulty when searching in Artstor Digital Library. Advanced search tools and facets (Classification, Date Range, Geography, and Collections) in Artstor are more robust when compared to Google Images. However, Google Images is generally easier to use since the sophisticated search engine allows for flexible and intuitive language. Google's use of metadata generated from file names and text surrounding an image is problematic, yet so is Artstor's lack of subject terms in many of the database's metadata image descriptions. The absence of subject terms in Artstor decreases the ability to search across collections and may hinder students more familiar with entering subject-related search terms.[8] Students should be made aware that there is no perfect "one-stop shop" for image searching.

Evaluating and interpreting images

Searching is an iterative process that requires evaluating results and refining the search until the desired image is obtained. Students may skip the process of evaluating images for use in art history research papers and presentations due to the easy access to a large quantity of images retrieved through search engines. The criteria for evaluating images includes checking the source reliability, accuracy, aesthetics, manipulation, and effectiveness for the research need.[9] Librarians can show the possibilities of the image resources to students and empower them to critically evaluate their findings to select the most accurate result. Just as students should evaluate resources for the purpose of supporting an argument on paper, they need to understand the importance of evaluating images and whether they add value to their research.

The misuse or misattribution of an image could result in unwanted consequences ranging from embarrassment to accusations of plagiarism.[10] One real-world example of the negative consequences of neglecting to evaluate an image came in early 2016 upon the death of Frank Sinatra, Jr. A television news station posted an image of an actor parodying his father, Frank Sinatra, Sr., when reporting his sudden death. Though it may seem like a simple mistake, the context of misreporting by a news station resulted in a loss of credibility, leaving a question about their ability to accurately report news, and possibly could have caused a loss of advertising revenue.[11] This example stresses the importance of carefully selecting and evaluating images.

Image information. The key to successfully finding and evaluating high-quality images on the web relies on image information, or metadata. Most web search engines rely on retrieval of images through file names, keywords used to describe the image, and text accompanying an image stating the creator, copyright, date of creation, location, and other sources of description. Keyword searching can be tricky, since a student does not necessarily know if the metadata provided is accurate—if information about the image is present at all. When the image search results for a work contain poor metadata, the student is left to infer image correctness without the necessary subject knowledge. In comparison, museums and libraries consistently use professional description standards, such as the Getty vocabularies and VRA Core, a metadata standard used to describe works of visual culture and images, allowing for the consistent use of title, date, creator, and subject in associated metadata.

Accuracy. Evaluating images for accuracy and quality can be challenging for students since the process relies on image characteristics rather than the traditional criteria found in text sources. Librarians can introduce and describe a set of criteria including color, size, format, metadata, hue, saturation, contrast, and brightness. Students should be taught to note the image source and owner of the image, as well as other clues to determine if anything has been done to alter the image, including cropping, recoloring, or contrasting.

Interpretation. There has been debate among librarians on how to approach interpreting images in the library classroom. Subject specialists in art may regularly teach the art of interpretation, whereas instruction librarians may feel uncomfortable assuming this role in the classroom. Generally, faculty are equipped best to teach students how to "read" images since they are the content experts and can relate the meaning of an image to the context of the course.[12] Further, it is difficult for librarians to teach these skills within the limitations of a single class session. Instead, librarians can teach students how to find, evaluate, and understand the legal and ethical use of images and focus sessions on the best practices for searching and evaluating images to begin the process of interpreting a work of art. Students should understand that the use and value of an image lies in its context. Understanding the historical and social contexts of an image, its intended audience, original purpose, and production are essential to helping students learn the value of analyzing and interpreting an image.

Ethical and legal use and citation of images

The Information Has Value threshold concept can be translated for students by stressing that images are a source of information and therefore have value. Students should learn that images have value as a commodity and are a form of intellectual property whose owner or creator controls its legal use. Students are accustomed to having immediate access to thousands of "free" images online and may not understand the difference between copyrighted, Creative Commons licensed, fair use, and public domain images. Students must learn how, and why, to give proper attribution and citation to the images they use in their papers and presentations.

Copyright and fair use. Copyright is a construct that gives exclusive rights to the owner of a creative work. The concept of fair use was created to allow exceptions and provide flexibility for educational and creative situations. *The Code of Best Practices in Fair Use for the Visual Arts*, published by the College Art Association in 2015, aims to provide best practices for using copyrighted images and other works in creative or scholarly work.[13] The Code offers guidelines for teaching about art and specifically mentions images. Though the Code is a resource on fair use geared toward art professionals, the criteria for teaching art also apply to student image use. The Code states images should accurately portray the work they represent, images should appear in non-pixelated form when projected on screen, and images should be accompanied by attribution to the work of art and augmented with all available metadata.[14] If librarians struggle to obtain faculty buy-in for offering visual literacy instruction in art history classes, this resource makes the case for the importance of critically sourcing and ethically using images in the classroom.

Fair use is crucial for using images in educational settings, since it allows students to incorporate copyrighted materials into their assignments as long as the finished product does not reach an audience beyond the classroom.

Creative Commons. The issues surrounding the copyright and fair use of images can be complicated and difficult to understand. Creative Commons was designed to alleviate some of the frustration caused by these issues by offering a way to differentiate images that can be used without violating copyright law.[15] Creative Commons is a nonprofit organization whose licensing works alongside copyright to make materials accessible and usable. The licenses assist researchers with the selection of content they know they can legally and ethically use. Creative Commons licensing is especially helpful for art historians, since it empowers artists to make their copyrighted work accessible and freely available for use. Many digital images are marked with one of six Creative Commons licenses, so librarians should show students how to locate Creative Commons licensed content and understand the license options provided to copyright holders. We have found that Creative Commons licensing helps students understand why some images are copyrighted and others are not and how to distinguish between them to become ethical and informed image users.

Citation. Librarians are deeply immersed in teaching students about ethically and legally citing information, but additional education is needed for students to fully understand the ethical and legal issues surrounding image use.[16] Presentations in art history rely on images as visual evidence for arguing an interpretation. As teaching librarians, we are often invited to watch student presentations and we frequently observe students using images with no citation information. Students are accustomed to citing print sources in their assignments, but rarely possess the skills to fully cite images. This issue can be alleviated by showing students how to properly cite images and what information is typically included in image citations. In subscription databases, metadata is often embedded and will download along with the image file. Students should be encouraged to store this information for images obtained elsewhere. Most standard citation formats provide formatting guidelines for citing images and other visual media, and librarians can show students the correct formatting for the required citation style. Teaching students that images are informational and require citation and attribution will reinforce the concept that images are valuable and essential resources for mastering the history of art.

Activities for librarians

At the Oxford College Library, we primarily teach one-shot information literacy classes. It can be challenging to incorporate activities focused on finding, evaluating, and ethically and legally using images within a single class period. The goal of the following activities is to encourage students to critically approach images as informational evidence within the discipline of art history. The activities are intentionally arranged to scaffold instruction throughout the students' degree program in art history.

Activity one. Assignment: The object of this activity is to compare the discoverability, accuracy, and provided information for images of a work of art using different resources to demonstrate issues finding images online.

Learning outcome: Students will be able to utilize critical inquiry skills in order to locate and source high-quality images.

1. Ask students to form teams to search for a well-known work of art, such as Vincent Van Gogh's *Starry Night*, using one of four image resources: Google Images, Flickr, museum website where the work is located, and a subscription image database like Artstor Digital Library. Tell students the goal is not simply to find an image of the work, but to describe the features of the image resource.
2. Once students have found the image of the work in the selected resources ask them to report their findings and share their observations with the class. Ask the following questions:
   - "What steps did you take to find the image?" Have students describe the keywords and refinements, if any, they used to locate the image.
   - "Did the image have any metadata or information about the image?" Have students state whether the image was accompanied by descriptive information, including the creator, title, date, medium, repository, image source, or permissions.
     a. Once each group has shared their findings with the class, ask students to describe the pros and cons (image quality, authority, image information, etc.) of using each image resource. Ask students to choose the best resource for finding an image of the selected work of art.

Assessment: Librarians can check for understanding and reinforce the lesson based on student responses to the questions during the discussion portion of the activity. Use exit papers, which require a response before students exit the class, and have students identify which image resource worked best for their search and why they thought it was most effective.

Activity two. Assignment: This activity uses the concept of image appropriation, or the act of re-using art objects or images with little alteration, to present real case studies related to image copyright and intellectual property. The goal of the exercise is to demonstrate the value of images to students. We like this activity because it uses real appropriation case studies to make the concept of copyright more approachable to students.

Learning outcome: Students will be able to articulate the ethical, legal, social, and economic issues surrounding the creation and use of images and visual media in order to use images ethically.
1. The concept of image appropriation will likely be new to most students and requires explanation. The Lynda.com course on Information Literacy has an excellent video designed to introduce the intricacies of art appropriation. This can be assigned to students prior to the class session as a flipped classroom technique.
2. Divide students into groups and give them real case studies related to image appropriation. Artists such as Shepard Fairey, Sherrie Levine, and Robert Colescott are great examples. Students should review information about the artist and compare the original work to the appropriated work.
3. Tell students to present their artist and case to the class, answering the following questions:
    - "What work did this artist appropriate?"
    - "Why do you think the artist appropriated this work?"
    - "Did any legal or ethical issues arise and, if so, how were they handled?"
    - "What steps would you take if you wanted to appropriate this work?"

Assessment: Polling and quizzes are great assessment strategies that provide real-time results. We recommend creating a quiz through Kahoot, a free online learning game, to assess understanding of copyright and fair use best practices.

Activity three. Assignment: This activity is designed for upper-level undergraduates or graduate students who require permission to legally use images in theses, dissertations, or publications. Art history majors will find the art of obtaining permissions a particularly useful skill if they go on to work in the museum or visual resources fields. The lesson, delivered in workshop format, will explain how to use images that require permission from the copyright owner. The goal is to guide students through the entire process of obtaining permissions.

Learning outcome: Students will be able to interpret need and evaluate criteria in order to acquire permission to legally use images in publications.
1. Have students identify an instance where they want to use an image. Unless stated otherwise, the image is probably protected by copyright, so they will need to seek permission.
2. Tell students to think about their terms and create a list. Where do you want to use the image? Do you want to modify it? Is this a one-time use or do you need to use the image for a particular length of time? Will you profit from use of the image? Who is your target audience?
3. Ask students to locate the image source and the contact information for the copyright owner. Show students where to find this information on most websites.

4. Instruct students to draft a request in writing for permissions for an image need. The request should include a brief introduction, title, and creator of the desired image, purpose of the requested use, terms and conditions of use, and how they plan to acknowledge the copyright owner.
5. Have students create a spreadsheet with image information, including title, date, artist, medium, repository, use, and permissions details. This will help students stay organized since the permissions process can take several weeks.
6. Using the information in the spreadsheet, have students practice citing images and documenting permissions for their research.

Assessment: Ask students to write about what remains unclear from the instruction session. Follow up with students who still have questions and help them seek alternative images if necessary.

Assessment. We believe that successful assessment goes beyond the confines of a one-shot session. As teaching librarians, we strive to be peer-evaluators alongside disciplinary faculty. We regularly observe and provide feedback at student presentations, which affords us the opportunity to emphasize information literacy threshold concepts on an as-needed basis. For example, librarians observing upper-level art history presentations can comment on the quality of images presented on slides and ensure that the proper citation information is included to reinforce the Information Has Value concept. We regularly meet with faculty to discuss the outcomes of research papers and other completed assignments to evaluate student work and assess the impact of information literacy instruction. This information is then used to adjust future instruction sessions.

Conclusion

The Framework and its focus on threshold concepts allows information literacy to be taught through a disciplinary lens. The application of threshold concept theory to information literacy instruction provides new opportunities to scaffold lessons and activities for all course levels. The Information Has Value concept as presented in the Framework is particularly valuable when applied to information and visual literacy instruction in the discipline of art history. When studying art history, students must understand that images are informational and have value since they are used to research and interpret works of art. Students should be prepared to critically engage with images in an academic context. Due to the risks of using digital images, including the prevalence of poor-quality images on the web, incomplete metadata, and copyright restrictions, librarians play a crucial role in introducing students to library resources for visual material, providing strategies to locate and evaluate high-quality images, and demonstrating the importance of ethically using and citing images.

Notes

1. Debora Shaw and Jennifer Wagelie. "Studying Artworks and Their Digital Copies: Valuing the Artist's Aura," *International Journal of Education through Art* 12, no. 1 (2016), 57–58. doi:10.1386/eta.12.1.57_1.
2. Ibid: 58–59.
3. Association of College and Research Libraries (ACRL), *Information Literacy Competency Standards for Higher Education*, 2000, http://www.ala.org/acrl/standards/informationliteracycompetency. The ACRL Board of Directors voted to officially rescind the Standards on June 25, 2016. The Standards will only remain on the ACRL website until July 1, 2017. ACRL encourages librarians to adopt the Framework as the basis for information literacy instruction.
4. ACRL, *Framework for Information Literacy for Higher Education*, February 2, 2015, http://www.ala.org/acrl/standards/ilframework. The Framework was officially adopted by the ACRL Board of Directors on January 11, 2016.
5. ACRL, *Visual Literacy Competency Standards for Visual Literacy*, October 2011, http://www.ala.org/acrl/standards/visualliteracy. The Visual Literacy Competency Standards were approved by the ACRL Board of Directors in October 2011 and act as a supplement to the Framework for multimodal information literacy instruction.
6. Benjamin R. Harris, "Blurring Borders, Visualizing Connections: Aligning Information and Visual Literacy Learning Outcomes," *Reference Services Review* 38, no. 4 (2010): 524–25. doi:10.1108/00907321011090700. Harris argues that it is vital to connect information literacy and visual literacy in library instruction.
7. Laurie Bridges and Tiah Edmunson-Morton, "Image-Seeking Preferences among Undergraduate Novice Researchers," *Evidence Based Library and Information Practice* 6, no. 1 (2011): 29–30. doi:10.18438/B82G9M. This study investigated the image-seeking preferences of freshman and supported our observations that students turn to Google as a starting point for their image needs.
8. Alyx Rossetti, "Subject Access and ARTstor," *Art Documentation: Journal of the Art Libraries Society of North America* 32, no. 2 (2013): 285.
9. Denise Hattwig, Kaila Bussert, Ann Medaille, and Joanna Burgess, "Visual Literacy Standards in Higher Education: New Opportunities for Libraries and Student Learning," *portal: Libraries and the Academy* 13, no. 1 (2013): 78–79. doi:10.1353/pla.2013.0008.
10. Patricia Bravender, Hazel Anne McClure, and Gayle Schaub, *Teaching Information Literacy Threshold Concepts: Lesson Plans for Librarians* (Chicago, IL: Association of College and Research Libraries, 2015), 146.
11. Lindsey Ellefson. "News Station Accidentally Shows Joe Piscopo While Trying to Honor Frank Sinatra Jr," *Mediaite*, March 17, 2016, http://www.mediaite.com/online/news-station-accidentally-shows-joe-piscopo-while-trying-to-honor-frank-sinatra-jr/.

12. Molly Schoen, "Teaching Visual Literacy Skills in a One-Shot Session," *Visual Resources Association Bulletin* 41, no. 1 (2015): 3. http://online.vraweb.org/vrab/vol41/iss1/6.
13. "Code of Best Practices in Fair Use for the Visual Arts," *College Art Association*, accessed June 15, 2016, http://www.collegeart.org/pdf/fair-use/best-practices-fair-use-visual-arts.pdf.
14. Ibid.
15. "About," *Creative Commons Corporation*, accessed June 14, 2016, https://creativecommons.org.
16. Hattwig et al., "Visual Literacy Standards in Higher Education," 82–84.

CHAPTER 11*

Mining for the Best Information Value with Geoscience Students

Susan Beth Wainscott and Joshua Bonde

Before a student can understand the social power of information, they must know that information has monetary value and is not always freely findable or available. Students may first experience this after graduation, when they lose immediate online access to their academic library resources. When recent graduates discover that personal access to some information required to succeed in their first professional role has been lost, it can be a rude awakening. Graduates without personal or employer funds to access these resources may feel cut off from trusted resources. In a knowledge-driven society, those with access to more and/or better information can gain more power and social capital. If faculty and librarians inform students before graduation that information often has a cost, and thus social power, and that ethical routes to access do exist post-graduation, each student has an opportunity to develop a personalized plan to access and use information in a more ethical manner.

The Internet allows easy access to a seemingly limitless universe of materials of varying information quality. While affiliated with an academic institution, students are more likely than ever to have web-based access to a wide variety of academic resources, particularly at larger and advanced degree granting institutions.[1] Scholarly databases and discovery service providers have increasingly adapted their products to meet users where they are—pre-

---

* This work is licensed under a Creative Commons Attribution-NonCommercial-NoDerivatives 4.0 License, CC BY-NC-ND (https://creativecommons.org/licenses/by-nc-nd/4.0/).

sumably on Internet search engines. Academic libraries strive to make access to their digital collections nearly effortless for students in the library, on campus computers, on mobile devices, and from remote locations.[2] Undergraduate students may become accustomed to easy, fairly seamless, anywhere, anytime access to academic information resources, and students may not realize that much of this scholarly information is provided to them via institutional purchase or subscription.

It is unlikely that students approaching graduation, and perhaps also their first professional job, consider that they are about to lose access to their academic library's resources. Discipline-specific databases and specialty publications are the most likely to be inaccessible without a subscription or per-use fee. These information-literate, well-informed library users are abruptly thrust into a state of library anxiety—specifically, resource anxiety[3]—just as they are launching their professional careers. Recent graduates in a variety of fields will desire access to information to fulfill their new professional workplace roles. The Project Information Literacy (PIL) Passage Studies found that of twenty-three interviewed employers of new college graduates, most rated as important the new hires' ability to search for information resources on the Internet.[4] Fewer of the interviewed employer representatives also rated as important the new hires' ability to search within academic search tools or corporate databases.[5] Recent college graduates interviewed during the PIL Passage Studies indicated that part of the difference in information seeking in the workplace compared to academic assignments in college was the lack of or decreased access to academic library resources and services.[6]

A more recent PIL Passage Studies report has also confirmed that loss of access to search tools and full-text for professional purposes can be frustrating for some recent graduates.[7] Half of the 1,651 respondents indicated that lack of access to college library databases made continued learning difficult.[8] This more recent report included interviews with alumni of our university (University of Nevada, Las Vegas) and nine other institutions. Indeed, anecdotal observations of the librarian had detected that recent STEM graduates at our institution had been contacting the library for continued remote access to search tools and full text materials that they had come to value. They often expressed shock upon finding that due to our current use policies and license agreements, they could now only get access to some of this university's digital library resources, and only through a physical visit to the campus and one of the guest use computer stations in any of the four library branch buildings. It seems likely that most of our undergraduate alumni may be surprised to learn that they have lost some of the easier routes of access to their former library's resources and that many other academic libraries do not offer access to unaffiliated persons.

How can librarians and instructors address this looming encounter with an apparently closed door? As mentioned earlier, the graduate's discovery of their current lack of easy access may cause them discomfort and frustration.[9] They now face uncertainty related to obtaining the information they need, and their view of the world is challenged. These are diagnostic characteristics of a potential threshold concept as described by Land, Meyer, and Flanagan: "Learning thresholds are often the points at which students experience difficulty and are often troublesome as they require a letting go of customary ways of seeing things, or prior familiar views."[10] Some students will have become aware that somebody pays for their access to some information, but others may be surprised and confused. They may feel powerless, and realize that information is a valuable tool that they require to achieve their desired outcomes.

Townsend, Hofer, Hanick, and Brunetti[11] describe how the realization that information often has a monetary value/cost can transform the learner's understanding that barriers to information may exist and that the choice to use each information source includes an economic decision. This adds an additional consideration and potential stressor to the information-seeking process. In response to this discomfort and stressful threat to their success and/or view of the world, learners may choose between a "flight or fight response."[12] In this information-seeking scenario, students may flee and return to easy-to-access sources, hoping for the best. Some may turn to materials that are of uncertain provenance or even those that are clearly pirated copies. Those who have grasped the value of these resources may be willing to fight and struggle and be willing to seek an ethical access route to the trusted resources they encountered in their academic studies.

The PIL Passage studies found 23 percent of the 1,651 recent graduates interviewed had used academic libraries for workplace information needs,[13] and 20 percent had sought out virtual or physical visits to academic libraries for personal information needs.[14] Had the other respondents simply gone without the information sources they suspected or knew existed, did they pay for access, or did they perhaps locate copies of the resources through questionable routes? Rather than allow our graduates to fall into an ocean of paywall links and be frustrated or tempted to seek out pirated versions of information sources, librarians and course instructors should provide ample warning and help each student create a personalized strategy as a life raft.

The importance of information access to geoscientists

In science, technology, engineering, and mathematics (STEM) disciplines such as geoscience, specialized subscription-based resources may contain highly relevant information that would be expensive to recreate with laboratory or field research data collection. Compared to other STEM disciplines, very old publications may remain relevant for current geoscience research.[15] Upper-level geoscience information literacy instruction often includes use of the advanced search features of specialized indices and emphasizes the importance of services such as interlibrary loan to provide timely access for students. Academic faculty and library instructors may emphasize these specialized resources because students are engaged in academic assignments that mimic research processes, and the students may also be involved in research activities. It is natural for academic faculty and academic librarians to wish to prepare students for academia if they may pursue advanced degree programs. However, many undergraduate geoscience students may instead go directly into professional practice after receiving their undergraduate degree. Academic faculty and librarians have an equal obligation to prepare students for this career path as well.

Many undergraduate and/or graduate students do not realize that if they attain employment in geoscience outside of an academic institution, they will still be required to research and compose literature reviews and reports. It becomes a culture shock for many when they realize that information is not as easily accessible to them upon graduation. Most entry-level positions for geology majors post-graduation involve a great deal of primary literature research. An informal survey of geoscience professionals by the geoscience professor author of this chapter verified that in their careers graduates will still need access to government reports, technical (peer-reviewed) literature, and maps. Many of these jobs are in the environmental consulting field, so recent graduates are tasked with researching new project areas, finding old maps, and other resources to better assess a project, including potential hazards. Therefore, literature search skills are a must-have for a geoscientist. However, in most job postings and subsequent interviews, the topic of research skills is rarely mentioned. Most of the time it is implicit in a student's research experience on their resume/CV in the form of authored products (conference abstracts, peer-reviewed papers, etc.). The ability to navigate the published literature is essential to the long-term success of a geologist. Additionally, access to information sources is unlikely to be part of the employer or graduate school selection process for new graduates. However, it could become a question posed during an interview or one of the criteria used to select among several graduate schools or positions, where they are expected to perform literature reviews to generate reports or research outputs.

This situation becomes an early career hurdle for geoscience graduates. They are still expected to conduct research but are no longer under the direct umbrella of their university's library. It seems that graduates from every field of the geosciences have to deal with this, with one glaring exception, which is the petroleum industry. The petroleum industry provides its geoscience workforce with access to technical literature, maps, and government reports as needed. All other fields are forced to make do. A recurring anecdote which arises in conversations between the geoscience professor and early career geologists is that they seek out local institutions of higher education to gain access to technical literature and map libraries. Those who are not near a college or university are forced to see what they can find online via popular search engines or via peer-to-peer exchange of full text files. In the professional world, completing a report with an incomplete literature review is not a satisfactory option, yet there is a concern that without easy access, some early career geologists may simply do without some sources. Without all pertinent literature, many of these projects could be at risk of bias toward only those sources which are more easily available to groups without subscription access. Authoring biased reports could damage a geologist's career prospects. As of 2015, the largest sector of employment for geology majors graduating with a bachelor of science (B.S.) is the environmental consulting industry.[16] The lack of access to information would seem to become less of a problem with advanced degrees, as the petroleum industry is the largest employer of those geologists graduating with a M.S. and academia being the largest employer of Ph.D.s.[17] The authors discussed these factors and modified an existing geoscience library session to focus on this looming loss of online access for students approaching graduation.

Information literacy instruction for Advanced Field Geology

The Advanced Field Geology course provided an opportunity to speak with upperclass Geoscience undergraduate students and help them to consider options for ethical access to discipline-specific information sources post-graduation. Geology 372: Advanced Field Geology is the capstone course/experience in order to obtain a B.S. degree in Geology from the University of Nevada, Las Vegas Geoscience Department. This is a course that requires students to do intensive field exercises and then synthesize that experience in the form of a professional-style geologic map and report. This is a traditional capstone for most geology departments across the United States, with 2,973 students reported enrolled in such courses for the year 2013, a 5 percent increase over 2012.[18] The ultimate reasoning behind this intensive course is to provide students who are near graduation with a real-world style project so that they can more easily transition into industry. It became apparent to course instructors that some of these upperclass students were very much lacking in two areas: 1) research skills, i.e., many of them did not know where to go to find technical literature, maps, or government reports, other than popular search engines; and 2) comprehension of the resources they would need upon completion of their degrees. As such, over the past three years, the Geoscience Department faculty have worked to incorporate a library experience into this capstone course.

In past semesters, the library session was a shortened version of a literature review workshop designed for new graduate students. That session was task-oriented and focused on best practices for use of discipline-specific databases provided by the University Libraries. Students were guided in exploration of advanced search tools and techniques and were shown how to quickly obtain full-text copies of articles. Subscriptions or per-copy fees for full-text were only mentioned when discussing interlibrary loan as something for students to avoid paying out of pocket. Seldom did students pose questions or discussion around access to materials or sharing of full-text file copies. Open-access publishing options and copyright status of federal or local government reports were not discussed.

In light of these aforementioned data and observations about the needs and struggles of recent graduates, in spring of 2016, the one-hour-long library session for Advanced Field Geology was revised to deliberately incorporate the information literacy threshold concept, Information has Value. We decided to make the students aware of the looming loss of access and start a conversation with an essential question about the value of information and a big idea related to continuing access to information once they graduate.[19] The session began with the librarian informing the class that after graduation, some library search tools and full-text article copies would become more difficult to access. Indeed, the tools and resources that they found most useful were the most likely to be subscription-based and would be least likely to be accessible from off campus once they graduated. The question framing the session was: What information sources will you need after you graduate, and how will you access them? As part of this session, we also sought to develop skills of immediate use to the students in their course assignment, such as evaluating and selecting appropriate databases, navigating tools to obtain full-text access, and using advanced search techniques.

To explore the utility and desirability of continued access to several search tools, the librarian then led the group in collaborative creation of a rubric to evaluate search tools, including free scholarly Internet search tools and academic indices that were free or subscription-based. The students collaboratively created a rubric that included five criteria: relevance of content searched/indexed, ease of initial search interface (keyword search), options to refine search results, accessibility of the search tool without a university account, and ease of access to full-text copies of content. The rubric included a three-point Likert scale with equal weight for each criterion.

Each team of three to five students each selected a unique search tool to evaluate. The five evaluated search tools were
- a free Internet search engine that returns scholarly material across many academic disciplines with links to open-access or freely available copies of full-text materials;
- a subscription-based, generalized index of scholarly materials across many academic disciplines with links to subscribed and open-access, full-text materials;
- a subscription-based, discipline-specialized index of historical and current geoscience scholarly materials without links to any full-text materials;
- a free discipline-specialized index to more current geoscience scholarly materials with links to subscribed and open-access, full-text materials; and
- a library discovery tool which aggregates results from several subscription-based indices, including scholarly and some popular materials, across many academic disciplines and with links to subscribed and open-access, full-text materials.

Each team then selected a unique topic to use as a sample search to evaluate their selected search tool.

Next, teams shared their evaluation results via a digital whiteboard, and the librarian led a brief class discussion about each search tool. The course instructor and librarian also shared recommendations for good searching and refinement of results within each search tool. Students then discussed ethical access to full-text articles, including a comparison of peer-to-peer sharing of subscription-based materials to music piracy. Access options were discussed, including an employer having a subscription for the organization, use of local public and academic libraries, interlibrary loan through a public library membership, and paying per article as needed. The closing statements from the librarian addressed the university's current practices for alumni access to university library resources, common interlibrary loan policies at public libraries, and how students might consider each of these to ethically address their future information needs.

Assessment of this library session was formative and based upon the authors' observations of each student's involvement in discussions to develop the rubric, how each team tested and evaluated their tool, and how engaged students were in the class discussion. The majority appeared to grasp that information has monetary value, and that each was at risk of losing easy access to useful tools and materials upon graduation. The session had no associated course assignment, yet the just-in-case topic framed with the student-focused, big idea had captured and held the students' attention. As we debriefed after the session, we decided upon several immediate changes for the next session.

Planned changes

We would keep some portions of the session, but there are a number of improvements that could be made in future semesters. The immediate changes include adding a discussion on useful resource types or formats for geoscientists, changing how copyright restrictions and licenses are discussed, removing a source of variation in search tool evaluations, and adding more discussion of how students can research their personal options for information access. Periodically, the lesson will need to be reviewed to ensure that descriptions of copyright guidelines, licensing practices, and alumni access policies are current. Larger changes might be prompted as the open-access publishing adoption rate within the geoscience discipline changes, or if we decide to add learning activities to explore the social or political ramifications of unequal access to subscription-based information. Each of these changes is discussed in more depth below.

Before the discussion about information access, we will add a short, facilitated class discussion about the wide variety of resource types (print and digital) that students are likely to need for this class project and in their careers. It is likely that in a group of twenty-five to thirty-five advanced undergraduate students, at least a few will have experience using maps, geographic datasets, materials property data, reference books, journal articles, conference proceedings, or technical reports. As our library doesn't have an extensive print or digital map collection, the librarian could briefly describe how to locate sources of print or digital maps and get access to them. This discussion could include an example of map use from the geoscience professor to serve as a demonstration that useful resources are worth the effort to obtain them.

We will keep the student-led rubric development and discussion about evaluating search tools. The student discussion that led to the rubric development was logical and robust. The class rubric closely mirrored the backup rubric the librarian prepared in advance. We will provide all teams with an identical keyword string to enter in their search tools to remove one source of variability in the rubric scores. The topic for this keyword string will be drawn from recent course discussions. If the search tools are selected in advance, the librarian will provide some baseline information to the class about each tool, describing what it indexes, what full-text materials it contains, and whether any of the product is currently available without subscription.

To ensure students have the background knowledge necessary to create their personal information access strategy, we will change how we approach the discussion of copyright restrictions and electronic resource licensing agreements. Instead of trying to help students interpret what the appropriate uses of the information resources might be, we will explain what types of information they need to request or locate in order to make informed decisions.

We will describe the difference between copyright restrictions and license agreements, and discuss the importance of license agreements for digital materials. We will remind students that these license agreements can be more restrictive than copyright, and each one that they accept when downloading a full-text resource may be different. The librarian will provide sample library statements about patron use of electronic resources that have licensing restrictions and a sample interlibrary loan disclaimer. This may be used during the library session or as a resource for a post-session assignment.

Finally, each year we will need to review the session lesson plan as copyright law and guidelines, electronic resource licensing practices, and library policies for alumni access at our institution change. The rate of adoption of open-access publishing and archiving models across the geosciences will also impact the discussion. If more geoscience information resources are published using open access, the importance of their findability will overtake the importance of full-text access. Free information resources are only useful if they can be discovered. Emphasis on search tool access and evaluation of search tool features will be increased in the session design as the rate of open-access publishing increases in the discipline.

Other possible changes

This session could also be expanded to discuss tools and strategies students can use to investigate their options for access based upon their planned geographic location and employer-provided resources. The class could discuss how each library resource will have a unique license negotiated between the provider and the entity paying the subscription fees. Students would be informed that these may not be the same for one resource at different types of libraries within each state or similar libraries in different states. Each library or information center that the students consider and ultimately use will likely have a statement about acceptable uses, cautioning users to be mindful of the copyright and licensing protections provided to the authors and provider of the resources.

Students should also be encouraged to read the licenses that they click through when accessing materials online, or that are appended to the materials they receive through interlibrary loan. An additional or alternative in the class learning activity could be for each student to locate the license for a particular resource and reflect upon what types of use/distribution they feel would be appropriate for that item. In a wrap-up discussion of that activity, students would be reminded that because these terms and guidelines may change over time, they should read the terms each time they have questions about acceptable uses or sharing of received items.

We could also expand the scope of the library activity to look beyond each individual's information access needs. As students realize and contemplate the impending loss of familiar route of access to library resources, at this point of stress and uncertainty they may experience the liminal state that is diagnostic of the troublesome nature of threshold concepts.[20] If they are crossing through this space of change and transformation, they may begin to question the systems and practices that result in cost and limited access to information and the impact this may have on themselves and on others.[21] We and others could also use this lesson and the students' discovery of a looming and potentially acute personal pain point as an opportunity to start a deeper reflection with our undergraduates about the power of information and how those without access to information are disadvantaged. The information access levels of employers in various geoscience subdisciplines may also change based upon economic forces and the affordability of corporate subscriptions. Thus, the power and resiliency of various employers may shift as their employees lose easy access to information, unless the employees have alternative strategies for access.

Potential library session assignments could include reflective writing, development of a personal access strategy, and evaluation of the power differentials among different organizations or groups.

Reflective writing assignment. A reflective writing assignment about the monetary value of information could be completed at the end of the library session. A variety of scenarios could be used to frame a reflection about how the value of information resources is reflected in their monetary cost, and how each student might rank the relative cost to benefit ratio of information sources for different purposes. Instructors and librarians could assess these reflections for evidence of learning of this threshold concept by looking for clues to the knowledge dispositions described in the Association of College and Research Libraries' Framework for Information Literacy for Higher Education (Framework): student agreement that information does have a monetary cost, statements indicating that students are evaluating the fairness of that cost, evidence that students are aware of the potential inaccessibility of some information resources, or student statements indicating the lack of access to individuals with less capital to spend on these resources.[22]

Personal information access plan assignment. If a points-bearing, summative assignment is desired, assessment could include creation of a personal information access strategy. These strategies could include a description of the local public and academic libraries near where the student hopes to reside in post-graduation, and an employer or graduate program they hope to be affiliated with. Students could research and describe what the local public library system(s) offer, what their posted use policies are, and describe the interlibrary loan program. The students could also describe what resources they expect to have through the employer or graduate program they hope to join. The resources of the nearest academic libraries and their community member use policies should also be described. This assignment addresses, in particular, the Framework knowledge practice related to recognizing issues related to lack of access to resources.[23] Assessment of these plans should focus on consideration of cost, risk of unethical access routes, and alternative access routes, but should not include making an overall judgement on the validity or legality of the student's plan to avoid implied approval by the institution on any questionable access options.

Beyond inclusion in this capstone course, the library session and the personal plan assignment could also be adapted for a wider audience and provided to seniors in a variety of disciplines as a lifelong learning workshop. Collaboration with other subject specialist librarians would be necessary to fully develop such a workshop to address specialty information formats, search tools, and the prevalence of open access publication or archiving. An assignment to create a personal information access plan would translate nicely to this audience, as would the reflective writing assignment about the impact of unequal information access. If this activity is completed within a course management system, students could download a copy of their response and potentially update it after graduation.

Diagnosing power differential assignments. To encourage students to further explore the notion that information has power, and develop the knowledge practices related to how groups of individuals may be underrepresented or systematically marginalized by differential information access,[24] students could be presented a scenario where a policy decision by a government agency is being evaluated for environmental and social impacts. The scenario could describe a differential in access to information among the policy stakeholders, including the types of impacted local community groups, as well as the agencies, resource extraction and mining corporations, and consulting firms that frequently employ geoscientists. A reflective writing piece could be used to explore the impact of the information access differential among the stakeholders, including the following questions: Who has access to information in a timely manner to address the science surrounding this policy issue? An open-ended question prompt could be, Is that fair? Why or why not? Who has the most power? Can this power differential be balanced in some ethical manner and by whom?

Reference consultations

In addition to the formal instruction described above, the personal information access plan could also be adapted to script format for reference consultations. These consultations could be with current students approaching graduation, alumni, or community members who are seeking access to academic information without a university affiliation. In academic settings, reference interactions often include informal instruction in order to improve the critical thinking and information literacy of our students and other patrons. While it may be difficult to overcome the affective struggles of a patron suddenly learning that the route to the information they seek may not be as immediate as they would prefer, a longer reference interaction or a follow-up appointment for a longer reference interaction can allow the space and time for the patron to develop a suitable information access plan.

Conclusion

Aware that students will encounter a point of frustration after graduating and losing familiar access routes to information, librarians and instructors should take advantage of this point of uncertainty to explore the threshold concept Information has Value. Rather than focus on their next assignment, library sessions for capstone courses such as this Advanced Field Geology course should also prepare students for their transition out of academia and into professional practice. While reinforcing more basic information literacy skills and knowledge, students can be provided a chance to become more expert information seekers and producers by exploring the notion that information value imbues it with power. Graduates who grasp the monetary value and social power of information access will be better able to navigate the information landscape. They will be equipped to be more savvy consumers and subscribers, will investigate their local academic and public libraries for access to professional and academic resources, and will seek out any employer information sources and services available to them.

If our students can access the information they need to hit the ground running at their new jobs, we believe it will increase their chances of success in their early careers. For those who continue with advanced degree programs, this session will provide a greater understanding of why university libraries cannot offer all the information resources directly, and how prospective graduate students can evaluate what library resources will be available to them at different institutions. For those graduates who have the opportunity to become authors, they will also be more aware of the potential cost to their desired readers when evaluating various publication options. Whether or not our new graduates become authors and publishers, it is our hope that we have opened their eyes to the systems that produce and make available the information that so fundamentally impacts their world.

Notes

1. Matthew P. Long and Roger C. Schonfeld, *Ithaka S+R US Library Survey 2013*, March 11, 2014, 38, doi:10.18665/sr.22787.
2. Larry Johnson, Samantha Adams Becker, Victoria Estrada, and Alex Freeman, *The NMC Horizon Report: 2015 Library Edition* (Austin, TX: The New Media Consortium, 2015), 16–18.
3. Anthony J. Onwuegbuzie, Qun G. Jiao, and Sharon L. Bostick, *Library Anxiety: Theory, Research, and Applications* (Lanham, MD: The Scarecrow Press, Inc., 2004), 38.
4. Alison J. Head, *Learning Curve: How College Graduates Solve Information Problems Once They Join the Workplace*, Project Information Literacy Research Report, October 15, 2012, 8, https://dx.doi.org/10.2139/ssrn.2165031.
5. Ibid.
6. Ibid., 17.
7. Alison J. Head, *Lifelong Learning Survey of Recent US College Graduates* (Ann Arbor, MI: Inter-university Consortium for Political and Social Research [distributor], February 22, 2016), 5, http://doi.org/10.3886/E100176V10.
8. Ibid., 54.
9. Ibid., 5.
10. Ray Land, Jan H. F. Meyer, and Michael T. Flanagan, eds., *Threshold Concepts in Practice*, (Rotterdam: Sense Publishers, 2016), xii.
11. Lori Townsend, Amy R. Hofer, Silvia Lin Hanick, and Korey Brunetti, "Threshold Concepts for Information Literacy: A Delphi Study," *Communications in Information Literacy* 10, no. 1 (2016), 35.
12. Terje Berg, Morten Erichsen, and Leif M. Hokstad, "Stuck at the Threshold: Which Strategies do Students Choose when Facing Liminality within Certain Disciplines at a Business School," in *Threshold Concepts in Practice*, eds. Ray Land, Jan H. F. Meyer, and Michael T. Flanagan (Rotterdam: Sense Publishers, 2016), 111–113.
13. Alison J. Head, *Lifelong Learning*, 34.
14. Ibid., 25.
15. Constance C. Gould and Karla Pearce, *Information Needs in the Sciences: An Assessment*. Report prepared for the Program for Research Information Management, The Research Libraries Group, Inc. (Mountain View, CA: Research Libraries Group, 1991), 35.
16. Carolyn Wilson, "Industries Hiring Recent Geoscience Graduates in 2015," *Geoscience Currents*, no. 108 (2016), 1.
17. Ibid.
18. Penelope Morton and Carolyn Wilson, "Field Camp Attendance Continues to Steadily Increase," *Geoscience Currents*, no. 82 (2013), 1.
19. Jay McTighe and Grant Wiggins, *Essential Questions: Opening Doors to Student Understanding* (Alexandria, VA: Association for Supervision and Curriculum Development, 2013), 12.
20. Jan H. F. Meyer and Ray Land, *Overcoming Barriers to Student Understanding: Threshold Concepts and Troublesome Knowledge* (New York, NY: Routledge, 2006), 19.
21. Townsend, et al., "Threshold Concepts for Information Literacy: A Delphi Study": 35; Association of College and Research Libraries (ACRL), *Framework for Infor-*

mation Literacy for Higher Education, February 2, 2015, http://www.ala.org/acrl/standards/ilframework.
22. ACRL, *Framework for Information Literacy for Higher Education*.
23. Ibid.
24. Ibid.

CHAPTER 12*

Teaching the Teachers:
The Value of Information for Educators

Jess Haigh

This chapter examines how a university subject librarian in the United Kingdom used the Association of College and Research Libraries (ACRL)'s threshold concepts as a jumping off point to designing information literacy skills training for classes of trainee teachers and other education and childhood studies students.

In the United Kingdom, the ACRL Framework for Information Literacy for Higher Education (Framework) is much discussed yet not formally implemented. Each university within the United Kingdom may have its own information literacy policies, but they are often informed by the Seven Pillars of Information Literacy, formulated by the Society of College, National and University Libraries (SCONUL), which represents all university libraries in the United Kingdom and Ireland.[1] The Seven Pillars model was first formulated in 1999 and has since been revised in 2011 and reviewed in 2015. The model recognises that the development of Information Literacy is not a linear process, using the metaphor of a series of pillars on which people can be higher or lower, depending on individual competency. Based on a series of statements related to competencies and understandings, the model theorizes that the more information literate a person, the more attributes they can display.

This librarian, however, found the theory of information literacy as a series of threshold concepts, rather than stated competencies to be learned and

---

* This work is licensed under a Creative Commons Attribution 4.0 License, CC BY (https://creativecommons.org/licenses/by/4.0/).

assessed through practical application, more valuable in planning teaching sessions, mostly supplementary, non-credit bearing information skills classes. This librarian's understanding of threshold concepts is that through the acquisition of knowledge or understanding, one steps through a metaphorical doorway from a previously perhaps misunderstood or comfortably uninformed place to a more enlightened, transformed way of knowing, even if that knowledge is troublesome.[2] The concept that one encounters on the threshold that leads to a greater understanding is one that can be then applied to other uses of the subject; for example, when learning to bake, once it is understood that it is heat that affects a food's texture, one can then apply this threshold concept to other applications of heat on a substance, such as hairstyling.

The Seven Pillars model, although revised to be more focused on learning through personal experiences, is still a model of definite capabilities that are then expected to be performed. The use of thresholds concepts as a learning framework returns the agency to students, allowing them to find their own conclusions about the application of that concept in their own and other's lives. The threshold concept Information Has Value, as described within the Framework, speaks of several dimensions of value, the understanding of which can then be applied to various situations, including within academia and within future teaching practices. The wider, more troublesome concepts raise ethical questions and force choices in the lives of the students who are thinking about them. Rather than just knowing a list of information dos and do nots, the student is fundamentally changed by their awareness of the concept and its implications within their own life. This approach to teaching was more relatable to this librarian in terms of her own journey of information literacy and education, as well as her preference for using a more critical pedagogical approach to her teaching.

This chapter focuses on the librarian's class application of the threshold concept Information Has Value. Once it is understood that information "possesses several dimensions of value," one can then apply this to thinking about how information can be used, or misused, withheld, bought, and sold.[3] A greater awareness of how personal creation of information is valuable to others as well as oneself is troublesome as it leads to questioning how one can or should have power over this, and can lead to a possible change in behavior.

This chapter examines the current information literacy skills of students and teacher trainees, instructing teacher trainees as an example of teaching practice, the use of critical pedagogy within library instruction and problems that may arise, and the context of Information Has Value within the classroom. The chapter also gives examples of using digital resources, including videos, within teaching sessions and describes a learning activity developed by this librarian specifically for trainee teachers.

This chapter focuses on the discipline of teacher training and childhood and education studies. This discipline supports students in becoming competent professionals working alongside children, young people, and adults in educational settings. This discipline values making a positive difference in the future lives of the people the students will be working with. Being able to debate and effectively challenge oppression and critique existing power structures are important skills that should be encouraged in trainee teachers and, in turn, their future students. By being able to answer questions relating to the commodification of personal information and intellectual property laws confidently, new teachers encourage their students to take information seriously as a commodity, and to value themselves as information producers. In addition, teachers must be aware of how online interactions influence their students as information producers and consumers and be able to guide young people in making positive choices about what personal information they reveal and discuss online. These skills are important to teachers in particular in order for them to understand the oppressions their students may be experiencing that will lead to their information access being marginalised. Teachers will also expect their students to use academic conventions, such as citing sources, and should understand why this happens first themselves if they are to encourage this behavior.

The skills of students and of trainee teachers

In 2011, United Kingdom think tank Demos published a report on the Internet use of young people. The literature reviewed, and their survey of 509 teachers in England and Wales showed, that while teenagers of that time were confident users of the Internet, they were not necessarily competent. Although most teachers reported that information found on the Internet is important in the formation of their students' beliefs, less than one in ten of these students ask, when using information found online, who made the website and why.[4]

The twelve- to eighteen-year-olds of 2011 are the trainee teachers of today, and there is little evidence that shows their digital and information literacies have improved. Godbey and Fabbi, for example, reported in 2014 that the majority of their research sample of teacher education students did not have the information literacy skills to navigate and appraise information available through the digital environment.[5] This is a concern, as without these skills trainee teachers will not be able to fulfill the value of their discipline: to make a positive difference to the future lives of their students.

Using a more critical pedagogy

When instructing teacher trainees, educational practitioners are demonstrating teaching in practice. This demonstration of practice can be used to communicate the experiences of teaching as a wider discipline. Librarians can be models for good teaching practice, while not being teachers themselves, in that they can use innovative and creative teaching methods to explore threshold concepts such as Information Has Value, which is a concept that can be interrelated with many disciplines and specific subjects. This gives student teachers an example of teaching outside of their subject specialty that still showcases positive pedagogical practices. It is therefore imperative that the education librarian makes informed choices about the teaching methods and pedagogies they use, as an educator modelling teaching. Furthermore, explaining the theories behind teaching styles and the content of the lessons enables these theories to be contextualised by experiences in the wider world, and to relate this discipline with wider educational practices, such as the practice of critical pedagogy.

Critical pedagogy is, first, the acknowledgment that traditional educational methods of teaching by rote, with the student passively absorbing information as communicated by the presumed authority figure of the teacher, are complicit in perpetuating oppression. In his exploration of critical information literacy, Elmborg describes traditional "banking" education methods as training students in capitalist ethics, becoming passive receivers of knowledge.[6] Cited by many as being first outlined by Freire in his 1967 work *Pedagogy of the Oppressed*, critical pedagogy actively reflects on and challenges oppression and its causes. Teachers and students meet on the same level and can engage in a dialogue that allows the students to critically reflect on their perceptions of reality.[7]

In a classroom using a critical pedagogy, students are given the opportunity to develop the knowledge and skills to question their own realities and engage in challenging social injustice. In examining the value of information, this could include appraising what information students have access to compared to other members of their communities, who owns or has influence on the information students use, and why that information is available.

In designing teaching sessions that aim to empower students with the ability to question assumed authorities, the use of the ACRL Framework is a good starting point. This is due to the Framework being composed of threshold concepts to be explored, as opposed to statements to be taught by rote or aptitudes that must be then assessed. While exploring the threshold concept Information Has Value, students could question how they value information both as a consumer and a producer. This may then lead to thinking about choices they have previously made about information production and publication, and how a greater understanding of the value of information can affect these choices in the future. The nature of threshold concepts means that, in designing instruction that incorporates them, the agency of learning is placed in the hands of the learner, rather than students learning something by rote.

In order for a learning environment to be truly critical, one must develop an approach based on the specific needs of the students involved in that particular environment.[8] Education students can have very specific needs; they must learn the practicalities of designing and implementing effective teaching sessions and the theories that underpin them, while also encountering positive models of teaching themselves in order to inform their future practice. A class session that incorporates a critical approach might include students exploring library systems and databases and presenting them to the class, reversing the power hierarchy between librarian and student. This demonstrates that students both have pre-existing knowledge of how to search and that they too can be competent demonstrators, as well as highlighting that their voice matters in the classroom.[9]

Problems that may arise

Students who may be unfamiliar with a critical approach to teaching may be reluctant to participate and even believe that the approach is ineffective. Many students unused to anything other than lecture style teaching methods are unable to view teaching practices, such as active learning, student story-led discussion, and critical information literacy, positively in terms of how engaged they feel they are and how much learning happens.[10] Students may feel uncomfortable without a checklist of recognizable learning goals or things that they will have been expected to memorize by the end of a session. In the case of teacher trainee students, explaining the pedagogical approach you are using not only makes the learning approaches used easier for students to accept, but also involves the students in reflecting on what paradigm they as future teachers will be embodying.

One of the most frustrating things for teaching librarians, especially if, like this librarian, one is a lecturer by nature, is knowing when and how to shut up. By structuring lessons around activities, videos, and class discussions, this librarian is attempting to force themselves to say very little; in this way, they are trying to not let an authoritative voice dictate student learning. By shutting up and allowing natural discussion and storytelling to happen in the classroom, perhaps guided by asking pertinent questions, the aim is for students to come to their own conclusions and develop their own values.

The argument for Information Has Value within the classroom

Within information literacy sessions, in order to explore the threshold concept Information Has Value, students should be able to discuss their own opinions and experiences about how information is created and consumed in their own lives, and, in the case of trainee teachers, in the lives of their future students. Through a facilitated, open discussion, students can learn from each other's wider experience the value of information in other spheres to their own.

The threshold concept Information Has Value is about gaining an awareness of how and why information can be used and to think more critically about who it is currently being used by, and how. Students, whose first experience with information having value may be in being warned against plagiarism, may find this troubling, as they may be used to an environment where sharing information without credit or reference is the norm. Without understanding why referencing within academia is important, students may struggle to include proper attribution and citation.

Without being able to appraise how and why the information gathered is available, there is a risk of being manipulated by those who control the publication or access of information. Members of marginalized communities, who may not have access to information sources available to other, more privileged groups, may be making important life and economic choices, such as what to buy or how to vote, based on restricted information. In an environment where information can seemingly be accessed and shared for free easily across several platforms, gaining an understanding of the value of information could be especially troublesome. Students may have never experienced information behind paywalls and may not appreciate the different source types and how they can be accessed. This knowledge of the value of information leads to an understanding of the rights and responsibilities of information consumers and creators, such as accrediting information used and deciding where and how to publish information created, as well as a greater understanding of what source types higher education library collections may be composed of.

Newly qualified teachers should be aware of the value of information if they are to successfully teach within the information society. Unless all teachers understand how information is restricted and how intellectual property laws and a lack of general open access stifle education to marginalized communities they will be unable to serve these communities fully in the future. Teachers should be able to have a dialogue with students about how they can make better informed choices about what information they use. Moreover, they should be prepared to make informed choices themselves about how they share information about their practice that allow for all communities to learn from them, for example, through publication in open-access publications. Exploring the threshold concept Information Has Value within the classroom would allow for trainee teachers to form their own ethical stances on information access, and where and how they would choose to publish their own work in the future.

Learning activity: Videos in learning digital literacy, online status, and value

In their 2011 report, Bartlett and Miller recommended that evaluating digital sources should become a core part of teacher training, with understanding search engines, propaganda techniques, and source attribution being taught as part of teacher training programs.[11] Through best practice use of digital sources within classroom teaching, librarians can demonstrate how they evaluate resources themselves.

Teaching resources should use the same techniques that are used by the trainees. As an example, YouTube, the second most popular website in the world, is also a very popular teaching tool. Within lessons, I often break up sessions with clips from YouTube videos or other video-sharing platforms, such as Vimeo. Not only is this an easy way to break up the sessions into manageable chunks, it also reinforces the lesson message and can kick-start discussions.

Using YouTube also helps in starting discussions about the commodification of personal information. In one class, when having to wait for a YouTube advertisement to play before a video, I asked the class what advertisements appear for them; this prompted a discussion on how this varied throughout the class based on their age. Through me explaining how search histories can be cached and used by websites to determine which advertisements are shown (Facebook showing your Amazon wishlist is an example), the trainee teachers become more aware about how their personal information and online interactions affect the information they receive online.

Librarians should be wary, however, as teaching using videos can lead to the assumption that everything the video says is true. The rise of people using face-to-camera videos, or vlogs, to learn about the world and make choices based on this learning is interesting, given the parallel rise of the theories underlining critical pedagogy within teacher education. Students spend their days engaged in critical discourse only to watch a "sage on the stage" at home by choice in their informal learning activities. The use of any teaching aid should be questioned within the classroom, to allow for trainee teachers to think critically about the use of it for their future classes. Videos can prompt discussions; they should not dictate learning.

Students often report that they regard YouTube as an information retrieval platform, rather than one they can collaboratively use to create content or to critically engage in.[12] Why not encourage students to participate in the online video culture themselves, as critical commenters or creators? YouTube can also be a place for critical thinking and appraisal of information, and by demonstrating the value of YouTube and other video sharing platforms to trainee teachers, librarians can more effectively use online sharing platforms as teaching tools.

Learning activity: Sources

Sources is a game I developed to help my teacher education students to think about issues of access to information sources. It involves students thinking critically about how information access affects people's choices regarding the information they use. The game is played cooperatively—everyone versus the board. This game therefore makes an excellent ice breaker as it gets students talking to each other and making decisions cooperatively.

Having trainee teachers think about access to information sources is important because unless teachers understand that not all access is equal, they will be unable to fully support the needs of the communities they will work with in the future. Otherwise, they will be ill-equipped to critically discuss with their students why some people are limited in their information access and how it affects their lives.

The game involves students first individually thinking about when and how they might want to access information, for example, in writing an essay, following a recipe, or finding a bus timetable. These instances are then written on Post-its (one instance per Post-it) and placed randomly on a grid placed on a table, a large piece of paper, or even the wall. This becomes your communal game board. Do not tell the students the purpose of this until after they have finished writing their Post-its.

Students then randomly pick a "character" card pre-made by the librarian. Characters have varying levels of information access. You could create different characters based on the communities your students are from or from marginalised communities you are aware of. Each character card lists the value of their access points, such as online access, library access, and educational institution. These access points are between 0 and 5 points. Some examples of characters' access points could be: Character A: Online Access (3), Educational Institution (2), Library Access (4), Information Literacy (4);

Character B: Online Access (5), Educational Institution (0), Library Access (0), Information Literacy (0).

Students will likely question why certain people have certain points, which could lead to a discussion on why levels of access are different. You could choose to write down student questions to return to a longer discussion after the game, or discuss as you go. Rather than answer students' questions directly, I ask them instead what they think. A student may ask why Character A has 4 online access points and Character B has 0, and instead of giving them a reason, I would open this out to the whole group, asking the broader question of what might limit Character B's access. I have had some players be very invested in their characters, creating lives for them based on their attributes.

The players can then buy "sources" cards, depending on the total value of their access points. Students can choose which of the following source cards they purchase: book, blog, general website, trade journal, academic journal, dictionary, or encyclopedia. You could adapt these sources to suit your library holdings, including a specialized database, for example. Source cards are worth varying points to better reflect the information environment, for example: a general website (1 point), an academic journal (3 points), etc. So, for example, a player with 10 access points in total could buy two source cards worth 3 points, and one source worth 4 points. These are then the source cards students play with; they cannot swap cards after this point in the game.

Players then place their source cards, in turn, on the game boards under examples where they think the information need matches the source used, with the player with the highest information literacy access points going first. Other players can challenge the source; if a challenge occurs, the group must reach a consensus as to whether the play is allowed. If the play is allowed, the student removes the Post-it with the information need from the board. The game ends when either the players use up all their source cards or every information need is removed from the board. If there are Post-its left on the board at the end of the game, the game has won, if all the Post-its have been removed, the group has won.

The aim of this game is, first, to get students talking about how they use information, what sources they use, and how this is different for others. Students then consider issues of access to information and how this varies, as well as how much certain information types may cost and how this affects satisfying their information needs. The game characters aim to represent the inequality of access that happens in the real world.

You can make various adjustments to this game depending on circumstances. Smaller groups could play from one large game board or you could split larger groups up to create game boards of their own. By having students first create their own game boards, the whole game revolves around their own information needs and experiences, central to the idea of locating learning in real life. You could also lead a discussion afterward on how the game could be made more equitable, for example, making the academic journals worth fewer points. This could initiate a discussion about open-access resources and paywalls.

When I ran this game in a workshop with some postgraduate teacher trainees, the response was very interesting, as the students became quite passionate about defending the sources they used for their information needs, and the longest discussions were about how they would justify using certain sources. When I then asked if they would expect their students to use those sources, their stance changed; trainee teachers that I have spoken to often have different perspectives of themselves as students to the student they themselves teach, or will be teaching in the future.

Students came out of the session thinking more about how access varies depending on institution: some students did not previously know that college libraries' online holdings are paid for by the college, rather than being free to external parties. If students have moved directly from high school to college, they may have very little understanding of communities without access to the Internet, library holdings, or paid-for content.

Most of the learning from this game comes out of the discussions. This is when it is important, as a facilitator, to allow students to lead discussions, to encourage storytelling and honesty, and to have a safe environment to be able to do this effectively. By using reflective questioning within conversations brought about by game playing, I am creating a playful, safe environment to have challenging discussions about troublesome threshold concepts, such as Information Has Value.

Conclusion

In this chapter I have explored my understanding of threshold concepts, how they relate to using a critical pedagogy within teaching, and how I apply this to teaching around the concept Information Has Value.

Through the critical discussion of information and its value, sparked by active teaching methods, including games and the use of digital resources, trainee teachers can move further through the threshold concept of Information Has Value. Using a critical approach to library instruction for trainee teachers is particularly important because it demonstrates pedagogy in practice, as well as allowing students to gain understanding informed by their own experiences.

Notes

1. Society of College, National and University Libraries (SCONUL), *Seven Pillars of Information Literacy*, 2016, http://www.sconul.ac.uk/page/seven-pillars-of-information-literacy.
2. Ray Land, "'There Could Be Trouble Ahead.' Threshold Concepts, Troublesome Knowledge and Information Literacy—a Current Debate," (presentation, LILAC 2015, Newcastle University, UK, April 8–10, 2015), http://archive.lilacconference.com/home/lilac-2015.
3. Association of College and Research Libraries (ACRL), *Framework for Information Literacy for Higher Education*, February 2, 2015, http://www.ala.org/acrl/standards/ilframework.
4. Jamie Bartlett and Carl Miller, *Truth, Lies and the Internet: A Report into Young People's Digital Fluency* (London: Demos, 2011), 5.
5. Samantha Godbey and Jennifer Fabbi, "Teaching Teachers: A Study of Factors Impacting the Information Literacy of Teacher Education Students," (presentation, European Conference on Information Literacy, Dubrovnik, Croatia, October 22, 2014).
6. James Elmborg, "Critical Information Literacy: Implications for Instructional Practice," *Journal of Academic Librarianship* 32, no. 2 (2006): 192.
7. Lane Wilkinson, "Paulo Freire, Critical Pedagogy, and Libraries," *Sense and Reference* blog, July 13, 2016, https://senseandreference.wordpress.com/2016/07/13/paulo-freire-critical-pedagogy-and-libraries/.
8. Lauren Smith, "Towards a Model of Critical Information Literacy Instruction for the Development of Political Agency," *Journal of Information Literacy* 7, no. 2 (2013): 15.
9. Eamon Tewell, "Putting Critical Information Literacy into Context: How and Why Librarians Adopt Critical Practices in Their Teaching," *In the Library with the Lead Pipe*, October 12, 2016, http://www.inthelibrarywiththeleadpipe.org/2016/putting-critical-information-literacy-into-context-how-and-why-librarians-adopt-critical-practices-in-their-teaching/.
10. Amy E. Covill, "College Students' Perceptions of the Traditional Lecture Method," *College Student Journal* 45, no. 1 (2011): 92.
11. Jamie Bartlett and Carl Miller, *Truth, Lies and the Internet*, 8.
12. Stefan Hrastinski and Naghmeh M. Aghaee, "How Are Campus Students Using Social Media to Support Their Studies? An Explorative Interview Study," *Education Information Technology* 17, no. 4 (2012): 451.

Research as Inquiry

Section Four

CHAPTER 13*

Empowering, Enlightening, and Energizing:
Research as Inquiry in Women's and Gender Studies

Juliann Couture and Sharon Ladenson

As practitioners of feminist pedagogy, women's and gender studies scholars facilitate a participatory and cooperative environment for teaching and learning. This empowers students to raise substantive questions about texts they read and to relate classroom concepts about gender roles and norms to their own experiences. Together, librarians and women's and gender studies scholars promote lifelong learning and inquiry beyond academia by placing high value on students' lived experiences.

The Research as Inquiry frame in the Framework for Information Literacy for Higher Education, which describes the research process as "iterative and depends upon asking increasingly complex or new questions," aligns with the women's and gender studies classroom environment, where students are encouraged to continuously raise critical questions.[1] This chapter explores how Research as Inquiry intersects with feminist pedagogy and applies within women's and gender studies. In this examination, the authors integrate women's and gender studies threshold concepts, including the social construction of gender, intersectionality, privilege and oppression, and feminist praxis into a disciplinary analysis of this information literacy concept.[2]

---

* This work is licensed under a Creative Commons Attribution 4.0 License, CC BY (https://creativecommons.org/licenses/by/4.0/).

The authors (two librarians) embrace authentic feminist practice that values the lived experience and use their own voices to reflect on how the Research as Inquiry frame shapes their work with women's and gender studies students and faculty. Suggestions for how to implement and assess the frame in women's and gender studies classes are discussed, including specific activities for raising critical questions as part of the iterative research process.

Theoretical foundation

Threshold concepts, Research as Inquiry, and women's and gender studies. The creation of the Information Literacy Framework for Higher Education (Framework) marked a transition from a standards-based skills focus to an adaptable and flexible conceptual approach.[3] The Framework puts forth six core concepts to serve as a foundation for how librarians teach, interact with students and faculty, and design curriculum. These core ideas were developed using a variety of educational approaches, most notably, threshold concept theory. This theory was developed by Meyer and Land, who established five characteristics of threshold concepts: transformative, troublesome, irreversible, integrative, and bounded to a specific field.[4] While this is an extensive theory that could be discussed in greater detail, we will instead focus on the Framework as signaling a significant pedagogical shift for librarians that has the greatest impact when situated within a discipline. In an essay examining the impact of the Framework, Pagowsky notes that regardless of educational theory, the document represents a shift toward "designing instruction with big ideas rather than skills-based curriculum."[5]

The Research as Inquiry frame describes experts as those who explore multiple perspectives, investigate gaps in previous research, and overall raise critical questions around lines of inquiry.[6] Key dispositions and knowledge practices outlined in the frame are particularly significant for the learning process in women's and gender studies, most notably valuing and developing intellectual curiosity, openly engaging with information, and becoming more comfortable with ambiguity. The application of these knowledge practices and dispositions beyond the classroom context is central to the Research as Inquiry frame.[7] Examining the Research as Inquiry frame in a disciplinary context requires further exploration of women's and gender studies programs and threshold concepts.

In a report for the National Women's Studies Association (NWSA), Levin explores teaching strategies, learning outcomes, and assessment plans that comprise women's studies programs across the United States.[8] In discussing distinctive learning processes for women's studies courses, it is noted that students are expected to link the intellectual with their personal experiences and are challenged to incorporate new knowledge. Additionally, characteristics of women's studies curricula include "teaching students a critical approach to knowledge rather than a common set of facts" while fostering a sense of social responsibility that extends beyond the academy. Consequently, classes themselves are "more participatory, experiential, diverse, and student-centered."[9]

Launius and Hassel used an extensive literature review, conversations with other faculty, their own research, and student learning assessment results to propose four threshold concepts for women's and gender studies: the social construction of gender, privilege and oppression, intersectionality, and feminist praxis.[10] Together, these transformative concepts provide the foundation needed to explore feminist scholarship. The social construction of gender is the premise that "gender and sex are distinct from each other, and that our gender identities are socially constructed and not immutable."[11] The concept of privilege and oppression examines interconnected structures of difference and inequality to illustrate how power operates in society. Intersectionality as a threshold concept explores how gender is just one aspect of feminist analysis. To fully examine the concepts of social construction and privilege and oppression, one must apply other categories of analysis including race, class, and age. Feminist praxis reinforces the connection women's and gender studies scholarship has with social justice by encouraging students to apply one's knowledge beyond the classroom to address inequities. While much of feminist scholarship places value in one's lived experiences, threshold concepts for women's and gender studies require a novice in the field to move from personal knowledge to examining larger structural issues. The process of situating one's lived experiences in the context of structural issues requires a paradigm shift that is often troublesome and transformative for learners.

Feminist pedagogy and critical inquiry. Encouraging students to actively shape their education by continuously raising critical questions is a key tenet of feminist pedagogy. Influenced by critical approaches to teaching and learning, feminist educators reject instructional approaches that encourage passive behavior.[12] Resisting educational practices that promote passivity, Freire shuns the "banking concept of education," in which "the teacher issues communiqués and makes deposits which the students patiently receive, memorize, and repeat."[13] Freire underscores the importance of developing a "critical consciousness," asserting that "knowledge emerges only through... the restless, impatient, continuing, hopeful inquiry human beings pursue in the world, with the world, and with each other."[14] Practitioners of feminist pedagogy reframe and expand upon Freire's notion of critical consciousness by raising awareness about gender inequality and encouraging students to question assumptions about gender norms. Feminist pedagogy has evolved from the second-wave feminist movement, which shaped social change in part by facilitating widespread consciousness-raising about oppression and gender discrimination. As Accardi notes, second-wave feminist activism focused on "all realms of a woman's life—the domestic sphere, the arts, music… [and] education was one arena that also saw activist energy and transformation. The conceptualization of feminist pedagogy was an effort to bring the women's movement into higher education."[15]

While feminist instructors encourage students to raise critical questions about gender roles and inequality, they also resist the banking concept holistically by broadly facilitating inquiry. When describing key tenets of feminist pedagogy, Bondy, Light, and Nicholas discuss the importance of developing a safe space for students to have substantive dialogue and debate, to identify and challenge assumptions, to "ask critical questions about the world around them, and [to] make connections between and among their learning experiences, often with a view to generate social change."[16] As feminist educators, Bell, Morrow, and Tastsoglou also emphasize the inquiry process, noting the importance of helping students to "develop critical-thinking skills, partly by using material in the classroom that challenges the status quo and partly through teaching students to question and analyze."[17]

Feminist pedagogy, critical information literacy, and Research as Inquiry. The feminist emphasis on inquiry aligns with critical approaches to teaching and learning in libraries. When discussing theory and practice of critical information literacy, Elmborg underscores the importance of consciousness-raising, which empowers students to "learn to take control of their lives and their own learning to become active agents, asking and answering questions that matter to them and the world around them."[18] While librarians have traditionally focused on helping with finding answers, the process of developing questions is central to critical information literacy. Simmons discusses how raising critical questions is a key area of the research process, noting the importance of asking questions about information and engaging with ideas in order to develop new knowledge.[19] Exploring the relationship between critical pedagogy, critical literacy, and information literacy, Jacobs underscores how the process of posing complex questions empowers students to play active and transformative roles, which ultimately extends learning beyond the classroom.[20] Hence, critical approaches to information literacy teaching and learning place a strong emphasis on developing and articulating substantive questions, and encouraging students to play active roles in their education and beyond by engaging in the ongoing process, as described by Freire, of restless, yet hopeful, inquiry.[21] As described in the Research as Inquiry frame, facilitating this process involves challenging students to appreciate and participate in complex dialogue and debate surrounding the creation of knowledge, in part by becoming intellectually curious and being open to seeking sources of information from diverse perspectives.

Reflections on facilitating the inquiry process

Sharon Ladenson. The Framework represents a shifting emphasis in teaching and learning in libraries. One of the key elements of the Framework involves encouraging students not only to be critical information consumers, but also active *producers* of information. The Research as Inquiry frame focuses on the iterative process of articulating thoughtful questions; encouraging students to continuously develop new and complex questions is a fundamental part of the process of developing knowledge.

Facilitating the process of developing critical questions is central to my teaching. Through researching and practicing feminist pedagogy, I also recognize that learning occurs collectively through open discussion and inquiry. Learning is an active, iterative, and continuous process, facilitated through practice and application of new concepts. Learning also occurs as a result of building on existing knowledge and experiences, and, consequently, the process is also personally meaningful.

I aim to cultivate a participatory and cooperative learning environment, building on the knowledge and questions shared by students about their research and information sources. When working with upper-level undergraduate and/or graduate women's and gender studies students, I often begin by asking them to write down and verbally share questions about their research, as well as their strategies for finding information. This activity not only facilitates the process of developing and articulating questions, but also frames information literacy sessions around student needs, which provides for a more targeted teaching and learning experience. For example, I have worked repeatedly with an upper-division undergraduate class at Michigan State focused broadly on gender and evolution; students are required to conduct semester-long group research projects. The faculty member brings her students to the library shortly after they have developed their research proposals, so the class has a good sense of the topics they are interested in exploring. During the 2015 fall semester, one group decided to focus on the evolution of diverse family structures, such as families with lesbian or gay parents, single-parent families, and adoptive families. When sharing their research questions, strategies, and sources, students from the group noted that they had managed to locate biographical and media sources, and were hoping to find empirical research articles as well. This led to questions and discussion about the value and use of diverse sources of knowledge. During this exercise, students demonstrated one of the key dispositions outlined in the Research as Inquiry frame: seeking and reflecting on multiple perspectives during the information-gathering process. I was also able to provide advice on locating empirical research articles on their topic, which addressed specific information-seeking needs.

I appreciate how the Framework shifts the conversation about teaching and learning in libraries from a skills-based approach to an emphasis on complex, sophisticated ideas surrounding research and information-seeking. For years prior to the development of the Framework, I have embraced feminist pedagogy and worked with faculty to facilitate the process of raising critical questions about research and information sources during information literacy sessions. The Research as Inquiry frame will provide a useful mechanism to continue to build and strengthen collaborative work with faculty to facilitate the process of exploring and engaging critically with information sources. Key dispositions outlined in the frame, such as valuing intellectual curiosity and being open to diverse perspectives, are aligned with a feminist pedagogical approach to teaching and learning, which is widely valued and practiced by women's and gender studies scholars.

Juliann Couture. When I began my career as an academic librarian with subject liaison information literacy instruction duties, I followed a general template of "things students should know about the library" instruction style. This approach was partially born out of a lack of teaching experience combined with finding my footing in an academic setting. While active learning components were integrated into my sessions, they did not foster the collaborative, problem-posing environment I aimed to cultivate and that I experienced as an undergraduate. How might I inspire that type of learning and inquiry in sessions I conducted?

In shifting my focus from a checklist of things to accomplish to facilitating the raising of critical questions, my interactions with instructors and students were altered. An integral part of my planning process has always included conversations with the instructor about goals and outcomes for a library instruction session. This discussion still occurs but no longer focuses on the performance of specific skills, such as locating two scholarly articles. Instead, the conversation centers around how to reinforce or build upon the concepts being addressed in the course, including how students are engaging in the inquiry process. These conversations ensure the success of the session by clarifying objectives and pedagogical approaches.

For an undergraduate women's and gender studies course focusing on women in the arts, my conversation with the instructor provided an opportunity to discuss the inquiry process and how it would lead to other concepts such as authority and information production. Our planning session led to a fruitful discussion about the aims of the course assignment, source type and number requirement, and how this related to feminist theory. Eventually, we decided to not prescribe a set number or type of sources but instead use the session to reinforce and expand on concepts addressed in earlier in the semester, such as synthesizing information from numerous disciplines. When the session occurred, the instructor and I worked collaboratively to facilitate students' inquiry on the production of literary and art criticism, gathering multiple perspectives, and determining the scope of their analysis. The Research as Inquiry frame provides a foundation for these discussions with instructors since it often leads into other concepts contained in the Framework.

Activities for facilitating the inquiry process

As practitioners of feminist pedagogy, the authors facilitate the process of raising critical questions during information literacy sessions. The Research as Inquiry frame provides a concrete mechanism for identifying specific behaviors and competencies acquired as a result of formulating such questions. The authors design and implement activities for developing and reinforcing knowledge practices and dispositions outlined in the Research as Inquiry frame, including valuing intellectual curiosity, maintaining a critical stance, and seeking multiple perspectives during the process of discovering and engaging with information sources.

Sharon Ladenson. Librarians can use activities for facilitating the inquiry process for women's and gender studies students at various levels in higher education. Working with first-year writing programs focused on inquiry provides an important opportunity to initially engage students in the process of raising questions as part of research and information seeking.

Students enrolled in Michigan State University's first-year writing program have had the opportunity to take introductory composition courses in various thematic tracks, such as American Radical Thought, Law and Justice in the United States, or Women in America. As the librarian for gender studies, I have collaborated with faculty members who teach the Women in America track. Inquiry ("a recursive process of posing, following, and answering questions") and discovery ("making new knowledge through [the] inquiry process") are key components of the first-year writing program at Michigan State.[22]

One of the exercises I have developed to support inquiry for first-year writing is a discussion-based activity and worksheet designed to facilitate the process of articulating critical questions about a specific information source. The activity involves distributing copies of a very short, provocative article on a topic relevant to the class.[23] One of the readings I have often used for this exercise is a *New York Times* opinion piece written by Judith Warner on "The Choice Myth."[24] The piece debunks myths and dispels stereotypes of stay-at-home-moms and explores various challenges that women continuously face when juggling paid work and family responsibilities. Warner also references several outside sources, such as a United States Census Bureau report, a research report by sociologists, and news media sources. After reading Warner's piece, students work in pairs to answer and raise critical questions about the article. Students identify questions that Warner raises about women's lack of support for balancing motherhood and paid work, and they also develop their own critical questions about challenges that mothers face in the paid workforce. Discussing Warner's article leads students to raise questions about social issues: for example, why various organizations lack sufficient resources to support families (such as child-care facilities on-site and flexible hours for staff). Students also explore how Warner frames the issues. For example, some students have raised questions about the author's narrow focus on heterosexual families. In addition, students identify outside sources referenced in Warner's piece and share examples of keywords for finding additional information on the topic explored in her article; this helps to underscore how a single source can be used as a launching point for finding additional information on a topic. During this exercise, students have demonstrated key knowledge practices and dispositions outlined in the Research as Inquiry frame, including maintaining a critical stance, valuing intellectual curiosity, assessing information sources for gaps and weaknesses, and seeking multiple perspectives as part of the research process. The activity also facilitates exploration of the concept of privilege and oppression, as students identify and discuss power structures that shape obstacles and challenges women face when lacking resources to balance paid work and family responsibilities. Students also explore the concept of intersectionality while discussing how racial identity and class status further limit women's options.

What are strategies for reinforcing the inquiry process for upper-division undergraduate students in women's and gender studies classes? Working with undergraduates at Michigan State in a third-year English class focused on women and literature provided another opportunity to facilitate the process of developing critical questions. Students were required to do analyses of specific texts by female authors and to incorporate outside sources of literary criticism into their work. In anticipation of the information literacy session, I spoke with the instructor, who expressed concerns about the work that her students had submitted previously. She explained that rather than engaging in critical analysis, students had been writing plot summaries. Reviewing the list of required texts for the class, I noted that students had read *The Handmaid's Tale* by Margaret Atwood. This novel presents a dystopian society in which fertile women are physically forced to bear children for the state. As the text has powerful and provocative themes, I decided to use it for the initial activity for the session with the English class. I asked students to reflect and raise questions about *The Handmaid's Tale*; for example, if they had the opportunity to talk with Margaret Atwood, what questions would they ask her about the plot, characters, and/or specific themes of the book? After generating and discussing critical questions, we explored resources for finding related literary criticism. Later in the semester, the instructor told me that the work of her students had improved, and indicated that the process of raising questions about *The Handmaid's Tale* helped her students to become more comfortable with critical analysis.

Juliann Couture. In the Women, Literature and the Arts course, students investigate a woman artist of their choosing, drawn from many art forms, including visual art, literature, and music. This lower-level undergraduate course examines women in literature and the performing arts and aims to emphasize cross-cultural and historical perspectives. The course counts as both a lower division elective course for the major and as a core-curriculum course for general education requirements, which results in a mix of women's and gender studies majors and students without prior exposure to disciplinary content.

In the course, students are exposed to the foundations of art and literary criticism as well as a few core feminist readings. Students' cumulative project is a research paper analyzing the work and life of a female artist from multiple perspectives. In conversations with the instructor, we identified the students' primary challenges as determining the appropriate scope for a thesis and synthesizing multiple perspectives. Students often resorted to summarizing the artists' life and work while struggling to analyze the work from different angles, such as class, race, ableism, or culture. Since the class was a mix of majors and non-majors, some students were more prepared to integrate women's and gender studies concepts into their work, specifically those of intersectionality and understanding structural issues around privilege and oppression.

To begin addressing these challenges, I designed a session aimed to encourage students to raise critical questions that led to deeper analysis of the artist's life and work. We began by discussing Frida Kahlo, an artist the students are familiar with and who is often used in class discussions throughout the semester. Taking an intersectional approach, we create questions as a class about different lenses with which to analyze Kahlo's life and work. How does Kahlo's Mexican heritage influence her work? Why is her work often analyzed in relation to her husband's? How does the meaning of her work shift if viewed through the lens of disability or her communist views? Through this collaborative exploration, different ways of examining the life and work of one artist arise and we discuss how multiple students could investigate the same artist but approach the project with different areas of inquiry and criticism. This portion of the session guides students through exploring multiple lenses of inquiry that can ultimately navigate the process of determining scope and articulating a clearly defined thesis. Additionally, this process reinforces the need to examine the artist on both a micro and macro level. After discussing this one example as a whole class, students pair up to explore their selected artists. Most students arrive at the session with an artist in mind but have not developed a specific line of inquiry. After sharing their selected artist with their partners, students are asked to respond to a few targeted prompts: What perspectives might you use to investigate this artist and her work including, but not limited to, historical, cultural, relational, ableism, economic, racial? What do you already know about the artist? How do you know it? What gaps might there be in this information? Where would you gather more information about this artist? While I provide these questions as a way to overcome the initial discussion barrier, most students readily engage with the process. When we come back together as a class to discuss the questions, what gaps of information exist, and the perspectives discussed, students drive the next phase of the session, which touches on information production, access, and authority.

Feminist Assessment

Many educators struggle to meaningfully examine learning in feminist classrooms while not reinforcing power structures inherent within assessment mechanisms. In *Students at the Center: Feminist Assessment*, Shapiro lays out guiding principles, starting with the core principle of questioning established evaluation practices.[25] The other principles include a student-centered, participatory approach, which is heavily shaped by feminist pedagogy and compatible with feminist activist beliefs. Finally, feminist assessment is not standardized but instead based on local context and needs.[26]

Keeping these principles in mind, how might one assess these inquiry-based activities from a feminist perspective? This is particularly challenging when information literacy instruction sessions are often limited to a one-shot interaction with a fifty- or seventy-five-minute time frame. As Accardi notes, "feminist assessment acknowledges the uniqueness of each learner and… traditional classroom assessment techniques are modified in ways that are explicitly feminist."[27] Since feminist pedagogy and women's and gender studies as a discipline value students' lived experiences, reflection is a key component of assessing a feminist classroom. One approach is to modify a traditional assessment practice, the one-minute paper. The one-minute paper often asks what the student learned and what is still unclear. In allocating a bit longer than one minute, the students could be asked to reflect on the class session and to describe their learning experience that day. The questions can be tailored to align with the knowledge practices in the frame. The students might be asked to reflect on how the scope of their research shifted based on the questions raised during the session or information located. This reflection practice aims to give students agency in the learning process.

Another way to assess student learning is to observe and examine how students compose and generate critical questions as well as how they negotiate those questions. Do they participate in the discussion? Are the students raising questions beyond the prompts given? Where were the barriers to the students raising critical questions? Were students seeking multiple perspectives? Are students struggling with uncertainty or not locating a straightforward answer? Observing the students' interactions could lead the librarian to identify more meaningful reflective questions throughout the session.

Conclusion

Taking a feminist pedagogical approach and critical stance when guiding the inquiry process does pose challenges for the planning and facilitation of information literacy instruction sessions. One of the biggest challenges the authors have encountered is student resistance to this type of learning. As hooks notes, "this type of learning process is very hard; it's painful and troubling" and that it may take a while for students to recognize the importance of what they've learned.[28] One strategy to ease students into this uncomfortable territory is to demystify the session. Discuss at the start of the session why it is being approached a certain way and clarify the benefits of the exercises. Engage in conversation with the class regarding how the process of raising critical questions can lead you to different directions that may create a more focused area of inquiry.

Approaching information literacy sessions with this stance also requires a shift in how one approaches instruction and how one negotiates the process with the course instructor. Some instructors will prefer an instruction session that provides students with a specific list of facts about the library and locating information. While this might occur, it is important to focus on a shifting emphasis toward a more engaged, critical session. For both authors, this has meant rethinking what needs to be included in a limited time frame. Is that database demonstration necessary in a fifty-minute session? What portions of a traditional one-shot could cut or covered by other formats, such as an online guide or tutorial? By rethinking our own approach to the sessions, we are able to shift our emphasis to facilitating the inquiry process and encouraging students as critical consumers and active producers of information.

The shift from a skills-based, standards approach to a focus on concepts and big ideas provides space to reimagine the librarian role as educator and examine our pedagogical approach. For the authors, this includes incorporating critical information literacy and feminist pedagogy in their practice and striving to integrate the Research as Inquiry frame and other information literacy concepts into the disciplinary curriculum. These approaches aim to guide learners through the process of raising critical questions and more fully engage in the inquiry process in all aspects of their lives.

Notes

1. Association of College and Research Libraries (ACRL), *Framework for Information Literacy for Higher Education*, February 2, 2015, http://www.ala.org/acrl/standards/ilframework.
2. Christie Launius and Holly Hassel, *Threshold Concepts in Women's and Gender Studies: Ways of Seeing, Thinking, and Knowing* (New York, NY: Routledge, 2015).
3. ACRL, *Framework for Information Literacy for Higher Education*.
4. Jan Meyer and Ray Land, *Threshold Concepts and Troublesome Knowledge: Linkages to Ways of Thinking and Practising within the Disciplines* (Edinburgh: University of Edinburgh, 2003).
5. Nicole Pagowsky, "A Pedagogy of Inquiry," *Communications in Information Literacy* 9, no. 2 (2015): 136.
6. ACRL, *Framework for Information Literacy for Higher Education*.
7. Ibid.
8. Amy K. Levin, "Questions for a New Century: Women's Studies and Integrative Learning," *College Park, MD: National Women's Studies Association*, 2007, http://www.nwsa.org/Files/Resources/WS_Integrative_Learning_Levine.pdf.
9. Ibid., 13.
10. Launius and Hassel, *Threshold Concepts in Women's and Gender Studies*, vii.
11. Ibid., 26.
12. Sharon Ladenson, "Paradigm Shift: Utilizing Critical Feminist Pedagogy in Library Instruction," in *Critical Library Instruction: Theories and Methods*, ed. M. Accardi, Emily Drabinski, and Alana Kumbier (Library Juice Press, 2010), 105–12.
13. Paulo Freire, *Pedagogy of the Oppressed*, 30th anniversary ed. (New York: Continuum, 2000), 72.
14. Ibid., 73.
15. Maria T. Accardi, *Feminist Pedagogy for Library Instruction*, Gender and Sexuality in Information Studies, number three (Sacramento, CA: Library Juice Press, 2013), 29–30.
16. Tracy Penny Light, Jane Nicholas, and Renee Bondy, "Introduction: Feminist Pedagogy in Higher Education," in *Feminist Pedagogy in Higher Education: Critical Theory and Practice*, ed. Tracy Penny Light, Jane Nicholas, and Renee Bondy (Waterloo, Ontario: Wilfried Laurier Univ. Press, 2015), 1–9.
17. Sandra Bell, Marina Morrow, and Evangelia Tastsoglou, "Teaching in Environments of Resistance: Toward a Critical, Feminist, and Antiracist Pedagogy," in *Meeting the Challenge: Innovative Feminist Pedagogies in Action*, ed. Maralee Mayberry and Ellen Cronan Rose (New York: Routledge, 1999), 23–46.
18. James Elmborg, "Critical Information Literacy: Implications for Instructional Practice," *The Journal of Academic Librarianship* 32, no. 2 (March 2006): 192–99, doi:10.1016/j.acalib.2005.12.004.

19. Michelle Holschuh Simmons, "Librarians as Disciplinary Discourse Mediators: Using Genre Theory to Move Toward Critical Information Literacy," *portal: Libraries and the Academy* 5, no. 3 (2005), 297–311, doi:10.1353/pla.2005.0041.
20. Heidi L. M. Jacobs, "Pedagogies of Possibility Within the Disciplines: Critical Information Literacy and Literatures in English," *Communications in Information Literacy* 8, no. 2 (2014), 192–207, http://files.eric.ed.gov/fulltext/EJ1089141.pdf.
21. Freire, *Pedagogy of the Oppressed*, 73.
22. "Department of Writing, Rhetoric, and American Cultures: FYW Learning Outcomes," accessed August 4, 2016, http://wrac.msu.edu/firstyearwriting/faculty/fyw-learning-outcomes/.
23. Sharon Ladenson, "Speaking Up: Using Feminist Pedagogy to Raise Critical Questions in the Information Literacy Classroom," in *Critical Library Pedagogy Handbook*, ed. Nicole Pagowsky and Kelly McElroy, vol. 2 (Chicago: Association of College and Research Libraries, 2016), 41–48.
24. Judith Warner, "The Choice Myth," *The New York Times*, October 8, 2009, http://opinionator.blogs.nytimes.com/2009/10/08/the-opt-out-myth/.
25. J.P. Shapiro, "What Is Feminist Assessment?" in *Students at the Center: Feminist Assessment*, ed. Caryn McTighe Musil (Washington, D.C.: Association of American Colleges, 1992), 29–37.
26. Ibid., 33.
27. Accardi, *Feminist Pedagogy for Library Instruction*, 76.
28. bell hooks, *Teaching to Transgress: Education as the Practice of Freedom* (New York: Routledge, 1994), 153.

CHAPTER 14

Framing the Visual Arts:
The Challenges of Applying the Research as Inquiry Concept to Studio Art Information and Visual Literacy

Marty Miller

The term "visual arts" encompasses a wide range of disciplines. Art history, architecture, ceramics, painting, fashion design, sculpture, interior design, printmaking, landscape architecture—all of these media are included on this broad description. Students working within these areas produce written, two-dimensional, and three-dimensional works. While subjects like art history require a great deal of "traditional" written research, others, including architecture and landscape architecture, balance writing with artistic output. By contrast, the focus for many studio courses is largely on the object rather than the research paper. This creates a unique challenge to information professionals when trying to provide effective research support.

When scanning the professional literature to date, it becomes apparent that almost all applications of the Framework for Information Literacy for Higher Education (Framework)[1] involve course content that includes some sort of written assignment to assess student learning. There is no discussion of its utilization with non-text-based projects. Many creative and effective approaches can be readily found for research papers, but when it comes to those courses that are primarily concerned with visualization and the physical act of artistic creation, examples of effective applications are few and far between. The Framework guidelines are meant to be flexible, rather than prescriptive sets of rules for students' academic success; however, an underlying assumption appears to be that the product of student research will take written form. This omits a significant student population from benefitting from the Framework guidelines. A printmaking course which, for example, has sixteen weeks to guide participants through the basic techniques of woodcuts, etching, dry point, and lithographic techniques, all leading up to a final review of an entire semester's work, will likely not have time for essays or ten-plus-page research papers. This is not to say that information gathering does not take place in the studio setting. It means that the information gathered, how it is used in an assignment, and even the assignment itself take on a different form. Furthermore, while traditional research relies on textual sources, studio art research relies a great deal on primary source material—that is, original artworks by other artists. The question that arises, then, is how librarians serving as liaisons in art departments may support this unique situation? How do they apply the Research as Inquiry frame when the research is rarely transformed into words on a page?

What is the threshold for art students?

Incoming students may come with assumptions that they know how to conduct research in the visual arts. To many it means finding an image on Google and simply giving the barest description of what is in the image or what the item appears to be. Beyond that, they may be confused when asked to analyze further. Rather than returning to the research process and seeking out additional sources of information that would provide a better understanding of the composition and its context, they may resort to "personalization" to fill this gap. For instance, they may begin to discuss how the work made them feel or a give a personal anecdote that, to them, makes the painting relatable, believing that this is what is meant by analysis. Some may try, consciously or unconsciously, to repeat the same design features over and over again, thinking that this also answers the charge of the assignment. An assignment that requires them to draw inspiration from a work may result in an almost carbon copy of the original, with a few minor changes or additions to the overall design, believing that this is the acceptable way to meet the requirement. The challenge here is to understand the difference between fact versus opinion and why the former carries more weight in the academic setting.

The concept of intellectual property can be difficult for the inexperienced visual researcher to grasp as well. Since paintings, architecture, and other visible art forms are very much in the public eye, students may not understand why attribution is necessary. After all, they may reason, everyone knows that Judy Chicago created the installation, "The Dinner Party," or that Frank Lloyd

Wright revolutionized the use of the cantilever in early twentieth-century architecture. If these works are so well known, why must they be attributed? Paradoxically, students may not realize that the "innovative" design element they believe they conceived of all on their own has, in fact, been long attributed to someone living and working several centuries ago. These are issues that the Framework can assist in resolving.

Complicating matters further, some visual arts instructors are also operating under the assumption that their students know how to conduct research successfully. Based on this assumption, they may not provide or have time to provide the necessary groundwork to guide students to a successful research outcome. Some may be unaware of the tools available in the library or be devoted to the notion that the only worthwhile information for their course can be found exclusively in a certain resource format, such as books. The librarian's task then becomes twofold: to assist the students and educate their instructors. To adequately address student needs, it is important to understand how and what kind of information is acquired and used in the arts disciplines.

Information gathering in the arts

While all disciplines require some form of interaction with text-based sources, a significant amount of visual arts research involves looking at works of art, either in physical or photographic form. In the case of art history, this may result in an essay or paper of some type. For a student in an oil painting class, it may influence or inform the style and content of a semester's worth of canvases.

Artists use primary visual resources to create new forms, styles, and techniques. Much like any other discipline, the process draws on the work of others, past and present. Artists study others in their field of concentration who share the same interests in themes, materials, and style. They may also venture into areas of expression that they are not familiar with, or particularly like, to experiment with an eye to improving or altering a particular aspect to suit their own preferences.

Museums and galleries are valuable sources of original artwork. They have been likened to libraries for the visual arts. Large city museums have collections that may range from prehistory to contemporary. Galleries tend to be more focused on a particular style, time period, artist, or group of artists. Artists' collectives may also have exhibition spaces that highlight their members' work. Students can visit these locations, not only to examine the collection but, in some cases, to listen to lectures and speak with the artists themselves. Direct communication with the artists can be invaluable when trying to discern the meaning of the content and the context in which the artists conceived their pieces.

In the case of large-scale installation pieces, students may need to move around the installation itself to make an accurate analysis of why and how the different parts have been assembled. In the case of paintings and prints, they may need to examine surfaces up close to discern the type of medium used and the manner in which it was the applied to the canvas or paper. These important details may be lost or obscured in a photographic reproduction. Multiple visits may be required to flesh out these impressions to capture all the work's elements that are relevant to the student's assignment requirements. This can be tricky, especially if the gallery rotates its exhibits on a regular basis or the piece is part of a traveling exhibition that charges an entrance fee or is on loan and therefore not part of the permanent collection.

Looking at a work of art in a gallery, in a museum, or in a photograph also makes its original context difficult to discern. For instance, the so-called Elgin marbles, originally brightly painted sculpture set several feet above the ground on the Temple of the Parthenon outside of Athens, Greece, are now exhibited at the British Museum. They are displayed at ground level, with many arms, heads, and other parts missing and almost all of the paint worn away. A reconstruction is required to give some idea of how these sculptures looked in the triangular space of the pediment, and even then it requires a fair amount of imagination to recreate the proper context.

The location or physical condition of an object is a potential barrier as well. Students may have neither the time nor the financial resources to travel thousands of miles overseas to view the original. Current world political conditions, security concerns, and military activities may preclude travel, regardless of time and financial ability to do so. The artwork may be undergoing very delicate and involved restoration, or access may be limited to professional scholars, by appointment only. Tragically, there are famous paintings, sculptures, etc., that no longer exist, whether they have been stolen, lost, or destroyed by natural or man-made disasters.

Given these limitations, print resources can prove to be invaluable for filling in the blanks. When the actual object is not physically present and the artist is unavailable, students can gather information via photographs and illustrations. This is not ideal because photographs tend to flatten and distort three-dimensional objects, subtly alter the colors, and disallow the ability to view the object from all available angles. However, the student can quickly record their initial visual impressions to refer to later. Also, whether the assignment culminates in a paper or an oral presentation or an object, some background information may be needed that can only be found by reading text accompanying the image. A reproduction provides more pictorial detail than a one-time sketch, much like a chapter in a book can supplement class notes.

Image databases, such as ARTStor, provide large collections of digitized photographs, covering the entirety of art history. Many databases offer the user the ability for focusing in on a particular section of a composition, thereby allowing for closer examination of brushwork, texture, color, and other smaller details. There may also be an option to gather several images together to be viewed side by side in small groups or folders, enhancing the ability to compare and contrast works that have some connection (historical, stylistic, subject matter) to one another. This is a more immediate information gathering practice, one that better suits the needs of the visual learner and practitioner. The textual information accompanying ARTStor images is kept to bare essentials: artist's name (if available), title, date, cultural affiliation, current location, as well as ownership and copyright information. This deficit can be supplemented with books and articles.

Finally, artists must be able to articulate why they have made certain design choices, to articulate the advantages of one technique over the other, and to explain the inspiration behind a composition. They must be able to present all these ideas in a coherent manner. This is often delivered in oral form in the studio classroom, either with or without an accompanying critique from the instructor and other students. Once a topic has been chosen, the next step is to begin the process of examining the work itself. This is when visual literacy comes into play.

Visual literacy: A brief description

What is visual literacy? Very simply put, it is the "reading" or decoding of images. It is the ability to analyze the various elements of a work of art to identify information and ideas contained therein and place them in context. There are a number of elements that students must consider in order to obtain an accurate analysis, including form, content, and context. This combination of mental as well as physical observation is what Amy Tucker refers to as "intelligent seeing."[2]

A major issue that confronts both instructors and librarians alike is the level of visual literacy students have acquired before they step into the college classroom. Although visual literacy is supposed to be a part of the pre-college curriculum, the concern with meeting other educational standards may push it down the ladder of importance. Primary and secondary art students are generally more focused on production rather than historical/contextual investigation. Although some will have good understanding of the larger history of art, many will have only a rudimentary concept of how to effectively look at and write about it. Often, their exposure to art has been predicated on the "I like/I don't like" approach without any sort of in-depth study of the various elements involved. There is a tendency to "personalize" their responses to art in that a charge to "describe what you see" leaves the door open for a great deal of personal interpretation, much of which will likely have little to do with the work's actual significance or purpose. What was meant to be a visual analysis will morph into a personal narrative about a memory that the composition sparks. As such, the narration becomes an opinion piece, revealing more about the student's likes and dislikes, rather than an exercise in learning about the image itself.

Analyzing art is a challenge, even for those who have had some early experience. The language of inquiry is different for the visual artist as well. The ability to translate a visual object into coherent prose or speech, creating an accurate picture for readers or observers, requires a great deal of practice. For the student who has not had to put what they see with their eyes into words, this is a daunting new problem, particularly if they have not been adequately trained in this type of analysis.

Analysis of the visual object. Form has a number of facets—color and value, line and shape, space, perspective, and the placement of all these elements as a whole to the overall composition. It is arguably the easiest part of the visual analysis process, since these facets are by and large easily identifiable by sight.

The next step is to look at the content of the piece. What sort of composition is it? Are there recognizable figures in it or is it entirely made up of lines, shapes, and colors? If there are figures, what are they and how are they arranged within the picture? What is the setting? What is the message that the artist may be trying to convey? Images from a particular part of the world and in a specific historical time period may have iconography and allusions that must be investigated more thoroughly to be decoded. As an example, the scenes in a medieval altarpiece may be crowded with symbols. Everything from the color of a garment, to a vase of flowers, to the furnishings of an interior scene can be a vehicle for religious messages. Examining the context or circumstances in which the artwork was created can assist in understanding why a composition looks the way it does. The challenge is to take all these characteristics of an artwork and translate them into a verbal or written description. A class may be given a selection of paintings from several different eras to analyze. All may have similar subjects, such as portraits of wealthy individuals. The assignment is to analyze these portraits, explaining how their appearance is representative of the culture or historical era in which they were produced.

Interpretation versus explanation. Edmund Burke Feldman defines interpretation as the viewer's understanding of a work of art, while explanation is the means by which this interpretation is made comprehensible to others.[3] He also identifies and defines fifteen different types of explanations that can be employed.[4] It is common for more than one type to come into play, depending on the unique characteristic of the work in question. For instance, the complex compositions of Faith Ringgold's story quilts utilize material, ideological, and technological types to convey the meaning behind the choice of quilt as medium, the social commentary on African-American life, as well as the skills needed to construct the entire piece.

Visual analysis in action. Studio courses rely on in-class evaluation and review to assess how well the student is progressing. Students must be able to articulate why certain choices in design, technique, and materials were used. While not delivered in written format, these short verbal presentations must be backed up by sound decision making, an understanding of the source material used to plan the design as well as background information on the artist, style, or other source of inspiration that help form the final product.

Peer-reviews are essential elements of the studio experience. Students will evaluate and critique each other's work, pointing out strengths in the piece as well as identifying elements that need improvement. This is essentially visual analysis put into action.

Research as Inquiry and visual literacy

The Framework is broad enough to accommodate many forms of research inquiry; however, at first glance, it would seem difficult to apply such concepts to an assignment which is meant to produce a two- or three-dimensional work of art. In the case of the Research as Inquiry frame,[5] it is tempting to view its knowledge practices as a process that ultimately leads to writing. Although not rigidly defined as such, research is commonly assumed to be the consulting of printed, textual sources, the taking of notes, and the presentation of compiled information in a written format. By contrast, art students prepare for assignments where the end product is visual, often requiring little if any writing during any part of the process. In this context, the challenge for the information professional becomes one of interpretation and application: How to adapt this frame to the gathering of visual information versus textual information? To assess how this works with visual arts research, it is useful to address a few of the Research as Inquiry frame's knowledge practices and dispositions.

The knowledge practices. Most of the frame's knowledge practices appear to fit both studio and non-studio art research, as well as complimenting visual literacy guidelines. Learning to "formulate questions for research based on information gaps or on reexamination of existing, possibly conflicting, information," to "determine an appropriate scope of investigation," and to "synthesize ideas gathered from multiple sources,"[6] are all practices that come into play in visual literacy instruction. If students are charged with studying a particular period of an artist's career, they must decide how much of that period can be reasonably covered in the time allotted, how many works to examine, and which works would be the best to use to meet assignment guidelines.[7] Analysis and interpretation can be easily applied to examining the minute details of an object as well as the content of a book or an article. As has been discussed earlier in this chapter, studio artists draw inspiration from a wide variety of sources, so synthesizing characteristics of each into a new composition is a natural outcome.

Some of the practices may appear less likely to address both studio and non-studio types of research. If the student is examining images or objects almost exclusively, the question may be how "use various research methods, based on need, circumstance, and type of inquiry" or "monitor gathered information and assess for gaps or weaknesses" come into play.[8] However, visual artists also must decide on the scope of their projects and the methods most likely to bring these to a successful end. They may need to explain to an instructor and their classmates why they made certain design choices, backing them up with information supporting these decisions. For instance, evaluating the efficacy of certain new, improved architectural materials for inclusion into a proposed building design or plants appropriate for the climate, soil, and space of a landscape architecture project are cases in point. These examples also speak to the need for simplifying complex information needs into smaller chunks, e.g., a specific building material or a specific plant.

The College Art Association (CAA) Standards for Bachelors in Arts, Fine Arts and Masters in Fine Arts degrees echo many of the practices.[9] These standards, like the Framework, are the scaffold on which art departments build effective, competitive programs to aid student success. Also like the Framework, they are not meant to be prescriptive, but to allow for the varied needs of individual departments. Informed aesthetic judgment and contextual awareness, and experience across other academic disciplines are emphasized as outcomes for successful degree completion. The CAA's exhibition statement encourages exhibitions as a means of "strengthen[ing] the ability to think critically, express ideas creatively, and work conceptually and with thematic consistency, professionalism and technical proficiency,"[10] goals that are supported by the scope, methods, organization, and synthesis-related practices.

Comparison of the CAA Standards with the Research as Inquiry Frame is useful in demonstrating the librarian's value to the visual arts faculty. For example, the CAA Standards emphasize that "BFA graduates should have the opportunity to develop technical competence, informed aesthetic judgment, and an understanding of the context in which contemporary work is created."[11] The librarian can then show how the Research as Inquiry frame supports these goals by engaging instructors in a discussion of the complementary knowledge practices.

The dispositions. By contrast, the frame's dispositions may be harder to reconcile with fine arts research. As with the knowledge practices, several of these dovetail directly with the standards for both visual literacy and the CAA Standards. Each charges the student with considering multiple sources and perspectives, valuing the research process, continuing to seek answers, and try out new, unfamiliar techniques to successfully complete course and degree goals. All these dispositions have obvious applications to any field in the arts.

Two of the dispositions, "appreciate that a question may appear to be simple but still disruptive and important to research" and "demonstrate intellectual humility (i.e., recognize their own intellectual or experiential limitations)" are not as obviously applicable.[12] However, they do come into play during the peer-review process. Students must be willing to take constructive criticism, to consider other perspectives and address questions about the motivations behind their designs from their classmates and instructors. Some will have experienced peer-reviews before, albeit perhaps not as thorough or as critical as those conducted in college-level reviews. They may not see how less-than-positive criticism is meant to help them to grow as artists. By assisting them in critiquing resources, deciding which are appropriate for an assignment, which are not, and why these judgments are made, the librarian can model the value of a review process. Intellectual humility also applies to the gaps in knowledge that students display when attempting to conduct an effective visual analysis or recognizing their limited understanding of visual literacy.

Difficulties arise for studio art students when it comes to addressing issues of intellectual property, ethical and legal issues surrounding the use of visual information, recognizing when they need help, and where to seek out research assistance. The librarian may create activities based on the "follow ethical and legal guidelines in gathering and using information"[13] disposition to foster a better understanding of how intellectual property issues may affect how much of a work they can ethically incorporate into their projects. Once the students' research needs are identified, the academic librarian, through the use of the appropriate practices and/or dispositions, can function as a vital part of the student's investigation process as well as being a contributor to his or her growth as a successful researcher.

The academic librarian's challenge

Owing to the information gathering habits discussed so far, students in the visual arts may bypass the librarian altogether. Reasons for this vary. A studio art student may assume that, since the assignment doesn't have a written element with source citations, a librarian's assistance isn't needed. They may not be aware of a liaison librarian's expertise in the art field and assume that the librarian can't help them. They may even be completely unaware of the art librarian's existence. This can also be true of studio arts faculty, so communicating with faculty is a vital first step in moving toward engaging with their courses.

The next issue is that of time. Faculty have limited time with which to instruct, evaluate, and grade their classes. Convincing them of the necessity to carve out twenty minutes to talk about library resources, let alone an entire fifty-minute class period, is difficult, particularly if the instructor in question has no idea what the art librarian can offer to support/enhance visual art students' research abilities. Embedding in the course, in this author's experience, is one way to allay the instructor's concerns about time constraints.

Although the success of the embedded librarian approach to instructional support and resulting positive impact on student writing is well documented, making a valid case for it in a studio arts course can be a challenge. It is vital to communicate the advantages of embedding with the instructor. For example, I have made the case that my physical presence in the classroom allows me to guide the students' research process immediately. I can also address individual students' research needs as they arise, which has a more positive impact on the development of their information gathering skills than a one-size-fits-all, one-shot instruction session. In this way, my instructional impact is enhanced and I take up less class time.

Another approach I have used involves creating supportive instructional materials for a visual analysis project. For example, students are asked to pick a ceramicist and draw inspiration from a particular piece for a hand-building project. By utilizing the visual analysis steps, the student will need to decide which elements of the artist's piece to retain and which to discard to create an entirely new work. This also provides an opportunity to discuss the differences between synthesizing certain elements from another artists' work, adapting them into new artistic forms, and outright copying. To illustrate this point, I have shown classes ARTStor photos of Chinese paintings side-by-side with works in the Orientalism movement of the nineteenth century. I then have pointed out the way the nineteenth-century artists adapted, reinterpreted, and sometimes misinterpreted certain elements in the Chinese works, creating a new and unique composition.

The flipped classroom method is another valuable tool in this context. The librarian, embedded or not, could work with the course instructor to formulate strategies for analyzing students' initial attempts at information gathering. A possible approach is to have the students explore how professional art photographers use Instagram to promote their work. They would be asked to narrow their focus to single artist, then choose and review one of the artist's photographs. The librarian could then facilitate a class discussion about how the students went about choosing photographs, what effect the Instagram platform had on their choice, and the ways in which they then set about decoding the image.

Student consultations are excellent opportunities to model visual literacy techniques as well as both knowledge practices and dispositions. Librarians can prepare for the consultation with all of these tools and guidelines in mind. Naturally, every student will have different research needs. They may be proficient in analyzing images and their content but unable to discern when further or alternative lines of inquiry are necessary. They may be proficient in searching an image database but unaware of the special features that allow them to zoom in on a particular aspect of the image to enhance small but important details, the careful study of which could alter the plan for their final project.

A variety of tools, outside of the realm of databases, can be called upon to address particular gaps in the student's level of visual literacy. The problem of context, for instance, may be explored, either in the classroom or in the consultation, through the use of video clips or virtual reality sites. The UNESCO Channel on YouTube has many excellent short clips of historically significant sites around the world, including the Mosque at Djenne in Mali, the Mogao Caves in China, and the Alhambra in Spain, to name a few.[14] Showing tourists and locals interacting with the architecture of the site provides valuable insight into the scale, design, and current status in the world community at large. The Lascaux Caves has a particularly excellent virtual tour, which leads the viewer through the entire complex, displaying the cave paintings as they would appear in the real cave. The viewer can pause the tour to examine individual paintings more closely and access additional facts about how they were created as well as possible interpretations of their meaning.[15]

Evaluation is considered by the CAA to be an inherent part of studio practice. The librarian may use those evaluation activities that have been factored in as a regular part of the class. For example, the peer-review process is one way to address the students' progress in the course as well as providing an opportunity to reinforce critical evaluation skills. By observing peer reviews, the students' projects are examined for weaknesses in technique, execution, and content. It can also be an immediate indicator as to whether research instruction during the semester has been effective. The faculty member can provide documentation through measuring the quality of student work as a whole, both before and after the librarian's inclusion in the research process. The librarian's challenge is to review this information, to identify what aspects of their instruction worked well and what did not adequately address students' research needs, and to develop more effective methods of applying the Research as Inquiry frame.

Conclusion

It is clear that the Research as Inquiry frame does, in fact, support the standards, goals, and research needs of students, faculty, and departments in the visual arts. The frame is constructed in such a way as to be adaptable and fluid. As such, it can support the process of visual research, literacy, and coursework, while aligning with departmental goals and national standards. Librarians have the ability to apply the frame to a wide range of instructional activities. The frame can guide both virtual and ground instruction activities, support both written and visual research processes, and allow for a great deal of experimentation and creativity.

This chapter modeled methods in which this threshold concept can be adapted to serve the needs of studio arts students and faculty. This can be accomplished by approaching the knowledge practices and dispositions of the Research as Inquiry frame as truly discipline-neutral. Redefining terms such as "information" to align with the terminology of visual inquiry common to the arts will assist the librarian in creating more effective information literacy instruction tools for studio art research support.

Traditional media will always be important to the studio curriculum. Increasing use of digital media and virtual design will create different avenues of inquiry and expression for students. The fluidity of the Research as Inquiry frame makes it possible to address the evolving research challenges that new, more technologically based techniques pose to visual arts research in the future.

Notes

1. Association of College and Research Libraries (ACRL), *Framework for Information Literacy for Higher Education*, February 2, 2015, http://www.ala.org/acrl/standards/ilframework.
2. Amy Tucker, *Visual Literacy: Writing About Art* (Boston: McGraw Hill, 2002), 25–26.
3. Edmund Burk Feldman, *Practical Art Criticism* (Englewood Cliffs, NJ: Prentice Hall, 1994), 52–55.
4. Ibid.
5. ACRL, *Framework for Information Literacy for Higher Education*.
6. Ibid.
7. Ibid.
8. Ibid.
9. College Art Association, *Standards for the Bachelor of Arts and Bachelor of Fine Arts in Studio Art*, last modified October 23, 2011, http://www.collegeart.org/guidelines/bfa; College Art Association, *MFA Standards*, last modified October 26, 2008, http://www.collegeart.org/guidelines/mfa.

10. College Art Association, *Standards for the Bachelor of Arts and Bachelor of Fine Arts in Studio Art*.
11. Ibid.
12. ACRL, *Framework for Information Literacy for Higher Education*.
13. Ibid.
14. UNESCO YouTube Channel, accessed June 2, 2016, https://www.youtube.com/user/unesco/.
15. Norbert Aujoulet, *Lascaux: A Visit to the Cave*, accessed June 2, 2016, http://www.lascaux.culture.fr/?lng=en#/en/00.xml.

CHAPTER 15*

Integrating the ACRL Threshold Concept Research as Inquiry into Baccalaureate Nursing Education

Kimberly J. Whalen and Suzanne E. Zentz

Introduction

Teaching information literacy skills to nursing students is a shared domain of nursing and library science faculty at Valparaiso University. This collaborative effort commenced in 2012 as faculty worked together to incorporate information literacy instruction within an undergraduate Introduction to Nursing Research for Evidence-Based Practice course. A deliberate effort was made to move away from the preexisting one-shot information science lecture provided by the librarian to multiple learning experiences with corresponding assignments aimed at building information skills of students over the semester. Positive student outcomes were achieved as students' grades on classroom assignments significantly improved. Gaining momentum from

---

* This work is licensed under a Creative Commons Attribution-NonCommercial-ShareAlike 4.0 License, CC BY-NC-SA (https://creativecommons.org/licenses/by-nc-sa/4.0/).

this initial work, nursing and library science faculty examined information literacy skills across the entire College of Nursing and Health Professions (CONHP) curriculum, which resulted in threading information literacy content with associated assignments throughout the sophomore, junior, and senior nursing courses.

Since the development of the ACRL Framework for Information Literacy for Higher Education in 2015, library faculty reevaluated information literacy education at the university and college levels.[1] The language of the Framework was adjusted and related learning outcomes were developed to fit the local learning community. Faculty developed curriculum maps to document the adjusted Framework concepts within common first-year and discipline-specific programs. This chapter describes the evaluation process and application of the Framework and specific threshold concept Research as Inquiry to the nursing discipline in general, as well as baccalaureate nursing courses within the CONHP. Specific assignments directed at reinforcing and mastering the Research as Inquiry frame within the baccalaureate nursing program are presented.

Information literacy and evidence-based practice in nursing

An expectation of baccalaureate nursing education is to prepare nurses to implement evidence-based practice (EBP). There are numerous definitions of EBP, but utilizing research information, applying clinical expertise, and considering patient values are typically common elements among definitions. EBP is a process by which nurses must gather, analyze, and synthesize the appropriate research evidence related to a clinical problem. Using their clinical expertise, nurses must apply this information to the specific patient, considering their preferences and values.[2] The EBP process, which is so vital to nursing practice, is dependent on the acquisition of information literacy skills.

Though not always identified as information literacy, nursing organizations have developed clinical practice standards that include information skill components. The American Association of Colleges of Nursing (AACN) has developed three sets of guidelines for baccalaureate, master's, and doctorate-level programs. These documents, entitled *The Essentials*, guide the development of nursing curricula and include recommendations of core knowledge required of nursing professionals at the various levels of education. At the baccalaureate level, nine essential outcomes are delineated.[3] Information literacy skills are included within these essential outcomes. For instance, Essential III, Scholarship, and Evidence-Based Practice emphasizes that nursing practice must be based on the best evidence. Specific program outcomes are stated reflecting information literacy skills that graduates of baccalaureate programs must achieve. Example outcomes related to information literacy skills include that graduates must be able to evaluate the credibility of sources, retrieve, appraise, and synthesize evidence to improve patient outcomes, integrate the evidence into patient care, and disseminate evidence.

Although the acquisition of information literacy skills is foundational to creating EBP, nurse educators have found teaching these skills to be rather daunting. Historically, emphasis has been placed on teaching the research process with less emphasis on how to access, appraise, synthesize, or utilize evidence. In recent years, nursing programs have begun to emphasize EBP and information literacy skill development within undergraduate nursing research courses.[4] Regardless of the level of EBP and information literacy instruction integrated within curricula, undergraduate nursing students habitually overestimate their information literacy skills, and some have negative attitudes regarding the need to be proficient at these skills.[5] Students struggle to formulate clinical questions, identify related keywords or standardized subject headings, craft effective search strategies within databases, and critically appraise and synthesize search results.

The difficulty in teaching EBP process skills within nursing education programs is evident when investigating practicing nurses' EBP knowledge. Over ten years ago, Pravikoff, Pierce, and Tanner surveyed 1,097 practicing nurses regarding their readiness to participate in EBP.[6] The researchers found that almost half of participants were not familiar with the term "evidence-based practice." Furthermore, more than half had never identified a clinical problem for research or searched a major database for evidence. Major barriers to implementing EBP identified by the nurses were a lack of time to implement and lack of value of the EBP process. Some movement has been made in recent years, as reflected in a descriptive survey performed by Melnyk and Fineout-Overholt.[7] Nurses who were members of the American Nurses Association were sent a survey aimed at assessing the current state of EBP implementation across the United States. Some findings from this more recent survey were more encouraging than the earlier findings. In the more recent study, nurses indicated wanting more education about and increased access to EBP information. Although nurses identified some of the same barriers to EBP as indicated in the earlier study, such as not enough time, knowledge, or support for EBP, nurses also indicated new barriers, such as lack of available evidence and resistance from colleagues. This shift indicates that nurses are interested in implementing EBP but need additional education and support to achieve this goal.

Nurse educators must ensure that baccalaureate-prepared nurses are not only knowledgeable of EBP but prepared to implement EBP. Thus curricula must be carefully designed to introduce foundational information literacy skills and concepts early in programs and gradually build to discipline-specific activities. Nursing and library science faculty who collaborate to design and implement a cohesive curriculum provide opportunities for students to practice these skills over time and thus facilitate students' ability to apply these skills to nursing practice.

Adaptation of ACRL Framework for Valparaiso community

While the new Framework and corresponding dispositions were being discussed within the broader information science discipline, Valparaiso University library faculty began internal discussions of how the Framework best suited the university's specific learning community. An Information Literacy Advisory Committee (IL Committee) comprised of six library faculty, the Director of Writing and the Director of Faculty Development was established along with a Curriculum Committee of six library faculty. The IL Committee agreed that a university-wide information literacy program based on the Framework should be developed. Building on IL Committee conversations, the Curriculum Committee met regularly to review the six original ACRL frames and develop a university-wide information literacy program, including objectives and learning indicators. The original frames, knowledge practices, and dispositions were adjusted, and an additional set of learning objectives for the Information Has Value frame were added to the Valparaiso University program document.[8]

Table 15.1. Valparaiso University Information Literacy Program Objectives, March 2015	
Valparaiso University Information Literacy Program Objectives	The information literate student:
1. Scholarship as Conversation	Recognizes that scholarship is an ongoing communal conversation in order to negotiate meaning and ethically contribute to the scholarly discourse
2. Research as Inquiry	Conducts research across a spectrum of inquiry in order to ask increasingly complex questions whose answers develop new questions or lines of inquiry

Table 15.1. Valparaiso University Information Literacy Program Objectives, March 2015	
3. Authority is Constructed and Contextual	Weighs markers of authority in order to determine whether a source satisfies the information need
4. Information Creation as a Process	Recognizes how a source's format is influenced by processes of creation, production, and dissemination in order to fully evaluate quality, relevance, and perspective
5. Searching as Strategic Exploration	Approaches information gathering with a sense of adventure, persistence, and flexibility in order to access a broad range of sources that informs the inquiry
6. Information Has Value	Operates within the information creation and dissemination value system in order to ethically participate in scholarly and social conversations through synthesis and attribution. Accepts that information, including personal information, can be a commodity in order to recognize bias, consider excluded perspectives within the information marketplace and curate digital footprints.

Research as Inquiry and nursing

Due to parallels between information literacy and the EBP process, the threshold concept Research as Inquiry, with corresponding knowledge practices and dispositions, can be used as a foundation for teaching components of the EBP process to undergraduate nursing students. According to Melnyk and Fineout-Overholt, there are seven critical steps of EBP: (0) creating a spirit of inquiry, (1) asking the clinical question, (2) searching for the best evidence, (3) appraising and synthesizing the evidence, (4) integrating the evidence with clinical expertise and patient preferences, (5) evaluating outcomes, and (6) disseminating outcomes.[9] The first four steps of the EBP process align nicely with the university's Research as Inquiry frame and learning indicators. Although Melnyk and Fineout-Overholt discussed the importance of laying the foundation for inquiry in the initial version of their EBP model, creating a spirit of inquiry was not identified as a specific step, due to the vital nature of this process, it was later added.

Table 15.2. Research as Inquiry within the Valparaiso University Information Literacy Program Objective and Learning Indicators, March 2015	
Valparaiso University Research as Inquiry	Conducts research across a spectrum of inquiry in order to ask increasingly complex questions whose answers develop new questions or lines of inquiry. a. Formulates questions for research based on information gaps or reexamination of existing, possibly conflicting, information b. Breaks complex questions into simple ones and focuses the scope of the research c. Uses a variety of research methods, based on need, circumstance, and type of inquiry d. Draws reasonable conclusions based on the analysis and interpretation of information e. Uses research appropriately to make decisions and take action (i.e., uses evidence to inform practice) f. Is willing to refine or change the direction, method, or scope of research based on new insights g. Demonstrates intellectual humility by recognizing their own intellectual or experiential limitations, interpreting results and making claims appropriate to their level of knowledge (e.g., student does not have expertise after a cursory encounter with information)

Step 0 of the EBP process, creating a spirit of inquiry, is foundational. For EBP to exist, the environment must be open to questioning. The culture must encourage asking, "Why?" Such an environment is consistent with educational settings. Liberal arts and sciences are the foundation of baccalaureate nursing programs. As part of the common first-year program, all Valparaiso University freshmen are encouraged to develop research questions and search for the best information to address their inquiries. As nursing students progress to discipline-specific courses in their sophomore year, questioning is encouraged and skills are refined. This initial stage of the EBP process is consistent with the Research as Inquiry frame, which welcomes questioning and anticipates disagreement. Mastery of this frame requires an open climate where differences can be discussed freely and new ideas are readily considered. Unfortunately, this milieu does not consistently transcend beyond educational institutions into healthcare organizations. Practicing nurses do not always feel free to question practice within healthcare organizations. When questioning is discouraged, and support is lacking, EBP is unlikely to be sustained; however, when nurses implement EBP in a supportive environment, quality patient care is achieved.[10] Educators must not only cultivate inquiry within students but also arm them with information about barriers to EBP in the real world and ideas to overcome them.

The next step of the EBP process, step 1, asking the clinical question, includes an iterative process of asking increasingly complex questions which are a direct parallel to the threshold concept of Research as Inquiry. Question formation typically begins with a general topic of concern or clinical problem and gradually morphs into a sophisticated question. A standard question format used in EBP is PICOT, which is an acronym that includes all the key components of a clinical question: population, intervention, comparison, outcome, and timeframe.[11] Identifying all these components focuses the clinical problem and thus the literature search. Searching for the best evidence, step 2 of the EBP process, involves finding the best information from a variety of sources to address a clinical problem. As students search, they modify their search elements until they have achieved their best search, which then can be duplicated in multiple information sources. A well-crafted PICOT question facilitates finding the best evidence to address a specific clinical problem. Reflection is a key component of this step. Each element of the PICOT question must be analyzed to determine the key factors regarding the clinical problem. There is overlap between the Research as Inquiry and Searching as Strategic Exploration frames in regard to the EBP process. Both frames address portions of step 2 of the EBP process, searching for the best evidence. Continual refinement of the PICOT or clinical question in regard to new evidence discovered while searching is a particular focus of Research as Inquiry.

Appraising and synthesizing the evidence, step 3 of the EBP process, and integrating the evidence with clinical expertise and patient preferences, step 4, directly engage the researcher with the evidence found. It is not enough to just locate evidence; the EBP process requires the appraisal, synthesis, and application of evidence to nursing practice. These EBP steps are fundamental to the Research as Inquiry and Searching as Strategic Exploration frames. Both frames address the need to draw reasonable conclusions based on the information found. Systematic reviews, integrative reviews, meta-analysis, and other forms of synthesis enable researchers to identify common research themes and findings efficiently. The Research as Inquiry frame encourages researchers to use information to take action. Depending on the clinical environment in which they practice, the evidence utilization elements of the EBP process can be a significant challenge for students and nurses.

Curriculum mapping of Research as Inquiry

To better understand how the Research as Inquiry frame was integrated within the undergraduate nursing program, a visual representation of the curriculum in the form of a curriculum map was developed. Curriculum maps document how information is scaffolded throughout a program. Specific information regarding introducing concepts, teaching content, administering assessments, and examining outcomes are documented.[12] Recent campus-wide assessment initiatives used curriculum mapping, which provided a common format to follow.

The curriculum map aligned Research as Inquiry student learning indicators and assessments with each baccalaureate nursing course. During development of the curriculum map, extensive discussion about indicators occurred until consensus was achieved regarding how to interpret the indicator for the nursing discipline. For instance, *indicator a: formulates questions for research based on information gaps or reexamination of existing, possibly conflicting, information*, was contemplated considerably until it was agreed that formulating questions would not be narrowly restricted to a formulation of formal clinical or PICOT questions. The interpretation used for nursing would include activities where students analyze broad topics and narrow them to more manageable sub-topics or specific clinical problems. Additionally, independent interpretations of *indicator e: uses research appropriately to make decisions and take action, i.e., uses evidence to inform practice*, initially varied. After much deliberation, it was agreed that "inform practice" would be applied to overall nursing practice and not limited only to an application within a clinical environment.

Through an examination of course syllabi, assignments, and library lesson plans for each course, the nursing and library science faculty determined how content was being delivered and scaffolded across the curriculum. These artifacts were analyzed to determine if Research as Inquiry concepts were introduced *I*, reinforced *R*, or mastered *M* within each course. Placing an I within the curriculum map indicates students are introduced to the concepts/skills. An R indicates the concept/skills are reinforced, and students are provided opportunities to practice. Placing an M within the map indicates students will have mastered the concepts/skills at an appropriate level. A similar exercise had been accomplished previously by the Curriculum Committee for common first-year programs. The committee determined that all Research as Inquiry learning indicators were introduced within the first-year. Nursing courses at Valparaiso University begin in the sophomore year, thus for this curriculum map, concepts were either reinforced or mastered within nursing courses. To determine which student learning indicators were achieved and at what level they were achieved within each nursing course, an independent analysis of course content was followed by the comparison of the individual assessments. If disagreements occurred, further re-evaluation of course artifacts and discussion took place until the pair reached consensus. Courses are noted by number in the map depicted in Table 3. The University uses a fairly standard system whereby courses numbered 200 are sophomore level, 300 are junior level, and 400 are senior level. Nursing 415 is entitled, Introduction to Nursing Research for Evidence-based Practice and contains much more comprehensive information regarding Research as Inquiry than previous courses. Nursing 460 Public Health Nursing is considered the capstone course of the program.

Table 15.3. Map of Research as Inquiry within select nursing courses

Research as Inquiry Student Learning Indicators	Undergraduate Nursing Courses								
	201	210	341	354	356	425	470	415	460
a. Formulates questions for research based on information gaps or reexamination of existing, possibly conflicting, information	R	R	R		R	R	R	M	M
b. Breaks complex questions into simple ones and focuses the scope of the research	R	R	R		R	R	R	M	M
c. Uses a variety of research methods, based on need, circumstance, and type of inquiry	R	R	R		R	R	R	M	M

Table 15.3. Map of Research as Inquiry within select nursing courses

Research as Inquiry Student Learning Indicators	Undergraduate Nursing Courses								
	201	210	341	354	356	425	470	415	460
d. Draws reasonable conclusions based on analysis and interpretation of information	R	R	R	R	R	R	R	M	M
e. Uses research appropriately to make decisions and take action		R	R	R	R	R		M	M
f. Is willing to refine or change the direction, method, or scope of research based on new insights	R	R	R			R	R	M	M
g. Demonstrates intellectual humility by recognizing own intellectual or experiential limitations, interpreting results and making claims appropriate to the level of knowledge	R	R	R	R	R	R	R	M	M

Teaching methods and assignments

Specific strategies targeted at reinforcing and mastering the Research as Inquiry frame are integrated throughout sophomore, junior, and senior-level nursing coursework. Direct responsibility for teaching and reinforcing content is shared. At times, library faculty directly engage with students, and in other instances, nursing faculty oversees activities and assessments with support from library faculty.

Sophomore level coursework within Nursing 201: Professional Role in Nursing and Nursing 210: Therapeutic Interventions for the Professional Nurse reinforce the Research as Inquiry concepts introduced in the common first-year programs and focus on the concept's specific role within nursing. In Nursing 201, small groups of students select a topic, such as the self-care of nurses, from a list provided by their professor. Students then identify, access, and utilize professional nursing information sources to develop a ten-minute presentation used to teach their peers about the topic. Groups are expected to determine the scope of research needed to develop an informative presentation for other sophomore nursing students. As each group becomes knowledgeable about their topic, they examine the information found for conflicts or gaps. Groups are required to identify and utilize at least one primary research or EBP article within their multiple references.

The nursing librarian meets with Nursing 201 students for fifty minutes. The session takes place in the library's computer classroom. Students prepare for the in-person session by: reading a PowerPoint that describes the nursing information publishing cycle; viewing brief videos about identifying keywords, using standardized CINAHL and MeSH subject headings, developing search strategies within journal databases and the library's discovery tool; and reading an explanation of key elements of a scholarly, peer-reviewed journal article. During the in-person session, each student is given a recent print nursing journal to evaluate. Class discussion focuses on how a spirit of inquiry within nursing is encouraged and supported within nursing journals and information sources. Another in-class activity gives students an opportunity to break a topic into keywords, brainstorm synonyms, and develop a search for information using multiple keywords, phrases, and limiters within the CINAHL database. Throughout the activity, the need to evaluate and continually adjust research strategies as knowledge of the topic develops is stressed. Students struggle to accept that the first search for information probably will not yield the most relevant results. Working together to adjust multiple inquiries exposes students to an iterative process.

Junior level coursework, including Nursing 341: Psychiatric Mental Health Nursing, Nursing 354: Nursing Care of Adults I, and Nursing 356: Nursing Care of Adults II, further reinforce Research as Inquiry concepts. In Nursing 354, the librarian meets with students for fifty minutes. The session takes place in the standard course classroom. Class discussion focuses on the importance of a spirit of inquiry within evidence-based practice as outlined by Melnyk and Fineout-Overholt.[13] Discussion focuses on the importance of evidence, how evidence is analyzed within nursing, and various evidence hierarchy systems common within nursing. During the session, each student is given a print copy of a Cochrane Library systematic review, an evidence summary from the Joanna Briggs Institute EBP Database, and a National Guideline Clearinghouse guideline summary to evaluate. At first, students find it difficult to understand why and how information is categorized as evidence. They question the need to search for evidence in sources other than CINAHL. While reviewing each evidence type, students recognize that new insights can be identified through the use of multiple information tools. Throughout the session, the importance of applying evidence to nursing practice is emphasized.

In Nursing 356, students identify a clinical nursing problem or nursing intervention they have witnessed within a clinical experience such as the best practice regarding urinary catheter removal. Students are expected to use a variety of research methods to identify the current state of evidence related to the problem or intervention. Students interpret the information found and describe how the research was or was not incorporated into the care of their patient. This experience can be troublesome for students as it brings to light the dichotomy between research and practice. The reflective elements of this assignment encourage students to utilize research to inform and potentially adjust future nursing practice.

Senior-level coursework within Nursing 425—Nursing Care of the Childrearing Family, Nursing 470: Management and Leadership Strategies for the Professional Nurse, Nursing 415: Introduction to Nursing Research for Evidence-based Practice, and Nursing 460: Public Health Nursing—enable students to practice and master Research as Inquiry concepts. Students in Nursing 415 are asked to research a specific clinical problem individually, document the search strategy used to find primary evidence, and reflect on the research process. Throughout the process, students focus the scope of their research on elements within the clinical problem. While conducting their research, students complete a systematic search worksheet which helps guide and record their process.[14] Reflecting on why evidence was selected, the difficulties encountered during the research process, and what the researcher will do differently the next time they conduct research helps students recognize the extent of their skills and opportunities for growth.

The culminating assignment in Nursing 415 requires students to work in groups on an evidence-based practice project. After groups are given a topic, they create a PICOT question, conduct an extensive search for varying levels of evidence, analyze findings, and compile an evidence summary of results. Transforming a topic into a PICOT question requires students to ask increasingly complex questions. For example, the topic of identifying intimate partner violence in pregnant women could result in the PICOT question, "In pregnant women, how does the use of an established screening tool as compared to an in-person interview identify intimate partner violence over a six month period?" Students must include all components of the PICOT question (population, intervention, comparison intervention, outcome, and timeframe) which results in an extremely targeted question that greatly facilitates their literature search. While synthesizing information found, students learn new insights which enable them to suggest a change in nursing practice or a need for further research on the topic. Groups complete a systematic search worksheet that records their process and requires reflection of their work. In addition to creating an evidence summary and documenting their research process, each group develops and presents a scholarly poster summarizing their work. These assignments, and other 400-level course assignments, encourage students to use a variety of research methods and regularly appraise the information found.

The nursing librarian meets with Nursing 415 classes multiple times during the semester. Two thirty-minute sessions take place in the standard course classroom, and two fifty-minute sessions take place in the library's computer classroom. A combination of lecture, small group instruction, and active learning exercises are utilized. During the first session, the discussion focuses on the importance of developing a systematic search for information across multiple information sources. The librarian reinforces systematic research methods within CINAHL, Medline, and other primary sources of information. In a large group, students brainstorm potential keywords, synonyms, and standardized subject headings. Students individually research a topic provided and document their research process and results. During the second session, systematic research methods within higher-level sources of information, such as The Cochrane Library, the Joanna Briggs Institute EBP Database, and the National Guideline Clearinghouse, are reinforced. Student volunteers demonstrate research strategies using multiple keywords, at least one subject heading, and multiple limiters across multiple information sources. Discussion focuses on the need to analyze and adjust the research process. Though similar content had been introduced and reinforced in sophomore and junior-level courses, students in their senior year still struggle to master these skills. Repeated exposure, practice, and reinforcement facilitates mastery of these abilities.

During the third session, student groups are assessed on their understanding of Research as Inquiry concepts and skills. Modeled after the television show *The Amazing Race*, groups compete to answer questions or demonstrate a process. Questions range from identifying appropriate MeSH headings within various information sources to leveling samples of evidence provided using a particular evidence hierarchy. Students reflect on the processes used to develop their conclusions. This session puts student skills on display and exposes areas in need of improvement, but since students are working in groups and the activity is not graded, the session is a safe environment for experimentation. During the fourth session, a mini-lecture on the importance of a systematic search is followed by small group activity. Student groups finalize their PICOT, brainstorm potential keywords, synonyms, and subject headings related to their PICOT, conduct preliminary research, analyze the information found, and reflect on their research processes. The librarian and nursing professor are both present in the library's computer classrooms to provide feedback. Groups often have difficulty revising their PICOT question as more evidence is identified. Frustration leads to the realization that the research process can be a time-consuming one. Groups, and individual members, "get it" at different times, which makes individualized follow-up instruction key to helping all progress throughout the process.

Since Research as Inquiry concepts have been scaffolded throughout the nursing curriculum, graduating nursing students should be able to demonstrate they have mastered the university's information literacy program objectives and indicators. Course assessments, whether administered by nursing faculty or library science faculty, in the form of papers, projects, presentations, quizzes, and examinations provide evidence of student learning.

Lessons learned from collaboration

Long before the Framework was introduced, nursing and library science faculty at Valparaiso University partnered to integrate and assess information literacy skills within the undergraduate nursing program. This five-year collaboration introduced both faculty groups to concepts, practices, and standards of another discipline. Working together to identify mutual expectations enabled faculty to learn about and speak a shared language. After the Framework was introduced, nursing and library science faculty evaluated the existing information literacy program using the new approach. The Framework was viewed as an adaption of the previous ACRL standards, not as an entirely new entity. Thus, it provided an alternative way to think about, talk about, and assess faculty work and student learning. Due to the Framework's less prescriptive and more conceptual nature, the frames easily translated to the nursing discipline. The Research as Inquiry frame more completely captures the complex iterative process inherent in this questioning phase and thus better aligns with the initial steps of nursing's EBP process. Additionally, the Framework's use of threshold concepts highlights those difficult skills that students typically struggle to master. Nursing students habitually underestimate the complexity of the EBP process. After multiple attempts and continual refinement, students begin to "get" the process. This cyclical nature was less evident in the ACRL standards. Although the standards were comprehensive in scope, they portrayed a more linear process that is less reflective of the EBP process.

In the end, faculty concluded that regardless of the label, whether a theory, a concept, a frame, a standard, or a step, the concepts defined within the Framework were being addressed within the existing nursing information literacy program. Although no major revisions to the information literacy program were warranted, use of the Framework validated the program's comprehensiveness.

Nursing, like library science, is a complex combination of theory and practical application. The university's Research as Inquiry frame, the overall ACRL Framework, the spirit of inquiry step within the EBP process, and the AACN Essentials for Baccalaureate Programs share similar complexities. To relate the Framework with student learning, librarians must first understand how information literacy applies to other disciplines. Once this groundwork is accomplished, information literacy skills can be integrated within specific programs of study and teaching methods and assignments to introduce, practice, and master the skills can be designed.

Lastly, assessment of student learning objectives by discipline and library faculty must be carried out continually to evaluate the effectiveness of the information literacy program. Utilizing common assessment tools, such as the university's curriculum mapping format, enables the work of the collaborating faculty to be incorporated into the broader university-wide assessment discussion.

Conclusion

Information literacy is as relevant to the nursing discipline as it is to the library science discipline. The Framework illuminates the similarities between library science's information literacy and nursing's EBP process. Key concepts that cause students to ponder and reflect are the focus of the Framework. This approach on threshold concepts facilitates collaboration between disciplines so that comprehensive information literacy programs for specific disciplines may be developed, implemented, and evaluated. Concepts and theories from disciplines outside of library science can be easily aligned with the Framework, allowing for the creation of information literacy programs that address multidisciplinary content. Integrating multiple learning experiences across curricula will build information literacy skills and facilitate students' ability to master critical EBP steps and the threshold concept of Research as Inquiry.

Notes

1. Association of College and Research Libraries (ACRL), *Framework for Information Literacy for Higher Education*, February 2, 2015, http://www.ala.org/acrl/standards/ilframework.
2. Nola A. Schmidt and Janet M. Brown, "What is Evidence-Based Practice?" in *Evidence-Based Practice for Nurses: Appraisal and Application of Research,* eds. Nola A. Schmidt and Janet M. Brown (Burlington: Jones & Bartlett Learning, 2015), 3–41.
3. American Association of Colleges of Nursing, *The Essentials of Baccalaureate Education for Professional Nursing Practice*, http://www.aacn.nche.edu/education-resources/essential-series.
4. Mary K. McCurry and Diane C. Martins, "Teaching Undergraduate Nursing Research: A Comparison of Traditional and Innovative Approaches for Success with Millennial Learners," *The Journal of Nursing Education* 49, no. 5 (2010): 276–279; Mary Anne Meeker, Janice M. Jones, and Nancy A. Flanagan, "Teaching Undergraduate Nursing Research from an Evidence-Based Practice Perspective," *The Journal of Nursing Education* 47, no. 8 (2008): 376–379; Regina M. Phillips and Susan H. Bonsteel, "The Faculty and Information Specialist Partnership: Stimulating Student Interest and Experiential Learning," *Nurse Educator* 35, no. 3 (2010): 136–138.
5. Denise R. Denison and Diane Montgomery, "Annoyance or Delight? College Students' Perspectives on Looking for Information," *Journal of Academic Librarianship* 38, no. 6 (2012): 380–90; Stephanie Rosenblatt, "They Can Find It, But They Don't Know What to Do With It: Describing the Use of Scholarly Literature by Undergraduate Students," *Journal of Information Literacy* 4, no. 2 (2010): 50–61.
6. Diane S. Pravikoff, Susan T. Pierce, and Annelle B. Tanner, "Evidence-Based Practice Readiness Study Supported by Academy Nursing Informatics Experts Panel," *Nursing Outlook* 53, no. 1 (2005): 49–50.
7. Bernadette Mazurek Melnyk, Ellen Fineout-Overholt, Lynn Gallagher-Ford, and Louise Kaplan, "The State of Evidence-Based Practice in US Nurses: Critical Implications for Nurse Leaders and Educators," *Journal of Nursing Administration* 42, no. 9 (2012): 410–417.
8. Valparaiso University Christopher Center Library Services, *Information Literacy Program Objectives and Learning Indicators*, http://libguides.valpo.edu/informationliteracy.
9. Bernadette Mazurek Melnyk and Ellen Fineout-Overholt, "Making the Case for Evidence-Based Practice and Cultivating a Spirit of Inquiry," in *Evidence-Based Practice in Nursing & Healthcare: A Guide to Best Practice,* eds. Bernadette Mazurek Melnyk and Ellen Fineout-Overholt (Philadelphia: Lippincott Williams & Wilkins, 2011), 3–24.
10. Bernadette Mazurek Melnyk, Ellen Fineout-Overholt, Susan B. Stillwell, and Kathleen M. Williamson, "Igniting a Spirit of Inquiry: An Essential Foundation for Evidence-Based Practice," *American Journal of Nursing* 109, no. 11 (2009): 49–52.
11. Susan B. Stillwell, Ellen Fineout-Overholt, Bernadette Mazurek Melnyk, and Kathleen M. Williamson, "Asking the Clinical Question: A Key Step in Evidence-Based Practice," *American Journal of Nursing* 110, no. 3 (2010): 58–61.
12. Grant Wiggins and Jay McTighe, *Schooling by Design: Mission, Action, and Achievement.* (Alexandria: Association for Supervision and Curriculum Development, 2007).

13. Mazurek Melnyk and Fineout-Overholt, "Making the Case for Evidence-Based Practice and Cultivating a Spirit of Inquiry."
14. Kimberly J. Whalen and Suzanne E. Zentz, "Teaching Systematic Searching in a Baccalaureate Nursing Research Course," *Worldviews on Evidence-Based Nursing* 12, no. 4 (2015): 246–248.

CHAPTER 16*

Action Research as Inquiry for Education Students

Samantha Godbey

As an education librarian and former teacher, when I consider the impact of the Framework for Information Literacy for Higher Education[1] (Framework) on my instruction, I consider its potential impact on my students in several different roles—as students, educators, and scholars. In fact, these roles overlap for my students during their degree programs, as most of them participate in field placements in K-12 schools while pursuing their degrees. Helping students gain the skills and confidence to approach research in their coursework and beyond is a key focus of my work, and the Research as Inquiry threshold concept stands out as significant and useful in approaching discussions about research with my students.

This threshold concept can be challenging to integrate into course assignments, as my undergraduate teacher education majors do few research-based assignments during their program. Resources are often provided to them, and the latter portion of their coursework emphasizes practical training via fieldwork and student teaching placements. I, however, firmly believe that we should ensure that all students are prepared to not only search but to do research, if not especially those professionals who will be teaching and working in other roles with our nation's children.

The University of Nevada, Las Vegas (UNLV), where I work, is situated in the center of the fifth largest school district in the nation and has one of the

---

* This work is licensed under a Creative Commons Attribution 4.0 License, CC BY (https://creativecommons.org/licenses/by/4.0/).

most diverse student bodies in the nation. The diversity of the student body and the school district was one of my main motivations in coming to this university. My own graduate studies in education prepared me to serve as an English teacher in multicultural, urban schools, so my approach to librarianship is reflective, critical, and grounded in an awareness of the diversity of student experiences and the wide-reaching impact of the work my students do.

At UNLV Libraries, our librarians strive to be partners in education. For me, engaging with the Framework is an opportunity to approach my work critically by actively considering what the troublesome points in learning are likely to be for my students—from undergraduate through doctoral students—and adjusting instruction accordingly. For librarians, asking a question and answering that question is rarely seen as a point-to-point process and, therefore, Research as Inquiry is one of the easiest of the Framework's threshold concepts for librarians themselves to grasp. However, for my outcomes-oriented students, this concept is more difficult. As articulated in the Framework, this threshold concept posits that: "Research is iterative and depends upon asking increasingly complex or new questions whose answers in turn develop additional questions or lines of inquiry in any field."[2]

That said, this threshold concept does pose challenges for librarians as well. In my experience, many librarians conflate the Research as Inquiry and Search as Strategic Exploration threshold concepts. To me, the distinction between research, i.e., the act of engaging in inquiry via formal and informal methods, and search, the act of locating sources, is a necessary and important one. Separating "research" from "search" provides an opportunity to separate the process of locating information from the processes by which we create new knowledge and understanding.

In this chapter, I explore Research as Inquiry within the context of the field of education by aligning this threshold concept with action and practitioner research, which are practiced in the field of education, as well as library and information science. I argue that the Research as Inquiry threshold concept offers a way of thinking about research that aligns with the values of both our fields and provides motivation for discussion about research. Furthermore, thinking of Research as Inquiry as a threshold concept acknowledges the troublesome nature of research itself and of accepting one's potential as a researcher and scholar. I conclude the chapter with suggestions for how one might approach incorporating this concept into one's instruction and other interactions with students from the undergraduate to graduate level.

Overview of Research as Inquiry

As I have already noted, Research as Inquiry presents a challenge to my students. Research has been defined as, "Study or investigation, in an organized and thorough manner, to establish concepts, principles, and facts."[3] This definition offers a traditional, linear vision of research that, while it accommodates the potential difficulty of the research process, establishes research as a direct process with a defined outcome. My students struggle with even this straightforward mode of research, particularly in how to be organized and thorough in their investigation of a topic. However, the threshold concept of Research as Inquiry problematizes this traditional notion of research by stating that research is iterative in nature. The frame refers to a "spectrum of inquiry" that ranges from simple to more sophisticated questions. Novice learners must "acquire strategic perspectives on inquiry and a greater repertoire of investigative methods" in order to successfully engage with this full spectrum of inquiry.[4] The strategies my students and professors frequently request for approaching even simple information searches can be applied across this spectrum of inquiry. Nonetheless, for many, accepting the idea of research as a more complex, inquiry-based practice remains difficult.

Key knowledge practices for this frame include formulating research questions, determining the scope of research, utilizing a variety of research methods to gather information, organizing that information, and drawing conclusions based on the synthesis, analysis, and interpretation of that information. Embedded within each of these knowledge practices is additional language that emphasizes the iterative, potentially complex process of meaningful research. For example, the knowledge practice regarding the formulation of questions states that this must be done "based on information gaps or on reexamination of existing, possibly conflicting, information." Questions must not be formed and left unexamined due to the information one discovers; they must, importantly, be reexamined and re-formed. The use of research methods should be "based on need, circumstance, and type of inquiry." The information gathered should be organized not only in logical but "meaningful" ways. Each of these knowledge practices leads a researcher to "consider research as open-ended exploration and engagement with information."[5]

As with students in many disciplines, the questions I am asked are often focused on the nuts and bolts of locating materials, usually articles, and are presented as "I need five articles on the topic of…" or "I need qualitative articles from the past five years on this topic for this age group." When my students are this assignment-focused, how can I prepare them to maintain intellectual curiosity in the face of the day-to-day challenges of teaching? Why should this matter to them? How can I motivate them to explore this troublesome concept?

Especially disruptive within this frame is the notion that there are "problems or questions in a discipline… that are open or unresolved," and that the "process of inquiry extends beyond the academic world to the community at large." It is in this idea that I find the Research as Inquiry threshold concept to be especially important to these education students who are studying and entering a field with so many unresolved questions, from what teaching strategies will be effective to larger educational policy issues. It is through helping education students to develop dispositions such as "valu[ing] intellectual curiosity in developing questions and learning new investigative methods"[6] that we can best prepare them to successfully engage in inquiry as postsecondary students and, as important, prepare them to engage in inquiry out in the field.

Research among educators

The importance of research and inquiry are documented in the field, notably within the Code of Ethics of the American Educational Research Association (AERA).[7] This code "sets forth the ethical principles and standards that govern the professional work of education researchers."[8] It is "intended to provide guidance that informs and is helpful to education researchers in their research, teaching, service, and related professional work," acknowledging the intertwined nature of those aspects of an educator's work.[9] I focus here on the AERA code and not any of the applicable accreditation or professional standards because I work with students preparing to become not only teachers but also administrators, counselors, higher education faculty and staff, and others. The common thread for all these future professional positions is the opportunity for research, and in particular the possibility for action research, particularly among those who do not pursue a traditional research-based degree such as a PhD.

The AERA Code of Ethics identifies five guiding principles for educational research: professional competence; integrity; professional, scientific, and scholarly responsibility; respect for people's rights, dignity, and diversity; and social responsibility. Within the first principle regarding professional competence, educational researchers "recognize the need for ongoing education in order to remain professionally competent; and they utilize the appropriate scientific, scholarly, professional, technical, and administrative resources needed to ensure competence in their professional activities."[10] In other words, educational researchers should continually attempt to increase their professional competence via research and scholarly activities. The fifth principle regarding social responsibility reminds educators of "their professional and scientific responsibility to the communities and societies in which they live and work. They apply and make public their knowledge in order to contribute to the public good. When undertaking research, they strive to advance scientific and scholarly knowledge and to serve the public good."[11]

Educational researchers are encouraged to see research as an integral part of their service to the profession. I highlight the first and last guiding principles due to their alignment with practitioner and action research.

Practitioner and action research

The term practitioner research is often used interchangeably with action research and will mostly be treated as such in this chapter. However, in the literature practitioner research is generally more broadly defined. Peter Jarvis, author of the seminal book on practitioner research, for example, defines practitioner-researchers simply as "practitioners who do research."[12] He notes that practitioner research is a logical outcome in professions such as education and nursing, in which the knowledge one gains during training is insufficient, as one must participate in ongoing learning during the practice of that profession.[13] The definitions of practitioner and action research are intertwined. Kemmis notes, for example, that "Action research aims at changing three things: practitioners' *practices*, their *understandings* of their practices, and the *conditions* in which they practice."[14]

I note the term practitioner research especially because of its use in the field of library science. Watson-Boone, for example, provides an overview of practitioner research and an analysis of twenty-four librarian practitioner-researcher articles, noting that practitioner-research is as well-aligned with librarianship as with nursing or education.[15] She lists six methods for practitioner-research, including action research and case studies, offering a guide for librarians seeking to pursue this kind of research. This is important, she argues, because "Practitioner research by academic librarians demonstrates, and acknowledges, involvement in a learning society."[16] Others have also highlighted the need for increased practitioner involvement in research among library and information science professionals,[17] stating that "The presence of librarian practitioner-researchers is crucial if evidence based library and information practice is to move forward in a practical as well as theoretical way."[18]

The term "action research" is most often applied specifically to teachers involved in conducting practitioner research in order to improve their practice. A teacher might, for example, conduct research within his or her classroom on methods to improve student engagement. Johnson defines action research as "the process of studying a real school or classroom situation to understand and improve the quality of actions or instruction."[19] Regardless of the field in which it is conducted, action research is intimately linked with the idea and goal of "change" and improvement.[20] Jacobs and Cooper, for example, note that "action research involves teachers in making change happen" with regard to their teaching and student learning.[21] Dickens and Watkins state that the essential goal of action research is "to improve and to involve."[22] Kemmis refers to action research as "a practice-changing practice."[23]

Several authors note the importance of action research in addressing the problem of the gap between theory and practice in education due to the fact that traditional research is limited to academics in research institutions.[24] Kemmis argues that action research is less about closing this gap and more accurately about "closing the gap between the *roles* of theorist and practitioner" in order to "give practitioners intellectual and moral control over their practice."[25] This type of research is less concerned than traditional research with generalizability and has been criticized as being less rigorous; however, action research can also be seen as more authentic and more directly representative of what is actually happening in the classroom.[26] Others have pointed out that action research also serves the very important purpose of empowering teachers[27] and that involving teachers in research increases ownership of classroom problems and increases the likelihood of their implementing research findings.[28]

Action research and Research as Inquiry

The Research as Inquiry frame states that research is iterative. Action research, as defined by Kurt Lewin, founder of action research, is also a recursive process. When writing about action research, authors refer to its cyclical nature with words such as cycles, spirals, and flows, noting that during the action research process, steps often need to be repeated.[29] Lewin described action research as consisting of a spiral of steps: "planning a change, putting the plan into action, observing what happened, and re-formulating the plan in the light of what had happened."[30] The cycle must be repeated as needed to arrive at the goal of action research, i.e., to improve one's practice. The spirals and cycles one finds in the literature on action research should not be seen as prescriptive, however. Kemmis, McTaggart, and Nixon, for example, note that action research does not usually fit into a tidy process, and in reality "is likely to be more fluid, open and responsive."[31] According to McTaggart, "The cyclic nature of the Lewinian approach recognizes the need for action plans to be flexible and responsive. Lewin recognized that, given the complexity of real social situations, in practice it is never possible to anticipate everything that needs to be done."[32] This cyclic idea aligns well with the Research as Inquiry idea that "research is iterative and depends upon asking increasingly complex or new questions whose answers in turn develop additional questions or lines of inquiry" and aligns with dispositions such as "consider[ing] research as open-ended exploration and engagement with information" and "valu[ing] persistence, adaptability, and flexibility" in the research process.[33] Emphasizing the iterative nature of research in general, and action research in particular, is especially notable given findings that recent graduates tend to complete tasks as quickly as possible, despite employers' need for them "to apply patience and persistence when solving information problems in the workplace."[34]

Additionally, this threshold concept refers to the extension of research to "the community at large" and notes that "the process of inquiry may focus upon personal, professional, or societal needs."[35] Parallels between this notion and the call to action inherent in action research are clear. Through action research, educators can actively grapple with the questions and problems of their profession and society. Also, while action research can be solitary and reflective, many authors encourage collaboration among practitioner- and action-researchers. The often collaborative nature of action research aligns with the statement within the Research as Inquiry frame that "Experts recognize the collaborative effort within a discipline to extend the knowledge in that field."[36]

Importance of action research to education students

Merging research and practice through action research is especially important given my students' values. Many come to the College of Education because of their commitment to social justice, and they are passionate about their profession. They care deeply about their future students and perceived disparities in the world, and many have overcome challenges in their own lives via education. Their emotional investment in the outcomes of their work as educators places an additional burden on them to succeed as students; however, for those students not enrolled in a doctoral program, research is often seen as separate from the practical side of career preparation. This is especially true for master's students, who often come to me overwhelmed by their capstone projects. Using action research as a model enables students to reconcile their identities as students with their future career as educators and education researchers. By embracing the idea of research as an iterative process that is a logical component of engaging in ongoing improvement, students can begin to think of themselves as researchers during their academic studies.

At my institution, students do some structured academic assignments with research components, i.e., locating and/or analyzing scholarly sources, in their first- and second-year courses, but they do little active work of locating sources in their upper-level coursework. Students are focused on fieldwork and practicum experiences that take them into local schools, and "scholarly" research is deemphasized. In focus groups I conducted with upper-level students, education students reported that in these courses they rarely need to find anything. If they need to use outside sources, they are provided by instructors. This lack of research-based assignments establishes a division between academic scholarship and the students' fieldwork experiences. Teaching students about research methods such as action research may help students understand the potential for integrating research and practice earlier on. Further, the discussion of action research as related to Research as Inquiry can help students to merge their identities as students and as teachers, i.e., to cultivate their identities as lifelong learners participating in ongoing inquiry.

It is imperative for colleges and schools of education to prepare students for research in order to cultivate what Davis refers to as "scholarly practitioners."[37] Davis also calls for a "paradigm shift from the notion of teachers as purveyors of knowledge to teachers as cocreators of knowledge." Discussing the Research as Inquiry threshold concept with education faculty and instructors provides a logical and useful approach to integrating library instruction into upper-level undergraduate courses and graduate courses. Drawing on the language of action research and using the need to prepare students as action researchers to justify an emphasis on this threshold concept allow librarians to demonstrate its relevance to faculty and students of education. Incorporating Research as Inquiry into interactions with students is possible, and even necessary, at each level.

Integrating Research as Inquiry

Undergraduate instruction. In undergraduate instruction, introducing the troublesome and cyclical nature of research is appropriate within lower-level courses such as first- and second-year seminars. In my own instruction, we have chosen to emphasize the threshold concepts of Scholarship as Conversation and Information Creation as a Process in disciplinary first- and second-year seminars in order to introduce students to specific concepts at strategic points in the curriculum. However, Research as Inquiry also has a place in instruction and conversations with these students.

First steps for introducing Research as Inquiry at this stage include introducing students to "ethical and legal guidelines in gathering and using information," and helping them to build a rapport with librarians to encourage them to "seek appropriate help when needed." Assignments at this level also often encourage students to "seek multiple perspectives during information gathering and assessment."[38] For example, in the first- and second-year seminar courses in our College of Education, students do a structured debate assignment and must use both outside sources and course readings. Students also explore a social issue related to a service learning experience. Students gather only three scholarly articles related to their topic, so the extent to which students can seek multiple perspectives or to which students must organize information in meaningful ways, both knowledge practices for this frame in the Framework, is limited. They can, however, work to break complex questions down in order to limit the scope of research to an appropriate level for this particular investigation. Providing action research as an example of the kind of research which students can conduct can help to give an example of how this knowledge can be applicable in the field.

In upper-level undergraduate courses, librarians might consider utilizing the connection between action research and Research as Inquiry in conversations with instructors working with courses concurrent with practicum and fieldwork assignments. We should pursue deliberate conversations with education instructors regarding the possibility of including assignments related to action research in these courses. Students need not actually implement action research projects at the undergraduate level. A first step in preparing them to conduct this kind of research later in the field is to help students become familiar with action research methods and projects by reading action research articles. In one course or assignment, students could be provided with action research articles. In a later course or assignment, students can learn strategies for locating these action research articles, thereby "acquir[ing] strategic perspectives on inquiry and a greater repertoire of investigative methods."[39] Even without conducting a study, students could develop a written research project proposal. In this proposal, students could articulate how they would strategically approach the project, including search strategies and a discussion of points in the process when their investigative methods and the research questions themselves might need to be reassessed. Search strategies should especially include databases such as ERIC, which will be available to students after graduation.

Graduate instruction. The approach to integrating Research as Inquiry will vary depending on the type of graduate degree a particular student is pursuing. Many doctoral programs have a traditional research focus, so a justification for studying research methods is less likely to be needed. These students are already aware that they need to participate in research, but at the same time, many are not sure how to begin. Helping these students to understand the iterative nature of research and how that is tied to yet distinct from search (and Searching as Strategic Exploration) is essential to doctoral student success. Addressing Research as Inquiry especially will help these students to progress from novice learners as they "acquire strategic perspectives on inquiry and a greater repertoire of investigative methods" to more experienced researchers who "value persistence, adaptability, and flexibility and recognize that ambiguity can benefit the research process."[40]

Grounding Research as Inquiry in action research is likely to be more applicable for master's students working on capstone papers and less extensive research projects than doctoral students. Librarians could utilize a similar approach to master's level instruction as with undergraduate instruction. Instruction with courses earlier in the program would emphasize an understanding of the iterative nature of research, the availability of help, and building the students' repertoire of investigative methods. Later in the program, assignments in which students locate and read action research articles, develop research plans, and potentially implement those research plans would best be aligned with this threshold concept.

Workshops. Workshops also offer opportunities for in-depth exploration of the Research as Inquiry threshold concept. I currently teach two graduate-level workshops that are well-aligned with Research as Inquiry. Neither is explicitly tied to action research, but they are worth noting here as examples of how to address this threshold concept with graduate students.

The first is a workshop on Conducting a Literature Review, in which we address both research (Research as Inquiry) and search (Searching as Strategic Exploration). I demonstrate and we practice specific search strategies, but we also discuss the term "research" and the iterative nature of research. Activities include students drawing a map of the research process, reflecting on challenging points in the research process and identifying strategies for adapting to those challenges, and discussing questions such as *What is the difference between research and search?*

I also lead a workshop on Critical Reading, in which I take students through a structured, iterative reading process through which students read and re-read a research article from their discipline. Students practice identifying a question and/or goal for approaching that text; they then skim the article and re-read the article strategically. We practice annotating and discuss ways of organizing the information acquired from the article. Students are interested in practical tips on annotation and file storage, but these are grounded in a broader discussion of research. In this workshop, we use the practice of reading a single article as the starting point for thinking about the research process as a whole. We focus on knowledge practices, such as articulating a research question, breaking complex questions down into more manageable components, and assessing gathered information, as applied to a single information source. We also discuss strategies for organizing the information they have found in meaningful ways, placing emphasis on the fact that there is no single correct way to organize information. Each person approaches a source differently, and since the research process involves revisiting the information and rethinking the research question itself, reorganizing the information found is often a natural step in the research process.

Research consultations. Finally, I use the research consultation space to explore this threshold concept, especially with graduate students. In my one-on-one consultations with students, I have deeper conversations with students about research and student/teacher identity while we do activities such as examine and rework research questions or discuss strategies for conducting a literature review. Graduate students, in my experience, are often ready to have these conversations and are not simply task- or assignment-driven in our session. Consultations are an especially effective venue for discussion of a threshold concept because the format allows me to communicate with each student as an individual with individual experiences. The research consultation is a valuable forum for acknowledging how "ambiguity can benefit the research process,"[41] even if it is frustrating. While this is not scalable for all my students, it is highly effective for those with whom I do interact, many of whom are struggling with finding their scholarly identity, and what I learn from individual students has influenced my instruction as well. These one-on-one conversations help me anticipate trouble areas in whole-class instruction, thereby increasing the relevance and quality of my instruction sessions.

Conclusion

In my work with education students, I am helping them to become comfortable with research, as messy as it is. I find the concept of Research as Inquiry useful in helping me to break down the complex concept of research into components that I can manageably include in instruction and broach in conversation with students at all levels. Maintaining an awareness of the kinds of research that are practiced in the field of education, and using action research as an example that aligns well with the notion of research as an iterative process, allows me to situate the potentially lofty, impractical notion of an information literacy threshold concept within a context relevant to my students' future work as educators.

And why does it matter that this is a threshold concept rather than a standard or proficiency? Assuming the mantle of a researcher is troublesome for students. Gaining the confidence, and acquiring and sustaining the motivation to conduct research at an appropriate level is not simply a proficiency in my mind. Thinking of this idea and approaching it as a threshold concept acknowledges the existence of a liminal space that students approach from different directions and move through at different paces. When students grasp this threshold concept, their professional identity will expand to include the role of information and research co-creator. Having already moved through this liminal space myself, I find the idea of research as an iterative inquiry process to be both obvious and exciting. I hope for my students to get there, too, to see themselves as capable of and excited about taking action through research—by engaging in the ongoing inquiry that will enable them to understand and improve the educational settings in which they will be working.

Notes

1. Association of College and Research Libraries (ACRL), *Framework for Information Literacy for Higher Education*, February 2, 2015, http://www.ala.org/acrl/standards/ilframework.
2. ACRL, Framework.
3. John W. Collins and Nancy P. O'Brien, eds., *The Greenwood Dictionary of Education*, 2nd ed. (Santa Barbara, CA: Greenwood, 2011), 400.
4. ACRL, Framework.
5. Ibid.
6. Ibid.
7. American Educational Research Association (AERA), "Code of Ethics," (Feb. 2011), accessed July 22, 2016, http://www.aera.net/Portals/38/docs/About_AERA/CodeOfEthics(1).pdf.
8. American Educational Research Association, "Professional Ethics," accessed July 22, 2016, http://www.aera.net/About-AERA/AERA-Rules-Policies/Professional-Ethics.
9. Ibid.
10. AERA, *Code of Ethics*, 146.
11. Ibid, 147.
12. Peter Jarvis, *The Practitioner-Researcher: Developing Theory from Practice*, 1st ed. (San Francisco: Jossey-Bass, 1999), xi.
13. For conceptual explorations of practitioner inquiry among educators, see the work of Marilyn Cochran-Smith and Susan L. Lytle, such as "Relationships of Knowledge and Practice: Teacher Learning in Communities," *Review of Research in Education* 24, (1999): 249–305, doi:10.2307/1167272.1999; and —, *Inquiry as Stance: Practitioner Research for the Next Generation* (New York: Teachers College Press, 2009).
14. Stephen Kemmis, "Action Research as a Practice-Based Practice," *Educational Action Research* 17, no. 3 (2009): 463, doi:10.1080/09650790903093284.
15. Rebecca Watson-Boone, "Academic Librarians as Practitioner-Researchers," *Journal of Academic Librarianship* 26, no. 2 (2000): 85–93.
16. Ibid: 91.
17. Gaby Haddow and Jane E. Klobas, "Communication of Research to Practice in Library and Information Science: Closing the Gap," *Library and Information Science Research* 26, no. 1 (2004): 29–43, doi:10.1016/j.lisr.2003.11.010; Virginia Wilson, "Formalized Curiosity: Reflecting on the Librarian Practitioner-Researcher," *Evidence Based Library and Information Practice* 8, no. 1 (2013): 111–117. For analyses of trends in LIS practitioner research, including prominent journals for these types of publications, see Charles R. Hildreth and Selenay Aytac, "Recent Library Practitioner Research: A Methodological Analysis and Critique," *Journal of Education for Library and Information Science* 48, no. 3 (2007): 236–258; Selenay Aytac and Bruce

Slutsky, "Published Librarian Research, 2008 through 2012: Analyses and Perspectives," *Collaborative Librarianship* 6, no. 4 (2014): 147–159.
18. Virginia Wilson, "Formalized Curiosity: Reflecting on the Librarian Practitioner-Researcher," *Evidence Based Library and Information Practice* 8, no. 1 (2013): 111–117.
19. Andrew P. Johnson, *A Short Guide to Action Research*, 4th ed. (Boston: Pearson, 2012), 16.
20. For a historical exploration of action research definitions, see: Linda Dickens and Karen Watkins, "Action Research: Rethinking Lewin," *Management Learning* 30, no. 2 (1999): 127–140.
21. Sister Mary Ann Jacobs and Bruce S. Cooper, *Action Research in the Classroom: Helping Teachers Assess and Improve their Work* (Lanham, MD: Rowman & Littlefield, 2016), 13.
22. Dickens and Watkins, "Action Research," 131.
23. Kemmis, "Action Research as a Practice-Based Practice," 463.
24. Stephen H. Davis, *Research and Practice in Education: The Search for Common Ground* (Lanham, MD: Rowman & Littlefield Education, 2008); Johnson, *A Short Guide to Action Research*; Jacobs and Cooper, *Action Research in the Classroom*; among others.
25. Kemmis, "Action Research as a Practice-Based Practice," 468.
26. These ideas are widely discussed in the literature on action research. For one example, see Jarvis, *The Practitioner-Researcher*, 99.
27. Johnson, *A Short Guide to Action Research*, 21.
28. Dickens and Watkins, "Action Research," 131.
29. For example, in Johnson, *A Short Guide to Action Research*.
30. Stephen Kemmis, Robin McTaggart, and Rhonda Nixon, *The Action Research Planner: Doing Critical Participatory Action Research* (Springer, 2014), 18.
31. Ibid.
32. Robin McTaggart, *Participatory Action Research: International Contexts and Consequences* (Albany, NY: State University of New York Press, 1997), 27.
33. ACRL, Framework.
34. Alison J. Head, "Learning Curve: How College Graduates Solve Information Problems Once They Join the Workplace," (October 16, 2012): 3, http://www.projectinfolit.org/uploads/2/7/5/4/27541717/pil_fall2012_workplacestudy_fullreport_revised.pdf.
35. ACRL, Framework.
36. Ibid.
37. Davis, *Research and Practice in Education*, 117.
38. ACRL, Framework.
39. Ibid.
40. Ibid.
41. Ibid.

Scholarship as Conversation

Section Five

CHAPTER 17*

Performance as Conversation:
Dialogic Aspects of Music Performance and Study

Rachel Elizabeth Scott

What does a photo have to do with a piece by Gershwin? A recently discovered photograph identified the pitches of taxi horns used in a 1929 performance of *An American in Paris* supervised by Gershwin. Scholars at University of Michigan's Gershwin Initiative have used this finding, in conjunction with a recording of the same performance, to justify the change from the traditional realization of the taxi horns for the new scholarly edition of this piece.[1] Flexibility is a requirement for the modern musicologist; discoveries and breakthroughs can come in a variety of formats, and not just printed music.

Although much of the classical music repertory is centuries old, musicians, musicologists, and fans participate in ongoing and lively conversations in an increasing variety of arenas. New insights on old works now surface thanks to technological innovations, from data-rich digital humanities projects to casual online forums, where media and text can be posted and discussed. The study and performance of a musical work—typically, the combination of sound, notation, and performance—is informed by a variety of sources in a wide array of formats.

---

* This work is licensed under a Creative Commons Attribution-NonCommercial-NoDerivatives 4.0 License, CC BY-NC-ND (https://creativecommons.org/licenses/by-nc-nd/4.0/).

The recently introduced Framework for Information Literacy for Higher Education (Framework) includes the frame "Scholarship as Conversation."[2] The frame highlights the ongoing, collaborative, and iterative nature of research processes. This frame, in addition to the Framework's emphasis on reflective practices, provides information professionals, students, and scholars alike with a structure with which to make sense of the complexity of music research and performance. As the interplay between audience and performer becomes increasingly dynamic and the potential sources for study multiply, librarians can help students negotiate this sustained, multi-format discourse.

Music as conversation

Conceptualizing Scholarship as Conversation will enable musicians to navigate the many considerations of how to perform or understand a piece. Unlike other disciplines, like law, in which consensus of field undergoes change slowly and only via codified processes, understanding of a musical work is subject to interpretation in uniquely personal ways and can change with each performance. Because music is primarily an aural and not a textual tradition, even recordings and notated music only lend so much permanence to a musical composition. With almost limitless ways to analyze a work or to realize the work in performance, musicians typically, if unwittingly, participate in conversations to negotiate meaning of musical works.

Traditionally, this "conversation" may have meant discussing the piece with a teacher, conductor, or other respected musician. It may also have entailed visiting the library to consult a scholarly edition and thematic catalog, listen to various recordings, and read relevant sections of the composer's biography. Traditional conversations were also social, discussing elements of performance with one's colleagues in a performance ensemble or with complete strangers in the audience of a performance venue. Historically, though, these conversations were among smaller groups in face-to-face interactions or via written correspondence, and both the variety and amount of musical information with which one came into contact were limited.

Now that compositional analysis, performance recordings, and a variety of scores can easily be found, uploaded, interacted with, and discussed online, the conversation is growing more dynamic, distributed, and complex. Music information in digital settings is rapidly changing, not fixed and controlled like traditional information sources. Increased interactivity and simplified web productivity tools mean that anyone has the potential to contribute to musical conversations online. Digital media of various kinds can be added to illustrate musical materials, creating an information-rich musical landscape. It is essential that novice researchers and musicians understand that the quality and authoritativeness of music sources must be evaluated; online availability or convenience does not necessarily recommend a resource.[3]

In order to fully appreciate the lifecycle of a given musical work, one must synthesize a variety of contemporary and historical recordings, scholarly, manuscript, and performing scores, composer biography, and other contextual information. Donald Krummel, noted musicologist and music librarian, wrote in 1982 that "the best way for any scholar to enter a field will always be bibliographically, through the activity of passing as much of the source material through his or her hands as possible."[4] While digital objects cannot necessarily be held in one's hands, the idea still proves true. In order to understand something well enough to make a scholarly or musical contribution, one must first read, listen to, see, and interact with as many of the extant materials as possible.

In a similar vein, this frame states, "developing familiarity with the sources of evidence, methods, and modes of discourse in the field assists novice learners to enter the conversation."[5] Knowledge of the variety of source material available and an understanding of how to use this material is essential to contributing to this discourse. Similarly, an appreciation of the various modes of discourse specific to music is essential to participating in this conversation. Music research is comprised of several specialties, including musicology and ethnomusicology, music therapy, music education, and music theory. Each of these subdisciplines has specific research methodologies, preferred source material, and scholarly processes and activities. However, recent music scholarship is increasingly interdisciplinary and may incorporate diverse modes of discourse. As modes of musical discourse diversify and become increasingly casual and participatory, contributing to scholarly conversations may become less intimidating to students and novice researchers.

Both the Framework in general and this frame in particular emphasize the interactive nature of scholarship. Students who have understood their only role in scholarship to be that of a passive consumer, using published research to support their arguments, are challenged to see themselves as participants in an ongoing conversation. Musicians, however, have a unique perspective on this interactivity. Musical performance is, after all, seldom performed in isolation; music is a conversation among composer, artist(s), and audience, among others. Musical performances may also be understood as a dialogue with the artist's perceived predecessors. Even when alone in a practice room, the musician is in dialogue with a composer's musical notation, a teacher's instruction, and a musical influence's interpretation. Where students in other disciplines might not actively contribute to or participate in their field until they enter graduate school or obtain a professional position, musicians learn from an early age to engage in the collaborative work of performance. While experts may have more confidence in their contributions to scholarly understanding of a musical work and a well-developed sense of their audience, students and amateur musicians now have online platforms from which to share and promote their performances and contributions. The possibility of posting one's performance or musical analysis and promptly receiving feedback from a variety of sources is a relatively new phenomenon for the novice researcher or amateur musician. Digital platforms have ushered in considerable changes, both in the size and diversity of audiences and in who can contribute.

This frame also highlights the interdisciplinary nature of research. One characteristic of expert researchers is their inclination to seek out diverse perspectives in order to conduct exhaustive research and to add depth of understanding to their research. Novice researchers may lack the deep subject knowledge to know when to step outside the boundaries of the discipline. They might also not know what questions to ask or be unable to appreciate the relative authoritativeness of various sources. Conducting research in many subdisciplines of music requires significant forays into other disciplines. Expert music researchers are familiar with expectations when incorporating outside perspectives into their research and know how to engage with extra-musical material when conducting music research.

According to this frame, "Providing attribution to relevant previous research is also an obligation of participation in the conversation. It enables the conversation to move forward and strengthens one's voice in the conversation."[6] Attribution has always been important to both musical performance and musicology. Many classical performers proudly trace their musical ancestry back to famous performers and pedagogues, claiming to be a musical descendent of so-and-so or a disciple of X-school of singing. Musicians may cite or signal their musical influences in their programmatic choices, elements of technique, or stylistic choices. This tracing of musical lineage may not be exactly what is meant by attribution in the Framework, in which learners credit others "through proper attribution or citation."[7] Although it espouses metaliteracy, the Framework focuses on text-based scholarship, which still comprises the bulk of the corpora. However, providing attribution, in music as in scholarship, helps others contextualize your contribution. Being able to recognize a musician or argument in a particular camp or school of thought is characteristic of someone with considerable experience and expertise.

Digital natives may struggle to understand traditional attribution. Classical and popular musics have long been sampled with and without attribution, but research has shown that students who have grown up in a "copy and paste" environment see fluidity of authorship.[8] Because of this fluidity, they may not appreciate the ways in which acknowledging the original context of content enriches one's use of it. In a recent study of undergraduate responses to the language and concepts in the Framework, one student used a musical example to highlight the dialogical interplay of scholarship: "Most musicians will say... the best musicians know how to borrow ideas. The same goes for creating other forms of content in our day and age. We're all offering our own input on their past works. It's an everlasting conversation!"[9] Musicians and musical scholars continue to draw heavily on the work of their predecessors. The increasing availability of music information, from authoritative to inaccurate, make this network of influence ever more complex to negotiate. Accordingly, it is essential that students learn to appropriate information ethically and with an understanding of its original context.

Teaching and assessing Scholarship as Conversation

In order to authentically teach and assess this frame, the academic librarian must collaborate with music classroom and studio faculty. Several studies of music information literacy have highlighted the need for instruction that is highly relevant and tailored to the specific needs of the class.[10] Accordingly, in order to specifically target and assess student understanding of the dialogic nature of music performance or study, the librarian must work closely with the classroom faculty to ensure that this content fits within the overall learning objectives of the course. The librarian should meet with the instructor and collect class syllabi, assignment descriptions, or performance assignments. Embracing the principles of backward design, the librarian should discuss and understand the instructor's desired results for the instruction session. By understanding the scope of course content, requirements for assignments, and instructor expectations, the librarian can better integrate the library instruction and assessment into the class.

In order for information literacy instruction to have immediacy for the students, it needs to be active and authentic. In an article in *Journal of Music History Pedagogy*, music librarian and musicologist Jennifer Oates emphasizes the importance of experiential learning in music library instruction: "Students are taught how to explore their intellectual curiosity by engaging in research and asking questions that require academic resources to answer them effectively."[11] Learning interventions should force students to critically evaluate and use resources in order to answer questions relevant to their personal or intellectual goals.

Regardless of the format of the instruction, the librarian can begin to introduce students to practices that will help them appreciate the dialogic nature of musical research and performance. Knowledge practices for Scholarship as Conversation include: properly citing others' work, contributing appropriately to the conversation, recognizing barriers to participation, analyzing others' contributions, recognizing the relative contribution of certain works to the discipline, identifying change in perspective, and appreciating the diversity of perspectives.[12] Not all of these knowledge practices can or should be introduced in a one-shot instruction session; the assignment and assessment section details some ways in which select knowledge practices might be incorporated in a single session. However, once the librarian has mapped out knowledge practices in relation to the instructional content, the overlapping nature of these practices should make the task of addressing multiple knowledge practices more approachable. Regardless of the knowledge practices targeted, instruction must allow students opportunity for engagement and reflection.

Unlike the *Information Literacy Competency Standards for Higher Education* (Standards), the Framework does not have built-in outcomes.[13] Where the Standards outline discrete and exhaustive competencies, the Framework identifies some potential dispositions and knowledge practices for each frame. I appreciate the knowledge practices as great fodder for thinking about long-term learning and find that they have helped me shift to a more student-centered pedagogy. The *Standards* were limiting; I felt compelled to stick to my script in order to ensure that the appropriate standards were taught and could be measured objectively. The *Framework's* interconnected frames and overlapping dispositions have heightened my awareness of the complexity entailed in knowledge construction and in measuring student learning. I have been forced to acknowledge that students will grapple with these information literacy practices at varying speeds and level of engagement long after a given library instruction session. There has also been debate about the frames as threshold concepts as defined by Meyers and Land.[14] Although I am not convinced that Scholarship as Conversation is particularly bounded, I do think "conversation" is a worthwhile metaphor for conceptualizing scholarship in many disciplines. Choosing conversation makes this frame accessible to and appropriate for novice and experts engaging in almost any type of scholarly work.

Accordingly, assessing Scholarship as Conversation may feel like an insurmountable challenge for librarians accustomed to the more prescriptive Standards. Oakleaf, however, offers some encouragement and several ideas for assessing the Frames at the program level:

> threshold concepts are very well suited to learning outcomes assessment, as long as the assessments permit the use of authentic assessment approaches, provide useful feedback to students to help them over the "stuck place," emphasize individual variation in the journey that students travel to achieve them, recognize that learners may redefine their sense of self, link learning and grading in meaningful ways,

organize programmatic assessment around transformational ideas, and support metacognition.[15]

What might this look like in the context of a single-shot library instruction session? The "troublesome" nature of threshold concepts make them challenging to teach and assess in a single session. Accordingly, instruction and assessment should be as personal, integrated, and open-ended as is practical. The instruction and assessment should support reflection and flexibility, convey to students that there are many ways to find, evaluate, and use information, and that awareness of one's findings and developing knowledge should inform one's strategy. Throughout the instruction and in assessment instruments, one should pose open-ended instead of multiple choice or fill-in-the-blank questions. Whenever possible, assessment should allow for individual variations rather than homogenize student understanding. This can be achieved by engaging music faculty to determine which information literacy concepts would best support their course objectives and collaborating to create a mutually beneficial assessment tool. When possible, one should provide feedback to students, offer to meet them individually, get to know them personally, and remind them of library services that support their ongoing learning.

The following section includes ideas for assignments and assessments based on the author's experience. Sample lesson plans for music education, musicology, and music business courses are not meant as exhaustive approaches to teaching this frame. Rather, they represent jumping-off points that should be revised based on one's own context and, ideally, informed with input from teaching faculty.

Assignment and assessment ideas

Music education: Conversation as pedagogy. Music librarians often teach music education majors in the context of a music history or research methods course. If the librarian has an opportunity to work with music education or music pedagogy students in a major-specific course, the librarian could introduce a discussion of the dialogical nature of pedagogy and show students some resources that model this approach in the context of applied music instruction. Two learning outcomes for this class might be:
- Students will find and access master classes in order to identify useful pedagogical techniques.
- Students will identify ways in which questions and conversation facilitate musicians' understanding in order to enhance their own instruction.

During the instruction, the librarian demonstrates how to find master classes and other instructional videos in MUSAIC, a free streaming video platform for classical music concerts, master classes, and interviews. In music, master classes are typically group classes in which an expert publicly works with a single student at a time on a prepared piece or excerpt. After watching part of a master class together, the instructor leads a discussion of how the teacher's question-posing and conversation improve the student's musical performance. The librarian ties this into the theme of "Scholarship as Conversation" and encourages students to seek out other resources that make this dialogue explicit. The master class viewed should provide the librarian with ample opportunities to highlight that musical works and music performance are both ongoing conversations, master classes are a venue for such conversations, and, finally, as future educators, students will facilitate these conversations and must understand the responsibilities and privilege thereof.

The librarian and instructor collaborate to plan and write an assessment of student learning. A possible assignment would require students to select and watch another master class and ask students to respond to the following questions in one-page essays.

1. Describe how the "master" uses dialogue to facilitate learning. Identify as many specific strategies as possible.
2. Which of these practices will you incorporate into your own instruction? How will you do so?
3. Reflect on the usefulness of the master/student dichotomy and identify one example of expertise that may be dismissed in this construct.

The assignment facilitates the following student practices: "seek out conversations taking place in their research area; see themselves as contributors to scholarship rather than only consumers of it; recognize that scholarly conversations take place in various venues… recognize that systems privilege authorities," all of which are dispositions for this frame.

Music students are familiar with the master class format and accustomed to streaming online media, but the casual venue for professional content is likely new. This assignment demonstrates that relevant, scholarly conversations can be found and hosted online. Although students might struggle to recognize that "systems privilege authorities," seeing the all-star line-up on MUSAIC makes the master/student dichotomy quite clear. Nonetheless, the media format makes it easy for students to hear, see, and observe master teaching techniques in action and begin to form ideas about how they might appropriate techniques and enter into the conversation. Furthermore, providing timely feedback on student essays reinforces the import of these practices and extends the librarian's dialogue with the student.

Musicology: Eavesdropping on scholarly conversations. One option for teaching this frame to musicology students over the course of a semester

would be to require students to subscribe to AMS-L, the email discussion list of the American Musicological Society. Subscribing to this list for a semester would teach students a great deal about the research methods, resources, and discourse employed by professional musicologists. Students would have the opportunity to eavesdrop on the conversation or to participate. The learning outcome for this instruction is:
- Students will evaluate email discussion list threads in order to identify characteristics of musicological scholarship.

Begin the instruction session by asking students to identify some of the traditional scholarly processes involved in music research. Present as a case study a recent example from AMS-L in which a *New York Times* article[16] about slavery and race in Mozart operas sparked multiple conversations, not only about the article, but about why a relevant letter to the editor would not be published and where else a rejoinder should appear. This case illustrates how scholarly conversations increasingly occur across various formats and venues, involve non-academicians, and are highly interactive. Use this or a similar case example to facilitate a discussion of how scholarly processes are evolving in light of digital media.

To assess this assignment, the librarian would only need to provide a prompt that promoted reflection and then provide written feedback on student responses. A sample prompt should include open-ended questions that allow students to articulate in their own words the nature and perceived value of the conversations fostered by this email discussion list. A sample prompt might read as follows: Please reflect on the various posts and conversations you've followed on AMS-L and respond to each of the following questions in one or two paragraphs:

1. What kinds of information have you seen posted to this email discussion list? Explain which are most useful to you and why.
2. Evaluate three or four Calls for Papers (CFP). Describe the characteristics of musicology scholarship as outlined in these CFP.
3. Look up the credentials of some of the more frequent posters. Who are these people? Who seems to be included in this forum and who is excluded? Why does this matter/what are the implications of exclusion?
4. What types of research methods were discussed or featured? Describe a digital musicology initiative that piqued your interest.

In addition to identifying the variety of ways in which this email discussion list facilitates conversation within the musicology community, this assignment should also open students' eyes to the diversity of musicology projects, papers, and initiatives. Exposing students to this diversity helps students see a role for themselves as contributors to the discipline. The list provides an appropriate opportunity to interact with prospective colleagues at various levels and, perhaps, to contribute to the conversation. By pausing to reflect on who might be excluded from participating, it forces students to recognize a variety of barriers to publishing in the field. As they reflect on participating authors and their messages, students will gain familiarity with the tone of the conversation and develop an awareness of the relative contributions of some authors.

Music business: Disruptive events in a sustained conversation. Music Business students have very different information needs than their peers in classical music programs. They frequently seek sales and other music industry data and may be less interested in engaging conceptually in information literacy topics. However, the following assignment might present an opportunity to encourage music business students to consider the ongoing and iterative nature of research. The learning outcome for this assignment is:

- Students will evaluate articles in order to identify how understanding of a disruptive event (in music business) has evolved over time.

To set up the activity, the librarian opens with a discussion of source evaluation and explains that the scholarly study of popular music is relatively new and necessarily interdisciplinary. By asking students, "Who is qualified to write authoritatively about music business?" and "Where can authoritative music business information be found?" the librarian encourages them to identify stakeholders in this conversation. If students can identify potential experts in the field (e.g., music producers, artists, fans, recording engineers) and explain when each might be authoritative and when their contributions might be less meaningful, they demonstrate a burgeoning understanding of the dynamic and contextual nature of authority in music business research.

The librarian asks students to form small groups and assign each a "disruptive event" in the field of music business. Examples of disruptive events and ideas might include: MP3, streaming platforms, Auto-Tune, Web 2.0, "Rockonomics" (relationship of declining record sales and rising ticket prices), and TV talent shows. The librarian provides each of the groups with two articles from different time periods or perspectives. Working in groups, students evaluate the two sources using a prompt that encourages reflection related to frame:

1. Who wrote each of these? List their qualifications to write on this topic.
2. What can you find about this journal/source? What barriers can you identify to publishing in it?
3. What external citations can you find in these articles? Explain how the respective author uses these citations (to provide evidence, to acknowledge its importance, to contest claim, etc.).
4. How has understanding of the topic changed over time?

These questions underscore several of the underlying features of Scholarship as Conversation: the ongoing and dynamic nature of inquiry, the hierarchy of scholarly contributions, the limitations to participation in certain venues, the diversity of perspectives and approaches, and, finally, the need for critical evaluation of all contributions. By walking around the room and providing feedback to the groups as they work, the librarian legitimizes their practice of critically evaluating sources and identifying competing understandings in published works. By modeling source evaluation, assigning group work, and exposing students to this ongoing conversation in two different forums, the librarian encourages students to enter the conversations surrounding their "disruptive event."

Conclusion

As musicians, music students have an inherent understanding of the conversational nature of any piece, scholarly or not. The above exercises are meant to help bring to the surface this innate understanding of the ongoing dialogue which surrounds all forms of music information production. This has implications for the performer's understanding of the musical works; only when this knowledge becomes explicit can musicians and music scholars fully leverage the complexity and richness of music information past and present. By demonstrating an understanding of a musical work's history, import, and contemporary understanding, the performer enters into the ongoing dialogue surrounding the works.

Conversation is a useful and accessible metaphor for explaining scholarly processes to music students. It has also been a valuable conceptual framework for me to apply not only in library instruction, but also to my own scholarly endeavors. Reflecting on Scholarship as Conversation has shaped my understanding of the various dialogues in which in which I must participate in order to contribute to library science practice and research. It has given me a new understanding of scholarly agency and encouraged me to participate more broadly in professional discourse.

Librarians' knowledge of subject resources and information literacy concepts that ground research practices make us well-situated to model the variety of sources and diversity of approaches that can inform musical performance and scholarship. By helping musicians recognize and understand the many voices engaged in these scholarly conversations, librarians' contributions can make a meaningful impact on the musician's stock-in-trade: performance.

Notes

1. Mark Clague, "1929 Gershwin Taxi Horn Photo Clarifies Mystery," *Gershwin Initiative blog,* March 5, 2016, http://www.music.umich.edu/ami/gershwin/?p=715.

2. Association of College & Research Libraries (ACRL), *Framework for Information Literacy for Higher Education*, February 2, 2015, http://www.ala.org/acrl/standards/ilframework.
3. Kirstin Dougan, "Music, YouTube, and Academic Libraries," *Notes* 72, no. 3 (2016): 491–508; Rachel E. Scott, "The Edition-Literate Singer: Edition Selection as an Information Literacy Competency," *Music Reference Services Quarterly* 16, no.3 (2013): 131–140.
4. D. W. Krummel, "The Bibliographical Prognosis," *The Journal of Musicology* 1, no. 1 (1982): 31.
5. ACRL, *Framework for Information Literacy for Higher Education*.
6. Ibid.
7. Ibid.
8. Mary R. Lea and Sylvia Jones, "Digital Literacies in Higher Education: Exploring Textual and Technological Practice," *Studies in Higher Education* 36, no. 4 (2011): 377–393; Dan Perkel, "Copy and Paste Literacy? Literacy Practices in the Production of a MySpace Profile," in *Informal Learning and Digital Media: Constructions, Contexts, Consequences*, eds. Kirsten Drotner, Hans Siggard Jensen, and Kim Schroeder (Newcastle, UK: Cambridge Scholars Press, 2008); John G. Palfrey and Urs Gasser, *Born Digital: Understanding the First Generation of Digital Natives* (New York: Basic Books, 2008), 111–129.
9. Rachel E. Scott, "Part 2. If We Frame It, They Will Respond: Undergraduate Student Responses to the Framework for Information Literacy for Higher Education," *The Reference Librarian* 58, no. 1 (2017): 19–32, doi:10.1080/02763877.2016.1196471.
10. Beth Christensen, "Warp, Weft, and Waffle: Weaving Information Literacy into an Undergraduate Music Curriculum," *Notes* 60, no. 3 (2004): 616–631; Victoria Vaughan and Kathleen A. Abromeit, "Info Lit and the Diva: Integrating Information Literacy into the Oberlin Conservatory of Music Opera Theater Department," *Notes* 60, no. 3 (2004): 632–652; Rachel E. Scott, "The Edition-Literate Singer: Edition Selection as an Information Literacy Competency," *Music Reference Services Quarterly* 16, no. 3 (2013): 131–140; Alessia Zanin-Yost and Christina L. Reitz, "Information Literacy in Music History: Fostering Success in Teaching and Learning," *Journal of Library Administration* 54, no. 7 (2014): 562–572.
11. Jennifer Oates, "Engaging with Research and Resources in Music Courses," *Journal of Music History Pedagogy* 4, no. 2 (2013): 284.
12. ACRL, *Framework for Information Literacy for Higher Education*.
13. Association of College & Research Libraries (ACRL), *Information Literacy Competency Standards for Higher Education*, 2000, http://www.ala.org/acrl/standards/informationliteracycompetency.
14. Jan Meyer and Ray Land, *Threshold Concepts and Troublesome Knowledge: Linkages to Ways of Thinking and Practising within the Disciplines*, Occasional Report 2, ETL Project (2002), http://www.ed.ac.uk/etl/publications.
15. Megan Oakleaf, "A Roadmap for Assessing Student Learning Using the New Framework for Information Literacy for Higher Education," *The Journal of Academic Librarianship* 5, no. 40 (2014): 511.
16. Zachary Woolf, "Can Opera Become an Agent of Change?" *New York Times*, July 15, 2016, http://www.nytimes.com/2016/07/17/arts/music/can-opera-become-an-agent-of-change-aix-en-provence-festival.html.

CHAPTER 18*

Framing the Talk:
Scholarship as Conversation in the Health Sciences

Candace Vance

Scholarship as Conversation, one of the threshold concepts in ACRL's Framework for Information Literacy for Higher Education, is and always will be an important concept for students to understand. The idea behind this frame has traditionally been introduced to students across the disciplines in the context of citing sources correctly, giving scholarly attribution, and avoiding plagiarism. These tenets are repeated in English class lectures, library orientations, as well as many other classes requiring research and writing. The Scholarship as Conversation frame continues to reflect these tenets in the knowledge practices; however, the frame has much broader implications that are crucial for students to employ as they continue their education and later when they enter their professions, such as following changes in scholarly perspectives over time on topics in their disciplines, seeking out different perspectives, and contributing to the scholarly conversation. If students fail to understand these broader implications, they are unlikely to find the idea of attribution important or meaningful.[1]

Information literacy for students in the health sciences has a particularly vital role as they acquire increasing responsibility in patient health care decisions. These students view this frame through the lens of evidence-based practice (EBP), which includes concepts such as study appraisal, clinical questioning, and understanding and applying the medical literature to health care decisions. The Framework for Information Literacy for Higher Education

---

* This work is licensed under a Creative Commons Attribution-NonCommercial-NoDerivatives 4.0 License, CC BY-NC-ND (https://creativecommons.org/licenses/by-nc-nd/4.0/).

(Framework)² offers a better correlation with EBP than perhaps the Information Literacy Competency Standards for Higher Education (Standards)³ did, directing Information Literacy (IL) instructors to expand beyond the skills-based approach (how to cite) to teaching information literacy competencies such as citation scanning, evaluating study design, and valuing user-created content. Many librarians have already done this or have been doing it all along, but the Framework unifies efforts and offers direction in *how* to do it.

Many health sciences librarians have also been emphasizing knowledge and comprehension over the acquisition of specific information literacy skills, but Knapp and Brower challenge health sciences librarians to be more thoughtful about incorporating the Framework as a means to improve their information literacy practices.[4] In the past, the Standards did not align very well with the EBP framework. Nancy Adams compared the two and found important concepts in EBP overlooked in the previous Standards. She determined that the Standards should include less reliance on authority as indicators of quality and more emphasis on question formulation and application of knowledge.[5] Perhaps health sciences librarians felt the gulf was too wide to be able to incorporate the two. The Framework, however, offers better alignment with many of the complex issues inherent in health science information literacy instruction and provides an outline of how to teach the complexities of evaluating and using information. Knapp and Brower recommend the Medical Library Association consider best practices for using the Framework in health science instruction and the possibility of officially adopting the new Framework.[6]

In the health sciences, Scholarship as Conversation highlights the community aspect of research, as well as its evolution. The directive of this frame is to instill in students an idea, which they often do not appreciate, of research as a "discursive practice in which ideas are formulated, debated, and weighed against one another over extended periods of time."[7] In this same vein, students must learn to view their own research and writing as participation in discourse and themselves as information creators.[8]

The Framework is based on several core concepts, which are organized into six frames, as well as two additional elements: knowledge practices and dispositions. Knowledge practices are "demonstrations of ways in which learners can increase their understanding of these information literacy concepts."[9] Dispositions "describe ways in which to address the affective, attitudinal, or valuing dimension of learning."[10] The knowledge practices for this frame also include discovering the many types of scholarship that make up disciplinary knowledge. Exercises and discussion should help develop this notion that scholarship is an ongoing conversation—a conversation where students can contribute and lend their voices and opinions, not merely accept or consume. This should be in accord with the knowledge practice to "contribute to scholarly conversation at an appropriate level, such as local online community, guided discussion, undergraduate research journal, conference presentation/poster session," as well as "identify barriers to entering scholarly conversation via various venues."[11] One of the Framework's dispositions identifies a barrier, requiring that students learn to "recognize that systems privilege authorities and that not having a fluency in the language and process of a discipline disempowers their ability to participate and engage."[12]

In our current society, where the public has entered many scientific conversations through blogs and social media, different types of authority are recognized by different segments of the community. In the vaccination and autism debate, scientists possess one type of authority and parents of autistic children possess another. Often, scientists communicate less effectively than advocacy groups. P.A. Offit laments the lack of communication skills of the scientific community, wishing they would do a better job of communicating theoretical risk and the difference between coincidence and causation. He states, "Once you raise the notion of a possibility of harm, it's hard for people to get that notion out of their head."[13]

Students should explore how the expansion of scholarly venues through weblogs, research repositories, and social media allow more opportunities for a larger variety of perspectives and participation, allowing students, community, and any other stakeholders to add their thoughts and opinions to the conversation.

Even if students currently lack the authority to participate in certain dialogues, we can help them develop the ability to critically evaluate the conversation and the contributions of those involved, with the understanding that they will need to eventually cross the threshold of identifying themselves as producers of knowledge, instead of just passive consumers.

Information literacy instruction at Murray State University

At Murray State University (MSU) Libraries, a four-year, public master's level institution with a recently added doctoral program in Nursing, the information literacy class evolved from a one-credit-hour, half-semester class to a three-credit-hour, full-semester class in 2010. In 2013, the MSU Libraries added an information literacy minor to the curriculum. One of the Information Literacy (INF) minor classes offered focuses on the health sciences. Some of these changes occurred alongside the ACRL's creation and adoption of the Framework. In the wake of these changes, we have been considering ways to move our information literacy instruction from teaching "library skills" in a one-hour class to trying to develop life-long learners in a newly expanded curriculum. The shift in the information literacy design encourages building a strong scaffold for students in one-shot instruction sessions as well—one that will allow them to develop an increasingly complex relationship with information over the course of their educational and professional careers, a tall order for a one-hour spot. In an effort to reach this goal, we have been working with faculty to build a scaffold of IL instruction to try and reach these outcomes, expanding students' IL skills as they move toward graduation.

Implementing the threshold concept

In our three-hour INF 101 class, we critically examine the 1998 retracted *Lancet* article by Andrew Wakefield, which proposed a connection between autism and the measles, mumps, and rubella vaccine (MMR). The social impact of the article, as well as the comments, retraction, and citation history of the study, serve as a significant and vivid example of the influence of scholarly conversation and the sense of accountability necessary when participating in scholarly discourse. In our class, we discuss the media's role in this conversation and how it led to user-generated content, creating a great deal of social unrest. The fallout was precipitous, leading to some parents deciding against childhood vaccinations, allowing new outbreaks of diseases previously considered eliminated in the United States and Great Britain, such as measles, whooping cough, and mumps.

In our INF class, we look at retracted articles and the importance of reading critically. This lesson maps well to the Scholarship as Conversation frame because it shows one way in which scholars formally communicate about published research. There are often published conversations before an article is retracted in the form of comments, replies, and expressions of concern. Comments can be substantive articles, letters, or editorials that challenge, refute, support, or expand upon another published item. The original author may often respond to the comments. Occasionally the journal will publish an "Expression of Concern" to draw attention to possible problems. So even before blogs, Twitter, and Facebook, students can see the scholarly discourse that occurred surrounding certain retracted or disputed articles.

In class, we go over the definitions of errata, so students will have a better understanding of why an article might be retracted. The National Library of Medicine (NLM) defines errata as any correction or corrigenda for any previously published articles. NLM states that articles may be retracted or withdrawn by authors, academic or institutional sponsor, editor, or publisher because of pervasive error or unsubstantiated or irreproducible data. NLM does not remove the citation for a retracted article, but updates the citation to indicate it has been retracted and links the original citation to the citation for the published retraction notice. Partial retractions occur when only a small part of an article needs to be corrected or removed.[14]

Class discussions include the fact that even though a scholar has conducted research and had an article published in a peer-reviewed journal, we as readers should not automatically accept it as a valid scientific study. Discussion includes coming up with the reasons why an article would be retracted, such as faulty logic or computation, accidental contamination, falsified or fabricated data, or honest error, scientific misconduct, or plagiarism. The discussion helps students understand how important it is to evaluate every article they read, regardless of the reputation of the journal that published it.

To emphasize this point, the INF students search Medline for the Wakefield article with very little or no prior knowledge of the content. They include "retracted publication" as a limit in in publication type and enter "Wakefield" as an author search and "autism" as a keyword search. Once they locate the correct citation entitled "Illeal-lymphoid-nodular hyperplasia, non-specific colitis, and pervasive developmental disorder in children,"[15] they must find the full-text of the article and answer several questions about the content of the article, such as: "What are the environmental triggers considered in the article?" and "What is the behavioral disorder under discussion in the article?" It takes careful reading to identify the answers. They must also evaluate the study design and number of children in the study, deciding whether the number of participants in the study (twelve) seems sufficient.

Another important aspect of Scholarship as Conversation is citation history or times cited. Students should develop the ability to identify key players and their perspectives on topics within their disciplines. The conversational aspect of science can also be illustrated by citation chaining and noting the number of times an article has been cited and by examining the articles that have cited it, as well as the bibliography. Students in the Nursing Leadership class often become discouraged over the lack of resources for their very narrow topics and may immediately want to change their focus. When they practice citation chaining using a citation index like Google Scholar or Web of Science, they are often relieved to discover articles they had not found previously, as well as discovering authorities on their topics and critical articles cited multiple times.

The Wakefield article has been cited in Google Scholar 2,549 times at this writing. After discussing scholarly impact in a previous class, the high citation count of the Wakefield article is a good example of negative impact. Articles can be cited because they are an example of misconduct, for example, or they can continue to be cited despite the retraction or cited without realizing it has been retracted. Budd, Sievert, and Schultz report that of 235 articles retracted during 1966–96, they were cited in total more than 2,000 times after their withdrawal with fewer than eight percent of the citations acknowledging the retraction.[16] Students often ask if it is acceptable to cite an article that is cited in another article. Citation scanning can help explain how consulting the original article can prevent problems, such as perpetuating incorrect citations, quotes, or continuing to cite articles that have been retracted.

Before searching for the Wakefield article, the class looks at "Retraction Watch" a blog first published by Ivan Oransky and Adam Marcus in 2010.[17] The purpose of the blog is to increase the transparency of the retraction process. Da Silva and Dobránszki state that retraction notices should inform the scientific community why a particular publication has been retracted and that retraction notices that don't fully explain the reasons behind a retraction serve as "a poor historical document."[18] They do not hold all parties accountable or inform the audience of the problem and reason. Da Silva and Dobránszki graph the inconsistencies across publishers and other entities regarding definitions of different errata.[19]

Do journals retract articles when a theory or evidence has been displaced? In 2005, JAMA published an article contending fetuses do not feel pain before the third trimester.[20] Newer studies propose that fetuses feel pain earlier. Howard Bauchner, Editor in Chief at *JAMA*, said the Lee et al. article should not be retracted, stating that review articles summarize the evidence available at the time "Although subsequently published reports may add to the existing evidence on a topic, or propose alternative theories, that new information does not require retraction of previous review articles. In addition there is no evidence supporting other issues that would necessitate retraction, such as fabrication or falsification."[21] This topic presents a good discussion topic for students to argue when a retraction is appropriate.

The last two questions on the homework assignment concern measles—when it was eliminated and how many cases were reported in the United States in 2015. Students learn that measles was eliminated in the United States in 2000, but because of fears surrounding the safety of the MMR vaccine, as well as fears regarding the levels of thimerosal in vaccines, there were outbreaks. In 2015, there were 189 cases of measles reported. In 2014, 667 cases were reported from twenty-seven states.[22] The majority of people who contracted measles were unvaccinated. Prior to the vaccine becoming available in 1963, three to four million cases were reported yearly in the U.S. with 450 deaths.[23] Other disease outbreaks occurred as well that were previously controlled or eliminated in the United States, including mumps, whooping cough, and Haemophilus Influenzae Type B (Hib).[24]

The fear of vaccination and the resulting return of deadly diseases shows how perceptions in scholarly thought can change over time. Sharon Kaufman draws a comparison between the "enduring belief in the vaccine-autism theory"[25] with what Ludwik Fleck calls "an event in the history of thought,"[26] a critical step in the way the perception of a scientific fact changes. In his book

Genesis and Development of a Scientific Fact, originally published in 1935, Fleck believed that scientific facts are not prior, fixed, and autonomously determinate features of an external world, but rather, "events in the history of thought." Fleck proposed that "Truth is not a convention, but rather one in historical perspective, an event in the history of thought."[27] Fleck argues that before a fact is even perceptible, "it must be in harmony with the prevailing thought style and aligned with the intellectual interest and other goals."[28] He describes the statement or belief that we call truth a "harmony of illusion," which relies on our current beliefs and experiences.[29] Scholarship as Conversation illustrates how our thoughts change as we move through different beliefs and experiences. So, once again, students must think critically to realize even science is a gray area, relying on perceptions and experiences, reluctant to change, and exists at any point in time within a "harmony of illusion."

Responsibility is a major concern of the frame, Scholarship as Conversation. "Understand the responsibility that comes with entering the conversation through participatory channels contributing to the conversation,"[30] is a disposition in this frame. In the vaccination and autism debate, the parents advocacy group, SafeMinds, promotes the idea that the thimerosal in vaccines causes autism by citing an article in *Medical Hypotheses* entitled "Autism: a novel form of mercury poisoning."[31] The journal admits that it accepts articles that are "probably untrue" and true to form; this article's theory was disproved but is still cited by advocacy groups.[32] Ludwik Fleck wrote that "there can be resistance to a prevailing thought style, only when striving for a goal."[33] In the vaccination/autism debate, the public health goal is the elimination of disease through the immunization program, now the accepted norm. The goal of autism advocacy groups, however, is discovering the cause of autism, so it can be eliminated. Both are worthy goals, but the advocacy groups, such as SafeMinds, are resistant to the prevailing thought style, believing immunization interferes with their goal of preventing autism and challenging the idea of a universal immunization program. They are entering the scholarly conversation, but in an irresponsible manner, by continuing to cite disproven theories.

Media's role in Scholarship as Conversation

We also look at the responsibility of the media and their role in the scholarly conversation in class. In the name of balance, media fuels the social media fire by giving equal time to both sides of an issue, despite potential harm through misinformation.[34] In the vaccine/autism debate, parent advocacy groups, such as Generation Rescue, arise from the fears and misinformation that media's need for balance and ratings produce. Listservs, chat rooms, blogs, and other social media perpetuate rumor and myth. Responsibility often falls away in social media venues. Students witness this every day in their personal lives. The knowledge practice of the Scholarship as Conversation frame encourages students to "critically evaluate contributions made by others in participatory information environments."[35]

In one assignment, students find a medical news article and compare it to the original article. They are asked which is the primary and which is the secondary source. The secondary news articles are written in a much easier to understand style and will usually cite the original article. This is another opportunity to remind students to try and cite the original work whenever possible. It also allows them to see how focus or meaning can change each time we take a step away from the original study or thought.

Scholarly perceptions can change for many other reasons. Students must think critically about topics to understand different ways in which misconceptions can occur. Autism diagnoses have risen in the United States from about .47 per 1,000 children in the 1980s to about 14.6 per 1,000 in 2012, according to the CDC.[36] The media and others may look first at environmental factors for the increase, overlooking the changes in the definition of autism. The DSM-5 changed the diagnosis to include four separate disorders: autistic disorder, Asperger's disorder, childhood disintegrative disorder, or pervasive developmental disorder. This change in diagnostic criteria accounts for at least part of the increased prevalence. In a Denmark study, Hansen et al reported that these changes accounted for 60 percent of the increase in the observed prevalence of Autistic Spectrum Disorder from 1980–1991.[37] Better screening, greater parent awareness, and more health professionals trained in the diagnosis of autism may also contribute to an increase in prevalence, but whether it accounts for all of the increase is highly doubtful.[38] Students are asked to critically evaluate everything they read in class. The statistics in this case are correct and seem to indicate a tremendous increase in autism, but students must learn to consider other factors that may not be readily apparent but critical nonetheless.

Conclusion

The consequences of misconceptions or misinformation, particularly in the areas of public health, can be dire, illustrating how important responsibility is in scholarly conversation. As parents worry and abstain or delay vaccinations, public health can be threatened. Low vaccination rates in states such as Oregon, California, and Colorado become problematic, especially when vaccination rates drop critically. When the "herd immunity threshold"[39] is reached, infection spreads. Because measles is very contagious, the immunity threshold needed to protect a community is high—95 percent. Diseases like polio, which are less contagious, have a threshold of 80 to 85 percent.[40]

The vaccine/autism debate offers one example of how the conversation of scholarship can impact society. Authorities come to the forefront and then recede. Parents want desperately to protect their children and are unsure who to trust. Scientists do little to reassure them because they tend to communicate within their own narrow areas of research and do little to reach out to the broader society. Meanwhile, advocacy groups and the media bombard parents with information that is difficult to ignore.

My hope is that this course, and the lesson based on the autism/vaccination debate, will be one, small, incremental step in helping our students incorporate the knowledge practices and dispositions of the Scholarship as Conversation frame into their information literacy knowledge base. An information-literate professional can be a voice of reason in critical health debates, such as the autism/vaccination one. Students may soon have the responsibility of calming fears regarding vaccinations or other health care related issues. They may also contribute to the conversation through published articles, social media, or presenting at professional meetings.

The autism/immunization debate lesson should help students realize the importance of following changes in scholarly perspective of evidence over time, as stated in the Frame's knowledge practices. The Wakefield article was published in 1998, when many of our students were infants or not even born yet. It took thirteen years of debate before *Lancet* officially retracted the article. Following, reading, and evaluating the validity of the comments and concerns regarding the article before it was retracted illustrates the value of seeking out different perspectives and interpretations, as stated in the Frame, before students come to their own conclusions.

The Scholarship as Conversation frame offers a more expansive view of this concept and serves as a helpful guide that educators and information literacy instructors may give students a better appreciation of the discursive practice of scholarship, as well as an understanding of their roles as contributors, evaluators, and interpreters. A better comprehension of the implications of this frame will help students appreciate the importance of the traditional information literacy skills, such as attribution, but more importantly, information literate students will ultimately be better health care providers because they will be better equipped to evaluate the available information and decide for themselves the current best evidence on any topic.

Notes

1. Alexander J. Carroll and Robin Dasler, "'Scholarship is a Conversation': Discourse, Attribution, and Twitter's Role in Information Literacy Instruction," *The Journal of Creative Library Practice* (2015), http://creativelibrarypractice.org/2015/03/.
2. Association of College and Research Libraries (ACRL), *Framework for Information*

Literacy for Higher Education, February 2, 2015, http://www.ala.org/acrl/standards/ilframework.
3. Association of College and Research Libraries (ACRL), *Information Literacy Competency Standards for Higher Education*, 2000, http://www.ala.org/acrl/standards/informationliteracycompetency.
4. Maureen Knapp and Stewart Brower, "The ACRL Framework for Information Literacy in Higher Education: Implications for Health Sciences Librarianship," *Medical Reference Services Quarterly* 33, no. 4 (2014): 467.
5. Nancy E. Adams, "A Comparison of Evidence-Based Practice and the ACRL Information Literacy Standards: Implications for Information Literacy Practice," *College & Research Libraries* 75, no. 2 (2014): 242.
6. Knapp and Brower, "The ACRL Framework for Information Literacy in Higher Education: Implications for Health Sciences Librarianship": 467.
7. ACRL, *Framework for Information Literacy for Higher Education*.
8. Carroll and Dasler, "Scholarship is a Conversation."
9. ACRL, *Framework for Information Literacy for Higher Education*, February 2, 2015, http://www.ala.org/acrl/standards/ilframework.
10. Ibid.
11. Ibid.
12. Ibid.
13. Liza Gross, "A Broken Trust: Lessons from the Vaccine–Autism Wars," *PLoS Biology* 7, no. 5 (2009): e1000114: 6.
14. National Library of Medicine, "Errata, Retractions, Partial Retractions, Corrected and Republished Articles, Duplicate Publications, Comments (Including Author Replies), Updates, Patient Summaries, and Republished (Reprinted) Articles Policy for MEDLINE," accessed September 15, 2016, https://www.nlm.nih.gov/pubs/factsheets/errata.html.
15. A. J. Wakefield et al., "Ileal-Lymphoid-Nodular Hyperplasia, Non-Specific Colitis, and Pervasive Developmental Disorder in Children," *Lancet* 351, no. 9103 (1998): 637–641. (Retracted Article. In *Lancet* 375, no. 9713, 2010: 445).
16. John M. Budd, MaryEllen Sievert, and Tom R. Schultz, "Phenomena of Retraction: Reasons for Retraction and Citations to the Publications," *JAMA* 280, no. 3 (1998): 296.
17. Craig Silverman, "Retraction Action: Oransky and Marcus Keep Tabs on Retracted Scientific Papers," *Columbia Journalism Review*, August 9, 2010, http://www.cjr.org/thezobservatory/retraction_action.php.
18. Jaime A. Teixeira da Silva and Judit Dobránszki, "Notices and Policies for Retractions, Expressions of Concern, Errata and Corrigenda: Their Importance, Content, and Context," *Science and Engineering Ethics* (2016): 1, doi:10.1007/s11948-016-9769-y.
19. Ibid.
20. Susan J. Lee et al., "Fetal Pain: A Systematic Multidisciplinary Review of the Evidence," *JAMA* 294, no. 8 (2005): 947–954.
21. Howard Bauchner, "JAMA: No Plan to Retract Article on Fetal Pain, Despite Outcry from Anti-Abortion Activists," June 15, 2016, http://retractionwatch.com/2016/06/15/jama-no-plan-to-retract-article-on-fetal-pain-despite-outcry-from-anti-abortion-activists/.
22. Centers for Disease Control and Prevention, "Measles: Cases and Outbreaks," last updated August 3, 2016, http://www.cdc.gov/measles/cases-outbreaks.html.

23. Gross, "A Broken Trust": e1000114. Fig. 2: 3.
24. Ibid, 2.
25. Sharon R. Kaufman, "Regarding the Rise in Autism: Vaccine Safety Doubt, Conditions of Inquiry, and the Shape of Freedom," *Ethos* 38, no. 1 (2010): 20.
26. Ludwik Fleck, trans. Frederick Bradley and Thaddeus J. Trenn, *Genesis and the Development of a Scientific Fact* (Chicago: University of Chicago Press, 1979), Kindle edition, chap. 4, sect. 4, location 1921.
27. Ibid, chap. 4, sect. 4, location 1971.
28. Ibid, chap. 4, sect. 4, location 963.
29. Ibid, chap. 2, sect. 3, location 233.
30. ACRL, *Framework for Information Literacy for Higher Education*.
31. S. Bernard et al., "Autism: A Novel Form of Mercury Poisoning," *Medical Hypotheses* 56, no. 4 (2001): 462–471.
32. Gross, "A Broken Trust": e1000114, 3.
33. Ludwik Fleck, trans. Frederick Bradley and Thaddeus J. Trenn. *Genesis and the Development of a Scientific Fact* (Chicago: University of Chicago Press, 1979), Kindle edition, chap. 4, sect. 3, location 1985.
34. Gross, "A Broken Trust": e1000114, 6.
35. ACRL, *Framework for Information Literacy for Higher Education*.
36. Centers for Disease Control and Prevention, "Autism Spectrum Disorder: Data and Statistics," last updated August 5, 2016, https://www.cdc.gov/ncbddd/autism/data.html.
37. Stefan N. Hansen, Diana E. Schendel, and Erik T. Parner, "Explaining the Increase in the Prevalence of Autism Spectrum Disorders the Proportion Attributable to Changes in Reporting Practices," *JAMA Pediatrics* 169, no. 1 (2015): 60.
38. Deborah L. Christensen, Jon Baio, Kim Van Naarden Braun, et al., "Prevalence and Characteristics of Autism Spectrum Disorder among Children Aged 8 Years – Autism and Developmental Disabilities Monitoring Network, 11 Sites, United States, 2012" *Morbidity and Mortality Weekly Report Surveillance Summaries*, 65 no. 3 (2016): 1–23, doi: http://dx.doi.org/10.15585/mmwr.ss6503a1.
39. Emily Willingham and Laura Helft, "What Is Herd Immunity?" *NOVA*, September 5, 2014, http://www.pbs.org/wgbh/nova/body/herd-immunity.html.
40. Ibid.

CHAPTER 19*

Widening the Threshold:
Using Scholarship as Conversation to Welcome Students to Science

Rebecca Kuglitsch

When thinking about the frames and how I might introduce them to science faculty and students, Scholarship as Conversation was one that seemed easy to understand but unlikely to resonate with them. As I read "… experts understand that a given issue may be characterized by several competing perspectives as part of an ongoing conversation in which information users and creators come together and negotiate meaning,"[1] I imagined it might not be easy to introduce to students of science and engineering, since a rather popular conception is that there are singular answers in science. As Graff and Birkenstein write, "Despite the importance of argument in scientific writing, newcomers to the genre often see it solely as a means for communicating uncontroversial, objective facts."[2] To my surprise, however, after speaking with students and faculty, this concept did resonate well, and I believe it can help us address some critical questions of importance to both scientists and students. In fact, it is a concept that can irreversibly transform how students see scientific research and themselves as participants in it. Seeing themselves as participants helps them through a threshold not only for information literacy but for research education as well.[3]

Anyone who has ever had a conversation about evolution, vaccines, or climate change has probably heard "but it's just a theory!" Expert scientists are comfortable with ambiguity and multiple answers. Thus, the gap between

---

* This work is licensed under a Creative Commons Attribution 4.0 License, CC BY (https://creativecommons.org/licenses/by/4.0/).

fact and conversation is not unfamiliar to scientists or students. But how do we bridge the gap between "it's just a theory" and expert comfort with ambiguity? The concept of scholarship as a conversation can help get us there. Moreover, opening the conversation with faculty members by acknowledging this gap can help librarians draw clear connections between their interest in enhancing students' information literacy and science faculty members' interest in scientific literacy. This point of connection can serve as a foundation for further discussion of information literacy.

Moreover, by positing scientific scholarly work as a conversation, something with expected conventions, styles, and approaches, we can help students begin to value their own potential contributions to the conversation and see themselves as contributors to and participants in science, rather than as outsiders looking in at an inhuman process that has always been driven by truth. By positing the scientific scholarship as a conversation, we can make it more vivid to students that science is a product of people. This both encourages students to feel like they could contribute to science—that their questions and unique perspectives have something to add to the conversation—and to feel that it is perhaps less intimidating and more meaningful.

What does Scholarship as a Conversation look like in the sciences?

Perhaps most challenging for many students accustomed to traditional methods of science and engineering is the idea of a lack of a single uncontested answer. While there is an active movement to increase active learning in the sciences and teach science in a way that encourages investigation rather than simple reception of facts, this change will take time to fully permeate the classroom. No matter how science is taught in the classroom, textbooks, the medium through which most students encounter science, also typically present science as an uncontested, non-controversial series of facts.[4] Or, textbooks may highlight occasional controversies as special features, which tends to visually suggest that argument is not a normal part of science but an exceptional one. As well as these aspects of presentation, there are aspects of science that functionally have single uncontested answers. A mouse is a mouse; an ecosystem is usually classifiable; water is a gas, liquid, or solid under knowable conditions. These facts form the foundation from which scientific investigation is conducted, but especially for students who are at the early stages of learning to become scientists, they can be mistaken for science. Thus, for many students understanding that there are complex problems with many possible perspectives is more difficult. But this is a key shift for students who want to join the scientific community of practice. "Creating and negotiating meaning" is a phrase that is not really commonly used in science, but which accurately describes the attempt to make sense of phenomena on the borders of our knowledge and understanding.[5] So what does it look like when a science or engineering student has grasped the concept that scholarship is a conversation?

Certainly, many of the knowledge practices listed in the Framework are quite directly and easily applicable to the scientific context: citing the contributing work of others, for example, or practicing contributing to the scholarly contribution at an appropriate level via poster sessions, presentations, or lab reports. However, some of the knowledge practices for this frame can be more challenging for students in the sciences to understand. For example, the knowledge practices "identify the contribution that particular articles, books, and other scholarly pieces make to disciplinary knowledge" (in a way more complex than venerating Darwin or Newton), or "summarize the changes in scholarly perspectives over time on a particular topic within a specific discipline," are not necessarily phrased in ways that are particularly resonant with the sciences, and moreover are challenging to students who may even struggle to read and understand complex technical peer-reviewed articles, the sciences' form of primary literature.[6] But thinking about these skills in the context of a literature review or a research proposal explaining how a new question arises out of existing research can help make them clearly relevant to students in the sciences. Similarly, recognizing that the conversation is not just scientists presenting facts to each other but rather a conversation with disputes that may be resolved, may take a field in a new direction, or may never be resolved is very challenging, particularly for students encountering the primary literature for the first time. Another key knowledge practice that students can find challenging is identifying barriers to participation in the conversation. Students may find it quite easy to identify material barriers to participation in the scholarly conversation of science—for example, lack of access to a lab, equipment, or software would be a challenge to participation in the scholarly conversation. But it can be more challenging for students to identify social barriers to participation, such as exclusion due to race, gender, sexual orientation, religion, and socioeconomic status, and yet it is key for students in the sciences to recognize that these barriers exist.

Learner dispositions for this frame identified in the Framework, too, range widely in their ease of applicability to the sciences. Recognizing that they are entering an unfinished conversation is likely to be challenging to students who perceive science as a series of fact-based, finished projects. Seeking out conversations taking place in a research area is something many undergraduate science students do, although they may struggle as undergraduates to seek out conversations in the peer-reviewed literature, rather than, say, a reputable magazine like *Scientific American* or *ScienceNews*. The emphasis on the peer-reviewed literature from professors and librarians, too, may make it hard for students to recognize that there are other venues to participate in the conversation, such as data sets, conferences, scholarly blogs, disciplinary listservs, and technical documentation.

But what I think is particularly key for making the conversation more inclusive is for students in the sciences to develop two dispositions in particular, to:
- "see themselves as contributors to scholarship rather than only consumers of it;"
- "recognize that systems privilege authorities and that not having a fluency in the language and process of a discipline disempowers their ability to participate and engage."[7]

The latter is a point students may particularly quickly understand, since their experience engaging with the peer-reviewed literature usually makes that point quite clearly. While students often appreciate and capitalize on the highly structured nature of peer-reviewed scientific articles to read just what they find essential, other aspects of the language and norms of the discipline can be frustrating and opaque. Struggling to cope with dense jargon, decoding graphs, and managing an extensive if precise and technical vocabulary, students are immediately and personally confronted with the challenge of entering a discipline without fluency.

Understanding that mastering the language of science is a key to entering the scientific conversation is a foundational part of students recognizing that they themselves can contribute knowledge, and it is also a way to relate the concept to faculty members who often have vivid memories of the experience of mastering the language of science. As Hope Jahren wrote in *Lab Girl*, reminiscing about learning to write as a faculty member, "I have become proficient at producing a rare species of prose capable of distilling ten years of work by five people into six published pages, written in a language that very few people can read and that no one ever speaks."[8] Instructors can conceptualize this challenge as learning a language to take part in a conversation. Students can then learn that this is a conversation with rules that are constructed by people. Consequently, students can also learn that those rules are therefore changeable if needed, and this can help students understand that their difficulties in joining the conversation, or following the conversations' rules, are not fundamental deficiencies of their own, but rather learned skills that challenge all nascent scientists. Knowing that the rules are changeable means students can perhaps better see a place for themselves in the conversation. Historically, the conversation of science has been shaped by a very narrow sliver of race, class, sexuality, and gender expectations. To know that the conversation is shaped, and that historically only certain participants—or in some cases participants able to present themselves in certain ways—were permitted to enter it, can help student see that the way science is investigated and communicated isn't inevitable, perfect, or permanent. It can help them see that science could use their voices, and that the questions and concerns they have to add to the conversation can shape and re-create the conversation. Seeing oneself as a contributor to knowledge is a threshold concept not just for information literacy but also for becoming a researcher, and offers another way for librarians to approach this frame in conversation with faculty members.[9]

Consequently, of the practices and dispositions in the frame Scholarship as Conversation, it is the practice of identifying barriers to participation and the dispositions of recognizing the ways systems privilege authority and of recognizing oneself as a contributor that I would like to focus on, both as a way of improving information literacy and as a way of making science more inclusive.

So how has the library community discussed Scholarship as a Conversation?

While some of the notions of who is permitted to join conversations, and the mechanism of the scientific conversation are less familiar to students, the notion of scholarship as a conversation has a long history both within and without the library. Indeed, one of the classic "how to write like a scholar" books is titled *They Say, I Say*, and its central framing device is derived from Kenneth Burke's ideas of scholarship as a conversational parlor.[10] In this conception, Burke presents scholarship as a long-running discussion taking place in a room, which the scholar can enter, then listen, contribute, and, eventually, depart: "Someone answers; you answer him; another comes to your defense…"[11]

Within the library scholarship, the idea of scholarship as a conversation has been explored both since and before the development of the Framework. Much of the pre-Framework conversation, like *They Say, I Say*, has focused on the conversation idea as a way of framing argumentative writing that empowers students and reframes sources as something integral to developing arguments, rather than as decorations added after an argument has been constructed. McMillen and Hill discussed the idea of research as a conversation in the context of a collaboration between the libraries and the composition program at the Oregon State University; they, too, frame the idea of research in terms of the Burkean parlor.[12] Atwood and Crosetto, for example, similarly explore teaching personal voice as part of library instruction in composition.[13] They suggest that librarians and composition instructors share a common goal of students developing a personal voice that yet acknowledges the existence of other arguments and evidence; I would go beyond this and say librarians and any instructor share this goal. Despite the relatively recent establishment of the Framework, the concept of scholarship as a conversation is certainly one familiar in the library world.

How has the scholarly conversation been shaped in science?

The conversational norm in science is rooted in a very particular genre, the peer-reviewed scholarly article. While there are other methods of communicating science, the peer-reviewed article has long established priority and seriousness of investigation. This format did not spring out of nothing; it developed from an epistolary tradition of scholarship, in which savants, scholars, and natural philosophers maintained a written conversation, also known as the invisible college.[14] These letters would have been circulated, broadening their audience beyond one or two, but still remaining relatively limited. Eventually, this tradition grew into a journal format, moving from the communications just of a scholarly society such as the Royal Society. While the journal format broadened the reach and opened the conversation, participants were still limited. Class, race, religion, sexual orientation, and gender presentation all constituted barriers to participation. The journal published the apparently objective word of gentleman, verified by experiment, in the form of the article.

Indeed, while the format of the journal article has changed since the first issue of the *Proceedings of the Royal Society*, the first English-language journal, and one that largely aligns with what we think of as science (though at the time it would have been termed natural philosophy), many of the underlying ideas remain. The veneer of objectivity remains an important part of scientific publishing: today's ideal journal still publishes the word verified by the experiment, pruned as cleanly as possible of any intrusions of the scientist's self.

One might argue that the stripping of the self from the article would allow the broadest possible participation. If scientific articles take no account of the self, then what could be easier to join from the margins? But this is a false premise. The person who writes the article participates in a community of practice, and the article is only the fruit of a long process of growth.

Ultimately, articles are inseparable from their authors, who must do research, process data, and write in the company of other humans and their attendant preconceptions and biases. Underlying the conversation of the article is a deeper daily conversation that does not allow full and equal participation. Scientists who transition genders recount experiences where their work is suddenly evaluated differently after transition. Ben Barres, for example, writes of a situation where he overhead a colleague, unaware of his transition, explain that Ben's work was much better than his sister's.[15] Yet the person who wrote it did not change. From the beginning, then, the journal article grew out of the written conversation of economically privileged white men who, at a minimum, presented as cisgender, heterosexual, and of the religious tradition most accepted in their home countries. There have always been exceptions and people who paid dearly to join the community, of course. But this is at the root.

Acknowledging that root can make it clear that structures that *still* do not fit a wide swathe of humanity do not fit because of a problem in the structure, rather than a problem with the humans who seek to participate. Understanding these barriers as constructions are essential for making it possible for students likely to be marginalized to see themselves as contributors to the scholarly conversation. So, by making it clear that the participants in the scholarly conversation are privileged in different ways, we can make science more welcoming. But how do we actually make this clear?

Exploring the conversation of science

When teaching, I approach these questions in several ways, depending on the amount of time available and the scope of a class session. In situations with repeated, long-term contact, one approach that has been successful is using an activity inspired by the BEAM method, which asks students to assess how citations are used, fitting them into one of four categories (Background, Exhibit, Argument, and Method).[16] I explored this approach in a biology course that is team taught with a colleague, where we had three sessions with upper division undergraduates. Our underlying approach is inspired by BEAM, although we modified the form greatly. Our goal is that at the end of the session students understand why a particular citation has been chosen. Rather than asking students to categorize citations into one of four categories, we simply asked small groups of students to look at particular sections of an article and identify why articles have been cited in each section. Because there is a fairly significant barrier to reading an entire article in class, we have typically sought to use an article students have already read and split the class up into at least four sections that each take responsibility for a section: the introduction, methods, results, and conclusion. Depending on the article and class, one might choose to swap the results section for the literature review. While each section has a set of tailored questions, there are one or two that are consistent throughout the exercise, asking students the general purpose of citations in that paragraph and asking them to select one citation and explore in depth why it might have been selected. By using a carefully selected article, one can elicit questions and conversations that give rise to reflection about who is participating in the conversation and how. For example, students notice when a particular person is repeatedly cited or when the author cites themselves frequently.

These observations serve as introductions to discussion about participation in the conversation of scholarship and how particular voices come be rendered important. For example, discussing self-citation prompted a conversation about how self-citation can lead to more citation by others and the way that particular behavior is gendered.[17] I asked students why self-citation might happen, and they identified several reasons, ranging from a narrow specialization in which there are no other experts, a research project building on past experiments, and also gendered behavior. Students reflected on issues of who is permitted to brag, to claim their own authority, and establish themselves as experts. Other questions raised by this citation analysis touched on status and class access to the conversation. For example, in a discussion about standard techniques for affixing motion-trackers to turtles, students wondered about laboratory technicians and their ability to participate in the conversation, when they noticed that in their experience it is lab techs who do much of this kind of work but are rarely credited as authors or invited to participate in larger conversations. This was an opportunity for students to reflect on how people might choose research collaborators, and indeed who counts as a collaborator. It sparked their beginning to think about how authorship credit is impacted by social expectations and biases. This, in turn, can help students see that citation and collaboration are not markers solely of virtue but of social forces.

Another activity that has worked well begins by exploring a controversy or question that is influenced by whose voice is privileged in science as a case study. Students might be given a short description of a scholarly scenario in which issues of identity are interwoven and a set of questions including:

- What is the current state of knowledge around the question?
- Who are the participants in investigating the question?
    - What stake do they have in it?
    - What perspectives and background do the participants bring to the question at hand?
    - How do they interact with each other?
- How do these perspectives and backgrounds enrich the conversation? How might they facilitate or obstruct entry into the scholarly conversation?
- What related questions remain unasked?

These scenarios might be current or they might take a more historical approach. Examples might include any of the following:

- the field of animal behavior, and how long it took to acknowledge, record, and investigate widespread and behaviorally important same-sex sexual behaviors in animals;[18]
- the field of Arctic ecology, and how long it is taking to integrate indigenous perspectives and what has consequently been missed when, for example, university climate change scholars assert that

indigenous populations have "little understanding of the history of the earth;"[19]
- human biology, exercise science,[20] and medical research,[21] in which typical subjects have until recently been male, to avoid the confusion that female hormones might add to research, ignoring the fact that male hormones exist and affect the body, and that half of most drug recipients will, in fact, not be male, leading to a limited understanding of male hormonal processes, and medications that may not work as expected in women;
- in medicine, where members of minority racial groups have long received subpar pain treatment.[22]

These activities are very structured and take place in a course where we have several sessions and a relatively free hand with content.

What can one do in one-shots or sessions where most of the content is fixed and pre-determined? A few well-placed discussion questions can at least raise awareness of the issues and is a method I commonly employ. Graff and Birkenstein suggest simply asking questions that frame a question in terms of a conversation; they suggest asking who an author is responding to, rather than what the author's argument is, for example.[23] They found that when phrased this way, students were able to participate in a more lively conversation where they intelligently questioned the author's point of view, discovered other alternative points of view, or developed their own unique views rather than painfully summarizing.[24] This method of foregrounding the academic conversation forces students to engage with the idea of authors as part of something larger, rather than isolated pieces. Librarians can take advantage of this approach. Discussing forward citation tracking is already a frequent part of my instruction in the sciences, given the emphasis on currency in the sciences, and it offers an opportunity to clearly raise questions about who is responding to whom and why. Making the approach more explicit helps highlight the idea of scholarship as a conversation. Using these small opportunities, we can intertwine conversations about why certain voices might be listened to above others in a standard discussion of forward and backward citation chaining. Why is someone's contribution to the conversation enshrined in a citation while others are not? Beyond relevance and currency, what other factors are brought to bear on who can participate? Understanding and identifying these factors can be a struggle for students when there is only time for short discussions, so it is important to have some guiding questions to elicit these points in the classroom. For students, once grasped, this point can encourage them to seek out additional points of view, searching beyond simply citation chaining backward and forward. Indeed, in my own practice as an author, I find thinking about these questions makes me more mindful of who I am citing and encourages me to search for more perspectives.

Assessment

I have found that more informal assessments work well to assess whether students are developing dispositions and knowledge practices that align with these ideas. Think-pair-share has been a particularly effective approach for formative assessment, since it gives students scope to explore their ideas. In this technique, students are asked to think about a question, discuss it with a partner, and then join a larger, full group conversation. Because this classroom assessment technique lets all the students engage and share their insights, and is especially well suited when a range of potential opinions and insights can be shared, it is a good fit for these courses.[25] Because students exchange and discuss opinions, it allows them to refine their thoughts and explore others' points of views, and in the sharing phase, it allows the librarian to hear student perspectives, assess the overall grasp of key ideas, address anything missing or misunderstood, and use the current conversation to segue into the next topic.[26] For this activity, I would expect to hear students identify both material and immaterial barriers to participation in science, in particular how language and stylistic conventions are useful both to present complex ideas concisely, but also function to exclude many participants from the conversation. Any of the questions used in the activities described above would be potentially applicable here, and librarians might also choose to ask students to take a moment at the end of a session to ask what, in particular, they can add to the conversation. What unique perspectives do they bring to science? In this case, I would hope to hear students reflect on how their experiences and concerns can bring a useful perspective to science and potentially address new questions.

If the context is one where the librarian has more time with the class, perhaps a credit course or a recurring session, another classroom assessment option that could work well is the invented dialogue. In this technique, described by Bowles-Terry and Kvenild, students are asked to create dialogues with an imagined partner in order to explain a challenging concept.[27] One might ask students, for example, to imagine they are explaining the habits and practices of participation in the scientific scholarly conversation to a newer student. If students have crossed or begun to cross this threshold, I would hope to see students identifying barriers, both material and immaterial, to participating in the scholarly conversation and explaining that scientists must learn particular language and conversational conventions to participate in the scholarly debate. This assessment demands time from the student and time from the teaching librarian to read, assess, and follow up with feedback, so it may be difficult to stage in one-shots or other short engagements.[28]

Conclusion

By explicitly discussing who participates in the scientific scholarly conversation, and how the conversation developed in a way that privileges certain voices, we can help students understand both how to work better within the system as it is, and how to think about possibilities for change and why there is an urgent need to broaden the pool of voices. While this is a narrow aspect of the frame Scholarship as Conversation, it is an aspect that can have a significant effect on students and is deeply transformative. Crossing the threshold of seeing themselves as participants in research is a transition for both nascent scientists developing their identity as a research and for students becoming information literate. Moreover, crossing this threshold can lead to a greater sense of inclusion and, consequently, increased retention of underrepresented students in the sciences. This retention can lead to wider pool of voices that will increase the scope of questions in the sciences, enhance the quality of work done, and simply make sure that more students have the opportunity to explore their interests in full.

Notes

1. Association of College and Research Libraries (ACRL), *Framework for Information Literacy for Higher Education*, February 2, 2015, http://www.ala.org/acrl/standards/ilframework.
2. Gerald Graff and Cathy Birkenstein, *They Say, I Say: The Moves That Matter in Academic Writing*, 2nd ed. (New York: W. W. Norton & Company, 2009), 158.
3. Kristine Alpi and Chad Hoggan, "Recognizing the Value of Threshold Concepts: Application of a Conceptual Tool to Professional Students Learning to Be Researchers," *The Reference Librarian* 57, no. 2 (April 2, 2016): 121–122, doi:10.1080/02763877.2016.1121070.
4. Graff and Birkenstein, *They Say, I Say*, 158.
5. ACRL, *Framework for Information Literacy for Higher Education*.
6. Ibid.
7. Ibid.
8. Hope Jahren, *Lab Girl* (New York: Alfred A. Knopf, 2016), 63.
9. Alpi and Hoggan, "Recognizing the Value of Threshold Concepts"; Margaret Kiley and Gina Wisker, "Threshold Concepts in Research Education and Evidence of Threshold Crossing," *Higher Education Research & Development* 28, no. 4 (August 1, 2009): 431–41, doi:10.1080/07294360903067930.
10. Graff and Birkenstein, *They Say, I Say*; Kenneth Burke, *The Philosophy of Literary Form: Studies in Symbolic Action* (Baton Rouge: Louisiana State University Press, 1941).
11. Burke, *The Philosophy of Literary Form*, 110.
12. Paula S. McMillen and Eric Hill, "Why Teach 'Research as a Conversation' in Freshman Composition Courses? A Metaphor to Help Librarians and Composition

Instructors Develop a Shared Model," *Research Strategies* 20, no. 1–2 (2004): 3–22, doi:10.1016/j.resstr.2005.07.005.
13. Thomas A. Atwood and Alice Crosetto, "How to Address 'I've Already Written My Paper, Now I Just Need to Find Some Sources': Teaching Personal Voice through Library Instruction," *College & Undergraduate Libraries* 16, no. 4 (2009): 322–28.
14. David A. Kronick, "The Commerce of Letters: Networks and 'Invisible Colleges' in Seventeenth- and Eighteenth-Century Europe," *The Library Quarterly: Information, Community, Policy* 71, no. 1 (2001): 28–43.
15. Ben A. Barres, "Does Gender Matter?," *Nature* 442, no. 7099 (July 13, 2006): 134, doi:10.1038/442133a.
16. Kate Rubick, "Flashlight: Using Bizup's BEAM to Illuminate the Rhetoric of Research," *Reference Services Review* 43, no. 1 (February 5, 2015): 98–111, doi:10.1108/RSR-10-2014-0047.
17. Robin Wilson, "Lowered Cites," *The Chronicle of Higher Education*, March 17, 2014, http://www.chronicle.com/article/New-Gender-Gap-in-Scholarship/145311.
18. Joan Roughgarden, *Evolution's Rainbow: Diversity, Gender, and Sexuality in Nature and People* (University of California Press, 2013).
19. Elaine Bielawski, "Inuit Indigenous Knowledge and Science in the Arctic," in *Naked Science: Anthropological Inquiry into Boundaries, Power and Knowledge*, ed. Laura Nader (New York: Routledge, 1996), 224.
20. Bethany Brookshire, "Women in Sports Are Often Underrepresented in Science," *Science News*, accessed June 18, 2016, https://www.sciencenews.org/blog/scicurious?mode=blog&context=131; Joseph T. Costello, Francois Bieuzen, and Chris M. Bleakley, "Where Are All the Female Participants in Sports and Exercise Medicine Research?," *European Journal of Sport Science* 14, no. 8 (November 17, 2014): 847–51, doi:10.1080/17461391.2014.911354.
21. Paula Johnson, Therese Fitzgerald, Alina Salganicoff, Susan F. Wood, and Jill M. Goldstein, *Sex-Specific Medical Research: Why Women's Health Can't Wait: A Report of the Mary Horrigan Connors Center for Women's Health & Gender Biology at Brigham and Women's Hospital* (Brigham and Women's Hospital, 2014), http://www.wisdombog.com/pdf/11200415250.pdf.
22. Vence L. Bonham, "Race, Ethnicity, and Pain Treatment: Striving to Understand the Causes and Solutions to the Disparities in Pain Treatment," *The Journal of Law, Medicine & Ethics* 28 (March 1, 2001): 52–68, doi:10.1111/j.1748-720X.2001.tb00039.x.
23. Graff and Birkenstein, *They Say, I Say*, 145–46.
24. Ibid.
25. Melissa Bowles-Terry and Cassandra Kvenild, *Classroom Assessment Techniques for Librarians* (Chicago, Illinois: Association of College and Research Libraries, 2015), 32.
26. Ibid., 34.
27. Ibid., 54.
28. Ibid., 56.

CHAPTER 20

Theater as a Conversation:
Threshold Concepts in the Performing Arts

Christina E. Dent

Working with first-year students in PA101: Languages of the Stage is always a bright spot for the teaching librarians in our library instruction program. What makes working with these courses such a dream is that the students by and large are willing and eager to engage. They actively listen. They raise their hands to answer questions. They ask questions. They will try to out-do each other in a think-pair-share activity. They *perform*.

For any librarian who has ever suffered through an hour-long one-shot filled with face-palmed heads and blank stares, what I am describing probably sounds like paradise. In a sense it is: we are instructing students who are often invested, lively, funny, and genuinely great to work with. The problem, however, becomes telling the difference between performance and learning.

One of the most exciting facets of the new Framework for Information Literacy in Higher Education (Framework) is the paradigm shift from distilling information literacy into a practical skill set as detailed in the Information Literacy Competency Standards for Higher Education to expanding the disciplinary function of information literacy into habits of mind and higher-order thinking, much like the top-tier attributes in the cognitive domain of Bloom's taxonomy.[1] In order to assist performing arts students with stepping into the conversations of their discipline, it is first necessary to help them realize that, for them, art and scholarship are intrinsically linked. Many theater students see themselves as performers first and scholars second, or worse, not as scholars at all. As teaching librarians, we need to design impactful learning experiences that will demonstrate to our students that research is critical to understanding art and, therefore, performing it. No actor undertakes a role without study; no director begins a production without a well-researched vision. Students must grasp this idea if they hope to progress within the discipline.

A historical conversation

Languages of the Stage is an introductory course to the performing arts major required of all first-year performing arts students. When I started at Emerson as the Instruction Librarian, PA101 was one of the first classes I inherited from my predecessor. The goal of the course is to: "[introduce] students to the various means of expression available to the art of the stage… [and] to the visual forms of artistic communication, their history, and the conventions of all theatrical forms."[2] Like many library instruction programs, we work to tie all of our library activities to a course assignment, so that students will find their library experience more meaningful. In PA101, this assignment is a midterm dramaturgical presentation on Tony Kushner's *Angels in America*. For these projects, PA101 students are assigned research topics pertinent to Kushner's play. Topics have included: Tony Kushner's life and aesthetic, Valium addiction, AIDS, Julius and Ethel Rosenberg, and the Red Scare. For those unfamiliar with dramaturgy, the *Dictionary of the Theatre* defines the term as "the technique of dramatic art which seeks to establish the principles of play construction, either inductively on the basis of actual examples or deductively on the basis of a system of abstract principles."[3] Students need to thoroughly research their topic and produce a ten-minute presentation discussing the influence the topic has on interpreting the play. They are required to use both primary and secondary sources and include a multi-media component in their presentations.

Prior to the adoption of the Framework, our primary student learning goal for PA101 workshops focused on introducing first-year performing arts students to subject-specific reference materials, i.e., encyclopedias, in order for them to find credible background information and primary sources on their dramaturgical topics. After a short presentation in which the librarian modeled steps of the research process, students were given a brief overview of how to navigate the library's website and were directed to a cart of reference books waiting at the front of the classroom. Because the librarian knew all of the topics in advance, reference materials were pulled on each subject; every student was able to begin researching their topic with a vetted source.

As a teaching model, this version of a one-shot workshop was fun and easy to prep. Model research presentations involved everything from understanding the socio-cultural history of Crown Heights, Brooklyn, as an insight into Anna Deveare Smith's *Fires in the Mirror* to reimagining Shakespeare's *Hamlet* staged during the French Revolution. Students generally responded favorably to this method as well. In their feedback surveys, students commented that they had a better grasp of the library resources available to them and that they felt more confident proceeding with their dramaturgy assignments.

Yet, when we attended student presentations to assess our instructional impact on the final products, the results were mixed. Some students made the most of the reference materials we had provided and even went beyond to find additional materials. Other students, despite having reference material handed to them, clearly chose instead to rely on Wikipedia entries to provide background information and historical context on their topics. Students included primary source materials—letters, photos, videos, etc.—but more often than not, these sources seemed tacked on and were not well-integrated into the presentation. For example, a student might present on the zeitgeist of gay culture under the Reagan administration and then show a YouTube clip from an early 1960s film reel on the dangers of homosexuality, as if the two eras were one and the same. We were left facing the question of how to push students toward a better understanding of the context of their research instead of just fact-finding.

A methodological conversation

In the spring of 2014, our library hosted its fifth iteration of a three-day faculty professional development workshop on information literacy. The goal of this workshop was to assist faculty in identifying ways of incorporating information literacy-based learning outcomes into their courses and assignments. Although the Framework had been drafted, it had not yet been finalized and adopted, so we did not share the document with our faculty. We did, however, share the pedagogical idea of threshold concepts with them, on which much of the theory within the Framework is based. One of the faculty participants was the course coordinator for PA101, an individual with whom I already had a good working relationship. After the workshop, we met to discuss changes to the library's intervention with PA101. I shared with him a draft of the Framework and asked him to identify what he saw as a bottleneck[4] to learning for his performing arts students. In essence, we were trying to better understand what was going wrong with the dramaturgical assignment.

My faculty friend explained that the point of the assignment and, in fact, the larger purpose of the course as a whole, was to introduce students to the phenomenology of theater and to help them identify the characteristics of the contemporary aesthetic. This meant getting students to connect research to understanding plays; that there is a place—an important one—for research in creating art. The barrier to student learning, as he saw it, was getting students to understand that the way people produce art is a direct result of how they see the world in any given time and place. Based on his experience in the classroom, this abstraction was the hardest element for his students to grasp.

Having shared the Framework with my PA101 colleague, we worked to identify which of the frames seemed best suited for helping students better understand this abstract concept. How could we get students to go beyond the surface research they were doing and instead realize that the *context* of the information they were researching was imperative to understanding *Angels in America*? Recontextualizing the abstract concepts of contemporary theater aestheticism within the Scholarship as a Conversation frame gave us a good starting point for revising our approach to the dramaturgical assignment and the accompanying library workshop. In particular, my colleague noted that having students "recognize they are often entering into an ongoing scholarly conversation and not a finished conversation" and "see themselves as contributors to scholarship rather than only consumers of it" best articulated the goals of the assignment.[5]

A theoretical conversation

How does one enter into a scholarly conversation? What are the conventions, the rules, so to speak? How does one begin to navigate the murky waters of what are often contradictory points of view? Especially when, in adolescence, those contradictions can become a source of anxiety?[6] In essence, how do we as teachers help our students "[develop] familiarity with the sources of evidence, methods, and modes of discourse in [their] field" in order to "[assist] novice learners to enter the conversation" as described within the frame of Scholarship as a Conversation?[7]

These questions are tricky in any discipline, but are particularly thorny in the field of performing arts. In *Artistic Literacy: Theatre Studies and a Contemporary Liberal Education*, Nancy Kindelan explores the frequently trivialized position of performing arts programs within the academy:

> [M]any educators from other academic backgrounds are operating under the perception that theatre programs are extracurricular—providers of campus "entertainment." As a result, many believe that theatre, as a discipline, is not on par with other academic fields and that the theatre curricu-

lum and its concomitant activities lack the intellectual rigor and substance to cultivate the critical skills, creative capacities, and learning strategies that are the key components of a contemporary liberal education.[8]

Kindelan further argues that theater studies programs are one of the few truly interdisciplinary majors within the performing arts. Expert dramaturgs researching for a production are no less diligent or scholarly than other researchers. Why should we not expect the same from theater students? Part of our role as teaching librarians, in partnership with our colleagues in the discipline, is to impart the value of research to the creation of art, to demonstrate that the two are inextricably linked. Reaching first-year performing arts students is an ideal starting point for this kind of cognitive transformation. Indeed, if cognitive behavioral theorists are correct, "advancing higher cognition in adolescence requires that we take advantage of the developing capacity of [the] adolescent brain to reason and to develop strategies, not simply train encoding and retrieval of discrete facts and knowledge that has been memorized."[9] We must begin to cultivate higher-order critical thinking skills, the habits of mind outlined within ACRL's new Framework.

To take this argument further into the performing arts discipline, I turn to Mikhail Bakhtin and his *Discourse in the Novel*. Though Bakhtin is investigating the novel, his exploration of language and dialogue are easily applicable to other artistic genres. When discussing his theory of "heteroglossia" within the novel, Bakhtin describes the "internal stratification present in every language at any given moment of its historical existence" that exists within the novel, further citing that "[t]he novel orchestrates all its themes, the totality of the world of objects and ideas depicted and expressed in it, by means of the social diversity of speech types [*raznorečie*] and by the differing individual voices that flourish under such conditions."[10] One can almost hear the cacophony of voices Bakhtin's description evokes. It is the din of many conversations taking place within a single body of work, not a single one of which can be ignored or important meaning is lost. We can translate this directly into theater, which is built from the dialogues between characters.

When studying a play, the scholar must first make sense of what the characters are saying to each other within the context of the work as a whole. On top of this, they must further explore the different languages present within and without the context of the play: the varied "speech types," including the author, the time in which the play was written, the political atmosphere, the setting, the history, etc. Bakhtin further explores what he calls "heterogeneous stylistic unities" that "combine to form a structured artistic system," what we identify as the genre of the novel.[11] The same is true for the dramatic genre; individual elements of a play "are subordinated to the higher stylistic unity of the work as a whole."[12] This is the kind of critical conceptualization our students need to be undertaking. Such a shift in thinking goes beyond a discrete skill set built upon finding, accessing, evaluating, and using information. In order to push our students to think in new ways, we as teachers need to think in new ways as well.

Bahktin's theories put the value of dramaturgical research into an important context, one that is reflected in the ACRL Framework. Nancy Kindelan, in her exploration of the cross-disciplinary value of theater studies, states that current educational research shows "High-Impact Educational Practices increase student engagement and retention. […] Through learning experiences that stress critical inquiry skills, information gathering, and interdisciplinary connections, students often explore diverse social issues with faculty, staff, and peers."[13] Kindelan goes on to state that at its heart, dramaturgical research is a prime example of this kind of valuable high-impact learning activity.

A practical conversation

In revising our library workshop, we not only needed to revisit our student learning outcomes, but we also needed to find ways to have students engage in the world of their profession and to see that world as their own. In other words, we needed to help them take ownership of the dramatic conversations they were learning about. For performing arts students, that ownership has deeply tangible aspects. Most students produce work for a single audience member: their professor. The conservatory aspects of our performing arts program, however, mean there are often very real possibilities that students will see their work, e.g., play interpretations, stage design, or dramaturgical research, translated into production. They have something out there in public view with their name on it. It is the ownership of ideas in the best sense of the word. In the performing arts, it is critical for students to own this beyond a skill to be used in college and then abandoned when test-taking and exams are done.

Like many librarians, though, we were hard-pressed to completely abandon a teaching model that had been sustainable for years. The pedagogical shift of the Framework loomed, and we felt daunted by the prospect of reinventing our entire instruction program. In using the Framework, however, we have found that total reinvention is not always necessary. Instead, we needed to move beyond the skills and standards-based instruction we were used to and begin to engage students to think about higher order habits of mind in the context of information literacy.

What we do now is not radically different from what we have done in the past, but our instruction has been recontextualized in light of the thresh-

old concepts outlined in the Framework. To do this, we modeled our transition after Pace and Middendorf's formula for overcoming learning obstacles (OLO) detailed in *Decoding the Disciplines*.[14] Their model is a cyclic process with seven steps; we modified our version to five steps for our collaborative work with faculty and translated the steps into these questions:
1. What is a threshold concept to learning in this class?
2. How does an expert do these things?
3. How can these tasks be explicitly modeled?
4. How will students practice these things and get feedback?
5. How well are students mastering these tasks?

Working through these questions with our PA101 faculty helped us redesign our workshop with the larger ideas of the Framework in mind.

First, using input from our performing arts colleague, we identified Scholarship as a Conversation as the main threshold concept for learning for our PA101 students. We opted to incorporate this frame into the notion of what our PA101 faculty call the "contemporary aesthetic"—that no artistic work exists in a vacuum and that every play is quintessentially a commentary on how the artist views the world in a given time and place. Theater is a conversation and is not devoid of scholarship.

Next, we needed to better understand how an expert might go through this process. I sat down with my performing arts colleague and asked him to detail his process for me. I realized that in our old instruction model, we relied on single modes of information, that of ahistorical encyclopedias that did not represent multiple points of view. As an expert, my colleague noted that he looked beyond background information; in fact, he usually went to primary source material first to get a better understanding of the world within a play in the context of its original milieu. From our own assessment of student presentations, we knew we needed to better incorporate the purpose of using primary sources.

Our current workshop model acts as our method for modeling research tasks to our students. Using Prezi to tell a story of research, we focus on *Fires in the Mirror*. We make the storytelling aspects much more interactive, however; we want our students to put themselves into the positions of researcher-storytellers as early on in the process as possible. For instance, one of the first visuals within the Prezi is a brief synopsis of the play pulled from Wikipedia. Frequently, students are not at all familiar with Deveare Smith's work, and this mirrors the experience of the professional dramaturg: they will not always know the play in advance. A student reads aloud the summary, and then we ask students to identify areas of research they would choose to pursue if they were researching the play. We visually trace some of these lines of inquiry through a variety of sources, such as subject-specific reference works, books, newspapers, and photo archives, while paying attention to the different voices providing information. In this sense, we are exposing students to the idea that research experts (dramaturgs) in their field (performing arts) "understand that a given issue may be characterized by several competing perspectives as part of an ongoing conversation in which information users and creators come together and negotiate meaning."[15]

The final step in the modeling process involves students putting themselves in the place of the expert researcher and taking some ownership of the information we have uncovered as a group. Deveare Smith's play premiered in 1992, more than twenty years ago. Yet they know this production is still staged and still must have meaning. One of the key ideas from the play concerns race relations in the Crown Heights neighborhood of Brooklyn. We ask students what they might consider if they were to restage this play for contemporary audiences, if any of the research on racial violence in the 1990s connects with anything they have encountered in the present day. Logical leaps to events like those in Ferguson, Missouri, and Baltimore, Maryland, quickly follow. Some students even transition their ideas into a global context, citing religion- and race-based violence around the world.

All of this becomes preparation for how they will themselves practice dramaturgical research. Students have already been assigned research topics related to Tony Kushner's *Angels in America*. Their task is to apply the same lines of inquiry they have seen modeled during the workshop to an investigation into their subject matter and to apply this information to a unique interpretation of Kushner's text. Remaining time is devoted to students beginning their research process. After the librarian presentation, students are given index cards with the call number of a book and sent into the stacks to retrieve the item. They are asked to pull the book and return to the classroom for a think-pair-share activity. Working in teams, students summarize the contents of the book in front of them and suggest ways in which it might be useful for someone researching for a production of *Angels in America*. Because PA101 is a required course that runs in both the Fall and Spring semesters, instruction librarians cannot assume students have had any previous library exposure. Physically retrieving items serves multiple purposes: first-year students are exposed to the library's layout, they get familiar with the Library of Congress call number system, and, ultimately, they share their findings with their peers.

In this exercise, students begin to embody what Thomas Mackey and Trudi Jacobson call a "networked learning environment" in their examination of information literacy as metaliteracy.[16] As before, librarians know these topics in advance and have selected texts that have relevance to all the topics students will be working on. As the groups share their findings, it quickly becomes apparent to the class that each book discussed has relevance to someone else's topic. Texts are passed around. Students also begin to make connections between texts, commenting that many books are relevant to multiple topics. For instance, a student tasked with researching the history of drag and camp culture will benefit most obviously from a book on gay cultural aesthetics, but they may also see that *The Encyclopedia of Lesbian, Gay, Bisexual, and Transgender History in America* can also provide nuanced insights into their area of inquiry. As students use their selected texts to begin their research, librarians talk with students one-on-one to answer any questions and to provide further guidance.

The end result of this practice remains the same; students must put together a ten-minute visual presentation discussing their research topic in the context of better understanding Kushner's play. This is what their professors will be assessing and grading and, as librarians, we can do the same. By attending these presentations, we have gotten a better sense of how students are engaging in the larger conversations about their topics. This kind of examination is vital to our pedagogical approach to teaching information literacy. We want to better understand the weaker aspects of our workshop in order to revise, improve, and help students move beyond the threshold for this concept in their discipline.

A final conversation

Little has changed in terms of the methodology of our workshop with PA101. What we have changed, however, is *how* we discuss research. We discuss *why* playwrights make the decisions they do, *why* directors make the choices they do, *why* actors perform roles in a certain way. The beauty of the Framework is that it allows us as teachers to consider the "why" of things, and to have our students do the same. At Emerson, our adaptation of the Framework into PA101 is an attempt to push beyond what Mackey and Jacobson describe as a "traditional emphasis on teaching discrete skills," and instead focus on pedagogy that "prepares individuals to take control of their learning by gaining a deeper understanding of what is needed to set and achieve goals."[17] Our focus has shifted to helping students make sense of the myriad conversations already taking place in the world of theater and art, and preparing students to take part in those conversations in meaningful ways.

Part of this process requires rethinking the role of the learner in the library classroom. Most of the teaching librarians I know are keen to adopt active learning methods like flipped classroom models or peer-teaching. But many of us are also hampered by the limitations placed upon us by our institutions, our faculty, even our own students. The Framework allows us an opportunity to redefine our roles as teachers and to rethink our expectations for our students. For Mackey and Jacobson, this is "the metaliterate learner":

> [T]he metaliterate learner is an active *participant* who is an effective *communicator* and *translator* of information. The metaliterate learner is the *author* of information in many forms [… and undergoes] the transformation of learner to *teacher* because the learning objectives support the self-empowering transfer of knowledge to others. The metaliterate learner is an effective *collaborator* within this context and works individually and in teams as a *producer* and *publisher* of information.[18]

What Mackey and Jacobson describe here, what they emphasize, is the creation of a learner who is both an active recipient and producer of information. Within various disciplines, this kind of author/producer/teacher takes on many forms; within performing arts, it is embodied in the role of the dramaturg. Moving forward with our collaborations with performing arts students and faculty, we want to emphasize these ideas of production and creation more and more, that the very heart of learning is much more than just the passive consumption of information. As librarians, we need to be the ones to start that conversation.

Notes

1. Benjamin Samuel Bloom, ed., *Taxonomy of Educational Objectives: The Classification of Educational Goals, Handbook 1–2* (New York: Longman, 1984).
2. Emerson College, *Undergraduate Catalog, 2015–2016* (Boston: Emerson College, 2015): 141, http://issuu.com/emersoncollege/docs/academics-undergraduate-catalogue-2/143?e=2168435/30808497.
3. Patrice Pavis, *Dictionary of the Theatre: Terms, Concepts and Analysis* (Toronto: University of Toronto Press, 1998), 124.
4. Joan Middendorf and David Pace, "Decoding the Disciplines: A Model for Helping Students Learn Disciplinary Ways of Thinking," *New Directions for Teaching & Learning* 98 (Summer 2004): 4–5.
5. Association of College and Research Libraries (ACRL), *Framework for Information Literacy for Higher Education*, February 2, 2015, http://www.ala.org/acrl/standards/ilframework.
6. There are any number of sources documenting cognitive development in late adolescence and early adulthood. For a good grounding in cognitive development, see: Valerie F. Reyna, Sandra B. Chapman, Michael R. Dougherty, and Jere Confrey, eds., *The Adolescent Brain: Learning, Reasoning, and Decision Making* (Washington, DC: American Psychological Association, 2012).
7. ACRL, *Framework*.
8. Nancy Kindelan, *Artistic Literacy: Theatre Studies and a Contemporary Liberal Education* (New York: Palgrave MacMillan, 2012), ix.
9. Reyna et al., eds., *The Adolescent Brain*, 5.

10. Mikhail M. Bakhtin, *The Dialogic Imagination: Four Essays*, ed. Michael Holquist (Austin, TX: University of Texas Press, 1981), 263.
11. Ibid., 262.
12. Ibid., 262.
13. Kindelan, *Artistic Literacy*, 78.
14. Middendorf and Pace, *Decoding the Disciplines*, 3.
15. ACRL, *Framework*.
16. Thomas P. Mackey and Trudy E. Jacobson, *Metaliteracy: Reinventing Information Literacy to Empower Learners* (Chicago: Neal-Schuman, 2014), 5–6.
17. Ibid., 9–10.
18. Ibid., 91.

Searching as Strategic Exploration

Section Six

CHAPTER 21*

From Novice to Nurse:
Searching For Patient Care Information as Strategic Exploration

Elizabeth Moreton and Jamie Conklin

Introduction

Nursing librarians partner with educators to ensure that students gain the skills, knowledge, and aptitudes needed to be both professional nurses and lifelong learners. Research and the search for best practices drive the current health care environment, requiring nurses to prove their competency with information skills for everything from job promotion to care improvement projects. The literature has consistently shown that nurses need information regarding medications, treatments, diseases, clinical procedures, and other point-of-care evidence, as well as patient education materials.[1] Despite this expectation, nurses lack time, search skills, and access to resources necessary for their information needs.[2] Nursing librarians can anticipate what students will need to know as practitioners, using the needs and information-seeking practices of nurses to guide learning objectives for students. Nursing librarians can work closely with faculty to plan instruction to ensure students know how to search efficiently and effectively, setting them up for future success as nurses.

---

* This work is licensed under a Creative Commons Attribution-NonCommercial 4.0 License, CC BY-NC (https://creativecommons.org/licenses/by-nc/4.0/).

The healthcare environment

Nursing educators readily partner with nursing librarians, especially for courses on evidence-based practice (EBP) that require the use of library resources and searching skills. EBP is defined as the "conscientious, explicit, and judicious use of current best evidence in making decisions about the care of individual patients" and entails "integrating individual clinical expertise with the best available external clinical evidence from systematic research."[3] EBP is described as a cycle with five steps that both begins and ends with a patient: ask a clinical research question (often about patient treatments), acquire the evidence with a thorough search, appraise the strength of the evidence, apply that evidence in patient care, and assess its effectiveness. This directly relates to information literacy, making it the perfect tool for health librarians to connect to practitioners, faculty, and students. By teaching Searching as Strategic Exploration from the ACRL Framework for Information Literacy for Higher Education,[4] nursing librarians can ensure that students and EBP practitioners can deftly navigate and analyze the literature to determine the best practices for patient care.

Teaching searching in nursing

The nursing curriculum. EBP is so widely accepted in the nursing community that several nursing associations have incorporated these skills into the framework of the nursing curriculum. The Searching as Strategic Exploration frame[5] ties directly to EBP, as shown in the following examples:

- The Essentials of Baccalaureate Education for Professional Nursing Practice: Essential III on Scholarship for EBP states that baccalaureate graduates should be prepared to "participate in the process of retrieval, appraisal, and synthesis of evidence in collaboration with other members of the healthcare team to improve patient outcomes."[6]
- Graduate-Level Quality and Safety Education for Nurses (QSEN) Competencies: The EBP competency requires that graduate students know how to identify and employ "efficient and effective search strategies to locate reliable sources of evidence" for focused clinical questions and that they "value development of search skills for locating evidence for best practice."[7]

EBP and the required search skills apply to all levels of nursing, from students to practicing nurses. Nursing librarians must consider the expectations for each and familiarize themselves with any curriculum standards that apply to their institutions.

Challenges. Faculty experience the same time, skill, and access barriers in incorporating EBP into the curriculum.[8] The curricula in many nursing schools revolve around clinical skills and caring for specific patient groups, leaving little dedicated time for EBP and searching. In one bachelor of science program, for example, junior nursing students take one EBP course and struggle to apply the concepts since they have little clinical experience.[9] We have also experienced the phenomenon of a single EBP course where we have been asked to teach the search process. It is encouraging that many faculty recognize the librarian's role in EBP as "the search expert who knows where and how to search;"[10] however, additional outreach opportunities exist because faculty do not always connect librarians' search expertise to their ability to apply those skills in teaching.[11]

Both EBP and literature searching have been identified as threshold concepts for nursing students.[12] Students encounter a disconnect between learning and practicing EBP and hold oversimplified views of EBP. They have trouble with the practical aspects of searching databases for evidence and understanding the need to use more advanced search skills.[13] This suggests there are opportunities for librarians and faculty to collaborate around these threshold concepts.

Our experience

Transforming our teaching. As new librarians with limited instruction experience, we dealt with our own set of challenges while our faculty and students faced barriers with EBP and literature searching. Although we knew how to search well, we recognized that our instructional approach was not as effective for students as it could be. We taught through traditional point-and-click demonstrations of how to use the catalog and databases. This approach mirrors parts of the second standard of the ACRL Information Literacy Competency Standards for Higher Education,[14] namely that students should be able to construct effective search strategies and retrieve information online. In our minds, if we showed the students these processes and they could replicate them, they succeeded in meeting the standard and we succeeded as teachers.

Students were not always able to replicate the processes we demonstrated, nor did they seem engaged in the classroom. Realizing this, we chose to participate in several professional development opportunities relating to our teaching role, both locally and at the ACRL 2013 conference. Topics included active learning, classroom assessment techniques, learning styles, and the threshold concepts. We found ourselves among faculty and librarians who asked bigger pedagogical questions, such as how students learn best, what knowledge gaps exist, how to try new instructional approaches, and how to assess those changes.

As ACRL developed and published the Framework, we shifted our teaching practice in several ways that aligned with this new approach. We put the student at the center of our teaching, pinpointing what was unfamiliar to them and what they needed to know. We realized that students varied in their knowledge practices and dispositions along the ACRL Framework distinctions between novice and expert learners; in addition, each student was on a unique learning trajectory based on a set of search practices, skills, and experiences. We realized we needed to modify instruction to reach all levels of learners.

The nursing student as a learner. The students themselves are a key component to the process of learning to search. Several studies have examined the link between higher emotional intelligence and students' performance in the clinical setting or in the classroom,[15] and while some found smaller correlation between the two, Fernandez et al.[16] found that emotional intelligence could be a "significant predictor of academic achievement" for some students.

Recognizing and working with students' affective needs are just as important as responding to their cognitive needs in learning. Students' affective domain can dictate how they listen and learn in the classroom, respond to the challenge of a muddy task, manage the anxiety and emotion of unfamiliar content, cope with stress, and seek help. Students who are frustrated with assignments or frustrated by concepts they do not understand may give up more easily when presented with the challenge of searching for their topic, rather than developing and testing a strategy for their searching. Librarians can present themselves as allies to students and lead them through the challenge of searching by demonstrating strategy while quelling the negative emotions they have about research.

The Searching as Strategic Exploration frame states that "experts realize that information searching is a contextualized, complex experience that affects—and is affected by—the cognitive, affective, and social dimensions of the searcher."[17] The students we teach are not yet at the expert level; however, we as instructors can help novice searchers recognize and reflect on what this means in terms of their search experiences.

Nursing students learn to care for specific types of patients through skill-based learning in which there is often a clear right or wrong approach to the technique. They practice their skills and patient interactions until they have learned the correct procedure. Students are expected to pass a National Council (of State Boards of Nursing) Licensure Examination (NCLEX) before they enter practice, and this exam is built around questions with clear correct or incorrect answers.

On the contrary, the search for literature is not straightforward. Rather than one correct approach, there are many search options and resources to choose—some more effective than others, and often depending on the information need. Students as novice searchers can be overwhelmed by the complexity of this task, and unfamiliar and complex searching can trigger emotional stress. In 1980, Shane described "Returning-To-School Syndrome" as a three-phase emotional journey nursing students go through; while phase one is the honeymoon phase, phase two causes conflict in which students are "stranger[s] in a strange land" and "no longer trust [their] own experience and knowledge to provide [them] with appropriate responses" to their concept of what nursing is.[18] In this phase, students often feel lost, alone, and incompetent.

As instructors, we can recognize this potential for frustration and find ways to make students more comfortable with the gray areas of searching, but this task is "neither easy nor painless."[19] Students may come to us with feelings of insecurity, frustration, or hostility about professors, courses, the curriculum, or even their own abilities, and we can earn their trust if we actively listen to their concerns, provide solutions or suggestions as we can, and act as advocates for them when needed. Librarians can help students to feel less alone by simply listening and sharing, whether convincing students of their own abilities or telling them other students share their struggles. Librarians can make use of the students' existing research frustrations (whether in one-on-one sessions or group office hours) by first allowing students to vent, then changing their perspective about themselves or about research. Resolving their emotional turmoil, students move to the third phase of Shane's syndrome, in which they experience reduced levels of anxiety and focus on what they can get out of the program rather than what is required of them.[20]

Another affective challenge is that students can see EBP courses as "dry and boring" or as a "distraction" from more clinically oriented courses.[21] They are unfamiliar with the excitement of strategic searches for evidence or the relevance of EBP for patient care, and they decide not to make the emotional investment in learning. We have bridged this divide by planning instruction around clinical case scenarios, which link clinical practice to the search process and demonstrate how health information has a direct impact on patient care.

Search as Exploration for novice through expert searchers

Nursing librarians encounter a diversity of student backgrounds and skill levels during instruction, so it can be helpful to review the curriculum and expectations of each program and tailor library instruction to the appropriate level (e.g., BSN, PhD, etc.). Students begin their nursing programs as freshmen or sophomores, often knowing little about nursing, the library, or the relevance of health information to their future work. Orienting students to the library and to the varieties of health information is a student-centered approach to beginner instruction. The use of case studies with patient stories provides a much-needed context for presenting students with the different types and uses of health information, including background information, reference sources, information for patients, drug information, and recent research. It also provides an opportunity to introduce a variety of health information resources, including the library catalog, websites, clinical tools, and databases, as well as a basic understanding of different search approaches.

Within the structure of the case study, librarians can have students compare the process of searching for patient information in MedlinePlus to the experience of finding drug information in a clinical tool. Students could then explore the same topic in a database like PubMed or the Cumulative Index of Nursing and Allied Health Literature (CINAHL). Not only will they be introduced to the variety of information producers, they will begin to connect information needs with specific search tools.

Students learning about EBP. Upper-level undergraduates and those enrolled in accelerated bachelor programs will either be starting or already immersed in their clinical experience, so librarians can capitalize on this by directly linking library instruction and search practices to clinical questions students have identified in practice. This way, instruction, much like EBP, will begin with both a patient and a specific question. Students can be directed to complete their clinical questions in PICO format, a recognized question framework that often includes a patient population, an intervention, a comparison, and one or more outcomes. Optionally, the format can also include timeframe, type of study, and setting, or PICOTTS. The components of the PICO act as a beginning search strategy, formulated before any mention of where to search. Note that some nursing faculty assign students to formulate PICO questions to bring to library instruction sessions; if so, librarians should take a little time to review them and address students' questions before teaching.

After question formulation, librarians can show students that searching is a systematic, strategic exploration with the goal of finding the most current and best available evidence on a topic. Librarians can prepare a sample search scenario to demonstrate searching for the most important components of the search first and then adapting it as needed. One way to do this would be to introduce students to the gold standard of searches: the Cochrane systematic review. These reviews provide high levels of evidence because they are collections of all the available research on a given topic, and they depend on well-planned and well-executed search strategies for specific clinical questions.

Having students read the methods section of a systematic review introduces them to the ideas of purposefully searching several databases and considering inclusion and exclusion criteria to narrow or limit a search.

Librarians can lead discussions about bias, asking students to consider how the selection of a particular resource over another would affect retrieved results and how publication bias occurs when published literature does not represent all the available studies. Similarly, searching haphazardly would introduce a search bias in that students would not retrieve all of the available studies on a particular topic. Overall, the idea of the gold standard exercise is not to have students replicate these high-level practices but to reassure them that a search can follow a systematic process, much like other clinical skills. Librarians can consider creating a search skills checklist to reinforce their instruction and to help students build lasting confidence in their search skills.

Students performing EBP. Graduate students face much higher expectations in terms of EBP than do undergraduates or even practitioners. Many faculty want students to create their own evidence reviews, guidelines, or even systematic reviews as part of their coursework and as firsthand experiences of the EBP process. In the healthcare field, these types of reviews regularly take months to years to complete when working as a team, but in graduate school they are often condensed into one semester (or less). Graduate students have a wide range of skill levels and knowledge and may benefit from a basic refresher on searching as well as step-by-step guidance on how to complete these complex projects.

The concept of higher levels of evidence and the steps to create that evidence are still foreign to most students at this level, despite many having had an introduction to EBP as undergraduates, so they must quickly learn what these types of evidence are while implementing their own research. Macbeth describes this problem where students are expected to know what they are trying to learn.[22] Students can feel rushed through the process, whether working as part of a team or solo, which can cause them to focus on simply getting the assignment done rather than understanding the purpose of each task or truly learning the steps.

In courses where EBP projects are common, librarians can take simple steps to make the process easier for students. They can assist graduate students in creating a search plan for their assignment. Smaller projects like a search protocol, evidence table, or evidence appraisal could fit into a variety of graduate courses, allowing students to get the full range of EBP experiences without feeling overwhelmed. Throughout these courses, librarians can provide highly detailed instruction for students as they perform the steps of EBP and explicitly discuss what distinguishes EBP from other searching strategies. Librarians should also teach search management strategies and describe the use of any specialized software or technology for the assigned project.

The librarian can step in as co-faculty or as a collaborator for graduate-level classes and offer supportive materials or consultations to assist students. Providing consultations in addition to office hours can help students feel more comfortable doing literature searching on their own topics and, in turn, refer their friends to the library as well. By becoming informed about program requirements and becoming more of a partner for graduate students, librarians can make intimidating theses and course projects more comfortable and achievable for students.

Addressing unique learning trajectories. Students within a program arrive at library instruction sessions with different levels of knowledge and interest in search practices. Some students may be attending school after years of nursing in the workforce, while others may be working their way through college as traditional students. To address varying skill levels, librarians can structure the session to first identify what students currently know and do, then use that as a basis to build on the knowledge practices and dispositions of the Searching as Strategic Exploration frame. This can be done through pre-work in a flipped classroom style or through an in-class activity at the beginning of the session. For example, task students with searching a given clinical question and documenting the search, including the sources used, the search strategy, and the length of time of both the search and the scan of results. If possible, have them record it visibly in the room, such as on a whiteboard. If not, gather the information and share it, if possible in aggregate form, and use the responses to generate a discussion of identified patterns, areas of strengths and weaknesses, consequences of chosen methods, and personal feelings toward searching (e.g., address fears and over- or under-confidence).

Alternately, ask students to write about or discuss their previous search experiences and how that may or may not differ from EBP. Areas to highlight would include scope, search comprehensiveness, and purpose. When we incorporated similar exercises into our instruction, we found that some students reconsidered searching with natural language; others stated that they would include controlled vocabularies such as PubMed's Medical Subject Headings (MeSH) in their future searches.

Our recommendations

There are both challenges and opportunities in teaching Searching as Strategic Exploration to nursing students, but it is certainly worthwhile to assist students in developing and fostering mental flexibility and persistence when faced with an information need. Doing so requires working directly with nursing faculty and students, as well as continually developing professionally as a librarian.

Working with faculty

Demonstrate your abilities to faculty. For librarians who want to be seen as experts in strategic searching, one of the best ways to gain recognition is to assist faculty with their own research. Once librarians are seen as experts, they can become part of the process of teaching students about EBP. Some librarians even act as co-faculty for EBP courses or as adjunct faculty in their discipline. Librarians can partner with faculty, nurses, or even student groups to perform and publish evidence reviews. With more practice working through the review process, librarians can pay close attention to the steps they follow and the tricks they use, and they can teach these shortcuts to students.

Revisit instruction goals and assess. Instruction can meet the learning objectives set by faculty and librarians, but it should be student-centered and tailored to the discipline. Practical, evidence-based assignments with a clinical focus can help nursing students understand the relevance of library instruction to their future and unify the goals of the nursing faculty and the librarian. Collaborate with faculty to develop instruction and assignments at the appropriate level and in the appropriate format for all involved—faculty, librarians, and students. Assess instruction and, if possible, assignments to determine how well students are grasping the covered material and to tweak troublesome portions. Use a variety of assessment techniques, from formal graded assignments to informal classroom techniques, like the muddiest point.[23] Librarians who integrate group activities or hands-on learning opportunities can easily monitor the progress of students and identify challenges the students face. Librarians can also ask faculty for permission to review final coursework, such as posters, papers, or portfolios, to identify the types and variety of evidence students included. If librarians have made an effort to integrate research skills at different levels of learning, assessment provides useful feedback on whether or not the identified learning objectives at each level are on target or need to be moved to a lower or higher level within the curriculum.

Integrate research skills in the curriculum and the classroom. There is so much to teach about searching health information sources that it is impossible to fit it into one session. Students would best be served by having research skills integrated throughout the program. One example of this is the University of Pittsburgh's integration of EBP skills throughout the entire nursing program, from year one to post-doctoral work, as described by Burke et al.[24] Nursing librarians can use the knowledge practices of the Searching as Strategic Exploration frame to link skills to appropriate points in the curriculum. For example, students can build on their ability to match information needs and search strategies to appropriate search tools. Beginning students can search e-books for background information, while more advanced students can search for practice guidelines in specific sites like the National Guidelines Clearinghouse. Librarians can use this approach to make the introduction to health information easier and to build a tiered-approach to teaching the mechanics of searching and the refinement and management of results.

Working with students

Support students with time and understanding. Simply recognizing that students are grappling with full course loads, clinical skill building, and the balance between academic, personal, and sometimes professional lives will enable librarians to empathize with those who seek their help. Librarians should schedule office hours at a time and in a location that is convenient for the students, whether in the School of Nursing or online. Be willing to dedicate time each week to meet with students, identify what their current search skills are, and help them build from there. Librarians can also partner with student-led health clinics, student interprofessional education groups or case competitions, and other student health initiatives to increase awareness of services and to emphasize support for students.

Give an abundance of examples. Nursing students are familiar with a style of learning in the clinical setting where they get instant feedback on whether their work is correct or incorrect. When class time prohibits reviewing student searches in real time, the use of plentiful examples can show students how to search and help them feel more comfortable. A useful technique is to demonstrate a failed search and discuss as a class how and why it failed, as well as how to improve it. Add interest and applicability through the use of non-health examples, such as by teaching the use of the "or" operator by having students stand as birthday months (e.g., October or November or December) are called out, thus demonstrating the concept of more results.

Incorporate reflection to enhance understanding. Including class time for reflection on search experiences helps students build their understanding of the search process. Encourage students to try new search strategies and to compare them to previously used strategies. Think out loud to show students how you approach a topic. For example, perform a search in PubMed using MeSH, note the publication dates of resulting articles, and then rerun the search with a combination of MeSH terms and keywords to show how the results would then include more recent literature because of indexing time. At the end of the session, ask students to jot down one or two ways they plan to improve their searches in the future to help them solidify what they learned and to promote behavior change.

Encourage self-efficacy. Nursing students need to build enough confidence in their individual skills so that they feel comfortable applying them in the workforce. Although many nurses work in teams, especially on EBP or quality improvement projects, they will need to search for evidence for their individual patients. Those who work in schools, home health, and other settings may work entirely on their own. It is crucial for librarians to help students develop the strategies that will allow them to adapt their knowledge to any future situation. Librarians can emphasize that first attempts at searching are rarely perfect and then equip students with skills to work past the troublesome parts of searching for health information. They can instill the belief that students have the knowledge and ability to find the information they need and encourage persistence in searching with a strategic approach.

Developing professionally as a librarian

Finally, we recommend that librarians carve out time to attend professional development opportunities, especially those that relate to effective instructional approaches. Experiment with different teaching techniques, technologies, and class exercises. Many times, nursing faculty are using different approaches to teaching and assessment than those traditionally used in library instruction, and adopting these can help students feel more familiar with the content and structure of the library session. Examples include utilizing stories and cases, prebriefing and debriefing students, creating opportunities for deliberate practice, encouraging reflection and metacognition, and more. Invite other librarians to watch you teach or to co-teach with you to give you feedback, and, when possible, assess student learning and use those assessments to reflect on and revitalize your instruction.

Notes

1. Martina A. Clarke et al., "Information Needs and Information-Seeking Behaviour Analysis of Primary Care Physicians and Nurses: A Literature Review," *Health Information & Libraries Journal* 30, no. 3 (2013): 178–90, doi: 10.1111/hir.12036.
2. April J. Schweikhard, "An Information Needs Assessment of School Nurses in a Metropolitan County," *Medical Reference Services Quarterly* 35, no. 1 (2016): 27–41, https://dx.doi.org/10.1080%2F02763869.2016.1117287; Michele Klein-Fedyshin, "Translating Evidence into Practice at the End-of-Life: Information Needs, Access and Usage by Hospice and Palliative Nurses," *Journal of Hospice & Palliative Nursing* 17, no. 1 (2015): 24–30, doi: 10.1097/njh.0000000000000117.
3. David L. Sackett et al., "Evidence Based Medicine: What It Is and What It Isn't," *BMJ* 312, no. 7023 (1996): 71, doi: 10.1136/bmj.312.7023.71.
4. Association of College and Research Libraries (ACRL), *Framework for Information Literacy for Higher Education*, February 2, 2015, http://www.ala.org/acrl/standards/ilframework.
5. Ibid.

6. American Association of Colleges of Nursing, "The Essentials of Baccalaureate Education for Professional Nursing Practice," 16, last updated October 20, 2008, http://www.aacnnursing.org/Portals/42/Publications/BaccEssentials08.pdf.
7. American Association of Colleges of Nursing QSEN Education Consortium, "Graduate-Level QSEN Competencies: Knowledge, Skills and Attitudes," 13, last updated September 24, 2012, http://www.aacn.nche.edu/faculty/qsen/competencies.pdf.
8. Jaynelle F. Stichler et al., "Faculty Knowledge, Attitudes, and Perceived Barriers to Teaching Evidence-Based Nursing," *Journal of Professional Nursing* 27, no. 2 (2011): 92–100, doi:10.1016/j.profnurs.2010.09.012.
9. Mary R. Boyd et al., "Using Debates to Teach Evidence-Based Practice in Large Online Courses," *Journal of Nursing Education* 54, no. 10 (2015): 578–82, doi: 10.3928/01484834-20150916-06.
10. Stephanie J. Schulte and Pamela J. Sherwill-Navarro, "Nursing Educators' Perceptions of Collaboration with Librarians," *Journal of the Medical Library Association* 97, no.1 (2009): 59, doi: 10.3163/1536-5050.97.1.013.
11. Ibid., 60.
12. Linda Martindale, "Threshold Concepts in Research and Evidence-Based Practice: Investigating Troublesome Learning for Undergraduate Nursing Students," Durham University, 2015, http://etheses.dur.ac.uk/10998/.
13. Ibid.
14. Association of College and Research Libraries (ACRL), *Information Literacy Competency Standards for Higher Education*, 2000, http://www.ala.org/acrl/standards/informationliteracycompetency.
15. Shaun Newsome, Arla L. Day, and Victor M. Catano, "Assessing the Predictive Validity of Emotional Intelligence," *Personality and Individual Differences* 29, no. 6 (2000): 1005–1016, doi: 10.1016/S0191-8869(99)00250-0; Raymond M. O'Connor, Jr. and Ian S. Little, "Revisiting the Predictive Validity of Emotional Intelligence: Self-Report Versus Ability-Based Measures," *Personality And Individual Differences* 35, no. 8 (December 2003): 1893–1902; Estelle Codier, Barbara M. Kooker, and Jan Shoultz, "Measuring the Emotional Intelligence of Clinical Staff Nurses: An Approach For Improving the Clinical Care Environment," *Nursing Administration Quarterly* 32, no. 1 (January 2008): 8–14, doi:10.1097/01.NAQ.0000305942.38816.3b; Estelle Codier, Barbara M. Kooker, and Jan Shoultz, "Emotional Intelligence, Performance, and Retention in Clinical Staff Nurses," *Nursing Administration Quarterly* 33, no. 4 (October 2009): 310–316, doi:10.1097/NAQ.0b013e3181b9dd5d; Jitna Por et al., "Emotional Intelligence: Its Relationship to Stress, Coping, Well-Being and Professional Performance in Nursing Students," *Nurse Education Today* 31, no. 8 (November 2011): 855–860; Kathryn Faguy, "Emotional Intelligence in Health Care," *Radiologic Technology* 83, no. 3 (January 2012): 237–253; Estelle Codier and Ellen Odell, "Measured Emotional Intelligence Ability and Grade Point Average in Nursing Students," *Nurse Education Today* 34, no. 4 (April 2014): 608–612, doi:10.1016/j.nedt.2013.06.007; Patricia A. Dwyer and Susan M. Hunter Revell, "Preparing Students for the Emotional Challenges of Nursing: An Integrative Review," *Journal of Nursing Education* 54, no. 1 (January 2015): 7–12, doi:10.3928/01484834-20141224-06.

16. Ritin Fernandez, Yenna Salamonson, and Rhonda Griffiths, "Emotional Intelligence as a Predictor of Academic Performance in First-Year Accelerated Graduate Entry Nursing Students," *Journal of Clinical Nursing* 21, no. 23/24 (2012): 3485–3492, doi:10.1111/j.1365-2702.2012.04199.x.
17. ACRL, *Framework for Information Literacy for Higher Education*.
18. Donea L. Shane, "The Returning-to-School Syndrome," *Nursing* 10, no. 6 (1980): 86, doi: 10.1097/00152193-198006000-00016.
19. Ibid.
20. Ibid.
21. Boyd et al., "Using Debates."
22. Karen P. MacBeth, "The Situated Achievements of Novices Learning Academic Writing as a Cultural Curriculum," (PhD diss., The Ohio State University, 2004), http://rave.ohiolink.edu/etdc/view?acc_num=osu1101244159.
23. Thomas A. Angelo and K. Patricia Cross, *Classroom Assessment Techniques: A Handbook for College Teachers* (San Francisco: Jossey-Bass Publishers, 1993).
24. Lora E. Burke et al., "Developing Research Competence to Support Evidence-Based Practice," *Journal of Professional Nursing* 21, no. 6 (2005): 358–363, doi:10.1016/j.profnurs.2005.10.011.

CHAPTER 22

Leveraging the Language of the Past:
Searching as Strategic Exploration in the Discipline of History

Jamie L. Emery

One of the unique challenges of historical research is the need for students to step outside of their present-day selves and utilize the language of the past in order to find relevant primary sources for their research. Students cannot expect to search early twentieth-century newspaper databases for "World War I" and find relevant articles on the then-named "Great War." Ascertaining which terms are most relevant for a particular topic within a certain historical period is an important part of the iterative process of searching for historical information. Students also need to recognize and make use of outdated, often derogatory terms for specific groups of people that were used in the past and be flexible enough to allow for spelling variations among and within texts, particularly those written prior to the nineteenth century. These discipline-specific challenges directly relate to the ACRL Framework for Information Literacy for Higher Education[1] frame Searching as Strategic Exploration and its threshold concept. Applying the frame's supportive knowledge practices and dispositions to the discipline of History can help librarians design meaningful instruction that introduces students to the particularly contextualized nature of searching in historical research.

Connecting the frame Searching as Strategic Exploration to the discipline

Threshold concept. The idea that "Searching for information is often nonlinear and iterative, requiring the evaluation of a range of information sources and the mental flexibility to pursue alternate avenues as new understanding develops"[2] is an incredibly important threshold concept in the discipline of History. It truly is a concept that must be grasped by students in order for them to find and access secondary sources in history and, more important, the difficult-to-find and access primary sources upon which historical research is based. It's a concept that is not grasped in one instruction session, but that once learned will not be unlearned. The iterative nature of searching and the need for students to exercise mental flexibility is particularly evident when searching for primary sources, as knowledge and understanding of the historical topic and period informs the terminology used to find materials as well as the resources selected for research.

Knowledge practices. As a result of their comprehension of this threshold concept, students in History develop the ability to closely read secondary or tertiary sources and use them to identify primary source texts and authors. They develop the ability to match leads to primary sources to appropriate search tools in order to access them. Students also develop the ability to brainstorm for historically appropriate keywords related to their topic, select research tools that fit their historical and geographical research needs, and utilize controlled vocabulary in library catalogs to find primary sources on their topic.

Dispositions. Over time, History students who've grasped this threshold concept will begin to think and act more like historians, carefully mining texts for leads to both primary and secondary sources for their research. When searching primary source databases, they will take into consideration the historical context of the materials they're searching in order to find relevant primary source information. Ideally, they will also become more perseverant searchers, adjusting and improving their searches as necessary without giving up and assuming there is no information on their topic. When encountering roadblocks in their research, they will seek and accept guidance from librarians as well as their History professors.

Foundational information needs and challenges related to the frame

As the History subject librarian at Saint Louis University, a Catholic, Jesuit University in St. Louis, Missouri that offers both undergraduate and graduate programs in History, I regularly meet with students in classroom and research consultation settings to provide information literacy instruction within the discipline of History. The research question I'm asked most frequently is, "How can I find primary sources on my topic?" Student research areas range from ancient history to medieval to early modern and modern history, but their core challenge is almost always related to finding primary sources.

While History students generally come to me already possessing a basic understanding of the difference between primary and secondary sources and familiarity with more common types of primary sources, they don't have the background knowledge to understand how primary sources are made available to researchers. For example, students studying ancient history don't realize that ancient Greek and Roman documents will be translated, collected, and published in print volumes collected by the library with much more recent publication dates than the original sources contained therein. They generally aren't aware of primary source collections that exist via their library in the circulating collection, special collections, archives, library databases, or on the Web. Bringing students up-to-speed on this foundational information is crucial to scaffolding instruction related to the frame Searching as Strategic Exploration.

In addition to lacking a foundational understanding of where primary sources typically can be found, students are generally incognizant of the idea that searching for information is an iterative process that requires multiple and varied searches targeted to specific resources for specific historical periods. They are quick to assume that there are no primary sources on their topic, rather than assuming that materials are available, but that they need to adjust what they're doing as searchers in order to tap into them. They have little understanding of how databases, catalogs, and other sources of information are organized and the existence of controlled or descriptive vocabulary is a new concept for them. They are also more likely to be willing to perform keyword searches on the Web or in library databases than recognize the value of mining secondary and tertiary sources for leads to primary sources.

The frame as inspiration for meaningful instructional design and assessment

The purpose of the Framework is to inspire and encourage librarians to center their information literacy pedagogy on the teaching of concepts, rather than skills. In this section, I describe three lessons that use the frame Searching as Strategic Exploration as inspiration within the discipline of History and focus on the development of primary source literacy. The knowledge practices and dispositions addressed by each lesson are indicated in Table 22.1.

Table 22.1. Searching as Strategic Exploration knowledge practices and dispositions 3 applied in Lessons 1–3.

Searching as Strategic Exploration	Lessons		
Knowledge Practices Learners who are developing their information literate abilities	1	2	3
☐ determine the initial scope of the task required to meet their information needs			
☐ identify interested parties, such as scholars, organizations, governments, and industries, who might produce information about a topic and then determine how to access that information		✓	
☐ utilize divergent (e.g., brainstorming) and convergent (e.g., selecting the best source) thinking when searching	✓		✓
☐ match information needs and search strategies to appropriate search tools	✓	✓	✓
☐ design and refine needs and search strategies as necessary, based on search results	✓		
☐ understand how information systems (i.e., collections of recorded information) are organized in order to access relevant information			✓
☐ use different types of searching language (e.g., controlled vocabulary, keywords, natural language) appropriately	✓		✓
☐ manage searching processes and results effectively			
Dispositions Learners who are developing their information literate abilities	✓		✓
☐ exhibit mental flexibility and creativity			
☐ understand that first attempts at searching do not always produce adequate results	✓		
☐ realize that information sources vary greatly in content and format and have varying relevance and value, depending on the needs and nature of the search		✓	✓
☐ seek guidance from experts, such as librarians, researchers, and professionals	✓	✓	✓
☐ recognize the value of browsing and other serendipitous methods of information gathering		✓	✓
☐ persist in the face of search challenges, and know when they have enough information to complete the information task	✓		

These practical applications of the Searching as Strategic Exploration frame are intended to serve as instructional templates that could be modified and used in any History course in which students need to find primary sources but are described within the context of a specific course for explanation purposes. They could be incorporated into one-shot instruction sessions or a credit-bearing information literacy course.

Lesson 1: Leveraging the language of the past. This lesson is designed to help students learn how to match their primary source information needs to appropriate search tools and challenge them to translate present-day language into historically accurate, context-specific language when searching primary source databases. It emphasizes the need for utilization of flexible terminology when searching texts from the past and demonstrates the iterative nature of searching for primary sources. To provide disciplinary context, it is presented as an instructional activity conducted with students in an undergraduate History course entitled "U.S. and the Middle East: Modern Connections" that covers relations between the two regions.

In order to frame this activity, the librarian asks students thought-provoking questions relevant to searching for primary sources for their course, using the Wiggins and McTighe "essential questions" model intended to stimulate thought and generate student questions while maintaining a deliberate focus on big ideas.[4] For example, the librarian may pose a hypothetical research scenario and ask students to "Imagine that you are researching U.S. involvement in the Israeli-Palestinian conflict and want to find primary sources on the Camp David Accords, the Egypt-Israel agreements brokered by Jimmy Carter and signed at Camp David on September 17, 1978.[5] What do you think would happen if you searched a twentieth-century U.S. newspaper database using the phrase 'Camp David Accords'?" After fielding student responses, the librarian demonstrates this search and shows that the first occurrence of this phrase doesn't appear in the database until two days after the signing of the accords. The librarian then asks, "Why do you think we're not finding older articles? Do you think that there weren't any articles published on this topic in these newspapers prior to September 19, 1978 or that we need to search differently in order to access them?" After fielding and incorporating student responses, the librarian then demonstrates that the alternate search "Carter and Israel and Egypt and Camp David" returns articles written during the twelve-day Camp David summit that led to the development of the peace accords. He or she explains that since the Camp David Accords didn't exist prior to September 17, 1978, one can't use that phrase to access earlier primary sources materials on that topic. Instead, researchers need to use terms that were used by journalists at the time to describe the meetings at Camp David.

The librarian then explains that another challenge and reality that researchers face when searching full-text collections of primary sources is that these sources reflect prejudices of their day. Students need to recognize this and in their searching utilize terminology commonly used during the period being researched, even derogatory names for specific groups of people we would never use today. Students may also need to allow for spelling variations in primary sources they're searching, particularly when searching texts written prior to the nineteenth century when spelling became more standardized.

The librarian then shares with the class a list of primary source databases relevant to their course and asks them to select one that fits the time period they're researching for their individual research project. He or she also introduces them to a shared online spreadsheet they'll use for an in-class activity. This spreadsheet, adapted from the CORA (Community of Online Research Assignments) Strategic Searching Spreadsheet activity,[6] should include categories similar to those listed in Table 22.2.

As each student completes one row of the spreadsheet, the librarian circulates around the room to help students and bring up things students should consider when brainstorming for alternate keywords on their topics. For example, "Was the event you're researching always called that?" or "Could the group of people you're researching have been referred to by another name during the period you're researching?"

It should be noted that some students may need to perform minimal outside research in order to create lists of terminology relevant to their search. For example, a student who is attempting to find primary sources related to Operation Torch, the British American invasion of French North Africa during World War II, may need to do additional research to discover that Operation Torch was originally called Operation Gymnast in order to proceed effectively with their research.[7] They may also need to search using more general terminology for the event and possibly include geographic names involved. Letting students know that this may be necessary and that it's okay to perform outside research using Google or another source is important.

Table 22.2. Sample spreadsheet template for Lesson 1

Name	Research topic	Database selected and why	Initial search strategy	Satisfied with results? yes/no and why	Alternate terms to use for searches	Second search strategy using alternate terms	Insert citation for the best primary source found	Librarian suggestions

For Lesson 1, assessment of student learning can include reviewing the contents of the activity spreadsheet and evaluating the change in students' search terms and strategies over the course of the exercise. Another option would be to teach students how to email database search histories to the librarian and use them to evaluate progressive student learning. Questions to ask oneself when evaluating either type of artifact include, "Did this student select an appropriate primary source database for their research needs based on their topic? Did they demonstrate the ability to generate relevant, alternate keywords related to their research topic and incorporate them into their searches? Did their searches improve over the course of their research session?"

Some librarians may be hesitant to bring up the use of derogatory terminology during an instruction session, with understandable concern about students' feelings and reactions. I can say though, that it is possible to do this effectively using general terms and allusions without making students visibly uncomfortable. In my experience, albeit not with a particularly diverse student body, addressing this historical reality hasn't been a problem. Students understand that biased terminology has been used throughout history. What needs to be explained is how this affects the historical research process.

Lesson 2: The value of close reading. This lesson is constructed to help students learn the value of closely reading secondary or tertiary sources in order to identify leads to primary sources. It models one way in which browsing for information sources can be a valuable means of information gathering and shapes student understanding of the relationship between primary and secondary sources. It is presented within the context of an undergraduate History course entitled "Religious Conversion in an Age of Empire" that covers the early modern period and extends through the nineteenth century.

To begin this lesson, the librarian engages students in a discussion of various methods of finding primary sources by asking, "How do you normally find primary sources for your history research projects?" Student responses will likely include the use of Google, course textbooks, and occasionally bibliographies. After acknowledging value in the methodologies suggested by students, the librarian offers that one easy way to find primary sources is to read secondary or tertiary sources very carefully, noting leads to primary sources. This explanation may pique student interest in this research method because it hinges upon the use of secondary sources, which students are generally more comfortable finding than primary sources.

The librarian breaks the class into small groups and shares with each an online, editable document that contains the text of a pre-selected secondary or tertiary source with relevance to the course. For example, in "Religious Conversion in the Age of Empire" the text could be an article from *History Review* entitled "The French Revolution and the Catholic Church."[8] Students in each small group work on their own computer but virtually share the document. The librarian asks students to carefully read the section of the article on the "Return of the Catholic Church" and highlight any possible leads to primary sources. These could include titles of specific texts or even vague mentions of primary source documents, as well as key authors or historical figures who may have written primary source materials related to this topic. They could also include references contained within the bibliography of the provided source. This portion of the activity challenges students to differentiate between primary and secondary sources within a bibliography, which can be difficult for those who have trouble deciphering bibliographic citations in general, much less within a specific historical context. Finally, the librarian asks students to add a comment to each highlighted primary source lead, explaining what search tool they would use to find this source.

After students complete this activity, they discuss in small groups the leads to primary sources they've identified and the search tools they believe they could use to find them. Small groups then share their findings with the class and the librarian compiles identified leads to primary sources and related search tools on a whiteboard. Finally, the librarian explains that this kind of close reading can be done with any source. This lesson represents a way of thinking that is foundational in the development of students' ability to think like a historian. He or she also mentions that this technique can be used to identify other secondary sources they may want to consult for their research.

Lesson 2 offers opportunities for assessment of student learning at three levels. The first level is the in-class comprehension check conducted as students share their leads to primary sources and related search tools with the class and the librarian records them. The second level is the evaluation of the students' highlighted texts and comments within the online documents using a rubric similar to that in Table 22.3.

Table 22.3. Sample assessment rubric for Lesson 2.			
Target Indicators	Beginning	Developing	Exemplary
Identifies leads to primary sources within a secondary source	Identifies some obvious primary sources with titles	Identifies some primary sources with titles and some alluded to	Identifies all primary sources with titles and all those alluded to in text

Table 22.3. Sample assessment rubric for Lesson 2.

Target Indicators	Beginning	Developing	Exemplary
Identifies interested parties who might have produced primary source information on a topic	Identifies parties described as authors who might have produced primary source information on topic	Identifies parties described as authors and some historical figures/groups who might have produced primary source information on topic	Identifies all parties described as authors and all historical figures/groups who may have produced primary source information on topic
Determines how to access primary sources identified via close reading activity	Determines how to access less than 40% of primary sources identified	Determines how to access 40–80% of primary sources identified	Determines how to access more than 80% of primary sources identified

The target indicators listed in the rubric above directly relate to several knowledge practices and dispositions that support the threshold concept that anchors Searching as Strategic Exploration. The first indicator relates to the disposition "exhibit mental flexibility and creativity."[9] The second and third indicators together relate to the knowledge practice "identify interested parties, such as scholars, organizations, governments, and industries, who might produce information on a topic and then determine how to access that information."[10] The third indicator also corresponds to a portion of the knowledge practice "match information needs and search strategies to appropriate search tools."[11]

The third opportunity for assessment is the evaluation of students' attitudes regarding the value of closely reading secondary or tertiary sources as a strategy for identifying primary sources. This evaluation closely relates to the Searching as Strategic Exploration disposition "Learners who are developing their information literate abilities… recognize the value of browsing and other serendipitous methods of information gathering"[12] and would likely detect a learner struggling to adjust their mindset to the threshold concept contained within Searching as Strategic Exploration. This assessment could take the form of a classroom opinion poll via the online document used for the small group activity, a paper or online form, a polling app, or even the simple raising of hands in the classroom. The sample questions in Figure 22.1 could be used in several polling formats.

FIGURE 22.1
Sample classroom poll questions for Lesson 2.

---

1. The close reading research method used in today's class is a valuable way to find primary sources.

| Strongly Disagree | Disagree | Don't Know | Agree | Strongly Agree |

2. Why or why not?

3. I would use this close reading research method to find primary sources in the future.

| Strongly Disagree | Disagree | Don't Know | Agree | Strongly Agree |

4. Why or why not?

It is important to recognize the benefit of assessing students' attitudes toward instruction in addition to student learning as described above. No matter how well students complete activities we give them, if they don't ultimately perceive the value in the research methods and concepts presented, they'll never use them again. Helping students understand the value of what they're learning and how it can be useful to them throughout their academic careers and beyond should be a priority for all instruction librarians.

Lesson 3: Metadata as search tool. Using a constructivist approach to learning, this lesson builds upon existing student knowledge of Twitter hashtags and actively involves students in the drawing of connections between them and the controlled vocabulary used in library catalogs.[13] More important, it introduces the idea that information sources are described in different ways in different databases of information and that recognizing and leveraging these descriptions is key to effective searching. For contextual purposes, it is presented below within the context of an undergraduate History course entitled "U.S. Civil War and Reconstruction, 1850–1877."

To begin, the librarian projects on a screen two lists of descriptive vocabulary relevant to the subject of the course and various kinds of primary source materials. A Twitter list includes hashtags such as #USCivilWar, as well as hashtags commonly used to tag primary sources, such as #primarysource, #primarysources, #diary, #journal, and #letters. A library catalog list includes Library of Congress subject headings such as United States—History—Civil War, 1861–1865 and Confederate States of America—History, as well as terms used to describe primary sources in library catalogs, such as personal narratives, sources, correspondence, interviews, diaries, letters, memoirs, documents, works, public opinion, foreign public opinion, doctrines, and writings.

The librarian draws a connection between the way in which Twitter users apply hashtags to tweets to identify them as being about a particular subject area and/or document type and librarians assign Library of Congress subject headings to items in library catalogs and add primary source descriptors to the subjects of those items that are primary sources. The librarian also draws the distinction between the crowdsourced, flexible, and sometimes temporary nature of hashtags used on Twitter and the stable, controlled vocabulary maintained by the Library of Congress.

The librarian acknowledges that Library of Congress subject headings are not particularly intuitive and are most easily discoverable by keyword searching within the library catalog, finding a relevant source on one's desired topic and then checking to see what Library of Congress subject headings are used to describe the source. The librarian recommends clicking on a relevant subject heading and examining the resultant list of subject headings for those with primary source indicators at the end of them. The librarian may also want to note that because these terms appear at the end of subject headings in library catalogs, they can also be included in keyword searches, although this method is imprecise, as these terms may be found in other contexts than subject headings.

The librarian then asks students to search both Twitter and the library catalog with the goal of identifying hashtags and Library of Congress subjects used to describe their research topic, using a worksheet provided (see Figure 2). Once students have completed this task, the librarian asks students to use the terminology on their list and provided by the librarian to find one post about a primary source related to their research topic on Twitter, one in the library catalog, and share both on Twitter along with a provided course hashtag. If students are unable to find a primary source on their topic, they are encouraged to ask the librarian for help. On Twitter, especially, it may be that there are no posts about primary sources related to a given topic. In that case, students are encouraged to find any tweet about their research topic.

FIGURE 22.2
Sample worksheet for Lesson 3.

How is Your Research Topic Described on Twitter and in the Library Catalog?

Search for your research topic on Twitter and in the library catalog. List parallel hashtags and Library of Congress subjects used to describe your research topic.

Twitter #s	Library Catalog Subjects

Lesson 3 offers several opportunities for the assessment of student learning. The first is the evaluation of students' brainstorming worksheets. Levels of student learning related to the threshold concept contained in Searching as Strategic Exploration in general, and the knowledge practice "use different types of searching language (e.g., controlled vocabulary, keywords, natural language) appropriately"[14] and the disposition "exhibit mental flexibility and creativity"[15] in particular, could be detected through use of a rubric that notes the number of relevant, accurate hashtags and Library of Congress subjects recorded by students.

The second opportunity for assessment is the review of student tweets about primary sources found using Twitter and the library catalog. The third opportunity is to pose reflection questions to students on Twitter using the course hashtag, which students answer on Twitter. Questions could include, "How do Library of Congress subject headings mirror hashtags on Twitter?" and "Why is it important to understand how information is described in different resources?" One could evaluate student responses using a rubric in order to detect the level of student learning related to the threshold concept. See Table 22.4. The target indicator used below directly relates to the threshold concept contained within Searching as Strategic Exploration and the knowledge practice "understand how information systems (i.e., collections of recorded information) are organized in order to access relevant information."[16]

Table 22.4. Sample assessment rubric for Lesson 3.

Target Indicator	Beginning	Developing	Exemplary
Recognizes the existence, variability, and value of descriptive vocabulary in information sources	Recognizes that information is described/tagged in information sources	Recognizes that information is described/tagged differently in different information sources	Recognizes that information is described/tagged differently in different information sources and that leveraging these descriptions is key to effective searching

It is important to acknowledge that the discussion of crowdsourced versus controlled vocabulary included in this lesson does cross over to address some elements of the frame Authority is Constructed and Contextual.[17] However, it is included only as an explanation of why Twitter hashtags are variable and Library of Congress subject headings are not. It should be noted, though, that just as elements of frames in the Framework overlap, many practical applications of the Framework will as well.

Conclusion

The lessons described above could easily be adapted to fit the needs of many History courses, and I encourage librarians to do so and make them their own. I suggest librarians use whatever databases, texts, social networks, technologies, and assessment methods best fit their own instructional outcomes and course contexts. What acceptable progress for students approaching a specific threshold concept will look like must be determined by each librarian and used to inform adaptation and assessment.

In order to describe these lessons to fellow librarians and course instructors, I'd suggest that librarians emphasize that in using these Framework-inspired lessons, they are able to teach students what they need to know for a specific assignment, such as how to find primary sources, but also make progress toward student understanding of a valuable threshold concept that once they grasp, they'll never lose. Over time, students will begin to approach their research as historians do, recognizing and adapting to the historical context of the content they're searching. They will become increasingly persistent researchers, revising their searches and employing alternate research methods when necessary, and seeking expert help rather than assuming relevant information isn't available.

Clearly the threshold concept contained within the Searching as Strategic Exploration frame has meaningful applications within the discipline of History, made even more challenging by the particularly contextual nature of historical research. What instruction librarians must remember when applying threshold concepts within any discipline is that they are, by definition, not quickly or easily grasped. They are big ideas that require multiple instructional exposures. It's important to acknowledge that no lesson plan, no matter how thoughtfully crafted, will be able to effectively address all knowledge practices and dispositions associated with any specific threshold concept. It's imperative that librarians use the Framework as inspiration to teach students meaningful, transferable concepts, but resist becoming overwhelmed by the comprehensiveness of the Framework as a whole. Focusing on addressing only the most relevant knowledge practices and dispositions to specific assignment, course, or program makes Framework-inspired information literacy instruction purposeful and achievable.

Notes

1. Association of College and Research Libraries (ACRL), *Framework for Information Literacy for Higher Education*, February 2, 2015, http://www.ala.org/acrl/standards/ilframework.
2. Ibid.
3. Ibid.
4. Grant Wiggins and Jay McTighe, *Understanding by Design* (Alexandria, VA: Association for Supervision and Curriculum Development, 2005), 105–25.
5. Brent Geary and Spencer C. Tucker, "Camp David Accords," in *The Encyclopedia of Middle East Wars: The United States in the Persian Gulf, Afghanistan, and Iraq Conflicts*, ed. Spencer C. Tucker (Santa Barbara, CA: ABC-CLIO, 2010), 255–257.
6. Carolyn Caffey Gardner, "Strategic Searching Spreadsheet," *CORA (Community of Online Research Assignments)*, November 5, 2015, http://www.projectcora.org/assignment/strategic-searching-spreadsheet.
7. Barbara Tomblin, *With Utmost Spirit: Allied Naval Operations in the Mediterranean, 1942–1945* (Lexington: The University Press of Kentucky, 2004), 6.
8. Gemma Betros, "The French Revolution and the Catholic Church," *History Review* 68 (2010): 16–21.
9. ACRL, *Framework for Information Literacy*.
10. Ibid.
11. Ibid.
12. Ibid.
13. Carol Kuhlthau, Leslie Maniotes, and Ann Caspari, *Guided Inquiry: Learning in the 21st Century* (Santa Barbara, CA: Libraries Unlimited, 2015), 15.
14. ACRL, *Framework for Information Literacy*.
15. Ibid.
16. Ibid.
17. Ibid.

CHAPTER 23*

Mapping the Chaos:
Building a Research Practice with Threshold Concepts in Studio Art Disciplines

Ashley Peterson

Art-making is an expression of the intellect. A viewer, observing a work of art, can guess at the physical labor required: sketches, models, editing, iterations, false starts. What about the intellectual labor? While not always apparent, this is no less vital a component than the manual skills required to make art.

I am a Research & Instruction Librarian at a small private art college. In this chapter, I explore the role of the academic art library, whose patrons express thinking, learning, and knowledge as visual art objects. A case study illustrates how the threshold concept Searching as Strategic Exploration from the ACRL Framework for Information Literacy for Higher Education,[1] along with other theoretical concepts and institutional goals, shape the integration of information literacy concepts into courses in studio art disciplines. I argue that librarians must assume a leading role in helping studio art students build research practices that inform and enrich their artistic practices, and in answering the question: What constitutes an information-literate artist?

---

* This work is licensed under a Creative Commons Attribution-NonCommercial-ShareAlike 4.0 License, CC BY-NC-SA (https://creativecommons.org/licenses/by-nc-sa/4.0/).

Artists and research

What is the role of research in the art-making process? Certainly, art can be a deeply personal expression or a display of in-born technical virtuosity, in which cases the need for gathering and synthesizing external information may not be apparent. However, in most academic studio art programs, students are encouraged to make art that is thoughtful, engaging, and in conversation with other art and ideas.

In his book *Art Practice as Research*, Graeme Sullivan argues that the "imaginative and intellectual work" that results in a work of art is a form of research.[2] In Sullivan's view, art is a document that expresses meaning and, potentially, new knowledge.[3] This suggests that an artwork, if it is the result of rigorous, careful research, is an important part of a scholarly conversation. In his article about the importance of forming good research questions to enrich the art-making process, George Petelin supports this notion when he claims that a work of art does not point toward an answer to the research question, but *is itself* the answer.[4]

If, following Petelin, research is an indelible part of artistic work,[5] it needs to be made visible and emphasized for students in studio art programs. It is within this process of inquiry, reflection, learning, and experimentation that librarians can situate themselves as an indispensable resource for student-artists.

The librarian's role

There is a long tradition of library support for visual arts-based research. Journals such as *Art Documentation*, *Art Libraries Journal*, and the *Visual Resources Association Bulletin* abound with case studies detailing thoughtful, creative approaches to working with academic studio art communities. These approaches come from all corners of librarianship, from technical services to digital humanities to research education. While all departments in a given academic library are essential to supporting community learning, this chapter will specifically address the role of librarians who work directly with patrons, one-on-one or in a classroom setting, to develop and hone their research abilities.

A crucial first step toward teaching research skills to visual artists is to understand how they find and use information in the creative process. William Hemmig provides a model for this in a pair of articles from 2008. In one, he conducts a study of academic literature addressing the information needs and information-seeking behavior of practicing visual artists. He concludes that the majority of these studies focus on how artists use libraries, rather than on how they more generally seek out information and conduct research.[6] Following this literature review, Hemmig conducted his own study of working artists and their information needs and drew several conclusions about how libraries can better serve this population.[7] Hemmig's work both illuminates some commonalities in artists' information needs[8] and demonstrates the importance of understanding the information needs of a user base within and, most crucially, beyond libraries.

In an academic art library context, it is of course useful to understand how students seek information and incorporate it into their creative processes. However, the end game is not to discover what students want and provide it; academic librarians need to assume a leading role in educating studio art students about effective research practices. Key to this is a strong alignment with faculty, both at the individual and administrative levels. Building trust and mutual respect between a librarian and an instructor is vital, as is the library's role in shaping the curriculum of an entire academic department or school. Increasingly, the art librarianship literature is arguing for this kind of collaborative, programmatic relationship.[9]

Information literacy at the School of the Museum of Fine Arts, Boston

The School of the Museum of Fine Arts (SMFA), Boston is a small private art college offering bachelor's and masters' degrees in studio art. To describe the SMFA Library's approach to information literacy education, it is crucial to begin with an overview of the curriculum. The case study outlined shortly is specific to the Bachelor of Fine Arts (BFA) degree program. BFA students are required to complete 76 studio art credits, as well as 14 academic courses at the SMFA or at Tufts University.[10] First-year BFA students are required to complete two courses in Writing and Composition, WRI 1 (or WRI 3, for English-language learners) and WRI 2. Instructors in each WRI 1, WRI 3, and WRI 2 class are required to work with a librarian to teach students research skills and information literacy concepts. Information literacy learning goals are determined in conjunction with the Writing and Composition program coordinator, and learning outcomes for class research sessions are set with the course instructors. Theoretically, these sessions are the first structured points of contact that BFA students have with SMFA library staff and resources. As yet, there is no structured point of contact between librarians and BFA students beyond the WRI classes, though many studio art and academic course instructors do schedule class visits to the SMFA Library. The goals and content of these sessions vary, but librarians always strive to align session content to course curriculum and to build on the foundational information literacy skills taught in the WRI classes.

Beyond considerations of curricular alignment, there are philosophical underpinnings to information literacy education at the SMFA. Of primary value is the acknowledgement of browsing and serendipitous discovery as legitimate and essential components of the research process. The research habits of SMFA community members, as observed by librarians and faculty, bear this out, as do trends observed broadly: William Hemmig notes at the conclusion of his literature review of artists' information-seeking habits that browsing is a crucial method of discovery for artists.[11] While art librarians have long understood the importance of chance encounters, librarianship in general is trending toward a more serious consideration of this phenomenon. In 2011, Birger Hjørland published a study of the library literature on browsing. He concludes that there have been very few attempts to understand and explicate browsing behavior and calls for a renewed effort to study it.[12] A similar plea is made in a recent conference paper about browsing and serendipitous discovery in the electronic environment. The authors maintain that as online searching has become an important method of information discovery, systems and tools have been designed that focus on search precision at the expense of the browsing experience.[13] They call for a new approach to online discovery, one that allows for multiple modes of information finding—"structured and unstructured, linear and serendipitous."[14] One desired outcome of browsing is, of course, serendipitous discovery: finding something illuminating, confounding, or just plain interesting that was not being consciously sought. Naresh Kumar Agarwal attempts to construct a definition of serendipity as it impacts information-finding. An important take-away from Agarwal's study is the notion that an unexpected discovery may not be of much importance to the research process in and of itself; what comes before and after a serendipitous encounter is just as important as that "aha!" moment.[15] Information-seekers should consciously open themselves to the serendipitous encounter, and following a discovery should thoughtfully consider *why* what they found has resonated and how it will be of value.

Another animating component of the SMFA Library's approach to information literacy is the notion of the library as cabinet of curiosities. Historically, cabinets of curiosities emerged in Europe in the early modern period (fifteenth through seventeenth centuries) and are the forerunners of the contemporary museum. Found mostly in the homes of the wealthy, these cabinets—which sometimes were literal cabinets and sometimes encompassed entire rooms—comprised collections of human-made and naturally occurring objects. Typically, the purpose of a cabinet was on the one hand to "define, discover, and possess" and to, via arrangement and juxtaposition, inscribe objects with layers of meaning that together suggest an overarching narrative of wonder.[16] Essentially, cabinets were a way for wealthy Europeans to order and make sense of their world, just as that world was expanding via discovery and exploration, both in terms of scientific thought and colonization.[17] Many contemporary thinkers see the curiosities cabinet as an apt metaphor for the process of research and knowledge creation, and it describes the function of many academic libraries: they are places where the juxtaposition of seemingly disparate things, when activated by a curious mind, can constitute new knowledge. This notion heavily informs how SMFA librarians encourage users to engage with libraries and approach the research process.

Why Searching as Strategic Exploration?

Librarians at the SMFA encourage students to be deliberate and metacognitive in their approach to research, and to carefully consider how it enriches their work. We want students to achieve this through the development of a research practice that informs, supports, and in some instances might *be* their artistic practice. The goal is not so much to show students the steps to do this (though that is part of it) as it is to help them develop the knowledge practices and dispositions required to develop a research practice. The ACRL's Framework for Information Literacy for Higher Education resonates with this approach, and has helped SMFA librarians situate our work within a larger conversation about information literacy in higher education.

Threshold concepts, one of the conceptual underpinnings of the Framework, provide a compelling avenue toward student mastery of information literacy. Given the foundations of research education at the SMFA, a concept that holds great relevance for our students is Searching as Strategic Exploration.[18] "Strategic exploration" is an apt way to describe how we encourage students to approach the artistic research process: *strategic* emphasizes the importance of being purposeful, productive, and self-reflexive, while *exploration* implies values that animate the entire endeavor—curiosity, creativity, and a sense of wonder. Where we see this as a potentially troublesome,[19] yet crucial concept is in the emphasis on the nonlinear, iterative, and serendipitous aspects of finding information. Speaking personally, I was well past my formal education and several years into my career before I realized that false starts, dead-ends, and "aimless wandering" through information during a research process are not wasteful or unproductive; they are essential to the final outcome. While so-called "experts" (art librarians, artists with a developed research practice) might acknowledge the importance of what can seem like creative wheel-spinning and embrace the complex connection between research and making, student-artists need to be deliberately led to this way of thinking. Many first-year BFA students come from an art-making background at the high school level that focuses on technique over concept, and the knowledge practices and dispositions that come with crossing the Searching as Strategic Exploration threshold are a means to a considered, critically engaged artistic practice.

Case study overview

During the spring 2016 semester, SMFA Librarians worked closely with a jewelry and small metals instructor to develop the research content of her Advanced Jewelry Studio/Seminar course. The seven students in this course were mostly in their third and fourth years of the BFA program, and one was a second-year MFA candidate. All had taken classes before in jewelry and small metals, and thus the focus of the seminar was less on technique and more on developing the conceptual ideas that shape their work and on independent studio time.

The librarians and the instructor collaboratively developed assignments and in-class activities to structure the development of student research practices. The overall learning goals for the research component of the course were for students to:
- build on the foundational information and visual literacy skills acquired in first-year writing courses;
- reframe engagement with research and library collections via browsing and serendipitous discovery;
- bring serious inquiry to artistic motivations; and
- cultivate a research practice that directly informs and enriches an artistic practice.

Since the fall 2014 semester and during each subsequent semester, SMFA Librarians have worked with this instructor to teach students research skills and information literacy concepts. Each time, previous efforts are evaluated and new ideas are implemented. The work done in the spring 2016 semester resulted from this iterative, reflexive process: what began in 2014 as a single meeting, in the library, with one of the instructor's classes evolved into a semester-long partnership where librarians help shape course content and meet with students several times, both in the library and in the classroom.

Another element new to the spring 2016 iteration is a focus on Searching as Strategic Exploration in shaping the assignments, activities, and overall learning goals for the course. One of the ways the librarians and the instructor agreed to approach teaching research is to illuminate and discuss the hidden labor that results in a "final" work of art. Research is an essential component of this labor, and we wanted to prompt students into considering and experiencing how, exactly, it shapes what they create. In order to help students cross the Searching as Strategic Exploration threshold—to take a considered, metacognitive approach to a process that is often messy, repetitive, and unpredictable—we identified some key knowledge practices and dispositions associated with this concept, which helped us develop course content. These include the "contextualized complex experience" of research, the "cognitive, affective, and social dimensions" of the researcher, the ability to toggle between divergent and convergent thinking during the search process, "mental flexibility and creativity," and recognizing the importance of browsing and serendipity.[20]

Building a research practice in Advanced Jewelry Studio/Seminar

On the first day of class, the instructor gave students a questionnaire that asked them to share how they typically conduct research, whether they have ever been asked to conduct research alongside their studio practices, and what they hope to accomplish in the course. The completed questionnaires were shared and discussed with the librarians. At the end of that first class period, students were given their first research assignment: visit the Museum of Fine Arts and select an object on display in the jewelry galleries; write a one-page response to it that includes at least some research; and make an object inspired by the piece, their research, and their reflections. The research requirements for the assignment were intentionally left vague, as one of the goals of the exercise was to observe how each student approached this component. Another goal was to make explicit the connection between learning and making, as this theme would be revisited and expanded upon throughout the course.

For the next research assignment, students were asked to take a self-guided field trip to a place relevant to the interests that inform their work. Students were free to choose where they visited; the only stipulation was that it must not be a place they'd been before. While at their chosen sites, students were required to visually document their visits, focusing on anything they found interesting, inspirational, or surprising. By requiring students to visit an unfamiliar place and pay attention to visual elements, the intent was that they would both position themselves for a potential serendipitous encounter and appreciate the visual elements of the research process. Following the field trips, students were asked to create a ten-minute slide presentation featuring images of their work prior to the course, images that relate to their research interests, images of other artists' work that they find inspiring or that they admire, and images from the field trip. This gave them an opportunity to visually express a coherent narrative of their interests, influences, and inspiration. The librarians were invited to class to observe and offer feedback on these presentations.

For the next research activity, librarians spent an entire class period (9 a.m. to 5 p.m., with a two-hour break for lunch) working with the students. In preparation for this class, students were asked to read "The Performance and Practice of Research in *A Cabinet of Curiosity: The Library's Dead Time*," an article about an art installation that investigates how the "materiality of information shapes the making of meaning."[21] The authors, who are also the artists, aimed to make visible the "dead time" or hidden labor that underlies the production of knowledge. Students were also required to complete a series of questions asking them to reflect on their research interests and practices (sample questions: "How did you approach the Museum of Fine Arts research exercise? What subjects or themes did you concentrate on in your presentations? What questions do you have of your own work?"), and to generate a list of twenty keywords associated with the subjects, themes, and questions defined.

The class session began in the classroom with a conversation about the assigned reading. Librarians came prepared with guiding questions and were delighted to find that the students generated discussion topics on their own. These included the aesthetic dimensions of research, the concept of "dead time" and hidden labor, the notion of libraries as curated spaces that reflect the goals and values of an institution, and how this might impact research and knowledge creation. Next, the librarians and instructor guided students in a mind-mapping exercise. Based on the keywords students generated, each used large sheets of paper and colorful writing implements to map out the links and connections among their interests. After about forty-five minutes, students switched mind maps with a partner and re-drew these associative webs for one other. The goal was to show students the social, collaborative dimensions of the research process. Following this, the entire class had the opportunity to examine each map and its re-drawn version and to ask questions or offer further ideas.

After the lunch break, the students, instructor, and librarians re-grouped in the library for what was termed an "Exploration Session." Starting with the keywords from their mind maps and the questions generated during the mapping/sharing exercise, students were turned loose in the library to find information to help them learn more about their research interests. At the outset, students were encouraged to try browsing as well as searching: perhaps note the call number of an interesting book title and spend several minutes scanning adjacent titles, or approach a new section of the library shelves, or browse the titles in the library catalog or databases that fall under a particular subject heading. To continue to foster a collaborative research environment and emphasize the social nature of knowledge creation, the mind-mapping partnerships were maintained; students were required to find at least one resource of interest for their partner. As the students found resources (often with the assistance of the librarians) they were asked to note book and article titles, names of artists or authors, any new information they discovered, and any questions they were left asking.

There were two follow-up assignments to the day-long mind mapping and library exploration sessions: an annotated bibliography and a cabinet of curiosities project. The annotated bibliography was intended to capture what students found during the library exploration and how each title supports their research. For the cabinet of curiosities assignment, students were asked to consider information that they found unexpectedly and that resonated with their interests, and to think again about why it is compelling. They were then asked to make visible the new ideas and knowledge generated so far in their research by making ten objects that together present a narrative about what each student is exploring. Students had two weeks to complete the cabinet assignment and present them in class for a mid-semester critique. The librarians participated in these critiques, which allowed us an opportunity to observe how connections were being forged between the research and making processes. Students' approaches to the project were varied: some used the opportunity to explore working in new materials or using familiar materials in new ways, others used object creation to explore and manifest new ideas, and some did both. One thing common to each project was the notion of "fearless experimentation" engendered by the assignment parameters: because two weeks is not a lot of time in which to create ten new art objects, students agreed that they worried less about the final outcome and instead focused on the experience of making. Students, librarians, and the instructor came to the conclusion that this constitutes a form of tactile, experiential research.

Following the cabinet of curiosities assignment, students had two more structured opportunities for outside research: a visit to the library at the Museum of Fine Arts (separate geographically and operationally from the SMFA Library), and a visit to the Department of Textile and Fashion Arts at the Museum of Fine Arts. Here they met with curators and were able to study objects from the collection. The SMFA librarians' last point of contact with the class came during the final critiques, where we had a chance to assess the progress students made in their research, observe and discuss how it informed their work, and identify who might still benefit from one-on-one research consultations with a librarian.

Assessment, debrief, and reflection

SMFA Librarians approach assessment as a means of evaluating student learning and improving our teaching practice. There were several points of assessment during this course that allowed the librarians to evaluate students' progress in their research practices:

- *Student feedback forms*: in addition to the first-day questionnaire asking students about the current state of their research habits and what they hoped to accomplish in the Advanced Jewelry Studio/Seminar course, a last-day questionnaire was distributed. This asked students to reflect on what they accomplished and how the various research activities contributed.
- *Assignments*: the work the students created was a visual manifestation of their progress, and librarians had the opportunity to observe this at two distinct points during the semester. The annotated bibliographies were also helpful for evaluating the quality of the information students were finding to support their research interests.
- *Critiques*: the mid-semester and final critiques were essential assessment opportunities. In addition to viewing work, librarians were able to hear about students' creative processes and conceptual justifications, and to ask further questions about the role research played in a final piece.
- *Debrief conversation*: during the last class session, librarians and the instructor engaged students in a conversation about the research content of the course—how it was and was not helpful to their work, and how things might be improved moving forward.

Feedback from the last-day questionnaire and the debrief conversation seem to suggest that for many students the goals of the course were met. Overall, there was consensus that the research component pushed them to consider resources and information they would not usually engage with, and that the collaborative nature of some of the research activities was very beneficial for discovering new ideas. Students agreed that the class engendered a comfort with the art-making process which, perhaps paradoxically, allowed them to start reaching better results once they were not as hung up on these results. Another interesting point raised was that students felt their time in the library, working with librarians, was made more productive by librarians' having seen examples of their work and having a visual understanding of their interests and what they are trying to accomplish. Regarding the impact of research on their work, students commented that it allowed them to formalize their own ideas about what they create and communicate these ideas with confidence, and to experiment with new materials and techniques.

Students also had great suggestions for improving the research experience. Many were overwhelmed by the volume of information found during the library exploration. While the annotated bibliography and cabinet of curiosities assignments were helpful in distilling the information somewhat, more time to read, reflect, and synthesize would have been appreciated. One student suggested, and many agreed, that the mind mapping exercise should have come earlier in the semester (it was conducted during the fourth week of class), so that everyone could immediately begin identifying their research interests and making connections. It was also suggested that making a second mind map, toward the end of the semester, and comparing it to the first iteration would be helpful. Students were pleased with how accessible and ready-to-help the librarians were, and it was agreed that moving forward, students in an intensive research seminar like this class should be required to meet one-on-one with a librarian to discuss their research agendas.

When the instructor and the librarians met to reflect on the course, we came to the conclusion that more thought should be given to how we assess the quality of research evident in students' artistic output. While to some extent this is necessarily a tricky endeavor—we are not interested in dictating what art "should" look like or represent—it is still, we believe, possible to develop a rubric for evaluating to what degree a piece or a body of work is the outcome of a thoughtful, rigorous research process. This is under consideration for subsequent semesters.

Overall, Searching as Strategic Exploration as a threshold concept proved an apt guiding principle for the research content of this course. We wanted students to recognize the complexities and the "dead time" of the research process and to value its importance in their own work. Key course components that drew from this concept were the variety of resources students explored (museum collections, library collections, print resources, visual resources), different ways of finding information (targeted browsing, open-ended browsing, directed searching, collaboration), multiple modes of connecting information and ideas to artistic output (concept mapping, slide presentations, the cabinet of curiosities project), and requiring students to pay attention to their own thought processes via reflection questions, group critiques, and the debrief conversation.[22] The concept of "strategic exploration" helped students observe and enact research as a nonlinear, iterative, and multimodal process essential to their artistic output.

Future directions

The librarians and the instructor feel very positive about the collaborative work done in the spring 2016 Advanced Jewelry Studio/Seminar course. We will continue to refine our approach, with the broader goal of reaching as many students as possible with these opportunities to develop their research skills and information literacy aptitude. To this end, discussions are underway regarding how the SMFA librarians will shape the research content of the Senior Thesis Program for the fall 2016 semester; the work done in the Seminar course will serve as a model. Senior Thesis is a year-long, research-and-writing intensive course that culminates in an artistic thesis project. As this program usually enrolls anywhere from one-third to one-half of the senior class, librarians see it as a productive focus of information literacy education.

In closing, it is worth noting that the SMFA is in some operational flux. Previously affiliated with the Museum of Fine Arts, Boston, as of July 2016 the School is under the management of Tufts University. At the time of writing this chapter, it remains to be seen how this new alignment will impact the degree programs, curriculum, or even the name of the SMFA. While the future is uncertain, SMFA librarians see this as an excellent opportunity to advocate for information literacy and research education as essential components of the revised studio art curriculum. Our accomplishments in the Advanced Jewelry course demonstrate that librarians can and should form robust, meaningful partnerships with faculty toward shaping studio art course content and overall student learning outcomes. The end result is art work that is thoughtful and research-driven, and artists who are critically engaged with their sources of inspiration and the scholarly conversation in visual art.

Notes

1. Association of College and Research Libraries (ACRL), *Framework for Information Literacy for Higher Education*, February 2, 2015, http://www.ala.org/acrl/standards/ilframework.
2. Graeme Sullivan, *Art Practice as Research: Inquiry in Visual Arts*. 2nd ed. (Thousand Oaks, CA: Sage Publications, 2010), xix.
3. Ibid., 72.
4. George Petelin, "Begging the Question: Performativity and Studio-Based Research," *Arts and Humanities in Higher Education* 13, no. 3 (July 1, 2014): 199.
5. Ibid., 193.
6. William S. Hemmig, "The Information-Seeking Behavior of Visual Artists: A Literature Review," *Journal of Documentation* 64, no. 3 (May 2008): 343–62.
7. William Hemmig, "An Empirical Study of the Information-Seeking Behavior of Practicing Visual Artists," *Journal of Documentation* 65, no. 4 (July 2009): 682–703.
8. Hemmig, "An Empirical Study of the Information-Seeking Behavior of Practicing Visual Artists," 683.
9. See for example: Larissa Garcia and Jessica Labatte. "Threshold Concepts as Metaphors for the Creative Process: Adapting the Framework for Information Literacy to Studio Art Classes." *Art Documentation: Journal of the Art Libraries Society of North America* 34, no. 2 (2015): 235–48.; and Kristina M. Keog and Stephen A. Pat-

10. ton. "Embedded Art Librarianship: Project Partnerships from Concept to Production." *Art Documentation: Journal of the Art Libraries Society of North America* 35, no. 1 (March 1, 2016): 144–63.
10. Currently, SMFA students receive their degrees through Tufts University and complete many of their academic credits through the Tufts School of Arts and Sciences. However, with the exception of dual enrollment students (who have been admitted to both schools), BFA and MFA students at the SMFA do not go through the Tufts application process and are not "officially" Tufts students. As of July 2016, the SMFA is operationally part of Tufts University; it remains to be seen how application and enrollment will change.
11. Hemmig, "The Information-Seeking Behavior of Visual Artists," 357.
12. Birger Hjørland, "The Importance of Theories of Knowledge: Browsing as an Example," *Journal of the American Society for Information Science and Technology* 62, no. 3 (March 1, 2011): 596.
13. Kate Joranson, Steven VanTuyl, and Nina Clements, "E-Browsing: Serendipity and Questions of Access and Discovery" in *Charleston Library Conference* (Charleston, SC: Purdue e-Pubs, 2013), 2.
14. Ibid., 7.
15. Naresh Kumar Agarwal, "Towards a Definition of Serendipity in Information Behaviour," *Information Research* 20, no. 3 (September 2015): 18.
16. Patrick Mauries, *Cabinets of Curiosities* (New York: Thames & Hudson Inc., 2002), 25.
17. It is important to pause and more fully acknowledge this link between cabinets of curiosities and the colonialist legacy of the Early Modern period; their histories are inextricable. Many of the objects collected in cabinets were symbolic of the "exotic" places and people newly "discovered" by European nations. The sense of wonder that cabinets were meant to engender often elided the brutal and deliberate erasure of the personhood of colonial subjects, reducing them and their cultures to "curiosities" to be collected. For an engaging and thoughtful examination of this phenomenon, see Stephen Greenblatt, *Marvelous Possessions: The Wonder of the New World* (Chicago: University of Chicago Press, 1991).
18. ACRL, *Framework for Information Literacy for Higher Education*.
19. For a definition of "troublesome" as it relates to threshold concepts, see Jan H. F. Meyer, and Ray Land, "Threshold Concepts and Troublesome Knowledge: An Introduction," in *Overcoming Barriers to Student Understanding: Threshold Concepts and Troublesome Knowledge*, eds. Jan H. F. Meyer and Ray Land (London: Routledge, 2006), 3–18.
20. ACRL, *Framework for Information Literacy for Higher Education*.
21. Bonnie Mak and Julia Pollack, "The Performance and Practice of Research in A Cabinet of Curiosity: The Library's Dead Time," *Art Documentation: Journal of the Art Libraries Society of North America* 32, no. 2 (2013): 202.
22. ACRL, *Framework for Information Literacy for Higher Education*.

CHAPTER 24*

Teaching Future Educators Exploration through Strategic Searching

Michelle Keba

As future teachers, students in the field of education will play a unique role as not only consumers but also disseminators of information. In order to succeed, these future teachers must become lifelong learners who can strategically search in a variety of information contexts. The newly adopted ACRL Framework for Information Literacy for Higher Education (Framework) can provide a structure for preparing these students to be lifelong, information literate learners. Based on a "cluster of interconnected core concepts" for information literacy, the Framework focuses on six key threshold concepts related to information, research, and scholarship.[1] First proposed by Meyer and Land, threshold concepts are "those ideas in any discipline that are passageways or portals to enlarged understanding or ways of thinking and practicing within that discipline."[2] By nature, threshold concepts are troublesome, transformative, and irreversible. These threshold concepts are not easy to grasp. However, once a learner understands a threshold concept, he or she has a transformed understanding of the field which cannot be unlearned or forgotten.

One of the six frames, Searching as Strategic Exploration, focuses on the idea that searching is "often nonlinear and iterative," and that learners need to

---

* This work is licensed under a Creative Commons Attribution-NonCommercial-NoDerivatives 4.0 License, CC BY-NC-ND (https://creativecommons.org/licenses/by-nc-nd/4.0/).

be willing to "pursue alternative avenues" in their searches.[3] This frame can be specifically tied to the field of education through the practice of culturally responsive teaching. Using the Searching as Strategic Exploration frame, librarians can prepare students to become culturally responsive teachers by showing them how to strategically gather reliable information about other cultures which they can use to expand their worldview and inform their future teaching styles. By showing students how to search strategically and to be critical of what they find, librarians not only teach the idea of culturally responsive teaching, but also the information literacy threshold concept Searching as Strategic Exploration.

In this chapter, I outline the threshold concept of Searching as Strategic Exploration within the context of the field of education. I then describe my experience teaching students how to search strategically for culturally relevant information about cultural groups they could be working with as teachers as an example of applying Searching as Strategic Exploration to a real-world situation.

Searching as strategic exploration

As students learn more about Searching as Strategic Exploration, they will come to understand that searching is a nonlinear process that must be revised and repeated based on new information they discover through their searches. They must be willing to pursue multiple lines of inquiry from a variety of information sources and to persist even when an initial search strategy fails.

According to the Framework, "learners who are developing their information literate abilities" as strategic searchers will express the following dispositions.[4] These students will be able to reflect on their information need and select appropriate information sources that will meet their need while understanding that each information source will vary in content and relevance to their topic. They will also "recognize the value of browsing and other serendipitous methods of information gathering"[5] as a search strategy in its own right and will be mentally flexible and persistent as they search, realizing that the first search they try will not always produce the best results. For this reason, they will not be afraid of failed searches or of reaching out to experts for assistance. Finally, they will be able to recognize when they have gathered sufficient resources to fulfill their information need.

Thinking about searching not as a set of discrete skills but rather as a transformational threshold concept has changed the way I think about and teach students how to search. As a threshold concept, we must first recognize that not just searching, but searching as way to explore strategically, is a troublesome concept. Novice learners will often want to find answers quickly with a single search. Revising search strategies and learning the most effective ways to search disparate information sources can be frustrating and intimidating.

It is important to address that with students from the beginning by explaining upfront that research is not a straightforward, linear process with a single answer. They must be intellectually tenacious and willing to press on even when a search strategy fails. Intellectual tenacity cannot be taught as a set of skills but rather demonstrated as a concept during instruction sessions, at the reference desk, and while working with students in one-on-one consultations.

Strategic searching within the field of education

There are many foundational theories within the field of education. While these theories can conflict at times, one value holds true for all educators. From behaviorists to constructivists to humanists, educators may debate *how* children learn, but all of them can agree that they want children to learn. Education majors want to know how they will be able to help their students succeed. They value straightforward information and strategies that will help them be effective teachers. Many students drawn to the teaching profession are also creative individuals who thrive on solving challenges. These values pair well with several of the dispositions associated with Searching as Strategic Exploration, including the abilities to "exhibit mental flexibility and creativity," "understand that first attempts at searching do not always produce adequate results," and "persist in the face of search challenges."[6]

In order to be strategic searchers within the field of education, students must learn that search is iterative. They need to try their search in more than one information source and be open to varying their search terms. In this way, they will learn that there is no single path for locating information,[7] but rather a series of forking paths which will give them a broader view of their subject area. This series of forking paths may seem intimidating to a novice searcher, so the concept of "strategic" searching must be emphasized. As strategic searchers, students develop a plan for their research and understand the information sources and vocabulary specific to their disciplines. By developing a plan and understanding the unique features of their discipline's most common sources, students will be prepared to search efficiently rather than wandering down every path they cross.

Culturally responsive teaching

In today's educational landscape, a discrepancy exists between the cultural backgrounds of teachers and their students. According to the U.S. Department of Education, in the 2011–2012 school year, approximately 52 percent of students identified as white, 24 percent as Hispanic, 16 percent as black, and 5 percent as Asian, whereas over 80 percent of teachers identified as white.[8] For all students to succeed, teachers must learn to utilize teaching styles that incorporate their students' cultural norms. This can be achieved through a practice referred to as culturally responsive teaching. Built on work by Ladson-Billings and Gay,[9] culturally responsive teaching is defined as "using knowledge of student cultures and modalities to select and apply strategies and resources for instruction, while engaging in self-reflection."[10] First proposed in the mid-1990s, culturally responsive teaching has gained prominence with the push to promote diversity and inclusivity in the classroom. At Palm Beach Atlantic University, culturally responsive teaching is taught in a required course for all elementary education majors: Cultural Dimensions of ESOL.

Culturally responsive teaching in practice

In practical application, the first step to becoming a culturally responsive teacher involves recognizing cultural differences without categorizing them as "good" or "bad."[11] By removing value judgments, teachers can begin to work with students of other cultures while trying to avoid imposing their own biases. Teachers can begin to recognize these cultural differences through engagement in self-reflection and active study of cultural diversity. It is in this active study of cultural diversity that future teachers can begin to apply the dispositions and knowledge practices of Searching as Strategic Exploration. They must be able to search for information about cultural norms of their future student populations in order to ultimately apply that knowledge to their teaching strategies.

Rather than teaching all students the same way, culturally responsive teachers will recognize that current teaching practices often reflect European American cultural values. For example, many teachers require students to maintain eye contact when they are being spoken to as a sign of attentiveness, but to an Apache student this may be perceived as staring, which could lead to resentment.[12] Through self-reflection, culturally responsive teachers can recognize what values they hold from their own culture, as well as how their cultural norms and values are reflected in their own teaching style and classroom policies.

In addition to self-reflection, Gay suggests that "teachers need to begin the process of becoming more caring and culturally competent by acquiring a knowledge base about ethnic and cultural diversity in education."[13] Teachers must actively acquire knowledge about other cultures in order to recognize what role culture plays in their classroom as well as to identify cultural disconnects. This knowledge base can be created through reading current research on cultural diversity as well as informal discussion with students and their families.

Curriculum selection. Once a teacher has recognized a disconnect between his or her cultural norms and those of the students he or she teaches, changes can be made. For example, materials can be selected which reflect the cultural experiences of all students. Rather than standing apart from the curriculum as a multicultural unit, a culturally responsive teacher will weave in materials that are relevant to all students throughout the entire curriculum.

Lesson modification. Culturally responsive teachers also reflect on the lessons they develop and the teaching strategies they employ. For example, group work can pose an initial challenge for some students, depending on how they have been raised to view collaboration. Gay expands on this idea in her book when she states, "Children who have been brought up to value the individual above the group are apt to experience difficulties—at least initially—when expected to collaborate with peers…. To enable these students to participate effectively in collaborative problem-solving projects, the culturally responsive teacher helps them understand not only how to participate in this type of instructional event, but also why it is important for them to adopt ways of learning that are culturally unfamiliar, perhaps even clashing."[14] For example, teachers can explicitly teach or model expected behaviors for group work as well as the value of working as a team. By anticipating cultural responses, teachers can prepare students for classroom activities which may conflict with their cultural norms or modify the lesson so that it accommodates different learning and cultural styles.

Searching strategically for culturally relevant information

As information professionals, librarians can teach future educators how to search strategically for culturally relevant information in order to build their "knowledge base about ethnic and cultural diversity in education" as suggested by Gay.[15] Through conversations with teaching faculty, provision of culturally relevant texts and direct instruction during library training, librarians can apply the knowledge practices and dispositions associated with Searching as Strategic Exploration to this process of building a knowledge base of culturally relevant information. For example, at my institution, I worked with a teaching faculty member to create an instruction session that would show future teachers how to search strategically for culturally relevant information.

Partnering with teaching faculty on an existing assignment. Teaching faculty can become a librarian's strongest ally in information literacy instruction. With a teaching faculty member's support, information literacy threshold concepts can be woven into the school's curriculum as well as specific research assignments for key courses. I have found that many professors in schools of education are receptive to partnering with librarians in order to promote information literacy and will become advocates to other professors once they see the value of well-planned library instruction sessions for their students.

In this case, a professor from the School of Education and Behavioral Studies reached out to me to see if I could conduct a library training session for her Cultural Dimensions of ESOL course. With a "CultureGram" assignment already in place, there was a ripe opportunity to pair the required course assignment with a library session about searching strategically for culturally relevant information.

For this course, students must work as a group to develop an in-depth culture study or "CultureGram." In their CultureGram, students must examine and evaluate culturally specific resources that influence the diversity of behaviors of K–12 students and parents in educational contexts. As they collect the information for their CultureGram, the students must also select a cultural informant to interview. They then compare the information they found through scholarly sources with the information they learned during the interview.

Identifying learning objectives. One of the first steps to take when creating an instruction session related to Searching as Strategic Exploration and culturally responsive teaching is to identify learning objectives students should achieve by the end of the session. Librarians teaching these sessions can use the knowledge practices and dispositions included in the Framework as a starting point, which can be modified for the individual needs and interests of the students at his or her university. For example, one of the knowledge practices for Searching as Strategic Exploration is to "identify interested parties, such as scholars, organizations, governments, and industries, who might produce information about a topic and then determine how to access that information."[16] In practice, this could be translated into a concrete learning outcome such as, "By the end of this session, students will be able to select an appropriate information source to meet their information need."

For my instruction session, I created three learning objectives related to searching strategically for culturally relevant information. Specifically, by the end of the session, I hoped that the students would be able to:
1. locate books and articles relevant to their self-selected culture;
2. critique the effectiveness of their search strategy; and
3. explain how they would modify their teaching styles based on the information they found.

In this case, the first two outcomes related directly to Searching as Strategic Exploration in that they require students to find resources and think critically about their strategies while the third outcome tied searching strategically to becoming a culturally responsive teacher.

Building the instruction session

Once I have worked with a faculty member to develop learning outcomes tied to a research assignment, I start to plan the content for the instruction session. For this session, I used the list of knowledge practices for Searching as Strategic Exploration included in the Framework to guide the content for the session. Each knowledge practice for Searching as Strategic Exploration is listed as a shortened heading and expanded upon below.

Determining initial scope. To begin searching strategically, students must identify the initial scope of their task. One way to generate interest in the topic of culturally responsive teaching, while also identifying the initial scope needed for the CultureGram assignment, is to have students self-reflect on their cultures. Wisniewski, Fawcett, Padak, and Rasinski suggest that students on the way to becoming culturally responsive teachers should begin by examining their own cultures.[17] Wisnieski et al. suggest having students make a list of all the words that come to mind when they think about their culture. Then, have students reflect on the list they have created, asking what they noticed about the list or if anything surprised them. This can help students begin to recognize which aspects of their own culture influence them, while also encouraging them to think about what aspects they will need to research about their selected culture group. This activity could be done at the beginning of the class as students walk into the room or as pre-work if time will be limited during a one-shot instruction session.

Identifying interested parties. As students begin to determine the initial scope of their information task, they must also start to think about which "interested parties, such as scholars, organizations, governments, and industries" might collect, analyze, and produce information on their topic.[18] As with all disciplines, information sources within the field of education vary in content and relevance depending on a student's information need. However, in this instruction session, I introduce two key sources run by the United States Department of Education's Institute of Education Sciences that provide complementary yet distinct information: the Educational Research Information Center (ERIC) and the National Center for Education Statistics (NCES).

ERIC contains education-focused journals, gray literature reports, and conference papers. Since its founding on May 15, 1964, ERIC has become the primary research repository for educational research.[19] As an open-access database, ERIC makes citation information accessible to researchers, policy makers, and the general public. For this reason, ERIC is one of the top databases for students in the field of education to know.

NCES is the "primary federal entity for collecting and analyzing data related to education in the U.S. and other nations."[20] The center also includes several studies from the Organisation for Economic Co-operation and Development (OECD), which offers a wealth of international information and statistics. In particular, the Teaching and Learning International Survey (TALIS) contains information about working and classroom conditions around the globe, including class size and teacher working hours.[21] By analyzing raw data about foreign classrooms, future educators can begin to picture the learning environments from which their students may be coming. With requirements from professors to find a certain number of "scholarly" sources, students are often hesitant to use websites for their papers. However, strategic searchers will learn that statistics are often recorded and reported by government entities such as NCES.

Utilizing divergent and convergent thinking. The Framework offers "brainstorming" as an example of divergent thinking and "selecting the best source" as an example of convergent thinking when searching.[22] These strategies will most likely resonate within many students in the field of education as brainstorming is a common activity for many subject areas. Students may already be familiar with the use of graphic organizers and mind mapping tools for brainstorming. However, librarians can show students how to use these tools to generate keywords and synonyms, as well as search strategies for their research topics.

Once students have completed the cultural self-reflection activity, I ask them to brainstorm where they might be able to find culturally relevant information. They will most likely suggest using the Internet and speaking to people from other cultures. However, at this point I introduce them to sources of information like ERIC and NCES. I also encourage students to brainstorm keywords they can use in their searches by asking them what components make up culture. We then discuss how these components can be incorporated into a search. I caution them that brainstorming will just get them started; once they begin their search, they can revise their keywords or incorporate controlled vocabulary from the databases and library catalog.

Matching information needs and strategies to search tools. Encyclopedias can offer a great place to start when searching for culturally relevant information. Though there is some danger of generalization when giving a broad overview of a subject, encyclopedias can give students a baseline knowledge of various cultures. In order to search strategically, students must learn that encyclopedias are only a jumping off point.

Three sets of encyclopedias have proved to be particularly useful to our students during their search to learn more about other cultures: *Countries and their Cultures* published by Macmillian, *Countries, Peoples & Cultures* published by Salem Press, and *Encyclopedia of World Cultures* published by G.K. Hall & Co.[23] As digital natives, many students may be unfamiliar with print encyclopedias like the sets mentioned above. While the first two are rather straightforward with countries listed either alphabetically or by region, the third set, *Encyclopedia of World Cultures,* can pose a challenge. This set is organized by ethnic group rather than by country, so students must first identify a region and then use a map located within the encyclopedia to determine which ethnic groups are located in their region. As they use these varied sets of encyclopedias, students will come to realize that information can be organized in a variety of manners, depending on the focus of the author.

Once students have some general ideas about a culture, they can expand their search to other sources, like books and articles, using keywords and ideas they have learned through the encyclopedias. Books can play an important role in deepening their knowledge of the culture while articles can provide in-depth case studies.

Designing and refining needs and strategies. In my instruction sessions, I encourage students to begin with a broad search. For example, their first search may just start with the keyword "culture." Once they begin to look through their search results, they can write down keywords related to culture and concepts they might want to use to narrow their topic. This is a good time to discuss Boolean logic, though I often explain the concept without actually using the term Boolean. We focus on the idea that the term AND will narrow a search while the term OR will broaden one. We talk about how using too many ANDs at first will probably be too specific and won't yield many results. However, if they already have too many results, we discuss adding more concepts or keywords to narrow the search. Showing this trial and error during the instruction session demonstrates to students that all search strategies need to be revised and modified based on the terms and keywords that come up in current literature on their topics. Students must not be afraid to revise failed search strategies. Librarians can model this as they teach by showing that every search will not work perfectly. Searches which are too broad can be narrowed with Boolean operators and specific subject headings, while searches which are too narrow can be expanded.

This is an excellent time to incorporate active learning into the library session. During practice time, students can search and fail in a controlled environment where a librarian is able to step in and assist as needed. Students need to go through the experience of trying and failing in order to learn intellectual persistence. However, with scaffolded support, students can experience the feeling of success while avoiding research frustration and burnout. For example, each team of students can start by doing a prepared search for a cultural group in an education database. Once they experience success during the search, the group can try a new search using their own keywords. Because the students are working in groups for this assignment, they can encourage each other as they search and offer each other feedback and ideas for other possible searches. Since these searches are conducted during class time, the librarian can check in with each group to check for misunderstandings or frustration. That way, students can conduct strategic searches in the class environment rather than failing and burning out on their own.

Understanding organizational structure of information systems. Understanding how information systems are structured is another key knowledge practice for accessing relevant information. For example, while a simple catalog search for the name of a country or culture will often yield results, students can also explore relevant Library of Congress Subject Headings to narrow their searches. For example, students can learn that the LC Subject Heading "Brazil—Social life and customs" will focus not just on Brazil but more narrowly on the social life and customs within the country. Relevant subject headings should be reviewed prior to the course, and any biased headings should be addressed and discussed during the session.

Using searching language appropriately. As strategic searchers, students must also learn the language of the ERIC database. One of ERIC's strongest features is the ERIC Thesaurus, which contains more than 11,000 subject headings.[24] Learning to use these subject terms in their research queries helps students narrow and refine their searches. Persistence is key when learning to use the ERIC Thesaurus, as students will realize that some subject headings will not match the terms they themselves use. For example, the ERIC Thesaurus uses the phrase "Parent Participation" rather than the term "Parental Involvement." Through engagement with the ERIC Thesaurus, students will learn that subject headings can provide the necessary terms for a more precise search. For example, the ERIC Thesaurus uses the specific phrase "School Holding Power" rather than the more ambiguous "Student Retention," which could refer to retention of information as well as retention related to being held back a grade. There are several subject headings listed in the ERIC thesaurus that will help students narrow their searches for culturally relevant information. "Cultural Differences," "Cultural Awareness," and "Cultural Background" are all terms used by ERIC to focus on the role of culture within education.

Managing searching processes and results effectively. As students search, they may become overwhelmed by the amount of results they find. While serendipitous discovery can lead to relevant results, it is important for students to keep track of what they found as well as how they found it. During the instruction session, I have students complete an exercise listing the most relevant source they found, how they found it, and a summary of the source.

Assessing the session

At the end of the session, each group gives a pop-up presentation where they identify the source they found, how they found the source, and how they would incorporate what they learned about the culture they were studying into their teaching style. These pop-up presentations allow the students to learn from each other and reflect on what worked and what didn't work as they searched. Since the assessment aligns to the learning outcomes for the session, I am able to determine whether each group has exceeded, met, or failed to meet the predetermined learning outcomes.

Presentation of source. Each group is instructed to share the most interesting resource they found during their search. Though evaluating information sources is not a key focus of the session, I ask the students to explain what made them think the resource they were sharing was a reliable source of information.

Critique of search strategy. While some groups may share articles and others books or encyclopedias, each team should explain their search strategies including which keywords they used and how they narrowed their searches. By presenting to their classmates, group members are able to critique their own strategies while reinforcing the idea that the best searches are refined and revised as needed during the search process.

Modification of teaching style. Once a group shares their information resource and search strategy, they are asked to explain how they would modify their teaching style based on the information they had discovered. For example, in one session, a group described an article they found explaining how schools in the Bahamas are more relationship-oriented than task-focused. They then spoke about how they could incorporate more relationship building in their classrooms instead of solely focusing on tasks.

Conclusion

Though the Framework for Information Literacy for Higher Education was only adopted in 2016, many of the threshold concepts, like Searching as Strategic Exploration, translate directly to the skills and ideas librarians have been teaching students for years. In order to excel as teachers and become lifelong learners, future educators must learn to identify information sources that will meet their needs and to be persistent and willing to revise their search strategies until their needs are met. Within the field of education, strategic searching can be directly applied to the search for culturally relevant information. Teachers must recognize how their own culture affects their teaching style and be willing to search strategically to learn more about their students' cultures. With this information, teachers can modify their lessons to be sensitive to all learners in their classrooms.

Notes

1. Association of College and Research Libraries (ACRL), *Framework for Information Literacy for Higher Education*, February 2, 2015, http://www.ala.org/acrl/standards/ilframework.
2. Ibid.
3. Ibid.
4. Ibid.
5. Ibid.
6. Ibid.
7. Patricia Bravender, Hazel McClure, and Gayle Schaub, *Threshold Concepts: Lesson Plans for Librarians* (Chicago: Association of College & Research Libraries, 2015), 106.
8. Thomas D. Snyder and Sally A. Dillow, "Digest of Education Statistics 2013 (NCES 2015-011)," *National Center for Education Statistics*, May 2015, http://nces.ed.gov/pubs2015/2015011.pdf.
9. Gloria Ladson-Billings, "Toward a Theory of Culturally Relevant Pedagogy," *American Educational Research Journal* 32, no. 3 (1995): 465–491; Geneva Gay, *Culturally Responsive Teaching: Theory, Practice and Research* (New York: Teachers College Press, 2000).
10. Robin Wisniewski, Gay Fawcett, Nancy D. Padak, and Timothy V. Rasinski, *Evidence-Based Instruction in Reading: A Professional Development Guide to Culturally Responsive Instruction* (Boston: Pearson Higher Ed., 2012), 3.
11. Ibid., 7.
12. Geneva Gay, *Culturally Responsive Teaching*, 22.
13. Ibid., 70.
14. Ibid., 108.
15. Ibid., 70.
16. ACRL, *Framework for Information Literacy for Higher Education*.
17. Wisniewski et al., *Evidence-Based Instruction in Reading: A Professional Development Guide to Culturally Responsive Instruction*, 8.
18. ACRL, *Framework for Information Literacy for Higher Education*.
19. "50 Years of ERIC: 1964–2014," *Education Resources Information Center*, accessed August 5, 2016, http://eric.ed.gov/pdf/ERIC_Retrospective.pdf.
20. "About Us," *National Center for Education Statistics*, accessed August 5, 2016, https://nces.ed.gov/about/.
21. "Teaching and Learning International Survey," *National Center for Education Statistics*, accessed August 5, 2016, https://nces.ed.gov/surveys/talis/index.asp.
22. ACRL, *Framework for Information Literacy for Higher Education*.
23. Melvin Ember and Carol R. Ember, eds., *Countries and their Cultures* (New York: Macmillan Reference USA, 2001); Michael Shally-Jensen, ed., *Countries, Peoples & Cultures* (Ipswich: Salem Press, 2015); David Levinson, ed., *Encyclopedia of World Cultures* (Boston: G.K. Hall & Co., 1991).
24. "Frequently Asked Questions," *Education Resources Information Center*, accessed August 5, 2016, https://eric.ed.gov/?faq.

CHAPTER 25

Threshold Concepts, Information Literacy, and Social Epistemology:
A Critical Perspective on the ACRL Framework with Reference to Psychology

Tony Anderson and Bill Johnston

Introduction

We have adopted the stance of "critical friends" in order to bring to bear our respective expertise in psychology, information literacy, and educational development to offer a supportive perspective on the Association of College and Research Libraries (ACRL) threshold concept project. We regard the ACRL Framework as a valuable work in progress and hope that our stance will be helpful in progressing understanding and adaptation of the Framework. We are aware of theoretical criticisms and qualifications that have been levelled at threshold concepts[1] and are agnostic on the issues involved, but we are sympathetic to the apparent utility of the threshold concept approach as a mechanism for encouraging lecturers and others to engage with educational development in their disciplines.

Consequently, we adopt both a critical stance to the terminology of threshold concepts and an investigatory interest in the possibility of identifying threshold concepts for psychology. This discussion is not simply about terminology but concerns the very notion of threshold concepts and what sort of mental entity they might be.

The chapter involves two main elements. First, we look at the notion of threshold concepts from a psychological perspective, which highlights some interesting issues about the very notion of threshold concepts. Second, we examine a suggested threshold concept within psychology, which is the idea that knowledge within the discipline is inherently uncertain and subject to change. This epistemological threshold concept, we argue, is particularly pertinent to an account of information searching in relation to student epistemological development and therefore relevant to ACRL's suggested threshold concept of Searching as Strategic Exploration.[2] Hopefully, readers will gain some insight into threshold concepts by considering a psychological perspective on the notion. We also hope that readers will gain by observing how we jointly attempt to combine the notion of threshold concepts in psychology with the threshold concepts for information literacy offered in the ACRL Framework for information literacy as a focus for a practical intervention in teaching. We explore the implications of this approach for teaching practice and suggest lines of research for further development.

Threshold concepts originated in pedagogical research on approaches to learning within the disciplines.[3] A key aspect of the research was the value placed on investigating the perceptions of experienced disciplinary teachers and, in particular, their observations of what particular disciplinary content students found difficult to understand. The researchers identified a number of features of learning, such as "troublesome knowledge" and a change in perspective following comprehension of the threshold concept, which have become the basic descriptive account of threshold concepts as a pedagogical construct. This work can be located in the field of educational development[4] and has become firmly established as an approach to educational development in universities. We see the ACRL Framework project as an important extension of this tradition.

ACRL has taken up the threshold concept approach as the major driver for revision of their account of information literacy (IL).[5] Interestingly, the ACRL approach to developing threshold concepts for IL used a Delphi technique among librarians[6] to bring forward candidate threshold concepts. This is an apparent departure from the original approach of researching the views of disciplinary academics, and may be significant in how threshold concepts are implemented in academic settings. For example, it may be that librarians will find it easier to collaborate with academics using the new ACRL Framework than the previous largely skills-based Standards. Space limitations preclude us from fully exploring the implications of ACRL's adoption of the threshold concept approach to teaching and learning in the disciplines, such as (1) the possibility that information literacy is a "discipline" in its own right; (2) the re-positioning of information literacy and the role of librarians in academic settings; and (3) the importance of fully engaging with threshold concepts as a pedagogical construct. In the meantime, we reprise two key, interlinked aspects of the ACRL approach.

ACRL and the changing pedagogical landscape

ACRL has acknowledged a significant shift in pedagogical practice on the part of teaching faculty in American universities over some fourteen years since the original Standards appeared in 2000. For example, examples of pedagogical change in the US include:
- student collaborative working
- undergraduate research
- integrative learning/learning communities/cross-disciplinary critical thinking
- focus on early years of degree programmes
- growth in professional Masters degrees
- IT
- blended learning
- MOOCs
- the "flipped classroom"
- focus on active, collaborative learning

What seems to be missing, in our view, is any underlying theory of the pedagogical nature of these particular changes. We address this here by discussing the importance of the students' developing epistemology and argue for pedagogical strategies of the sort described by Tanner[7] to nurture such development.[8]

ACRL and threshold concepts

ACRL threshold concepts are intimately linked to the ACRL analysis of the changing pedagogical landscape in US Higher Education. ACRL describes threshold concepts as demanding, conceptual portals, which students must pass through in order to achieve higher levels of disciplinary understanding. Threshold concepts are presented as transformative, integrative, irreversible, bounded, and troublesome. While the ACRL Framework provides elaboration of each concept, there is clear scope for analysis and constructive critique. Our contribution focuses upon ACRL's suggested threshold concept of Searching as Strategic Exploration and draws upon the notion of social epistemology.[9]

The ACRL website notes that "Searching for information is often non-linear and iterative, requiring the evaluation of a broad range of information sources and the mental flexibility to pursue alternate avenues as new understanding is developed."[10] It further notes a number of knowledge practices and dispositions that are required for effective searching, including:
- determining the scope of the search;
- identifying sources who might produce relevant material;
- designing and refining information needs and search strategies and modifying these as necessary based on search results;
- effectively managing search processes and results;
- exhibiting mental flexibility and creativity;
- understanding that first attempts at searching do not always yield the best results; and
- persisting in the face of challenges, and knowing when they have enough information to complete their information task.

We entirely agree with all of the above stipulations and those others that are not reproduced here because of space limitations. The ACRL Framework notes that searchers, particularly novice searchers, will fall short on some of these requirements and research evidence bears this out. The process of search by students has been studied extensively and several significant problems documented.[11] For example, Halverson et al.[12] found that the criteria which students used to evaluate and select information were sometimes less than optimal in that they occasionally relied upon criteria that were, strictly speaking, non-relevant, such as the information's readability or its superficial aesthetic features. Likewise, Attar[13] observed adults' use of and reaction to websites, and noted that some users found it difficult to distinguish between an "official" organizational website and a page written by an individual, for example. Jones and Allen[14] noted a number of difficulties experienced by students in their search processes, such as where to start and how many journal articles to use. Hofer, Whitmire, and Anderson, Johnston, and MacDonald[15] noted a number of problems, such as difficulty in deciding the trustworthiness of particular sources, and all of these authors linked the problems noted to epistemological difficulties. In short, everyday academic tasks, such as writing essays, require students to approach their search process in a systematic, strategic, self-regulated and critical way, yet in doing so they have to make judgements that they find tricky. For example: What is good quality material? How do I identify sources that I can regard as trustworthy? How much material is enough for the current purposes? How do I deal with contradictions arising across different sources? And so on.

It is clear that the processes described immediately above are fundamental to all academic disciplines. Does this necessarily mean that Searching as

Strategic Exploration is indeed an example of a threshold concept, as asserted by ACRL? In adopting our stance as critical friends, we sought to critically examine the very notion of the threshold concept and did so with reference to an academic discipline, Psychology, that was familiar to one of us (Anderson). Having clarified the notion of the threshold concept for ourselves, we then return to the issue of Searching as Strategic Exploration as a putative threshold concept.

Threshold concepts in Psychology

The fundamental claim of the theory of threshold concepts—that there exist key ideas that act as a gateway to thinking about a knowledge domain in an entirely new and much more accurate way—is at first sight very appealing, in that it implies that identification of any such concepts within a given discipline coupled with concerted research on how best to get such concepts across to students and thereafter deploying this pedagogical knowledge assiduously, will have a profound, transformative effect on students' understanding. It is not hard to understand the attractiveness of such a notion to those of us who (sometimes struggle to) help students to learn and ultimately to join their disciplinary community. The example of a threshold concept that is perhaps most familiar in the literature is the notion of opportunity costs within Economics; however, given that neither of us is an economist, we hesitate to undertake an analysis of this supposed threshold concept. Instead, we would like to offer a critical analysis of the notion of the threshold concept using an example from psychology, a discipline with which we could claim rather greater familiarity.

The language of threshold concepts

Before we even do that, however, it is worth pondering the terms "threshold" and "concept." The notion of a "threshold" is metaphorical. The threshold of a front door, for example, is the point at which we might see outward from the building to the wider world beyond. This clever metaphor underlines the idea of a learner being on the brink of apprehending a much bigger "picture." The second term, "concept," is also worth pondering, and is intended (we presume) to be much less metaphorical. It is widely used informally to refer to any kind of ideational content. However, other more specific senses of "concept" exist; see Rowbottom for an interesting discussion of different senses of the word "concept."[16] To consider the different possible senses of the word "concept," we would argue, is not mere academic nitpicking but necessary clarification of exactly what kind of thing it is that students are struggling to comprehend and that educators themselves are struggling to teach. Threshold concepts are therefore difficult for both students from the point of view of learning and educators from the point of view of devising suitable pedagogies.

One specific use of the term "concept" comes from cognitive psychology, and in that body of literature a concept is a mental category to which we assign particular instances. Thus, if we perceive a particular object as a chair, i.e., assign it to the category "chair," we know what it can be used for, how we should interact with it, and so on, by virtue of its belonging to a class of things with common properties and functions. By having a generic concept of chair, we simplify our processing of the many instances of that concept that we will encounter, such as dining chairs, lounge chairs, desk chairs, deck chairs, and so on, and thus we do not have to treat every new object that we encounter as if we had never encountered it before—that is, as a completely new object requiring full analysis. The saving of mental effort that this affords—so-called "cognitive economy"—is immediately obvious.

Thus, concepts as conceived within classical cognitive psychology are regarded as a categorization tool with which to simplify our experience of the myriad objects that we encounter and operate at a relatively low level, although they are complex enough in themselves. However, we suspect that the notion of "concept" used within threshold concept theory is something at a rather greater level of complexity.

A search of the literature for suggested threshold concepts within psychology yielded surprisingly sparse results. For example, MacAndrews, Spedding, and Jamieson[17] asked students and lecturers in Geography, Medical Sciences, and Psychology to reflect on difficult aspects of their teaching or learning, in the hope of identifying threshold concepts, but this resulted in the interviewees focusing on generic skills rather than discipline-based threshold concepts. This led us to ponder the question: What would we nominate from first principles as candidate threshold concepts within psychology? We intend to produce a fuller discussion of possible threshold concepts within Psychology (Anderson and Johnston, forthcoming), but one example that sprang readily to mind given our interests in information literacy and critical thinking merits extended discussion here. It seemed to us that a key requirement for an idea to count as an example of a threshold concept is that the grasping of the idea should have profound consequences for the student's understanding of much subsequent material, implying that the concept is transformative for the student, and both of these properties are certainly the case for our proposed threshold concept.

A candidate threshold concept within Psychology

The example of a possible threshold concept within Psychology that sprang to our minds is one that has very direct relevance to threshold concepts within information literacy. It is the idea of *epistemological evaluativism*. There is a substantial body of research within Psychology on students' ideas about knowledge.[18] That literature appears to show that beginning undergraduate students have a dualistic, right versus wrong or realist epistemology in which ideas are regarded as being either correct or incorrect; that is, ideas are seen as either corresponding to supposed states of affairs in the world, or not. Later, the students develop a multiplist epistemology in which alternative ideas are seen as equally valid. Later still, they develop a fully evaluativist epistemology in which competing ideas are classified as stronger or weaker depending on the evidence base that supports them. Such epistemological variation has profound implications for students' learning of a discipline and even of the way in which they will read textbooks, react to teaching methods involving peer interaction, or conduct literature searches.[19] The notion that academic theories are abstractions that might not have corresponding concrete equivalents in the world—that a theory is only as good as what evidence is there to support it—is epistemologically quite sophisticated. Anderson and Johnston[20] argue that a dualist, right versus wrong epistemology could prove to be associated with particularly poor literature search strategies. After all, if a student genuinely believes that there is a single definite "right" answer to an issue, and that that "right" answer has already been found, what is the point of further searching? And indeed, several authors[21] have noted exactly such phenomena in students' search strategies. On the other hand, a fully evaluativist epistemology requires students to access all available ideas on the subject, critically evaluate their supporting evidence, and arrive at a weighed conclusion as to which theory is the best supported, as matters currently stand. This process of weighing up the rival theories and choosing the best-supported among them would undoubtedly be a very complex one; the investigation of students' heuristics for doing this is, we would contend, an important topic for further research.

We would therefore claim that *the student's state of epistemological development is fundamental for their information literacy, and that the greatest degree of epistemological sophistication—an evaluativist epistemology—should itself count as a threshold concept.* Once the evaluativist perspective on knowledge is grasped, all knowledge is seen in a new way—not as an absolute, immutable truth that corresponds to a state of affairs in the world, but as malleable and changeable in the light of any new evidence received.

Nothing is absolutely certain, and the application of critical thought is a routine requirement when considering any knowledge claim. This means that epistemological evaluativism meets the criteria for being an example of a threshold concept. It is difficult to get one's head around it in the first instance, the empirical evidence suggesting that several years of Higher Education are required, and even after that a fully evaluativist position is not necessarily guaranteed. It is transformational in that the way the world (of knowledge) is seen is radically different compared to the way it was perceived when the former epistemological dualism held sway. Finally, it is irreversible. Once knowledge comes to be seen as tentative and changeable, it is difficult or impossible to return to seeing it as fixed and a simple matter of correspondent truth.

It is worth exploring further the implications of the different epistemological positions for Search as Strategic Exploration. First of all, take the notion of search itself: it implies a purposive, active process in which a number, quite possibly a large number, of options are to be examined. Taking the notion of a purposive, active stance first, for an epistemological dualist, a more passive orientation might seem reasonable given that this viewpoint conceives of the learning situation as one in which an "expert" communicates or transmits "the truth," whether that be in a lecture or via the pages of a book. The evaluativist, on the other hand, recognises the need for a much more active approach toward the available information and, in particular, finding information on the different competing ideas in the area in question, evaluating these, and selecting that thought to be most compelling overall—a necessarily active set of processes.

Turning to the issue of search, to the epistemological dualist holding a black or white, right or wrong view of knowledge, the very notion of search might not seem to be entirely relevant: what is required is to establish the "truth" from an authoritative source, such as a textbook or a lecturer; there is only one theme to be established, the "correct" one. To the epistemological evaluativist, on the other hand, the notion of search is central: *there is a need to establish how many theoretical positions exist on an issue and what items of evidence have accrued within the literature in support of each. These have to be found, evaluated, and their implications weighed up.*

Then there is the issue of strategy, which implies the existence of a number of usable mechanisms for obtaining relevant information, and a carefully considered process of selection among those mechanisms constrained by the purposes of the student. Epistemological dualism, with its emphasis on truth and authority, could be expected to be associated with a narrow range of strategies focusing on finding authoritative sources and consulting them. Epistemological evaluativism, on the other hand, could be expected to be associated with an awareness of what are the stronger and weaker forms of evidence within a discipline, and an awareness of the varying reputability and trustworthiness of different kinds of information sources.

Thus, we would expect the epistemological evaluativist to distinguish, in the case of psychology, among experimental, correlational, and anecdotal or qualitative evidence and assess their relative merits in particular cases. In addition, we would expect an epistemological evaluativist to employ relevant information search strategies, such as: to seek out refereed journal articles or articles in particular types of journal—for example, those that are peer reviewed, or those that publish only literature reviews; and to constrain their searches in terms of time windows—for example, by restricting search to the most recent few years to establish the latest thinking on an issue, and so on. In other words, we would expect the evaluativist to deploy a much broader range of strategies compared to the dualist.

The term "exploration" implies a degree of tentativeness allied to purposiveness, plus some awareness of the scope of particular keywords and combinations of keywords that enable an engagement with the knowledge that is afforded by the database being searched. A willingness to change the focus of search and, if necessary, to start afresh entirely are the hallmarks of exploration. We would expect the epistemological dualist to engage in a "depth first" search of a narrow range of ideas starting with textbooks and lecture notes as sources, whereas the evaluativist would be expected to engage with a wider range of options using a "breadth-first" search from the start and to occasionally change direction, dropping entire lines of inquiry, if necessary. All of these considerations imply that even if the dualist is taught to have facility in the technicalities of searching any given database, this would not guarantee thorough search or genuinely *strategic* exploration; that is, the strategy adopted is ultimately an epistemologically driven one, and a less sophisticated epistemology will be associated with fewer, and/or less sophisticated, strategies. For example, identifying search terms would require thought about what knowledge is being sought—i.e., the nature and quality of the knowledge matters; it is not simply a matter of finding a bibliographic reference.

However, the epistemological ideas required for successful information literacy go beyond ideas about the nature of knowledge itself to ideas about the nature of knowing and therefore implicate what has been termed "social epistemology."[22] This explicitly social dimension to knowledge and belief is exemplified by the fact that most of us rely most of the time on acknowledged experts to tell us what is true. This social dimension to epistemology is very broad-ranging, covering everything from the processes of knowledge acquisition and theory acceptance in science to the acceptance as true of an item of information by an individual. It squarely implicates the role of social factors and social institutions in people's acquisition of knowledge from other people, whether directly or indirectly via for example books or the Internet.

We would argue that *all* of the threshold concepts suggested by ACRL implicate student epistemology—and *social* epistemology—as conceptually fundamental. However, we do not have sufficient space within the present chapter to spell out the implications of epistemological development for each of the threshold concepts suggested by ACRL. For example, the idea that "authority is constructed and contextual" seems to us to immediately and directly implicate notions of social epistemology. Likewise, the idea of "information creation," as opposed to simply "finding out," is rich with epistemological implications. However, we would emphasize our fundamental claim that the ACRL threshold concepts themselves presuppose other, epistemological threshold concepts—in this case, evaluativist ideas about the nature of knowledge, and that the latter constitute the appropriate level at which to design and implement educational interventions intended to improve information literacy. To summarize, we have contrasted the two most extremely different epistemological positions taken by students, one involving belief that definite, correct versus incorrect knowledge exists, and the other involving the belief that all knowledge is tentative and that only the best supported ideas should provisionally be accepted as true. We have argued that these different positions have strong implications for Searching as a Strategic Exploration. The kinds of nonlinear, iterative searches involving the evaluation of a range of information sources and the use of mental flexibility to pursue alternate avenues as new understanding is developed, as advocated by ACRL as optimal types of search, are, we argue, uniquely associated with the most sophisticated, evaluative epistemology. That, in turn, implies that teaching interventions aimed at improving searching behaviour have to be designed to explicitly address epistemological issues.

We have discussed epistemological evaluativism as a putative example of a threshold concept at length to justify two claims about threshold concepts. First, if we accept that the idea of epistemological evaluativism is a threshold concept within psychology, it is a "concept" at an altogether greater level of complexity than the classical notion of a concept as a category. This level of ideational complexity seems to us more akin to the notion of a "mental model"[23] which has an inner "relation-structure" among its elements and the possibility of manipulation of these elements of mental models to allow prediction and explanation of events in the world. The fundamental idea of mental model theory is that thought does not merely construct and interrogate static representations of information but takes the form of working models that parallel the reality that is being modelled.

For example, imagine a psychology student with a fully evaluative epistemology who is searching for information related to a particular issue. Such a student would have an awareness of the scope of particular search terms and of the breadth of inclusivity of particular databases, such that it would be possible for such a student to anticipate, via manipulation of the mental model that underpins the epistemological evaluativist stance, which strategies would be likely to yield greater or lesser numbers of "hits" of varying degrees of dependability of provenance. For example: "If I use this search term rather than that search term and restrict the search to peer reviewed journals only, I will get fewer hits but they will be more relevant and of better quality." This knowledge of the effects of particular strategies and of how multiple variables will interact with each other would seem to us to be more dynamic and model-based than static.

Suppose further that such a student encounters a particular publication. He or she might note its support for a particular theoretical position and initially evaluate it positively for having an experiment-based methodology, i.e., one which, if properly conducted, could in principle yield information about causal relationships among variables. But he or she might also note caveats, such that it has been carried out with a demographically restricted sample, it might usefully have deployed control groups to fully eliminate possible alternative conclusions, and there might also be doubts about the ecological validity of the experimental procedure. A weighed conclusion as to how convincing it is overall as support for the theory would then be required. That weighing process would continue for all articles supporting each of the competing theories, and some sort of more global weighing process would ultimately have to take place in which each theory and all of its supporting evidence were compared with the other(s). It is again clear to us that such a process is far more complex than a simple concept-as-a-categorization device as conceived of within psychology; being able to envision the status of evidence in support of a theory when multiple considerations have to be weighed against each other clearly implies a much more dynamic, modelling type of process. The term "threshold concepts" is by now probably too well established within the literature for the "concept" element to be replaced by "model" or "idea," but we believe that such a change would lead to more accurate terminology. We would go so far as to claim that describing this mental activity as any kind of "concept" misleads us into thinking that it is much simpler than it in fact is.

The example also illustrates a second important point. It is clear that the idea of epistemological evaluativism is absolutely fundamental to psychology: psychologists need to fully understand the epistemological status of knowledge published within psychological research journals, otherwise they will find aspects of the research literature within their own subject difficult if not impossible to interpret. For example, apparent contradictions across sources will seem baffling to someone with a dualist epistemology and impossible to resolve within a multiplist epistemology. However, the important point to note here is that the very notion of epistemology is not itself psychological; it is fundamentally philosophical, leading to the paradox that a threshold concept in one discipline actually belongs in a very real sense to another.

A final, and quite profound, point is that although we have argued for the importance of epistemological thinking for Searching as Strategic Exploration within the context of psychology, it is in fact something of a universal across all academic disciplines: while disciplines vary in terms of what types of evidence count as good quality evidence, ultimately in all cases an epistemologically evaluativist stance is the most sophisticated one. Even in long-established scientific disciplines, such as physics and chemistry, which are underpinned by well-supported bodies of theory such as the atomic theory of matter, those at the "cutting edge" of research in the discipline nevertheless regard even such well-established theories as potentially susceptible to replacement in the event of a newer, more inclusive theory of greater explanatory power emerging, leading in extreme cases to "scientific revolutions."[24] This evaluativist way of thinking, cutting as it does across disciplinary boundaries, offers the exciting possibility of common perspectives on information literacy across disciplines.

The above considerations naturally raise the question: In the light of these variations in epistemological thinking, how do we design curricula to help encourage the development of an evaluativist epistemology and, therefore, encourage the student to undertake searching as a process of genuinely strategic exploration? We explore this issue in the next section.

Implications for curriculum practice

We have argued elsewhere[25] that effective instruction in information literacy requires explicit attention to epistemological issues, metacognition, and critical thinking. We suggest that a social constructivist approach to pedagogy[26] based in problem-based, peer-interaction type teaching and learning settings, with extensive use of metacognitive prompting of the type advocated by Tanner,[27] would be a good way forward. This approach would have several important implications:

1. The traditional "one-shot" approach in which search mechanisms are presented within one session of teaching will not in itself be sufficient. The one-shot teaching scenario remains a basis of practice for instructional librarians in many universities, despite its limitations. Lecturers can reinforce this situation by assuming that a few sessions on particular information sources and relevant searching practices are enough for their students and do not release course time for more sophisticated interventions. However, the literature reviewed above implies that multiple sessions, with time between to allow a phase of reflection, would be needed.
2. Design of the learning content would need to be a collaborative effort involving both library staff and subject area academics, and ideally

would need to link in with the disciplinary content being studied alongside the information literacy material.
3. Since the existing research literature suggests that epistemological growth happens slowly, developing a curriculum across year groups would be advisable. We suggest the development of new course designs that consider issues around information literacy alongside the relevant disciplinary content. Assessment would be a key element of our approach to course design.[28]
4. Educational development would be implicated. Staff development would be required so that the design of the information literacy-related teaching and learning activities were optimized. Educational staff development is typically described as the provision of development opportunities for those who support learning and teaching in the university. In this case, the development would be in the capability of supporting the implementation of information literacy within the institution.
5. Organizational development would therefore also be required in terms of developing the institutional strategic policy and executive-level management of teaching. The assumptions are that the status quo is no longer an option in the present circumstances and improving information literacy education is part of necessary change within higher education.

The above outline is consonant with the work of Wiggins and McTighe, Hepworth and Walton, and Secker and Coonan.[29]

Conclusions

We agree that the idea of threshold concepts has potential value for educators, and ACRL's embracing of the notion is both understandable and in many ways useful: it focusses very much on what has to be learned and specifies the required capabilities very clearly. We do, however, question whether the activities identified by ACRL as candidate threshold concepts are in fact threshold concepts in themselves, and suggest that what underpins the ACRL "threshold concepts" is a specific type of epistemology, and that that particular epistemological level (epistemological evaluativism) is the level of threshold concept that should be addressed by learning and teaching interventions. We argue that searching will only take the form of a truly strategic exploration in the case of students who hold an evaluativist epistemology—only if the student believes that all knowledge is tentative and dependent on evidential support will active searching for multiple competing theoretical positions and a process of carefully weighed selection among them take place. We further argue that traditional one-shot teaching slots for information literacy are therefore entirely inadequate; that the teaching of information literacy concepts should be integrated with disciplinary material across the years of the typical undergraduate degree; that explicit attention should be given to epistemological issues within the information-literacy-plus-disciplinary-material teaching; that peer- and problem-based learning is a useful vehicle for inculcating the relevant ideas; and that explicit metacognitive prompting along the lines used by Tanner[30] in biology education would be an important addition to any teaching intervention. These suggestions[31] imply the need for a research program examining the effectiveness of such an approach and evaluating it against currently existing standard practice.

Acknowledgements

We would like to thank the editors for their thoughtful comments on an earlier draft of this chapter, and to thank Kay Anderson for her help with the preparation of the final manuscript.

Notes

1. Darrell P. Rowbottom, "Demystifying Threshold Concepts," *Journal of Philosophy of Education*, 41, no. 2 (2007): 263–70; Malcolm Tight, "Theory Development and Application in Higher Education Research: The Case of Threshold Concepts," in *Theory and Method in Higher Education Research II: International Perspectives on Higher Education Research*, vol. 10 (Emerald Group Publishing Limited, 2014): 249–67.
2. Anthony Anderson and Bill Johnston, *From Information Literacy to Social Epistemology: Insights from Psychology* (Chandos, 2016).
3. Jan H. F. Meyer and Ray Land, "Threshold Concepts and Troublesome Knowledge: Linkages to Ways of Thinking and Practising Within the Disciplines," in *Improving Student Learning: Improving Student Learning Theory and Practice—Ten Years On*, ed. Chris Rust (Oxford: Oxford Centre for Staff Development, 2003); —, "Threshold Concepts and Troublesome Knowledge (2): Epistemological Considerations and a Conceptual Framework for Teaching and Learning," *Higher Education* 49 no. 3 (2005): 373–88.
4. John B. Biggs, *Teaching for Quality Learning at University: What the Student Does* (Maidenhead: Open University Press, 2011); Noel Entwhistle and Peter Tomlinson, eds., *Student Learning and University Teaching: British Journal of Educational Psychology Monograph Series II, 4* (The British Psychological Society, 2007): 1–18; Tight, "Theory Development and Application in Higher Education Research."
5. Korey Brunetti, Amy R. Hofer, and Lori Townsend, "Interdisciplinarity and Information Literacy Instruction: A Threshold Concepts Approach," in *Threshold Concepts: From Personal Practice to Communities of Practice, Proceedings of the National Academy's Sixth Annual Conference and the Fourth Biennial Threshold Concepts Conference*, eds. Catherine O'Mahony, Avril Buchanan, Mary O'Rourke, and Bettie Higgs (Cork, Ireland: NAIRTL, 2014), 89–93, http://www.nairtl.ie/

documents/EPub_2012Proceedings.pdf#page=99; Megan Oakleaf, "A Roadmap for Assessing Student Learning Using the New Framework for Information Literacy for Higher Education," *The Journal of Academic Librarianship*, 40 no. 5 (2014): 510–14.
6. Association of College and Research Libraries (ACRL), *Framework for Information Literacy for Higher Education*, February 2, 2015, http://www.ala.org/acrl/standards/ilframework.
7. Kimberly D. Tanner, "Promoting Student Metacognition," *CBE-Life Sciences Education*, 11, no. 2 (2012): 113–20.
8. Anderson and Johnston, *From Information Literacy to Social Epistemology*.
9. Ibid.; Margaret E. Egan and Jesse H. Shera, "Foundations of a Theory of Bibliography," *The Library Quarterly*, 22, no. 2 (1952): 125–37; Jesse H. Shera "Social Epistemology, General Semantics and Librarianship," *Wilson Library Bulletin*, 35, no. 3 (1961): 767–70; Don Fallis, "Social Epistemology and Information Science," *Annual Review of Information Science and Technology*, 40, no. 1 (2006): 475–519.
10. Searching as Strategic Exploration, accessed 20 May 2016, https://sites.google.com/site/acrlframework/searching-as-strategic-exploration.
11. Dena Attar, "Dismay and Disappointment: Perspectives of Inexperienced Adult Learners on Becoming Webpage Readers," *International Journal of Educational Research*, 43, no. 7–8 (2005): 495–508; Sarah K. Brem, Janet Russell, and Lisa Weems, "Science on the Web: Student Evaluations of Scientific Arguments," *Discourse Processes*, 32, no. 2–3 (2001): 191–213; Kristy L. Halverson, Marcelle A. Siegel, and Sharyn K. Freyermuth, "Non-Science Majors' Critical Evaluation of Websites in a Biotechnology Course," *Journal of Science Education and Technology*, 19, no. 6 (2010): 612–20.
12. Halverson, Siegel, and Freyermouth, "Non-Science Majors' Critical Evaluation of Websites."
13. Attar, "Dismay and Disappointment."
14. Steve Jones and Julie Allen, "Evaluating Psychology Library Skills and Experiences," *Psychology Teaching Review*, 18, no. 2 (2012): 94–115.
15. Barbara K. Hofer, "Epistemological Understanding as a Metacognitive Process: Thinking Aloud During Online Searching," *Educational Psychologist*, 39, no. 1 (2004): 43–55; Ethelene Whitmire, "Epistemological Beliefs and the Information-Seeking Behavior of Undergraduates," *Library and Information Science Research*, 25 (2003): 127–42; Anthony Anderson, Bill Johnston, and Alexandra McDonald, "Information Literacy in Adult Returner Students," *Library and Information Review*, 37, no. 114 (2013): 55–73.
16. Rowbottom, "Demystifying Threshold Concepts"; Tight, "Theory Development and Application in Higher Education Research."
17. Siobhan B. G. MacAndrew, Nicholas Spedding, and Susan Jamieson, "How Was It for You? A Cross-Disciplinary Study of 'Troublesome Knowledge' as Identified by Undergraduate Students and Lecturers in Geography, Medical Science and Psychology," September 2011, https://repository.abertay.ac.uk/jspui/bitstream/handle/10373/1219/.
18. Hofer, "Epistemological Understanding as a Metacognitive Process"; Deanna Kuhn, Richard Cheney, and Michael Weinstock, "The Development of Epistemological Understanding," *Cognitive Development* 15, no. 3 (2000): 309–328; William

G. Perry, Jr., *Forms of Intellectual and Ethical Development in the College Years: A Scheme* (San Francisco: Jossey-Bass, 1970).
19. Whitmire, "Epistemological Beliefs and the Information-seeking Behavior of Undergraduates"; Anderson and Johnston, *From Information Literacy to Social Epistemology*.
20. Anderson and Johnston, *From Information Literacy to Social Epistemology*.
21. Whitmire, "Epistemological Beliefs and the Information-Seeking Behavior of Undergraduates"; Jones and Allen, "Evaluating Psychology Library Skills and Experiences."
22. Anderson and Johnston, *From Information Literacy to Social Epistemology*; Egan and Shera, "Foundations of a Theory of Bibliography"; Shera "Social Epistemology, General Semantics and Librarianship"; Fallis "Social Epistemology and Information Science."
23. Phillip N. Johnson-Laird, *Mental Models* (Cambridge: Cambridge University Press, 1983); Kenneth Craik, *The Nature of Explanation* (Cambridge: Cambridge University Press, 1943).
24. Thomas S. Kuhn, *The Structure of Scientific Revolutions* (Chicago: University of Chicago Press, 1962).
25. Anderson and Johnston, *From Information Literacy to Social Epistemology*.
26. Ibid.
27. Tanner, "Promoting Student Metacognition."
28. Anderson and Johnston, *From Information Literacy to Social Epistemology*.
29. Grant Wiggins and Jay McTighe, *Understanding by Design* (Alexandria, VA: Association for Supervision and Curriculum Development, 2005); Mark Hepworth and Geoff Walton, Teaching Information Literacy for Inquiry-Based Learning (Oxford: Chandos Publishing, 2009); Jane Secker and Emma Coonan, eds., *Rethinking Information Literacy: A Practical Framework for Supporting Learning* (London: Facet Publishing, 2013).
30. Tanner, "Promoting Student Metacognition."
31. Anderson and Johnston, *From Information Literacy to Social Epistemology*.

Bibliography

Bravender, Patricia, Hazel McClure, and Gayle Schaub, eds. *Teaching Information Literacy Threshold Concepts: Lesson Plans for Librarians*. Chicago, IL: Association of College and Research Libraries, 2015.

Flanagan, Michael T. "Threshold Concepts: Undergraduate Teaching, Postgraduate Training, Professional Development and School Education: A Short Introduction and a Bibliography." Accessed May 5, 2017. http://www.ee.ucl.ac.uk/~mflanaga/thresholds.html.

Land, Ray, Jan H. F. Meyer, and Jan Smith, eds. *Threshold Concepts Within the Disciplines*. Rotterdam: Sense Publishers, 2008.

Land, Ray, Jan H. F. Meyer, and Michael T. Flanagan, eds. *Threshold Concepts in Practice*. Rotterdam, Boston & Taipei: Sense Publishers, 2016.

Mackey, Thomas P., and Trudi E. Jacobson. "Reframing Information Literacy as a Metaliteracy." *College and Research Libraries* 72, no. 1 (2011): 62–78. doi: 10.5860/crl-76r1.

Meyer, Jan H. F. "Helping Our Students: Learning, Metalearning, and Threshold Concepts." In *Taking Stock: Research on Teaching and Learning in Higher Education*, edited by Julia Christensen Hughes and Joy Mighty, 197–213. Montreal: McGill-Queen's University Press, 2010.

Meyer, Jan H. F., Ray Land, and Caroline Baillie, eds. *Threshold Concepts and Transformational Learning*. Rotterdam, Boston & Taipei: Sense Publishers, 2010.

Townsend, Lori, Amy R. Hofer, Silvia Lin Hanick, and Korey Brunetti. "Identifying Threshold Concepts for Information Literacy: A Delphi Study." *Communications in Information Literacy* 10, no. 1 (2016): 23–49.

About the Authors

Tony Anderson. Tony Anderson is a senior teaching fellow in the School of Psychological Sciences and Health and Vice-Dean (Academic) of the Faculty of Humanities and Social Sciences at the University of Strathclyde. Tony's initial research interests in language understanding in dialogue developed over thirty years into an interest the effect of peer interaction on learning, both from the point of view of learning discipline content and of thinking skills, such as critical thinking.

Catherine Baird. Catherine Baird is the online and outreach services librarian at Montclair State University, where she is also the liaison to education, counseling, and modern languages. She holds an MLIS from the University of Western Ontario and an MA from the University of British Columbia. Catherine's research interests include information literacy, information behavior, and online teaching and learning.

Courtney Baron. Courtney Baron is the teaching and learning librarian at Oxford College of Emory University. She leads the Research Practices team and coordinates the instruction program for the Oxford College Library. She received her bachelor of arts in classical archaeology and Latin from the University of Georgia and a Master of Library and Information Science from Valdosta State University. Courtney's research interests include critical librarianship, visual literacy, information literacy instruction, and providing library services to the arts and humanities.

Christopher Bishop. Christopher Bishop is the user services librarian for the McCain Library at Agnes Scott College. In addition to the coordination and management of the Access Services department, Christopher shares library instruction responsibilities for undergraduate students. His areas of interest include instructional design for first-year students, mentoring programs geared toward senior seminar students, incorporating gaming strategies to improve instructional delivery, and improving communication between Reference and Access Services staff to better assist patron needs.

About the Authors

Joshua Bonde. Joshua Bonde is an assistant professor in residence in the Geoscience Department at UNLV. He also serves as Director of Conservation and Research at the Las Vegas Natural History Museum and is a paleontology research associate for the Nevada State Museum in Carson City. Dr. Bonde received his BS in biology at the University of Nevada-Reno, MS in earth sciences at Montana State University-Bozeman, and his PhD in geoscience at UNLV. His research focuses on the interaction of life and geology across the state of Nevada.

Callie Wiygul Branstiter. Callie Wiygul Branstiter is the undergraduate engagement librarian at the University of Kansas. Her scholarly interests include information literacy, application of the Framework in undergraduate curriculum, social justice in academic libraries, library anxiety and social engagement for international students and first-generation college students, and digital humanities for undergraduate students. She previously was a first-year academic librarian blogger for ACRLog.

Jamie Conklin. Jamie Conklin is a research and education librarian at the Duke Medical Center Library and the liaison to the School of Nursing at Duke University. She received her master's degree in library and information science from Florida State University. Jamie's interests include evidence-based practice in nursing education, evidence-based teaching, and open access to scholarly communication and instructional resources.

Juliann Couture. Juliann Couture is an assistant professor and interdisciplinary social sciences librarian at the University of Colorado Boulder. Her research interests include examining information literacy in social science disciplines, specifically focused on anthropology and women and gender studies. She currently serves on the ACRL Women and Gender Studies Section's Instruction committee which is creating a discipline-specific framework.

Christina E. Dent. Christina E. Dent holds an MA in literature from the University of Connecticut and an MFA in creative writing from Emerson College. Before beginning her career at the Iwasaki Library at Emerson College in 2006, she taught extensively as an adjunct professor of literature and composition at institutions all over New England.

Jamie Emery. Jamie L. Emery is a research and instruction librarian and associate professor at Saint Louis University. She is the author of "The Expanding Role of Information Literacy in the Freshman Writing Program at Saint Louis University: A Case Study" published in *Curriculum-Based Library Instruction: From Cultivating Faculty Relationships to Assessment* and co-author of "Pay Attention to the Data Behind the Curtain: Leveraging LibGuides Analytics for Maximum Impact" published in *Innovative LibGuides Applications: Real World Examples*.

Beate Gersch. Beate Gersch is assistant professor and coordinator of instruction services at the University of Akron Libraries, where she also serves as liaison to the School of Communication and the Department of Modern Languages. She holds a PhD in media studies from the University of Oregon, an MLIS from Kent State University, and an MA in American Studies from the Freie Universität Berlin, Germany. Her current research explores the intersection of communication models and information literacy.

Samantha Godbey. Samantha Godbey, education librarian and assistant professor at the University of Nevada, Las Vegas, earned her MLIS from San Jose State University and MA in education from the University of California at Berkeley. Prior to becoming a librarian, Samantha was a high school English teacher in Berkeley, California, and served as a Peace Corps volunteer in the Russian Far East. Her research focuses on information literacy instruction and assessment. She is also co-editor of *Journal of Research in Technical Careers*, an open-access journal.

Xan Goodman. Xan Goodman is a health sciences librarian at the University of Nevada, Las Vegas where she supports the Schools of Allied Health, Community Health Sciences, and Nursing. She earned her master's degree in library and information science from Wayne State University. Xan's research agenda focuses on assessment, information literacy, teaching practice, and cultural competence.

Jess Haigh. Jess Haigh is subject librarian for the School of Education and Professional Development at the University of Huddersfield. She is a member of the committee of the Academic and Research Libraries Group for Yorkshire and Humberside, and co-founded LISDIS, the conference which showcases LIS masters dissertations in the UK. Her research currently focuses on collaboratively designing learning interventions that enhance students critical reading and writing. She is also interested in storytelling as educational practice.

Rebecca Halpern. Rebecca Halpern is the teaching and learning services coordinator for the Claremont Colleges Library. She was a member of the inaugural cohort of the Institute for Research Design in Librarianship, where she completed a project exploring the efficacy of activity-based learning in online classrooms in reducing information anxiety. Her research interests are at the intersections of public policy, critical education theories, and library services for underrepresented groups. She is a member of the editorial board for the collaboratively peer-reviewed and open access journal *Hybrid Pedagogy*.

Megan Heuer. Megan Heuer is the head of information literacy and the communication arts librarian at Southern Methodist University, where she has developed an information literacy certificate program for advertising students. She serves on the Communication Studies Committee for the ACRL Education and Behavioral Sciences Section, which is currently developing a discipline-specific version of the *ACRL Framework* for journalism. Her research interests include the transfer of information literacy skills as well as workplace information literacy. She has an MLIS from the University of North Texas (2013) and an MM from Yale University (2002).

Jonathan Howell. Jonathan Howell holds a PhD from Cornell University and is an assistant professor of linguistics at Montclair State University. Dr. Howell's digital humanities project, "Harvesting Speech Datasets for Linguistic Research on the Web," was a recipient of the first international Digging into Data Challenge award funded by the National Science Foundation and the Social Sciences and Humanities Research Council of Canada. His research interests include speech prosody, information literacy and quantitative literacy.

Heidi Johnson. Heidi Johnson is social sciences librarian at the University of Nevada, Las Vegas University Libraries, where she is the liaison to anthropology, political science, and sociology. In addition to her MS in library and information science, Heidi has an MA in political theory, postmodernism, and feminisms from University of Illinois Springfield. Heidi's research interests include critical librarianship, critical information literacy, and, more generally, social and political theory as it impacts librarianship.

Bill Johnston. Bill Johnston is an honorary research fellow in the School of Psychological Sciences and Health at the University of Strathclyde. Before retiring in 2010, Bill was senior lecturer and assistant director at Strathclyde's Centre for Academic Practice and Learning Enhancement. His academic interests include information literacy, strategic academic development, the first-year experience at university, and curriculum and course design. At an earlier stage in his career, Bill was a professional librarian and worked in both public and academic library settings.

Michelle Keba. Michelle Keba is an assistant reference librarian for education and behavioral studies at Palm Beach Atlantic University. Prior to becoming a librarian, Michelle served as a fifth and sixth grade English language arts teacher in South Texas through the Teach for America program. In 2015, she and her co-workers won the Association of College and Research Libraries Instruction Section Innovation Award for their work creating LibraryLearn, a mobile-first platform for storing and displaying instructional videos.

Rebecca Kuglitsch. Rebecca Kuglitsch is the head of the Gemmill Library of Engineering, Mathematics & Physics at the University of Colorado Boulder. Her research interests center around information literacy in the sciences, transferability, and the intersection of science literacy and information literacy.

Sharon Ladenson. Sharon Ladenson is gender and communication studies librarian at Michigan State University. She has written on feminist pedagogy and information literacy as a contributor to the 2016 *Critical Library Pedagogy Handbook* from the Association of College & Research Libraries (ACRL), and to the 2010 Library Juice Press book, *Critical Library Instruction: Theories & Methods*. Ms. Ladenson serves on the Instruction Committee within the ACRL Women & Gender Studies Section, which is developing a discipline-specific framework for information literacy.

Marty Miller. Marty (Margaret) Miller is the art and design librarian at Louisiana State University. She is the subject liaison for the College of Art and Design, which includes the Schools of Art, Architecture, Interior Design and Landscape Architecture. Prior to her time at LSU, she has worked in art museum, private school, and community college libraries. In addition to her Master of Library Science from Emporia State University, she holds a master's degree in art history from the University of Kansas and a bachelor of arts from Bethany College at Lindsborg, Kansas. Her research interests include visual literacy, new and emerging instruction techniques for visual learners, and the history of art librarianship.

Elizabeth Moreton. Elizabeth Moreton is the librarian for nursing at the UNC School of Nursing and UNC Hospitals in Chapel Hill, NC. She first developed her interest in information literacy, health sciences librarianship, and evidence-based practice while earning her MLS at Indiana University Bloomington. Elizabeth is an advocate for student-centered librarianship, reducing library anxiety, and having a little fun. Elizabeth also dabbles in user experience, process improvement, outreach, the maker movement, and she is secretly a craft fiend.

Ellen Neufeld. Ellen Neufeld is the deputy director of the Library at Oxford College of Emory University. She oversees the library's Dynamic Content & Systems, serves as a personal librarian to a variety of faculty, teaches undergraduates and serves on numerous committees both at Oxford and with the

University libraries. She received a BS in journalism from the University of Tennessee and an MS in library science from the University of North Texas.

Ashley Peterson. Ashley Peterson is a research and instruction librarian at the School of the Museum of Fine Arts at Tufts University, located in Boston. Her research interests include critical and feminist pedagogies, artists' information-seeking behavior, visual literacy, the history of visual display, and feminist art historical methodologies.

Jessica Robinson. Jessica Robinson is the assistant college librarian of finance and operations at Oxford College of Emory University. Jessica started working at the Oxford College Library in 2007 and her responsibilities include Hub of Living and Learning team leader, Student Employee Team leader, and personal librarian to biology, academic services and campus life, astronomy, chemistry, math, physics, and the Center for Healthful Living faculty. Jessica received a Bachelor of Business Administration in marketing from Valdosta State University, and Master of Science in Library Science from the University of Alabama. She works very closely with the dean of the library to oversee the day-to-day function and financial operations of the library.

Rachel Scott. Rachel Elizabeth Scott is assistant professor and integrated library systems librarian at the University of Memphis. She is co-editor of *Music Reference Services Quarterly* and her research focuses on the intersection of information literacy and music bibliography. She has recently published chapters in ACRL, Facet, Rowman & Littlefield, and Theatre Library Association anthologies and articles in *Communications in Information Literacy, Music Reference Services Quarterly, The Reference Librarian,* and *Tennessee Libraries.*

Christina Sheley. Christina Sheley is the head of the Business/SPEA Information Commons at Indiana University-Bloomington, a position she had held for five years. She holds a BS in psychology and communications and an MS in library science from Indiana University. Her research interests include information-seeking behavior in professional programs, workplace information literacy, academic library management, and library service development.

Anna Smedley-López. Anna C. Smedley-Lopez, PhD, is an assistant professor in residence in the Department of Sociology at the University of Nevada, Las Vegas, where she has been faculty since 2014. Dr. Smedley-López has an interdisciplinary background in sociology, women's studies, and social work that informs her research, service, and work in the classroom. Dr. Smedley-López is the program coordinator for the Service Learning Initiative for Community Engagement in Sociology (SLICES) and her work focuses on racial justice.

Michelle Twait. Michelle Twait is a reference librarian and associate professor at Gustavus Adolphus College in St. Peter, Minnesota. She obtained her MS in LIS from the University of Illinois at Urbana-Champaign and her MA in Educational Psychology from the University of Minnesota. Michelle is a member of the American Library Association and Minnesota Library Association. Her research interests include information-seeking behavior, mentoring in libraries, the psychology of decision making, and US women's labor history.

Candace Vance. Candace Vance is an assistant professor and research and instruction librarian at Murray State University, where she is a liaison to the School of Nursing and Health Professions and the Department of English. Her research and teaching interests include scientific scholarly communication, scholarly impact, open access, and scientific misconduct. Candace holds a master's degree in information sciences and an MFA in creative writing and has recently co-authored a book with one of her colleagues on scientific scholarly communication.

Susan Beth Wainscott. Susan Beth Wainscott is the engineering librarian, formerly the STEM librarian, for the University of Nevada, Las Vegas University Libraries. She holds a Master of Library and Information Science from San Jose State University and a master of science in biological sciences from Illinois State University. Her current research interests include information literacy instruction and assessment, specifically the impact of student affect on learning.

Alexander Watkins. Alexander Watkins is an assistant professor and art and architecture librarian at the University of Colorado Boulder. He received master's degrees in the history of art and design and library and information science from Pratt Institute. His research has focused on improving information literacy education in the visual arts.

Kimberly J. Whalen. Kim Whalen is an associate professor of library services and the health sciences librarian at Valparaiso University in Indiana. In her role, Kim is the liaison to nursing, healthcare administration/leadership, health sciences, psychology, and counseling. Kim is also the liaison to the University's Career Center and the manager of the library's Foundation Center Funding Information Network collection. Before becoming a librarian in 2002, Kim had a career in marketing, fundraising, and nonprofit management.

Suzanne E. Zentz. Suzanne Zentz is an associate professor and assistant dean of undergraduate nursing at Valparaiso University, College of Nursing and Health Professions. She teaches a variety of courses in both the undergraduate and graduate programs. Her areas of interest include pediatric nursing,

nursing education, evidence-based practice, and information literacy. Suzanne has published articles in a variety of professional nursing publications and serves as a peer reviewer for *Journal of Pediatric Nursing and Journal of Nursing Education.*